Perspectives on Urban Society

Perspectives on Urban Society

From Preindustrial to Postindustrial

Edited by
Efren N. Padilla
California State University, East Bay

Boston • New York • San Francisco
Mexico City • Montreal • Toronto • London • Madrid • Munich • Paris
Hong Kong • Singapore • Tokyo • Cape Town • Sydney

Senior Series Editor: *Jeff Lasser*
Series Editorial Assistant: *Heather McNally*
Senior Marketing Manager: *Kelly May*
Editorial-Production Service: *Omegatype Typography, Inc.*
Composition Buyer: *Linda Cox*
Manufacturing Buyer: *JoAnne Sweeney*
Electronic Composition: *Omegatype Typography, Inc.*
Cover Administrator: *Joel Gendron*

For related titles and support materials, visit our online catalog at www.ablongman.com.

Between the time website information is gathered and then published, it is not unusual for some sites to have closed. Also, the transcription of URLs can result in typographical errors. The publisher would appreciate notification where these errors occur so that they may be corrected in subsequent editions.

Library of Congress Cataloging-in-Publication Data

Perspectives on urban society : from preindustrial to postindustrial : [anthology] / Efren N. Padilla.—1st ed.
   p. cm.
Includes bibliographical references.
ISBN 0-205-37453-0 (pbk.)
  1. Cities and towns—History. 2. Sociology, Urban. I. Padilla, Efren N.

HT111.P473 2006
307.7609—dc22

                    2005053097

Printed in the United States of America
10 9 8 7 6 5 4 3 2 1   10 09 08 07 06 05

Contents

Preface

Understanding the city is not only an academic necessity, but is also a practical necessity for everyone. It is practical in the sense that the city is now almost synonymous with society at large. It has increasingly become the typical habitat affecting everyone. We have become accustomed to the fact that most of us no longer work on the land. In fact, most of us now live in cities rather than in small rural communities. For example, in 1900, 14 percent of the world's population lived in cities; in 1950, 29 percent lived in cities; and in 1990, 43 percent lived in cities. It is projected that 61 percent of the world's population will live in cities by 2025. These percentages stagger the mind, especially when viewed in relation to the world's total population. In 1960, there were only about 3 billion people in the world. In 1990, the world's population reached 5.3 billion. Between these two dates the population increased an average of 80 million people annually or 220,000 daily. After 1990, 93 million people were being added annually or more than 250,000 daily. It is projected that the earth's population will reach 10 billion people in the year 2050.

Notably, the distribution of people living in cities varies from country to country. Developing societies presently house 40 percent of the world's population in cities, while industrialized societies house 73 percent of the world's population in cities. Specifically, North America hit the 73 percent urban population mark in 1980 and is projected to reach 78 percent by the year 2025. If this growth rate continues, by the year 2050 about 70 percent of the world's projected population of 10 billion people will live in cities.

This is the inescapable condition of our contemporary way of life. The growth of the city is inevitable—there is no going back. It is anachronistic to imagine or to think that a rural society is a current or future possibility. The city will continue to march in its progressive steps. It will remain the locus for the invention and production of ideas and their applications and will thereby expand its role of providing alternative solutions to the unending needs of an exploding population. For better or for worse, the majority of us will live the expanse of our lives in the city.

But what does it mean to live in the city? This is a core question, not only for students of urban society, but also for laypeople. I suggest that to live in the city is to recognize its problems as well as its prospects. Charles Dickens alluded to this idea in the opening paragraph of *A Tale of Two Cities:*

> It was the best of times, it was the worst of times, it was the age of wisdom, it was the age of foolishness, it was the epoch of belief, it was the epoch of incredulity, it was the season of Light, it was the season of Darkness, it was the spring of hope, it was the winter of despair, we had everything before us, we had nothing before

us, we were all going direct to Heaven, we were all going direct the other way—in short, the period was so far like the present period, that some of its noisiest authorities insisted on its being received, for good or for evil, in the superlative degree of comparison only.

There is little question that the many social issues and problems we face today, such as poverty, unemployment, educational inequality, drug abuse, juvenile delinquency, mental illness, homelessness, road rage, drive-by shooting, family violence, and racial violence are matters of human behavior and relationships that plague city life. And yet, to live and grow in the city is to learn in a very personal way not only its problems, but also its prospects. The city has inspired freedom, rationality, and innovation from its citizens and they, in turn, have created material wealth, abundance, and leisure. Indeed, there is no doubt that the city has been, and still is, the economic crucible in which the production, distribution, and consumption of goods and services have provided us with unimaginable benefits and conveniences in life.

In order to address a growing interest in understanding the city, this collection of essays leads us into three objectives. First, it introduces us to a diverse body of literature that expresses a common concern for the spatial and aspatial dimensions of the city. Second, it provides us with recent materials that specifically deal with contemporary issues of city life. Third, it presents perspectives or theories of the city that guide us to discover the urban processes and outcomes that affect our day-to-day living.

Hopefully, as we progress to a more in-depth study of the city, our efforts will allow us to clearly view the problems as well as the prospects of our new urban landscape. To use a common expression, there is nothing as practical as a good theory.

Acknowledgments

As always, this edited volume is a product of the efforts of many people. I am grateful to the authors and original publishers of these selections for important information and helpful viewpoints. My students in Urban Sociology, Human Ecology, and Urban and Regional Planning have been unwitting but necessary collaborators through the years as they have participated in discussions of many issues that now await the reader. To them, I give my thanks. I would also like to thank the reviewers of this book for their comments: Harold S. Bershady, University of Pennsylvania; Townsand Price-Spratlen, The Ohio State University; and Leslie F. Uljee, University of Houston, Clear Lake.

E. N. P.

Perspectives on Urban Society

Introduction

The appearance and growth of cities is an object of continued investigation by urban theorists and urban practitioners alike. This includes continued interest in cities as centers of civilized life. The reason for this is that cities have not always existed, therefore, their origins have been associated with the birth of civilization. Interestingly, the word *civilization* comes from the Latin word *civis* which literally means "citification." Sometimes people use the word *civilized* to mean "courteous" or "polite," yet civilized people are not necessarily more courteous or polite than the so-called uncivilized ones. In fact, civilizations like traditional Egypt and China practiced human sacrifice; imperial Rome engaged in gladiatorial spectacles; and colonial Spain and France "hamleted" their colonies to pacify the natives. What makes the civilized distinct from the uncivilized is not so much its claim to moral ascendancy, but its production of complex divisions of labor, social organization, scientific research, and technical skills that the latter lacks.

As centers of civilization, the enormous significance of cities in determining the patterns or modes of a different way of life is obvious. The very term *city* represents both spatial and aspatial dimensions that generally underpin fundamental changes in human society. Spatially, the city is organized as a malleable yet structured space that exhibits multiple geometric patterns (e.g., gridiron, circular-radial, square, rectilineal, or hexagonal). Aspatially, the city is symbolized as a mosaic of social and economic conditions that reflects the social class, cultural identities, and social interactions of the times.

In order to capture the many changes that the city has undergone since its inception, this volume will address three distinct archetypes that merit particular mention—the preindustrial city, the industrial city, and the postindustrial city. To understand the city in its manifold transformations, it is useful to divide economic production into four sectors—primary, secondary, tertiary, and quarternary. The idea underlying such division is the assumption that the heart of the city is fundamentally economic in nature. As economic production shifts from one sector to another, it identifies *what* is produced, *how* it is produced, and *where* it is produced.

Of course, this is not to say that cities only engage in the production of a single economic sector. What is important to note is the degree to which one economic sector dominates over other economic sectors in terms of product (what), innovation (how), and location (where). *In short, economic production defines the limits of urban development.*

Although it is a crude criterion to use, the distinction between economic sectors is critical because it allows us to compare and contrast the different urban archetypes. The **primary sector** of economic production includes agriculture, fishing, forestry, mining, and related activities. However, with the increasing use of machineries and factories, economic production is drawn into the **secondary sector,** which relies on the conversion of raw materials into manufactured and industrial goods. The **tertiary sector,** on the other hand, depends on providing services to others. Financial, real estate, banking, managerial, and clerical occupations are types of work included in this sector. The **quarternary sector** refers to economic production associated with advances in information and communication technology.

In order to highlight the role of these sectors in the transformation of the city, let us consider the following. In 1996, only 3 percent of the labor force in the United States engaged in agriculture as compared to 69 percent in 1840. The decline in the share of agricultural labor signaled the shift from the primary sector to the secondary sector. As the primary sector declined, industries and factories that turned raw materials into manufactured and industrial products became the main engines of economic growth. More recently, there is a movement away from the secondary sector toward the tertiary and quarternary sectors as many workers find themselves employed in large organizations and corporations.

As early as the 1960s, the share of the tertiary sector increased to 62 percent compared to 48 percent in 1930. To date, almost 75 percent of the labor force in the United States works in tertiary and quarternary sectors of the economy. For example, three of the largest corporations in the United States currently employ about 2 million people. Wal-Mart has 1.2 million employees, General Motors has 388,000, and IBM has 316,303 employees. The federal government of the United States currently employs 3 million people and the state and local governments employ an additional 14.4 million people.

The deindustrialization of labor, that is, the tertiarization and quarternarization of labor, gave rise to the phenomenon of the knowledge-based postindustrial city, which now cradles the technological brainforce rather than the old smokestack elites of North America. The leading postindustrial center in the world today is Silicon Valley in northern California. Situated at the southern tip of the San Francisco Bay Area, this urban area (which now covers cities such as Newark, Fremont, Milpitas, Santa Clara, San Jose, Los Gatos, Cupertino, Sunnyvale, Mountain View, Palo Alto, Menlo Park, and Redwood) is known as the high-tech capital of the world. This urban type is also emerging in other U.S. cities like Chicago, Seattle, San Diego, Phoenix, Austin, Raleigh, Atlanta, St. Paul, Dearborn, Dayton, New York, and Cambridge.

Using this criterion of economic production, we can now make sense of the various urban archetypes. The **preindustrial city** lasted from 3,500 B.C. until the mid-eighteenth century and may be paradigmatically represented by the Mesopotamian experience, the Hellenic experience, and the Medieval experience. It mainly relied on the production of primary products by utilizing domesticated animals, canal irrigation, and wooden and metal tools. Thus, the majority of its population engaged in agriculture.

The **industrial city** lasted from the late 1600s until after World War II. Initially, it was tied with the Industrial Revolution (the dramatic economic and technological innovations that occurred in England during the period of 1760 to 1830) and, consequently, associated with the processes of industrial production and modernization. This postagricultural city produced secondary goods using machinery and mass labor in a factory setting. Over time, two labor processes guided the modern success of this **factory system. Fordism** was the principle of mass production based on the assembly line technique pioneered by Henry Ford, and **Taylorism** was the principle of industrial efficiency based on scientific management developed by Winslow Taylor.

The **postindustrial city** began in Post-World War II, a period that saw a dramatic growth in the television industry, and later, in the computer industry. Televisions and computers revolutionized access to information and communication in many forms and ushered us into the process of postmodernization commonly referred to as the **Information Age.** Rather than rely on modern industrial production, the city now concentrates on the productive activities of the tertiary and quarternary sectors. This means that the postindustrial city organizes its production system around the principles of increasing service activities, maximizing knowledge-based productivity, and expanding information-rich occupations.

To date, its labor processes, unlike the mass production of the modern standard and the consumption of the factory system, now depend on the **flexible production system.** Two of the principles that guide its postmodern success are **product differentiation,** the specialization and personalization of consumer goods and services, and **niche marketing,** the strategy of targeting consumers based on a specific characteristic or combinations of characteristics associated with age, gender, race, ethnicity, lifestyle, and social class.

The various sectoral shifts demonstrate the fundamental lesson that as the old era ends, a new era begins. In the same way that the primary sector gave way to the secondary sector, and the secondary sector to the tertiary and quarternary sectors, so the traditional gave way to the modern, and now, the modern to the postmodern. In short, the preindustrial city gave way to the industrial city, and the industrial city to the postindustrial city.

The Preindustrial City

In discussing the origins of cities, urban theorists frequently differentiate between the single culture–hearth theory and the multiple culture–hearth theory. The former hypothesizes that cities originated in the fertile crescent of Mesopotamia. Mesopotamia (modern day Iraq) literally means "the land between the rivers" (the Euphrates and the Tigris). The single **culture–hearth theory** suggests that the urban form diffused from this region to the great riverine depressions of the Nile Valley, Indus Valley, China Yellow River Valley, and the hinterlands of Mesoamerica.

The single culture–hearth theory argues that the construction of similar spatial designs are too distinct and too specific to have developed accidentally. Take, for example, the Incas in Peru, the Aztecs in Mexico, and the Mayas of the Yucatan, who all built pyramid structures, temples, palaces, towers, storehouses, and fortifications. It is therefore impossible for these civilizations to have developed independently without external influences.

The **multiple culture–hearth theory**, on the other hand, contends that cities in these various regions developed independently. Considering gaps in urban formation spanning several millennia that probably would have allowed for the Mesopotamian influence to spread, still, it insists that the lines of transportation and communication from the various regions did not develop at a level that would have facilitated the migration or exchange of people and information.

Although this debate remains unsettled, the Mesopotamian experience, which produced one of the most well-known ancient civilizations with a literate, preindustrial culture and highly developed social institutions, is widely regarded as the paradigm of incipient urbanization.

Why Mesopotamia? According to Scriptures, God originally created humankind by forming a clay figure and breathing life into it. The Scriptures also summarize the beginning and end of human existence as follows: "From dust thou art, to dust thou returnest." This reference to clay as a metaphor for life and death is by no means accidental. Clay holds the fertile topsoil that nourishes the crops and animals that people throughout the centuries depended on for their very life and survival.

By around 3,500 B.C., some inhabitants of southern Mesopotamia had already begun working with clay. They realized that they could build structures by making clay into rectangular blocks of varied sizes and shapes, and then attaching them on top of one another. In this way, they constructed defensive walls, towers, monumental buildings, and homes. They formed clay into flat tablets, providing a useful surface on which to record transactions, payments, taxes, laws, and rituals. They created cooking utensils and storage vessels by drying the clay with fire. They expressed their artistic views by sculpting clay into animal and human figures. As a metaphor, clay provides the key through which we may infer the beginnings of civilization. Using the same metaphor, we might say that it is through clay that our first cities were created.

Part One brings together selected essays that provide perspectives on the genesis, as well as the different transformations, of the preindustrial city. Although the selected essays represent different historical time frames, they are not meant to chronologically or geographically locate preindustrial cities.

V. Gordon Childe's essay, *The Urban Revolution,* lists and discusses the principal features of a complex process sometimes referred to as the **urban revolution.** These features include dense aggregations of people, craft specialization, social stratification, central authority, monumental buildings, foreign trade, use of writing and mathematics, development of applied sciences, artistic expressions, and group membership based on residence rather than kinship.

Gideon Sjoberg's essay, *The Preindustrial Society,* compares and contrasts the preindustrial city with the industrial city in terms of ecological and economic organizations and postulates that industrialization is the key variable in accounting for the distinction between the two.

In *The Sumerians,* Samuel Noah Kramer discusses the Mesopotamian urban experience, which consists of integrating isolated settlements into self-governing cities that united for defense, religion, and commerce under the leadership of a chief priest or king.

Kwang-chih Chang's essay, *The Emergence of Civilization in China,* portrays the Shang as builders of the first verifiable civilization in China (1850 B.C.) that organized its cities into religious, economic, and political networks influenced by the social hierarchy of classes.

In *Tenochtitlán,* Jorge E. Hardoy represents the grandeur of pre-Columbian cities (1325 A.D.) in terms of city planning and design that reflects the great foundation of Indian civilizations in Mesoamerica.

Jacob Burckhardt's essay, *The Polis,* exemplifies the transformation of the preindustrial city from a theological economy into a political economy. The Greek **polis,** which means "fortified citadel," represented a new form of government and a new idea of citizenship that allowed the Greeks to transition from a mere agrarian life into a predominantly urban life.

L. Benevolo's essay, *European Cities in the Middle Ages,* examines how the **bourgeoisie,** composed primarily of artisans and merchants, organized themselves into *guilds* and *societies* through which they gave the city-state a new sense of vitality. Adapting their spatial and aspatial settings to the nature of their geography and economic circumstances, the new movement created three prominent urban forms—the Italian **comune,** the French **bastide,** and the Spanish **poblacion.**

In *Architecture and Urban Growth,* Josef W. Konvitz discusses Renaissance architecture and urban growth as reactions against the Medieval city-building layout and design and traces evolution toward the vernacular and utilitarian city-building methods.

1

The Urban Revolution

V. Gordon Childe

The concept of "city" is notoriously hard to define. The aim of the present essay is to present the city historically—or rather prehistorically—as the resultant and symbol of a "revolution" that initiated a new economic stage in the evolution of society. The word "revolution" must not of course be taken as denoting a sudden violent catastrophe; it is here used for the culmination of a progressive change in the economic structure and social organisation of communities that caused, or was accompanied by, a dramatic increase in the population affected—an increase that would appear as an obvious bend in the population graph were vital statistics available. Just such a bend is observable at the time of the Industrial Revolution in England. Though not demonstrable statistically, comparable changes of direction must have occurred at two earlier points in the demographic history of Britain and other regions. Though perhaps less sharp and less durable, these too should indicate equally revolutionary changes in economy. They may then be regarded likewise as marking transitions between stages in economic and social development.

Sociologists and ethnographers last century classified existing pre-industrial societies in a hierarchy of three evolutionary stages, denominated respectively "savagery," "barbarism" and "civilisation." If they be defined by suitably selected criteria, the logical hierarchy of stages can be transformed into a temporal sequence of ages, proved archaeologically to follow one another in the same order wherever they occur. Savagery and barbarism are conveniently recognized and appropriately defined by the methods adopted for procuring food. Savages live exclusively on wild food obtained by collecting, hunting or fishing. Barbarians on the contrary at least supplement these natural resources by cultivating edible plants and—in the Old World north of the Tropics—also by breeding animals for food.

"The Urban Revolution" by V. Gordon Childe from *Town Planning Review*, Vol. 21, 1950, pp. 3–9, 11–17. Reprinted by permission of Liverpool University Press.

Throughout the Pleistocene Period—the Palaeolithic Age of archaeologists—all known human societies were savage in the foregoing sense, and a few savage tribes have survived in out of the way parts to the present day. In the archaeological record barbarism began less than ten thousand years ago with the Neolithic Age of archaeologists. It thus represents a later, as well as a higher stage, than savagery. Civilization cannot be defined in quite such simple terms. Etymologically the word is connected with "city," and sure enough life in cities begins with this stage. But "city" is itself ambiguous so archaeologists like to use "writing" as a criterion of civilization; it should be easily recognizable and proves to be a reliable index to more profound characters. Note, however, that, because a people is said to be civilized or literate, it does not follow that all its members can read and write, nor that they all lived in cities. Now there is no recorded instance of a community of savages civilizing themselves, adopting urban life or inventing a script. Wherever cities have been built, villages of preliterate farmers existed previously (save perhaps where an already civilized people have colonized uninhabited tracts). So civilization, wherever and whenever it arose, succeeded barbarism.

We have seen that a revolution as here defined should be reflected in the population statistics. In the case of the Urban Revolution the increase was mainly accounted for by the multiplication of the numbers of persons living together, i.e., in a single built-up area. The first cities represented settlement units of hitherto unprecedented size. Of course it was not just their size that constituted their distinctive character. We shall find that by modern standards they appeared ridiculously small and we might meet agglomerations of population today to which the name city would have to be refused. Yet a certain size of settlement and density of population, is an essential feature of civilization.

Now the density of population is determined by the food supply which in turn is limited by natural resources, the techniques for their exploitation and the means of transport and food-preservation available. The last factors have proved to be variables in the course of human history, and the technique of obtaining food has already been used to distinguish the consecutive stages termed savagery and barbarism. Under the gathering economy of savagery population was always exceedingly sparse. In aboriginal America the carrying capacity of normal unimproved land seems to have been from .05 to .10 per square mile. Only under exceptionally favourable conditions did the fishing tribes of the Northwest Pacific coast attain densities of over one human to the square mile. As far as we can guess from the extant remains, population densities in palaeolithic and pre-neolithic Europe were less than the normal American. Moreover such hunters and collectors usually live in small roving bands. At best several bands may come together for quite brief periods on ceremonial occasions such as the Australian corroborrees. Only in exceptionally favoured regions can fishing tribes establish anything like villages. Some settlements on the Pacific coasts comprised thirty or so substantial and durable houses, accommodating groups of several hundred persons. But even these villages were only occupied during the winter; for the rest of the year their inhabitants dispersed in smaller groups. Nothing comparable has been found in pre-neolithic times in the Old World.

The Neolithic Revolution certainly allowed an expansion of population and enormously increased the carrying capacity of suitable land. On the Pacific Islands neolithic societies today attain a density of 30 or more persons to the square mile. In pre-Columbian North America, however, where the land is not obviously restricted by surrounding seas, the maximum density recorded is just under 2 to the square mile.

Neolithic farmers could of course, and certainly did, live together in permanent villages, though, owing to the extravagant rural economy generally practised, unless the crops were watered by irrigation, the villages had to be shifted at least every twenty years. But on the whole the growth of population was not reflected so much in the enlargement of the settlement unit as in a multiplication of settlements. In ethnography neolithic villages can boast only a few hundred inhabitants (a couple of "pueblos" in New Mexico house over a thousand, but perhaps they cannot be regarded as neolithic). In prehistoric Europe the largest neolithic village yet known, Barkaer in Jutland, comprised 52 small, one-roomed dwellings, but 16 to 30 houses was a more normal figure; so the average local group in neolithic times would average 200 to 400 members.

These low figures are of course the result of technical limitations. In the absence of wheeled vehicles and roads for the transport of bulky crops men had to live within easy walking distance of their cultivations. At the same time the normal rural economy of the Neolithic Age, what is now termed slash-and-burnt or jhumming, condemns much more than half the arable land to lie fallow so that large areas were required. As soon as the population of a settlement rose above the numbers that could be supported from the accessible land, the excess had to hive off and found a new settlement.

The Neolithic Revolution had other consequences beside increasing the population, and their exploitation might in the end help to provide for the surplus increase. The new economy allowed, and indeed required, the farmer to produce every year more food than was needed to keep him and his family alive. In other words it made possible the regular production of a social surplus. Owing to the low efficiency of neolithic technique, the surplus produced was insignificant at first, but it could be increased till it demanded a reorganization of society.

Now in any Stone Age society, palaeolithic or neolithic, savage or barbarian, everybody can at least in theory make at home the few indispensible tools, the modest cloths and the simple ornaments everyone requires. But every member of the local community, not disqualified by age, must contribute actively to the communal food supply by personally collecting, hunting, fishing, gardening or herding. As long as this holds good, there can be no full-time specialists, no persons nor class of persons who depend for their livelihood on food produced by others and secured in exchange for material or immaterial goods or services.

We find indeed to day among Stone Age barbarians and even savages expert craftsmen (for instance flint-knappers among the Ona of Tierra del Fuego), men who claim to be experts in magic, and even chiefs. In palaeolithic Europe too there is some evidence for magicians and indications of chieftainship in pre-neolithic times. But on closer observation we discover that today these experts are not full-time specialists. The Ona flintworker must spend most of his time hunting; he only adds to his diet and his prestige by making arrowheads for clients who reward him with presents. Similarly a pre-Columbian chief, though entitled to customary gifts and services from his followers, must still personally lead hunting and fishing expeditions and indeed could only maintain his authority by his industry and prowess in these pursuits. The same holds good of barbarian societies that are still in the neolithic stage, like the Polynesians where industry in gardening takes the place of prowess in hunting. The reason is that there simply will not be enough food to go round unless every member of the group contributes to the supply. The social surplus is not big enough to feed idle mouths.

Social division of labour, save those rudiments imposed by age and sex, is thus impossible. On the contrary community of employment, the common absorbtion in obtaining food by similar devices guarantees a certain solidarity to the group. For co-operation is essential to secure food and shelter and for defence against foes, human and subhuman. This identity of economic interests and pursuits is echoed and magnified by identity of language, custom and belief; rigid conformity is enforced as effectively as industry in the common quest for food. But conformity and industrious co-operation need no State organization to maintain them. The local group usually consists either of a single clan (persons who believe themselves descended from a common ancestor or who have earned a mystical claim to such descent by ceremonial adoption) or a group of clans related by habitual intermarriage. And the sentiment of kinship is reinforced or supplemented by common rites focussed on some ancestral shrine or sacred place. Archaeology can provide no evidence for kinship organization, but shrines occupied the central place in preliterate villages in Mesopotamia, and the long barrow, a collective tomb that overlooks the presumed site of most neolithic villages in Britain, may well have been also the ancestral shrine on which converged the emotions and ceremonial activities of the villagers below. However, the solidarity thus idealized and concretely symbolized, is really based on the same principles as that of a pack of wolves or a herd of sheep; Durkheim has called it "mechanical."

Now among some advanced barbarians (for instance tattooers or woodcarvers among the Maori) still technologically neolithic we find expert craftsmen tending towards the status of full-time professionals, but only at the cost of breaking away from the local community. If no single village can produce a surplus large enough to feed a full-time specialist all the year round, each should produce enough to keep him a week or so. By going round from village to village an expert might thus live entirely from his craft. Such itinerants will lose their membership of the sedentary kinship group. They may in the end form an analogous organization of their own—a craft clan, which, if it remain hereditary, may become a caste, or, if it recruit its members mainly by adoption (apprenticeship throughout Antiquity and the Middle Age was just temporary adoption), may turn into a guild. But such specialists, by emancipation from kinship ties, have also forfeited the protection of the kinship organization which alone under barbarism, guaranteed to its members security of person and property. Society must be reorganized to accommodate and protect them.

In pre-history specialization of labour presumably began with similar itinerant experts. Archaeological proof is hardly to be expected, but in ethnography metal-workers are nearly always full time specialists. And in Europe at the beginning of the Bronze Age metal seems to have been worked and purveyed by perambulating smiths who seem to have functioned like tinkers and other itinerants of much more recent times. Though there is no such positive evidence, the same probably happened in Asia at the beginning of metallurgy. There must of course have been in addition other specialist craftsmen whom, as the Polynesian example warns us, archaeologists could not recognize because they worked in perishable materials. One result of the Urban Revolution will be to rescue such specialists from nomadism and to guarantee them security in a new social organization.

About 5,000 years ago irrigation cultivation (combined with stock-breeding and fishing) in the valleys of the Nile, the Tigris-Euphrates and the Indus had begun to yield a social surplus, large enough to support a number of resident specialists who were themselves released from food-production. Water-transport, supplemented in Mesopotamia and the Indus valley by wheeled vehicles and even in Egypt by pack animals, made it easy to gather food stuffs at a few centres. At the same time dependence on river water for the irrigation of the crops restricted the cultivable areas while the necessity of canalizing the waters and protecting habitations against annual floods encouraged the aggregation of population. Thus arose the first cities—units of settlement ten times as great as any known neolithic village. It can be argued that all cities in the old world are offshoots of those of Egypt, Mesopotamia and the Indus basin. So the latter need not be taken into account if a minimum definition of civilization is to be inferred from a comparison of its independent manifestations.

But some three millennia later cities arose in Central America, and it is impossible to prove that the Mayas owed anything directly to the urban civilizations of the Old World. Their achievements must therefore be taken into account in our comparison, and their inclusion seriously complicates the task of defining the essential preconditions for the Urban Revolution. In the Old World the rural economy which yielded the surplus was based on the cultivation of cereals combined with stock-breeding. But this economy had been made more efficient as a result of the adoption of irrigation (allowing cultivation without prolonged fallow periods) and of important inventions and discoveries—metallurgy, the plough, the sailing boat and the wheel. None of these devices was known to the Mayas; they bred no animals for milk or meat; though they cultivated the cereal maize, they used the same sort of slash-and-burn method as neolithic farmers in prehistoric Europe or in the Pacific Islands today. Hence the minimum definition of a city, the greatest factor common to the Old World and the New will be substantially reduced and impoverished by the inclusion of the Maya. Nevertheless ten rather abstract criteria, all deducible from archaeological data, serve to distinguish even the earliest cities from any older or contemporary village.

(1) In point of size the first cities must have been more extensive and more densely populated than any previous settlements, although considerably smaller than many villages today. It is indeed only in Mesopotamia and India that the first

urban populations can be estimated with any confidence or precision. There excavation has been sufficiently extensive and intensive to reveal both the total area and the density of building in sample quarters and in both respects has disclosed significant agreement with the less industrialized Oriental cities today. The population of Sumerian cities, thus calculated, ranged between 7,000 and 20,000; Harappa and Mohenjo-daro in the Indus valley must have approximated to the higher figure. We can only infer that Egyptian and Maya cities were of comparable magnitude from the scale of public works, presumably executed by urban populations.

(2) In composition and function the urban population already differed from that of any village. Very likely indeed most citizens were still also peasants, harvesting the lands and waters adjacent to the city. But all cities must have accommodated in addition classes who did not themselves procure their own food by agriculture, stock-breeding, fishing or collecting—full-time specialist craftsmen, transport workers, merchants, officials and priests. All these were of course supported by the surplus produced by the peasants living in the city and in dependent villages, but they did not secure their share directly by exchanging their products or services for grains or fish with individual peasants.

(3) Each primary producer paid over the tiny surplus he could wring from the soil with his still very limited technical equipment as tithe or tax to an imaginary deity or a divine king who thus concentrated the surplus. Without this concentration, owing to the low productivity of the rural economy, no effective capital would have been available.

(4) Truly monumental public buildings not only distinguish each known city from any village but also symbolize the concentration of the social surplus. Every Sumerian city was from the first dominated by one or more stately temples, centrally situated on a brick platform raised above the surrounding dwellings and usually connected with an artificial mountain, the staged tower or ziggurat. But attached to the temples, were workshops and magazines, and an important appurtenance of each principal temple was a great granary. Harappa, in the Indus basin, was dominated by an artificial citadel, girt with a massive rampart of kiln-baked bricks, containing presumably a palace and immediately overlooking an enormous granary and the barracks of artizans. No early temples nor palaces have been excavated in Egypt, but the whole Nile valley was dominated by the gigantic tombs of the divine pharaohs while royal granaries are attested from the literary record. Finally the Maya cities are known almost exclusively from the temples and pyramids of sculptured stone round which they grew up.

Hence in Sumer the social surplus was first effectively concentrated in the hands of a god and stored in his granary. That was probably true in Central America while in Egypt the pharaoh (king) was himself a god. But of course the imaginary deities were served by quite real priests who, besides celebrating elaborate and often sanguinary rites in their honour, administered their divine masters' earthly estates. In Sumer indeed the god very soon, if not even before the revolution, shared his wealth and power with a mortal viceregent, the "City-King," who acted as civil ruler and leader in war. The divine pharaoh was naturally assisted by a whole hierarchy of officials.

(5) All those not engaged in food-production were of course supported in the first instance by the surplus accumulated in temple or royal granaries and were thus dependent on temple or court. But naturally priests, civil and military leaders and officials absorbed a major share of the concentrated surplus and thus formed a "ruling class." Unlike a palaeolithic magician or a neolithic chief, they were, as an Egyptian scribe actually put it, "exempt from all manual tasks." On the other hand, the lower classes were not only guaranteed peace and security, but were relieved from intellectual tasks which many find more irksome than any physical labour. Besides reassuring the masses that the sun was going to rise next day and the river would flood again next year (people who have not five thousand years of recorded experience of natural uniformities behind them are really worried about such matters!), the ruling classes did confer substantial benefits upon their subjects in the way of planning and organization.

(6) They were in fact compelled to invent systems of recording and exact, but practically useful, sciences. The mere administration of the vast revenues of a Sumerian temple or an Egyptian pharaoh by a perpetual corporation of priests or officials obliged its members to devise conventional methods of recording that should be intelligible to all their colleagues and successors, that is, to invent systems of writing and numeral notation. Writing is thus a significant, as well as a convenient, mark of civilization. But while writing is a trait common to Egypt, Mesopotamia, the Indus valley and Central America, the characters themselves were different in each region and so were the normal writing materials—papyrus in Egypt, clay in Mesopotamia. The engraved seals or stelae that provide the sole extant evidence for early Indus and Maya writing, no more represent the normal vehicles for the scripts than do the comparable documents from Egypt and Sumer.

(7) The invention of writing—or shall we say the inventions of scripts—enabled the leisured clerks to proceed to the elaboration of exact and predictive sciences—arithmetic, geometry and astronomy. Obviously beneficial and explicitly attested by the Egyptian and Maya documents was the correct determination of the tropic year and the creation of a calendar. For it enabled the rulers to regulate successfully the cycle of agricultural operations. But once more the Egyptian, Maya and Babylonian calendars were as different as any systems based on a single natural unit could be. Calendrical and mathematical sciences are common features of the earliest civilizations and they too are corollaries of the archaeologists' criterion, writing.

(8) Other specialists, supported by the concentrated social surplus, gave a new direction to artistic expression. Savages even in palaeolithic times had tried, sometimes with astonishing success, to depict animals and even men as they saw them—concretely and naturalistically. Neolithic peasants never did that; they hardly ever tried to represent natural objects, but preferred to symbolize them by abstract geometrical patterns which at most may suggest by a few traits a fantastical man or beast or plant. But Egyptian, Sumerian, Indus and Maya artist-craftsmen—full-time sculptors, painters, or seal-engravers—began once more to carve, model or draw likenesses of persons or things, but no longer with the naive naturalism of

the hunter, but according to conceptualized and sophisticated styles which differ in each of the four urban centres.

(9) A further part of the concentrated social surplus was used to pay for the importation of raw materials, needed for industry or cult and not available locally. Regular "foreign" trade over quite long distances was a feature of all early civilizations and, though common enough among barbarians later, is not certainly attested in the Old World before 3,000 B.C. nor in the New before the Maya "empire." Thereafter regular trade extended from Egypt at least as far as Byblos on the Syrian coast while Mesopotamia was related by commerce with the Indus valley. While the objects of international trade were at first mainly "luxuries," they already included industrial materials, in the Old World notably metal the place of which in the New was perhaps taken by obsidian. To this extent the first cities were dependent for vital materials on long distance trade as no neolithic village ever was.

(10) So in the city, specialist craftsmen were both provided with raw materials needed for the employment of their skill and also guaranteed security in a State organization based now on residence rather than kinship. Itinerancy was no longer obligatory. The city was a community to which a craftsman could belong politically as well as economically.

Yet in return for security they became dependent on temple or court and were relegated to the lower classes. The peasant masses gained even less material advantages; in Egypt for instance metal did not replace the old stone and wood tools for agricultural work. Yet, however imperfectly, even the earliest urban communities must have been held together by a sort of solidarity missing from any neolithic village. Peasants, craftsmen, priests and rulers form a community, not only by reason of identity of language and belief, but also because each performs mutually complementary functions, needed for the well-being (as redefined under civilization) of the whole. In fact the earliest cities illustrate a first approximation to an organic solidarity based upon a functional complementarity and interdependence between all its members such as subsist between the constituent cells of an organism. Of course this was only a very distant approximation. However necessary the concentration of the surplus really were with the existing forces of production, there seemed a glaring conflict on economic interests between the tiny ruling class, who annexed the bulk of the social surplus, and the vast majority who were left with a bare subsistence and effectively excluded from the spiritual benefits of civilization. So solidarity had still to be maintained by the ideological devices appropriate to the mechanical solidarity of barbarism as expressed in the pre-eminence of the temple or the sepulchral shrine, and now supplemented by the force of the new State organization. There could be no room for sceptics or sectaries in the oldest cities.

These ten traits exhaust the factors common to the oldest cities that archaeology, at best helped out with fragmentary and often ambiguous written sources, can detect. No specific elements of town planning for example can be proved characteristic of all such cities; for on the one hand the Egyptian and Maya cities have not yet been excavated; on the other neolithic villages were often walled, an elaborate system of sewers drained the Orcadian hamlet of Skara Brae; two-storeyed houses were built in pre-Columbian *pueblos,* and so on.

The common factors are quite abstract. Concretely Egyptian, Sumerian, Indus and Maya civilizations were as different as the plans of their temples, the signs of their scripts and their artistic conventions. In view of this divergence and because there is so far no evidence for a temporal priority of one Old World centre (for instance, Egypt) over the rest nor yet for contact between Central America and any other urban centre, the four revolutions just considered may be regarded as mutually independent. On the contrary, all later civilizations in the Old World may in a sense be regarded as lineal descendants of those of Egypt, Mesopotamia or the Indus.

But this was not a case of like producing like. The maritime civilizations of Bronze Age Crete or classical Greece for example, to say nothing of our own, differ more from their reputed ancestors than these did among themselves. But the urban revolutions that gave them birth did not start from scratch. They could and probably did draw upon the capital accumulated in the three allegedly primary centres. That is most obvious in the case of cultural capital. Even today we use the Egyptians' calendar and the Sumerians' divisions of the day and the hour. Our European ancestors did not have to invent for themselves these divisions of time nor repeat the observations on which they are based; they took over—and very slightly improved systems elaborated 5,000 years ago! But the same is in a sense true of material capital as well. The Egyptians, the Sumerians and the Indus people had accumulated vast reserves of surplus food. At the same time they had to import from abroad necessary raw materials like metals and building timber as well as "luxuries." Communities controlling these natural resources could in exchange claim a slice of the urban surplus. They could use it as capital to support full-time specialists—craftsmen or rulers—until the latters' achievement in technique and organization had so enriched barbarian economies that they too could produce a substantial surplus in their turn.

2

The Preindustrial City

Gideon Sjoberg

In the past few decades social scientists have been conducting field studies in a number of relatively non-Westernized cities. Their recently acquired knowledge of North Africa and various parts of Asia, combined with what was already learned, clearly indicates that these cities are not like typical cities of the United States and other highly industrialized areas but are much more like those of medieval Europe. Such communities are termed herein "preindustrial," for they have arisen without stimulus from that form of production which we associate with the European industrial revolution.

Recently Foster, in a most informative article, took cognizance of the preindustrial city.[1] His primary emphasis was upon the peasantry (which he calls "folk"); but he recognized this to be part of a broader social structure which includes the preindustrial city. He noted certain similarities between the peasantry and the city's lower class. Likewise the present author sought to analyze the total society of which the peasantry and the preindustrial city are integral parts.[2] For want of a better term this was called "feudal." Like Redfield's folk (or "primitive") society, the feudal order is highly stable and sacred; in contrast, however, it has a complex social organization. It is characterized by highly developed state and educational and/or religious institutions and by a rigid class structure.

Thus far no one has analyzed the preindustrial city per se, especially as it differs from the industrial-urban community, although Weber, Tönnies, and a few others perceived differences between the two. Yet such a survey is needed for the understanding of urban development in so-called underdeveloped countries and,

"The Preindustrial City" from *American Journal of Sociology*, Vol. 60, March 1955, pp. 438–445. Reprinted by permission of The University of Chicago Press and the author.

for that matter, in parts of Europe. Such is the goal of this [reading]. The typological analysis should also serve as a guide to future research.

Ecological Organization

Preindustrial cities depend for their existence upon food and raw materials obtained from without; for this reason they are marketing centers. And they serve as centers for handicraft manufacturing. In addition, they fulfil important political, religious, and educational functions. Some cities have become specialized; for example, Benares in India and Karbala in Iraq are best known as religious communities, and Peiping in China as a locus for political and educational activities.

The proportion of urbanites relative to the peasant population is small, in some societies about 10 per cent, even though a few preindustrial cities have attained populations of 100,000 or more. Growth has been by slow accretion. These characteristics are due to the nonindustrial nature of the total social order. The amount of surplus food available to support an urban population has been limited by the unmechanized agriculture, transportation facilities utilizing primarily human or animal power, and inefficient methods of food preservation and storage.

The internal arrangement of the preindustrial city, in the nature of the case, is closely related to the city's economic and social structure.[3] Most streets are mere passageways for people and for animals used in transport. Buildings are low and crowded together. The congested conditions, combined with limited scientific knowledge, have fostered serious, sanitation problems.

More significant is the rigid social segregation which typically has led to the formation of "quarters" or "wards." In some cities (e.g., Fez, Morocco, and Aleppo, Syria) these were sealed off from each other by walls, whose gates were locked at night. The quarters reflect the sharp local social divisions. Thus ethnic groups live in special sections. And the occupational groupings, some being at the same time ethnic in character, typically reside apart from one another. Often a special street or sector of the city is occupied almost exclusively by members of a particular trade; cities in such divergent cultures as medieval Europe and modern Afghanistan contain streets with names like "street of the goldsmiths." Lower-class and especially "outcaste" groups live on the city's periphery, at a distance from the primary centers of activity. Social segregation, the limited transportation facilities, the modicum of residential mobility, and the cramped living quarters have encouraged the development of well-defined neighborhoods which are almost primary groups.

Despite rigid segregation the evidence suggests no real specialization of land use such as is functionally necessary in industrial-urban communities. In medieval Europe and in other areas city dwellings often serve as workshops, and religious structures are used as schools or marketing centers.[4]

Finally, the "business district" does not hold the position of dominance that it enjoys in the industrial-urban community. Thus, in the Middle East the principal mosque, or in medieval Europe the cathedral, is usually the focal point of community life. The center of Peiping is the Forbidden City.

Economic Organization

The economy of the preindustrial city diverges sharply from that of the modern industrial center. The prime difference is the absence in the former of industrialism which may be defined as that system of production in which *inanimate* sources of power are used to multiply human effort. Preindustrial cities depend for the production of goods and services upon *animate* (human or animal) sources of energy—applied either directly or indirectly through such mechanical devices as hammers, pulleys, and wheels. The industrial-urban community, on the other hand, employs inanimate generators of power such as electricity and steam which greatly enhance the productive capacity of urbanites. This basically new form of energy production, one which requires for its development and survival a special kind of institutional complex, effects striking changes in the ecological, economic, and social organization of cities in which it has become dominant.

Other facets of the economy of the preindustrial city are associated with its particular system of production. There is little fragmentation or specialization of work. The handicraftsman participates in nearly every phase of the manufacture of an article, often carrying out the work in his own home or in a small shop near by and, within the limits of certain guild and community regulations, maintaining direct control over conditions of work and methods of production.

In industrial cities, on the other hand, the complex division of labor requires a specialized managerial group, often extra-community in character, whose primary function is to direct and control others. And for the supervision and co-ordination of the activities of workers, a "factory system" has been developed, something typically lacking in preindustrial cities. (Occasionally centralized production is found in preindustrial cities—e.g., where the state organized slaves for large-scale construction projects.) Most commercial activities, also, are conducted in preindustrial cities by individuals without a highly formalized organization; for example, the craftsman has frequently been responsible for the marketing of his own products. With a few exceptions, the preindustrial community cannot support a large group of middlemen.

The various occupations are organized into what have been termed "guilds."[5] These strive to encompass all, except the elite, who are gainfully employed in some economic activity. Guilds have existed for merchants and handicraft workers (e.g., goldsmiths and weavers) as well as for servants, entertainers, and even beggars and thieves. Typically the guilds operate only within the local community, and there are no large-scale economic organizations such as those in industrial cities which link their members to their fellows in other communities.

Guild membership and apprenticeship are prerequisites to the practice of almost any occupation, a circumstance obviously leading to monopolization. To a degree these organizations regulate the work of their members and the price of their products and services. And the guilds recruit workers into specific occupations, typically selecting them according to such particularistic criteria as kinship rather than universalistic standards.

The guilds are integrated with still other elements of the city's social structure. They perform certain religious functions; for example, in medieval European,

Chinese, and Middle Eastern cities each guild had its "patron saint" and held periodic festivals in his honor. And, by assisting members in time of trouble, the guilds serve as social security agencies.

The economic structure of the preindustrial city functions with little rationality, judged by industrial-urban standards. This is shown in the general non-standardization of manufacturing methods as well as in the products and is even more evident in marketing. In preindustrial cities throughout the world a fixed price is rare; buyer and seller settle their bargain by haggling. (Of course, there are limits above which customers will not buy and below which merchants will not sell.) Often business is conducted in a leisurely manner, money not being the only desired end.

Furthermore, the sorting of goods according to size, weight, and quality is not common. Typical is the adulteration and spoilage of produce. And weights and measures are not standardized: variations exist not only between one city and the next but also within communities, for often different guilds employ their own systems. Within a single city there may be different kinds of currency, which, with the poorly developed accounting and credit systems, signalize a modicum of rationality in the whole of economic action in preindustrial cities.[6]

Social Organization

The economic system of the preindustrial city, based as it has been upon animate sources of power, articulates with a characteristic class structure and family, religious, educational, and governmental systems.

Of the class structure, the most striking component is a literate elite controlling and depending for its existence upon the mass of the populace, even in the traditional cities of India with their caste system. The elite is composed of individuals holding positions in the governmental, religious, and/or educational institutions of the larger society, although at times groups such as large absentee landlords have belonged to it. At the opposite pole are the masses, comprising such groups as handicraft workers whose goods and services are produced primarily for the elite's benefit.[7] Between the elite and the lower class is a rather sharp schism, but in both groups there are gradations in rank. The members of the elite belong to the "correct" families and enjoy power, property, and certain highly valued personal attributes. Their position, moreover, is legitimized by sacred writings.

Social mobility in this city is minimal; the only real threat to the elite comes from the outside—not from the city's lower classes. And a middle class—so typical of industrial-urban communities, where it can be considered the "dominant" class—is not known in the preindustrial city. The system of production in the larger society provides goods, including food, and services in sufficient amounts to support only a small group of leisured individuals; under these conditions an urban middle class, a semileisured group, cannot arise. Nor are a middle class and extensive social mobility essential to the maintenance of the economic system.

Significant is the role of the marginal or "outcaste" groups (e.g., the Eta of Japan), which are not an integral part of the dominant social system. Typically they rank lower than the urban lower class, performing tasks considered especially degrading, such as burying the dead. Slaves, beggars, and the like are outcastes in most preindustrial cities. Even such groups as professional entertainers and itinerant merchants are often viewed as outcastes, for their rovings expose them to "foreign" ideas from which the dominant social group seeks to isolate itself. Actually many outcaste groups, including some of those mentioned above, are ethnic groups, a fact which further intensifies their isolation. (A few, like the Jews in the predominantly Muslim cities of North Africa, have their own small literate religious elite which, however, enjoys no significant political power in the city as a whole.)

An assumption of many urban sociologists is that a small, unstable kinship group, notably the conjugal unit, is a necessary correlate of city life. But this premise does not hold for preindustrial cities.[8] At times sociologists and anthropologists, when generalizing about various traditional societies, have imputed to peasants typically urban kinship patterns. Actually, in these societies the ideal forms of kinship and family life are most closely approximated by members of the urban literate elite, who are best able to fulfil the exacting requirements of the sacred writings. Kinship and the ability to perpetuate one's lineage are accorded marked prestige in preindustrial cities. Children, especially sons, are highly valued, and polygamy or concubinage or adoption help to assure the attainment of large families. The preeminence of kinship is apparent even in those preindustrial cities where divorce is permitted. Thus, among the urban Muslims or urban Chinese divorce is not an index of disorganization; here, conjugal ties are loose and distinctly subordinate to the bonds of kinship, and each member of a dissolved conjugal unit typically is absorbed by his kin group. Marriage, a prerequisite to adult status in the preindustrial city, is entered upon at an early age and is arranged between families rather than romantically, by individuals.

The kinship and familial organization displays some rigid patterns of sex and age differentiation whose universality in preindustrial cities has generally been overlooked. A woman, especially of the upper class, ideally performs few significant functions outside the home. She is clearly subordinate to males, especially her father or husband. Recent evidence indicates that this is true even for such a city as Lhasa, Tibet, where women supposedly have had high status.[9] The isolation of women from public life has in some cases been extreme. In nineteenth-century Seoul, Korea, "respectable" women appeared on the streets only during certain hours of the night when men were supposed to stay at home.[10] Those women in preindustrial cities who evade some of the stricter requirements are members of certain marginal groups (e.g., entertainers) or of the lower class. The role of the urban lower-class woman typically resembles that of the peasant rather than the urban upper-class woman. Industrialization, by creating demands and opportunities for their employment outside the home, is causing significant changes in the status of women as well as in the whole of the kinship system in urban areas.

A formalized system of age grading is an effective mechanism of social control in preindustrial cities. Among siblings the eldest son is privileged. And children and youth are subordinate to parents and other adults. This, combined with early marriage, inhibits the development of a "youth culture." On the other hand, older persons hold considerable power and prestige, a fact contributing to the slow pace of change.

As noted above, kinship is functionally integrated with social class. It also reinforces and is reinforced by the economic organization: the occupations, through the guilds, select their members primarily on the basis of kinship, and much of the work is carried on in the home or immediate vicinity. Such conditions are not functional to the requirements of a highly industrialized society.

The kinship system in the preindustrial city also articulates with a special kind of religious system, whose formal organization reaches fullest development among members of the literate elite.[11] The city is the seat of the key religious functionaries whose actions set standards for the rest of society. The urban lower class, like the peasantry, does not possess the education or the means to maintain all the exacting norms prescribed by the sacred writings. Yet the religious system influences the city's entire social structure. (Typically, within the preindustrial city one religion is dominant; however, certain minority groups adhere to their own beliefs.) Unlike the situation in industrial cities, religious activity is not separate from other social action but permeates family, economic, governmental, and other activities. Daily life is pervaded with religious significance. Especially important are periodic public festivals and ceremonies like Ramadan in Muslim cities. Even distinctly ethnic outcaste groups can through their own religious festivals maintain solidarity.

Magic, too, is interwoven with economic, familial, and other social activities. Divination is commonly employed for determining the "correct" action on critical occasions; for example, in traditional Japanese and Chinese cities, the selection of marriage partners. And nonscientific procedures are widely employed to treat illness among all elements of the population of the preindustrial city.

Formal education typically is restricted to the male elite, its purpose being to train individuals for positions in the governmental, educational, or religious hierarchies. The economy of preindustrial cities does not require mass literacy, nor, in fact, does the system of production provide the leisure so necessary for the acquisition of formal education. Considerable time is needed merely to learn the written language, which often is quite different from that spoken. The teacher occupies a position of honor, primarily because of the prestige of all learning and especially of knowledge of the sacred literature, and learning is traditional and characteristically based upon sacred writings.[12] Students are expected to memorize rather than evaluate and initiate, even in institutions of higher learning.

Since preindustrial cities have no agencies of mass communication, they are relatively isolated from one another. Moreover, the masses within a city are isolated from the elite. The former must rely upon verbal communication, which is formalized in special groups such as storytellers or their counterparts. Through verse and song these transmit upper-class tradition to nonliterate individuals.

The formal government of the preindustrial city is the province of the elite and is closely integrated with the educational and religious systems. It performs two principal functions: exacting tribute from the city's masses to support the activities of the elite and maintaining law and order through a "police force" (at times a branch of the army) and a court system. The police force exists primarily for the control of "outsiders," and the courts support custom and the rule of the sacred literature, a code of enacted legislation typically being absent.

In actual practice little reliance is placed upon formal machinery for regulating social life.[13] Much more significant are the informal controls exerted by the kinship, guild, and religious systems, and here, of course, personal standing is decisive. Status distinctions are visibly correlated with personal attributes, chiefly speech, dress, and personal mannerisms which proclaim ethnic group, occupation, age, sex, and social class. In nineteenth-century Seoul, not only did the upper-class mode of dress differ considerably from that of the masses, but speech varied according to social class, the verb forms and pronouns depending upon whether the speaker ranked higher or lower or was the equal of the person being addressed.[14] Obviously, then, escape from one's role is difficult, even in the street crowds. The individual is ever conscious of his specific rights and duties. All these things conserve the social order in the preindustrial city despite its heterogeneity.

Conclusions

Throughout this [reading] there is the assumption that certain structural elements are universal for all urban centers. This study's hypothesis is that their form in the preindustrial city is fundamentally distinct from that in the industrial-urban community. A considerable body of data not only from medieval Europe, which is somewhat atypical,[15] but from a variety of cultures supports this point of view. Emphasis has been upon the static features of preindustrial city life. But even those preindustrial cities which have undergone considerable change approach the ideal type. For one thing, social change is of such a nature that it is not usually perceived by the general populace.

Most cities of the preindustrial type have been located in Europe or Asia. Even though Athens and Rome and the large commercial centers of Europe prior to the industrial revolution displayed certain unique features, they fit the preindustrial type quite well.[16] And many traditional Latin-American cities are quite like it, although deviations exist, for, excluding pre-Columbian cities, these were affected to some degree by the industrial revolution soon after their establishment.

It is postulated that industrialization is a key variable accounting for the distinctions between preindustrial and industrial cities. The type of social structure required to develop and maintain a form of production utilizing inanimate sources of power is quite unlike that in the preindustrial city.[17] At the very least, extensive industrialization requires a rational, centralized, extra-community economic organization in which recruitment is based more upon universalism than on particularism, a class system which stresses achievement rather than ascription, a small and flexible kinship system, a system of mass education which emphasizes universalistic rather than particularistic criteria, and mass communication. Modification in any one of these elements affects the others and induces changes in other systems such as those of religion and social control as well. Industrialization, moreover, not only requires a special kind of social structure within the urban community but provides the means necessary for its establishment.

Anthropologists and sociologists will in the future devote increased attention to the study of cities throughout the world. They must therefore recognize that the particular kind of social structure found in cities in the United States is not typical of all societies. Miner's recent study of Timbuctoo,[18] which contains much excellent data, points to the need for recognition of the preindustrial city. His emphasis upon the folk-urban continuum diverted him from an equally significant problem: How does Timbuctoo differ from modern industrial cities in its ecological, economic, and social structure? Society there seems even more sacred and organized than Miner admits.[19] For example, he used divorce as an index of disorganization, but in Muslim society divorce within certain rules is justified by the sacred literature. The studies of Hsu and Fried would have considerably more significance had the authors perceived the generality of their findings. And, once the general structure of the preindustrial city is understood, the specific cultural deviations become more meaningful.

Beals notes the importance of the city as a center of acculturation.[20] But an understanding of this process is impossible without some knowledge of the preindustrial city's social structure. Although industrialization is clearly advancing throughout most of the world, the social structure of preindustrial civilizations is conservative; often resisting the introduction of numerous industrial forms. Certainly many cities of Europe (e.g., in France or Spain) are not so fully industrialized as some presume; a number of preindustrial patterns remain. The persistence of preindustrial elements is also evident in cities of North Africa and many parts of Asia; for example, in India and Japan,[21] even though great social change is currently taking place. And the Latin-American city of Merida, which Redfield studied, had many preindustrial traits.[22] A conscious awareness of the ecological, economic, and social structure of the preindustrial city should do much to further the development of comparative urban community studies.

Notes

1. George M. Foster, "What Is Folk Culture?" *American Anthropologist*, LV (1953), 159–73.

2. Gideon Sjoberg, "Folk and 'Feudal' Societies," *American Journal of Sociology*, LVIII (1952), 231–39.

3. Sociologists have devoted almost no attention to the ecology of preindustrial centers. However, works of other social scientists do provide some valuable preliminary data. See, e.g., Marcel Clerget, *Le Caire: Étude de géographie urbaine et d'histoire économique* (2 vols.; Cairo: E. & R. Schindler, 1934); Robert E. Dickinson, *The West European City* (London: Routledge & Kegan Paul, 1951); Roger Le Tourneau, *Fès: Avant le protectorat* (Casablanca: Société Marocaine de Librairie et d'Édition, 1949); Edward W. Lane, *Cairo Fifty Years Ago* (London: John Murray, 1896); J. Sauvaget, *Alep* (Paris: Librairie Orientaliste Paul Geuthner, 1941); J. Weulersse, "Antioche: Essai de géographie urbaine," *Bulletin d'études orientales*, IV (1934), 27–79; Jean Kennedy, *Here Is India* (New York: Charles Scribner's Sons, 1945); and relevant articles in American geographical journals.

4. Dickinson, *op. cit.*, p. 27; O. H. K. Spate, *India and Pakistan* (London: Methuen & Co., 1954), p. 183.

5. For a discussion of guilds and other facets of the preindustrial city's economy see, e.g., J. S. Burgess, *The Guilds of Peking* (New York: Columbia University Press, 1928); Edward T. Williams, *China, Yesterday and Today* (5th ed.; New York: Thomas Y. Crowell Co., 1932); T'ai-ch'u Liao, "The Apprentices in Chengtu during and after the War," *Yenching Journal of Social Studies,* IV (1948), 90–106; H. A. R. Gibb and Harold Bowen, *Islamic Society and the West* (London: Oxford University Press, 1950), Vol. I, Part I, chap. vi; Le Tourneau, *op. cit.;* Clerget, *op. cit.;* James W. Thompson and Edgar N. Johnson, *An Introduction to Medieval Europe* (New York: W. W. Norton Co., 1937), chap. xx; Sylvia L. Thrupp, "Medieval Gilds Reconsidered," *Journal of Economic History,* II (1942), 161–73.

6. For an extreme example of unstandardized currency cf. Robert Coltman, Jr., *The Chinese* (Philadelphia: F. A. Davis, 1891), p. 52. In some traditional societies (e.g., China) the state has sought to standardize economic action in the city by setting up standard systems of currency and/or weights and measures; these efforts, however, generally proved ineffective. Inconsistent policies in taxation, too, hinder the development of a "rational" economy.

7. The status of the true merchant in the preindustrial city, ideally, has been low; in medieval Europe and China many merchants were considered "outcastes." However, in some preindustrial cities a few wealthy merchants have acquired considerable power even though their role has not been highly valued. Even then most of their prestige has come through participation in religious, governmental, or educational activities, which have been highly valued (see, e.g., Ping-ti Ho, "The Salt Merchants of Yang-Chou: A Study of Commercial Capitalism in Eighteenth-Century China," *Harvard Journal of Asiatic Studies,* XVII [1954], 130–68).

8. For materials on the kinship system and age and sex differentiation see, e.g., Le Tourneau, *op. cit.;* Edward W. Lane, *The Manners and Customs of the Modern Egyptians* (3d ed.; New York: E. P. Dutton Co., 1923); C. Snouck Hurgronje, *Mekka in the Latter Part of the Nineteenth Century,* trans. J. H. Monahan (London: Luzac, 1931); Horace Miner, *The Primitive City of Timbuctoo* (Princeton: Princeton University Press, 1953); Alice M. Bacon, *Japanese Girls and Women* (rev. ed.; Boston: Houghton Mifflin Co., 1902); J. S. Burgess, "Community Organization in China," *Far Eastern Survey,* XIV (1945), 371–73; Morton H. Fried, *Fabric of Chinese Society* (New York: Frederick A. Praeger, 1953); Francis L. K. Hsu, *Under the Ancestors' Shadow* (New York: Columbia University Press, 1948); Cornelius Osgood, *The Koreans and Their Culture* (New York: Ronald Press, 1951), chap. viii; Jukichi Inouye, *Home Life in Tokyo* (2d ed.; Tokyo: Tokyo Printing Co., 1911).

9. Tsung-Lien Shen and Shen-Chi Liu, *Tibet and the Tibetans* (Stanford: Stanford University Press, 1953), pp. 143–44.

10. Osgood, *op. cit.,* p. 146.

11. For information on various aspects of religious behavior see, e.g., Le Tourneau, *op. cit.;* Miner, *op. cit.;* Lane, *Manners and Customs;* Hurgronje, *op. cit.;* André Chouraqui, *Les Juifs d'Afrique du Nord* (Paris: Presses Universitaires de France, 1952); Justus Doolittle, *Social Life of the Chinese* (London: Sampson Low, 1868); John K. Shryock, *The Temples of Anking and Their Cults* (Paris: Privately printed, 1931); Derk Bodde (ed.), *Annual Customs and Festivals in Peking* (Peiping: Henri Vetch, 1936); Edwin Benson, *Life in a Medieval City* (New York: Macmillan Co., 1920); Hsu, *op. cit.*

12. Le Tourneau, *op. cit.,* Part VI; Lane, *Manners and Customs,* chap. ii; Charles Bell, *The People of Tibet* (Oxford: Clarendon Press, 1928), chap. xix; O. Olufsen, *The Emir of Bokhara and His Country* (London: William Heinemann, 1911), chap. ix; Doolittle, *op. cit.*

13. Carleton Coon, *Caravan: The Story of the Middle East* (New York: Henry Holt & Co., 1951), p. 259; George W. Gilmore, *Korea from Its Capital* (Philadelphia: Presbyterian Board of Publication, 1892), pp. 51–52.

14. Osgood, *op. cit.,* chap. viii; Gilmore, *op. cit.,* chap. iv.

15. Henri Pirenne, in *Medieval Cities* (Princeton: Princeton University Press, 1925), and others have noted that European cities grew up in opposition to and were separate from the greater society. But this thesis has been overstated for medieval Europe. Most preindustrial cities are integral parts of broader social structures.

16. Some of these cities made extensive use of water power, which possibly fostered deviations from the type.

17. For a discussion of the institutional prerequisites of industrialization see, e.g., Bert F. Hoselitz, "Social Structure and Economic Growth," *Economia internazionale,* VI (1953), 52–77, and Marion J. Levy, "Some Sources of the Vulnerability of the Structures of Relatively Non-industrialized Societies to Those of Highly Industrialized Societies," in Bert F. Hoselitz (ed.), *The Progress of Underdeveloped Areas* (Chicago: University of Chicago Press, 1952), pp. 114 ff.

18. *Op. cit.*

19. This point seems to have been perceived also by Asael T. Hansen in his review of Horace Miner's *The Primitive City of Timbuctoo, American Journal of Sociology,* LIX (1954), 501–2.

20. Ralph L. Beals, "Urbanism, Urbanization and Acculturation," *American Anthropologist,* LIII (1951), 1–10.

21. See, e.g., D. R. Gadgil, *Poona: A Socio-economic Survey* (Poona: Gokhale Institute of Politics and Economics, 1952), Part II; N. V. Sovani, *Social Survey of Kolhapur City* (Poona: Gokhale Institute of Politics and Economics, 1951), Vol. II; Noel P. Gist, "Caste Differentials in South India," *American Sociological Review,* XIX (1954), 126–37; John Campbell Pelzel, "Social Stratification in Japanese Urban Economic Life" (unpublished Ph.D. dissertation, Harvard University, Department of Social Relations, 1950).

22. Robert Redfield, *The Folk Culture of Yucatan* (Chicago: University of Chicago Press, 1941).

3

The Sumerians

Samuel Noah Kramer

The Tigris-Euphrates plain is a hot, arid land. Six thousand years ago it was a wind-swept barren. It had no minerals, almost no stone, no trees, practically no building material of any kind. It has been described as a land with "the hand of God against it." Yet it was in this desolate region that man built what was probably the first high civilization. Here were born the inventions of writing, farming technology, architecture, the first codes of law, the first cities. Perhaps the very poverty of the land provided the stimulus that mothered these inventions. But the main credit must go to the people who created them—a most remarkable people called the Sumerians.

These Sumerians, as now revealed by long archaeological research, were a surprisingly modern folk. In many ways they were like the pioneers who built the U.S.—practical, ambitious, enterprising, jealous of their personal rights, technologically inventive. Having no stone or timber, they built with marsh reeds and river mud, invented the brick mold and erected cities of baked clay. They canalled the waters of the Tigris and Euphrates rivers into the arid fields and turned Sumer into a veritable Garden of Eden. To manage their irrigation systems they originated regional government, thus emerging from the petty social order of the family and village to the city-state. They created a written language and committed it to permanent clay tablets. They traded their grain surpluses to distant peoples for metals and other materials they lacked. By the third millennium B.C. the culture and civilization of Sumer, a country about the size of the state of Massachusetts, had spread its influence over the whole Middle East, from India to the Mediterranean. And there is hardly an area of our culture today—in mathematics or philosophy, literature or architecture, finance or education, law or politics, religion or folklore—that does not owe some of its origins to the Sumerians.

One might suppose that the story of the Sumerians and their accomplishments would be one of the most celebrated in history. But the astonishing fact is that until about a century ago the modern world had no idea that Sumer or its people had ever existed. For more than 2,000 years they had simply vanished from the human record. Babylonia and ancient Egypt were known to every history student, but the earlier Sumerians were buried and forgotten. Now, thanks to a century of archaeological labor and to the Sumerians' own cuneiform tablets, we have come to know them intimately—as well as or better than any other people of the early history of mankind. The story of how the lost Sumerian civilization was discovered is itself a remarkable chapter. This article will review briefly how the history of the Sumerians was resurrected and what we have learned about them.

The Cuneiform Tablets

Modern archaeologists began to dig in Mesopotamia for its ancient civilizations around a century ago. They were looking for the cities of the Assyrians and Babylonians, who of course were well known from Biblical and Greek literature. As the world knows, the diggers soon came upon incredibly rich finds. At the sites of Nineveh and other ancient Assyrian cities they unearthed many clay tablets inscribed with the wedge-shaped writing called cuneiform. This script was taken to be the invention of the Assyrians. Since the Assyrians were apparently a Semitic people, the language was assumed to be Semitic. But few clues were available for decipherment of the strange cuneiform script.

Then came a development which was to be as important a key to discovery in Mesopotamia as the famous Rosetta Stone in Egypt. In western Persia, notably on the Rock of Behistun, European scholars found some cuneiform inscriptions in three languages. They identified one of the languages as Old Persian, another as Elamite, and the third as the language of the Assyrian tablets. The way was now open to decipher the cuneiform writing—first the Old Persian, then the Assyrian, of which it was apparently a translation.

When scholars finally deciphered the "Assyrian" script, they discovered that the cuneiform writing could not have been originated by the Assyrian Semites. Its symbols, which were not alphabetic but syllabic and ideographic, apparently were derived from non-Semitic rather than Semitic words. And many of the cuneiform tablets turned out to be written in a language without any Semitic characteristics whatever. The archaeologists had to conclude, therefore, that the Assyrians had taken over the cuneiform script from a people who had lived in the region before them.

Who were this people? Jules Oppert, a leading 19th-century investigator of ancient Mesopotamia, found a clue to their name in certain inscriptions which referred to the "King of Sumer and Akkad." He concluded that Akkad was the northern part of the country (indeed, the Assyrians and Babylonians are now called Akkadians), and that Sumer was the southern part, inhabited by the people who spoke the non-Semitic language and had invented cuneiform writing.

So it was that the Sumerians were rediscovered after 2,000 years of oblivion. Oppert resurrected their name in 1869. In the following decades French, American, Anglo-American and German expeditions uncovered the buried Sumerian cities— Lagash, Nippur, Shuruppak, Kish, Ur (Ur of the Chaldees in the Bible), Erech, Asmar and so on. The excavation of ancient Sumer has proceeded almost continuously for three quarters of a century; even during World War II the Iraqi went on digging at a few sites. These historic explorations have recovered hundreds of thousands of Sumerian tablets, great temples, monuments, tombs, sculptures, paintings, tools, irrigation systems and remnants of almost every aspect of the Sumerian culture. As a result we have a fairly complete picture of what life in Sumer was like 5,000 years ago. We know something about how the Sumerians looked (from their statues); we know a good deal about their houses and palaces, their tools and weapons, their art and musical instruments, their jewels and ornaments, their skills and crafts, their industry and commerce, their *belles lettres* and government, their schools and temples, their loves and hates, their kings and history.

The Peoples of Sumer

Let us run quickly over the history. The area where the Sumerians lived is lower Mesopotamia, from Baghdad down to the Persian Gulf. . . . It is reasonably certain that the Sumerians themselves were not the first settlers in this region. Just as the Indian names Mississippi, Massachusetts, etc., show that North America was inhabited before the English-speaking settlers came, so we know that the Sumerians were preceded in Mesopotamia by another people because the ancient names of the Tigris and Euphrates rivers (*Idigna* and *Buranun*), and even the names of the Sumerian cities (Nippur, Ur, Kish, etc.), are not Sumerian words. The city names must be derived from villages inhabited by the earlier people.

The same kind of clue—words that turn up in the Sumerian writing but are plainly not Sumerian in origin—tells us something about those first settlers in Sumer. As Benno Landsberger of the University of Chicago, one of the keenest minds in cuneiform research, has shown, among these pre-Sumerian words are those for farmer, herdsman, fisherman, plow, metal smith, carpenter, weaver, potter, mason and perhaps even merchant. It follows that the predecessors of the Sumerians must already have developed a fairly advanced civilization. This is confirmed by excavations of their stone implements and pottery.

The dates of Sumer's early history have always been surrounded with uncertainty, and they have not been satisfactorily settled by tests with the new method of radiocarbon dating. According to the best present estimates, the first settlers occupied the area some time before 4000 B.C.; new geological evidence indicates that the lower Tigris-Euphrates Valley, once covered by the Persian Gulf, became an inhabitable land well before that date. Be that as it may, it seems that the people called Sumerians did not arrive in the region until nearly 3000 B.C. just where they came from is in doubt, but there is some reason to believe that their original home had been in the neighborhood of a city called Aratta, which may have been near the Caspian Sea: Sumerian epic poets sang glowingly of Aratta, and its people were said to speak the Sumerian language.

Wherever the Sumerians came from, they brought a creative spirit and an extraordinary surge of progress to the land of Sumer. Uniting with the people who already inhabited it, they developed a rich and powerful civilization. Not long after they arrived, a king called Etana became the ruler of all Sumer: he is described in Sumerian literature as "the man who stabilized all the lands," and he may therefore be the first empire builder in human history. Sumer reached its fullest flowering around 2500 B.C., when its people had developed the cuneiform symbols and thereby originated their finest gift to civilization—the gift of written communication and history. Their own history came to an end some 800 years later: about 1720 B.C. In that year Hammurabi of Babylon won control of the country, and Sumer disappeared in a Babylonian kingdom.

Life in Sumer

The Sumerians' writings and disinterred cities, as I have said, make it possible to reconstruct their life in great detail. Their civilization rested on agriculture and fishing. Among their inventions were the wagon wheel, the plow and the sailboat, but their science and engineering went far beyond these elementary tools. For irrigation the Sumerians built intricate systems of canals, dikes, weirs and reservoirs. They developed measuring and surveying instruments, and a sexagesimal number system (*i.e.,* based on the number 60) with a place notation device not unlike our decimal system. Their farming was highly sophisticated: among their tablets is a veritable farmer's almanac of instructions in agriculture.

In the crafts, the Sumerians' inventions included the potter's wheel, metal casting (of copper and bronze), riveting, soldering, engraving, cloth fulling, bleaching and dyeing. They manufactured paints, leather, cosmetics, perfumes and drugs. Prescriptions recorded on some of their tablets show that the Sumerian physician had command of a large assortment of *materia medica,* prepared from plants, animals and inorganic sources.

Although the Sumerians' economy was primarily agricultural, their life was centered mainly in the cities. Here lived many of the farmers, herdsmen and fishermen, as well as merchants, craftsmen, architects, doctors, scribes, soldiers and priests. Artisans and traveling merchants sold their products in the central town market, and were paid in kind or in money—usually silver coin in the form of a disk or ring. The dozen or so cities in Sumer probably ranged from 10,000 to 50,000 in population. Each was enclosed by a wall and surrounded with suburban villages and hamlets.

The dominant feature of every Sumerian city was a massive temple mounted on a high terrace. It usually had the form of a ziggurat, Sumer's most distinctive contribution to religious architecture. This is a pyramidal tower with a series of ascending terraces winding around the outside. To break the unattractive blankness of the temple's mud-brick walls, the Sumerian architects introduced buttresses and recesses, and they also beautified the building with columns decorated in colored mosaics. Inside the temple were rooms for the priests and a central shrine with a niche for the statue of the god. Each city in Sumer had a different tutelary god, and the Sumerians considered the city the god's property. Thus the city of Nippur, for example, belonged to Enlil, the god of the air. Nippur became Sumer's chief religious and cultural center, and Enlil was elevated to the highest rank as father of all the gods.

Originally the cities were governed by the citizens themselves, presided over by a governor of their selection. On all important decisions the citizens met in an assembly divided into two chambers—the "elders" and the "men." But for military reasons they gradually relinquished this democratic system. Each city acquired a ruler—at first elected, later hereditary—who organized its defense against the other cities and against foreign invaders. In the course of time the king rivaled the city's religious leaders in wealth and influence. The rulers of Sumer's dozen or so city-states also contended with one another for control of the whole country, and the history of Sumer is largely a record of bitter conflicts among its cities, which eventually led to its downfall.

The life of the individual citizen in a Sumerian city was remarkably free and prosperous. The poorest citizen managed to own a farm and cattle or a house and garden. To be sure, slavery was permitted, and a man could sell his children or his entire family to pay off his debts. But even slaves had certain legal rights: they could engage in business, borrow money and buy their freedom. (The average price for an adult slave was 10 shekels—less than the price of an ass.) The great majority of Sumerians were free citizens, going about their business and the pursuit of happiness with a minimum of restrictions. This did not, however, apply to children, who were under the absolute authority of their parents, could be disinherited or sold into slavery, and had to marry mates chosen by the parents. But in the normal course of events Sumerian families cherished their children and were knit closely together by love and mutual obligations. Women had many legal rights, including the right to hold property and engage in business. A man could divorce his wife on comparatively slender grounds, or, if they had no children, he was allowed to take a second wife.

Most Sumerian families lived in a one-story, mud-brick house consisting of several rooms grouped around an open court. The well-to-do had two-story houses of about a dozen rooms, plastered and whitewashed inside and out; these houses boasted servants' rooms and sometimes even a private chapel. Often the house had a mausoleum in the basement where the family buried its dead. The Sumerians believed that the souls of the dead traveled to a nether world where existence continued more or less as on earth. They therefore buried pots, tools, weapons and jewels with the dead. When a king died, the palace sometimes buried with him some of his courtiers and servants and even his chariot and animals.

Sumerian men were often clean-shaven, but many of them wore a long beard and had long hair parted in the middle. In early times their usual dress was a flounced skirt and felt cloak; later these were replaced by a long shirt and a big fringed shawl draped over the left shoulder, leaving the right arm bare. The common dress for women was a long shawl covering the body from head to foot, except for the right shoulder. Women usually braided their hair into a heavy pigtail and wound it around the head, but on important occasions they wore elaborate headdresses consisting of ribbons, beads and pendants.

Music apparently occupied a large place in the life of the Sumerians—at home, in school and in the temple. Beautifully constructed harps and lyres were found in the royal tombs at Ur. Research has also turned up references to drums, tambourines, reed and metal pipes, and hymns written on tablets. Some of the important personages in the palaces and temples of the Sumerian cities were musicians.

The Sumerians cannot be said to have produced any great art, but they did show considerable skill in carving and sculpture. Perhaps their most original contribution to the graphic arts was the cylinder seal—a stone cylinder with a carved design which was impressed in clay by rolling the cylinder over it. These designs, or seals, appear on clay tablets, jar covers and so on. They depict scenes such as a king on the battlefield, a shepherd defending his flock from wild beasts, heraldic arrangements of animals. Eventually the Sumerians settled on one favorite seal design which became almost their trademark—a scene showing a worshipper being presented to a god by his personal good angel.

Religion

The Sumerians lived by a simple, fatalistic theology. They believed that the universe and their personal lives were ruled by living gods, invisible to mortal eyes. The chief gods were those of water, earth, air and heaven, named respectively Enki, Ki, Enlil and An. From a primeval sea were created the earth, the atmosphere, the gods and sky, the sun, moon, planets and stars, and finally life. There were gods in charge of the sun, moon and planets, of winds and storms; of rivers and mountains, of cities and states, of farms and irrigation ditches, of the pickax, brick mold and plow. The major gods established a set of unchangeable laws which must be obeyed willy-nilly by everything and everybody. Thus the Sumerians were untroubled by any question of free will. Man existed to please and serve the gods, and his life followed their divine orders. Because the great gods were far away in the distant sky and had more important matters to attend to, each person appealed to a particular personal god, a "good angel," through whom he sought salvation. Not that the people neglected regular public devotions to the gods. In the Sumerian temples a court of professionals, including priests, priestesses, musicians and eunuchs, offered daily libations and sacrifices of animal and vegetable fats. There were also periodic feasts and celebrations, of which the most important was a royal ceremony ushering in each new year.

This ceremony is traceable to the cycle of nature in Mesopotamia. Every summer, in the hot, parched months, all vegetation died and animal life languished. In the autumn the land began to revive and bloom again. The Sumerian theology explained these events by supposing that the god of vegetation retired to the nether world in the summer and returned to the earth around the time of the new year; his sexual reunion with his wife Inanna, the goddess of love and procreation, then restored fertility to the land. To celebrate this revival and ensure fecundity, the Sumerians each year staged a marriage ceremony between their king, as the risen god, and a priestess representing the goddess Inanna. The marriage was made an occasion of prolonged festival, ritual, music and rejoicing.

The Sumerians considered themselves to be a chosen people, in more intimate contact with the gods than was the rest of mankind. Nevertheless they had a moving vision of all mankind living in peace and security, united by a universal faith and perhaps even by a universal language. Curiously, they projected this vision into the past, into a long-gone golden age, rather than into the future. As a Sumerian poet put it:

> *Once upon a time there was no snake, there was no scorpion,*
> *There was no hyena, there was no lion,*
> *There was no wild dog, no wolf*
> *There was no fear, no terror,*
> *Man had no rival.*
>
> *Once upon a time . . .*
> *The whole universe, the people in unison,*
> *To Enlil in one tongue gave praise.*

To students of the ancient religions of the Near East, much of the Sumerian cosmology and theology is easily recognizable. The order of the universe's creation, the Job-like resignation of sinful and mortal man to the will of the gods, the mystic tale of the dying god and his triumphant resurrection, the Aphrodite-like goddess Inanna, the ideals of "humaneness"—these and many other features of the Sumerian creed survive without much change in the later religions of the ancient world. Indeed, the very name of the Sumerian dying god, Dumuzi, endures as Biblical Tammuz, whose descent to the nether regions was still mourned by the women of Jerusalem in the days of the prophet Ezekiel. It is not too much to say that, with the decipherment of the Sumerian tablets, we can now trace many of the roots of man's major religious creeds back to Sumer.

Cuneiform

But the Sumerians' chief contribution to civilization was their invention of writing. Their cuneiform script is the earliest known system of writing in man's history. The cuneiform system served as the main tool of written communication throughout western Asia for some 2,000 years—long after the Sumerians themselves had disappeared. Without it, mankind's cultural progress would certainly have been much delayed.

The Sumerian script began as a set of pictographic signs devised by temple administrators and priests to keep track of the temple's resources and activities.

EARLIEST PICTOGRAPHS (3000 B.C.)	DENOTATION OF PICTOGRAPHS	PICTOGRAPHS IN ROTATED POSITION	CUNEIFORM SIGNS CA. 1900 B.C.	BASIC LOGOGRAPHIC VALUES		ADDITIONAL LOGOGRAPHIC VALUES		SYLLABARY (PHONETIC VALUES)
				READING	MEANING	READING	MEANING	
	HEAD AND BODY OF A MAN			LÚ	MAN			
	HEAD WITH MOUTH INDICATED			KA	MOUTH	KIRI₃ ZÚ GÙ DUG₄ INIM	NOSE TEETH VOICE TO SPEAK WORD	KA ZÚ
	BOWL OF FOOD			NINDA	FOOD, BREAD	NÍG GAR	THING TO PLACE	
	MOUTH + FOOD			KÚ	TO EAT	ŠAGAR	HUNGER	
	STREAM OF WATER			A	WATER	DURU₅	MOIST	A
	MOUTH + WATER			NAG	TO DRINK	EMMEN	THIRST	
	FISH			KUA	FISH			KU₆ HA
	BIRD			MUŠEN	BIRD			HU PAG
	HEAD OF AN ASS			ANŠE	ASS			
	EAR OF BARLEY			ŠE	BARLEY			ŠE

EVOLUTION OF SUMERIAN WRITING is outlined in the chart at left. The earliest pictographs were inscribed vertically on tablets. Around 2800 B.C. the direction of this writing was changed from vertical to horizontal, with a corresponding rotation of the pictographs. The pictographs were now reduced to collections of linear strokes made by a stylus which had a triangular point. Some of these cuneiform signs are logographic, *i.e.*, each sign represents a spoken word. Some of the signs represent more than one word;

They inscribed the signs in clay with a reed stylus, and this accounts for the curious wedge-shaped characters. In the course of the centuries Sumerian scholars developed the signs into purely phonetic symbols representing words or syllables.

More than 90 per cent of the tablets that have been excavated in Sumer are economic, legal and administrative documents, not unlike the commercial and governmental records of our own day. But some 5,000 of the finds are literary

CUNEIFORM SIGNS	TRANSLITERATION	TRANSLATION
	AMA-AR-GI$_4$	FREEDOM
	ARHUŠ	COMPASSION
	DINGIR	GOD, GODDESS
	DUB-SAR	SCRIBE
	É-DUB-BA	SCHOOL, ACADEMY
	HÉ-GÁL	PLENTY, PROSPERITY
	ME	DIVINE LAWS
	NAM-LÚ-LU$_7$	HUMANITY, HUMANENESS
	NAM-LUGAL	KINGSHIP
	NAM-TAR	FATE, DESTINY
	NÍG-GA	PROPERTY
	NÍG-GE-NA	TRUTH
	NÍG-SI-SÁ	JUSTICE
	SAG-GÍG	BLACK-HEADED ONES, THE SUMERIAN PEOPLE
	UKKIN	ASSEMBLY

some are syllabic, *i.e.,* they also represent syllables. The accents and subscript numbers on the modern transliteration of the cuneiform signs are used by modern scholars to distinguish between signs having the same pronunciation but different meanings. In the chart at right are 15 cuneiform words, their transliteration and their English translation.

works: myths and epic tales, hymns and lamentations, proverbs, fables, essays. They qualify as man's oldest known literature—nearly 1,000 years older than the *Iliad* and the Hebrew Bible. In addition the tablets include a number of Sumerian "textbooks," listing the names of trees, birds, insects, minerals, cities, countries and so forth. There are even commemorative narratives which constitute mankind's first writing of history.

From the Sumerians' invention of writing grew the first formal system of education—another milestone in human intellectual progress. They set up "professional" schools to train scribes, secretaries and administrators; in time these vocational schools became also centers of culture where scholars, scientists and poets devoted their lives to learning and teaching.

The head of the school was called "the school father"; the pupils, "school sons." Among the faculty members were "the man in charge of drawing," "the man in charge of Sumerian," "the man in charge of the whip." There was no sparing of the rod. The curriculum consisted in copying and memorizing the lists of words and names on the textbook tablets, in studying and composing poetic narratives, hymns and essays and in mastering mathematical tables and problems, including tables of square, and cube roots.

Teachers in ancient Sumer seem to have been treated not unlike their counterparts in the U.S. today: their salaries were low and they were looked upon with a mixture of respect and contempt. The Sumerians were an aggressive people, prizing wealth, renown and social prestige. As their tablets suggest, they were far more concerned with accounts than with academic learning.

Their restless ambition and aggressive spirit are reflected in the bitter rivalry among their cities and kings. The history of Sumer is a story of wars in which one city after another rose to ascendancy over the country. Although there are many gaps in our information, we can reconstruct the main outlines of that history from references in the tablets. The first recorded ruler of Sumer, as I have mentioned, was Etana, king of Kish. Probably not long afterward a king of Erech by the name of Meskiaggasher founded a dynasty which ruled the whole region from the Mediterranean to the Zagros Mountains northeast of Sumer. The city of Kish then rose to dominance again, only to be supplanted by the city of Ur, whose first king, Mesannepadda, is said to have ruled for 80 years and made Ur the capital of Sumer. After Mesannepadda's death, Sumer again came under the rule of the city of Erech, under a king named Gilgamesh who became the supreme hero of Sumerian history—a brave, adventurous figure whose deeds were celebrated throughout the ancient world of western Asia. The next great ruler who appears in the record was Lugalannemundu of the City of Adab; he is reported to have ruled 90 years and to have controlled an empire extending far beyond Sumer. But his empire also fell apart, and a king of Kish named Mesilim became the dominant figure in Sumer. Later rule over the country was won by the city of Lagash. The last ruler of the Lagash dynasty, a king named Urukagina, has the distinction of being the first recorded social reformer. He suppressed the city's harsh bureaucracy, reduced taxes, and brought relief to widows, orphans and the poor. One of King Urukagina's inscriptions contains the word "freedom"—the first appearance of this word in man's history. But within less than 10 years a king of the neighboring city of Umma overthrew Urukagina and put the city of Lagash to the torch.

4

Tenochtitlán

Jorge E. Hardoy

The Layout of the City

Seen against the tranquil surface of the lagoon, and backed by a distant circle of snowy mountain peaks shrouded in clouds through which rose Popocatépetl and its smaller neighbor, Iztaccíhuatl, the city at the beginning of the fifteenth century must have appeared as a level expanse, trees sprinkled along its canals and muddy banks extending in all directions.

A century later, Tenochtitlán, or at least its center, had changed radically. In the middle of what had once been the principal island, now the precinct of the Great Teocalli, rose the pyramidal mass of the Templo Mayor, thirty meters high and attracting all eyes. Beyond it, Tlatelolco's recently completed temple could be seen.[1] All over the city minor pyramids marked the centers of the twenty wards into which the Aztec capital was divided. The general impression was one of a city which had gradually acquired a workable, if incomplete, urban plan. From maps, archeological excavations in various sectors of the present day city, lucky finds unearthed during construction of modern public works, and the chronicles and histories of the sixteenth century, we can envision a city laid out in rather rudimentary form. But it was certainly a city where a general layout and a traffic system was emerging to satisfy the needs of a large population and a traffic consisting entirely of pedestrians and canoes.

The reports of the first Spaniards who came upon the city agree. Cortés, describing it in the second of his *Cartas de Relación* says, "Its streets, that is the principal ones, are very wide and very straight, and these and all the rest, are made half of earth and the other half of water, on which they travel in their canoes. All the streets have openings at intervals through which water passes from one side to another, and over all these openings, some being very wide, they have bridges of very wide and long beams, so well made and sturdy that ten horsemen side by side might pass" (Cortés, 1961).

The Conquistador Anónimo also remembers, "the beautiful and wide streets" characteristic of Tenochtitlán and of "all the other towns which we have said are on this lake, in that part having sweet water." Lack of any references to secondary streets does not alter my impression that the plan of the major part of the city was regular, or becoming increasingly regular, canals alternating with paths or roads of earth built on embankments. This would have been essential in order to make maximum use of land which was scarce and difficult to wrest from the lake. We must also remember that in a society in which the head of each family was responsible to his clan for the productivity of the parcel of land allotted him, the *chinampas* would have been subject to logical and equitable distribution.

Tenochtitlán's plan is not always precise, either in its larger layouts or in the details of the outlines of its better built districts. This was probably due more to a lack of adequate instruments for measuring, or disinterest in greater precision, than to a disregard for a scheme which would have offered the inhabitants maximum advantage of the scarce available land.

Architecture of the Indian civilizations of Mesoamerica generally lacked the precision of measurement seen in Egyptian architecture. In spite of outstanding mathematical and astronomical knowledge, the Indian civilizations could not overcome the absence of stable materials with which they could repeat certain measurements exactly. Axial compositions, however, were common in Mesoamerica, and Indian architects excelled in designing large structural groupings to be built on flat land. These gradually gave rise to building complexes of an urban character, laid out with unquestionable symmetry and precision. Even in those ceremonial centers constructed on the uneven terrain of Chiapas and the Petén, Maya architects employed quadrangles to set out groups of temples and principal buildings. Use of partial axes was common in these groups of structures as well as large axes of composition in relating the variety of structures forming a ceremonial center to each other. Tikal is a clear example of this principle as are Nakum, Yaxhá, Naranjo, and other less important ceremonial centers.

We can see the culmination of this type of design in Tulum where, on a site removed from their decaying ceremonial centers, the Maya adopted what I believe was their first deliberate urban plan.

All cultures dependent for subsistence and economic development, from their early evolution, on intensive cultivation of land requiring drainage and irrigation, have quickly learned the importance of a regular layout which permits maximum profit from this land. The first known urban planning on a large scale appeared in the Middle and Near East among the cultures that had developed in river valleys. Certainly in America, the logical evolution of various cultures as they adapted to environmental conditions elicited solutions similar to those evolved by the river cultures of India, the Indus and Mesopotamia thousands of years before.

Tenochtitlán was no exception. A spontaneous but ordered plan emerged in all the new districts that were continually being added to the city, and the Aztecs probably repartitioned and redistributed sectors in the peripheral areas which were periodically devastated by floods. This, I believe, explains the unceasing re-arrangement of the original layout, which was probably more disorderly than the one the Spaniards saw. And this, too, I feel, was how the districts of Tenochtitlán were connected, following the general outlines imposed both by the causeways, which determined the two main axes of the city's orientation, and by the regular base of the central precinct occupied by the temples. We are not dealing with a precise gridiron as we find in Greek or Roman cities, nor even a regular plan such as the Inca developed in some of their new settlements. Instead we see a pattern adopted progressively as extensions were added to the city.

Tenochtitlán had two principal routes or axes which crossed near the geo-graphical center at a point at the base of the Templo Mayor's stairway. These two streets, converging on the solid ground of the original island, were continuations of the causeways which served the dual purpose of crossing the lake and avoiding the swampy *chinampa* areas. The causeways not only connected the city with the mainland towns but also acted as dikes to contain floods.

One of the axes crossed the city from north to south, and in turn was di-vided into north and south sections. The largest section, running south from the Sacred Precinct to Ixtapalapa, was the route by which Cortés and his men entered Tenochtitlán. It was formed by two branch roads, originating at the cities of Ixtapa-lapa and Coyoacán, which joined into a single road about two kilometers from the coast. From the juncture of the roads to the southern bank of the island was about six and one-half kilometers, eight in all to the center of the city.[2] The causeway to Ixtapalapa was built around the year 1429 by order of King Itzcóatl (Galindo y Villa, 1955).

The causeway to Tepeyac started at the Sacred Precinct and ran north. It was not as straight as the first one and crossed the city to the east of Tlatelolco's market. At approximately two kilometers from its point of origin, it veered northeast, pass-ing through the last *chinampa* districts near the shore, and crossed over the lake to the city of Tepeyac, a distance of some four kilometers. Another causeway con-nected Tlatelolco with points on the shore to the northwest.

The two most important causeways ran from the center of Tlatelolco and Tenochtitlán westward to Tlacopán. The latter was formed by two branch roads, one which started at Chapultepec and the second at Tlacopán. Both converged at about 2,500 meters from the shoreline, near the island of Mazatzintanalco.[3] It was along this causeway that the aqueduct to bring fresh water from Chapultepec's spring to Tenochtitlán was built.

These three causeways were fundamental in determining the plan of the later Spanish city. In fact, the modern streets of República Argentina and Seminario co-incide with the north-south axis of the Aztec city, and the Calle de Tacuba with the western causeway. A fourth short causeway went from the center of the city to the eastern shore of the island where it came to an end at the canoe port.

These causeways captured the attention of the Spanish. Cortés tells us that the city "has four entrances, all man-made causeways, as wide as two lance lengths" (Cortés, 1961). Díaz del Castillo adds that on the way to Tenochtitlán from Ixtapalapa "we went on the causeway before us, which is eight paces wide, and goes so straight to the City of Mexico that it seems to me that it turns hardly at all" (Díaz del Castillo, 1955).[4]

All of the causeways were defended by openings, cutting across them from one side to another, which could only be crossed by drawbridges. These openings also served to regulate the water level in the fresh water lake created artificially between the shore and the north-south causeway. The causeway to Ixtapalapa probably had only one opening, formed by the irrigation canal bounding Moctezuma's New Houses and Tenochtitlán's main plaza to the south. It was, however, defended by "a bulwark of stone . . . with two towers on the sides" (Herrera, 1945). It was next to these "little towers," as Bernal Díaz del Castillo calls them (actually the Fort Xoloc shown in Cortés' map) that the Spanish conquistador had, in November 1519, his first meeting with the Aztec king.

The two main axes determined the direction of the city's major streets and canals. According to Orozco y Berra's reconstruction, the center of Tlatelolco and the western causeway from Tlacopán joined a few meters to the west of the Great Teocalli of Tenochtitlán via two streets which ran parallel to the north-south axis or causeway from Tepeyac. Tenochtitlán had few streets but canals crossed it in all directions, especially on the outskirts of the city. In the center and in the older, more densely populated districts, streets of packed earth alternated with canals in an apparently intentional, parallel arrangement.

We may wonder if Tenochtitlán reflected the urban life that was beginning to develop on the central plateau of Mexico, whether the Aztec capital's plan and urban elements were repeated in the smaller towns of the Valley, or whether Tenochtitlán was an exception because of its location, size, rapid development, and political importance. Aside from the conditions imposed by Tenochtitlán's very location, we have reason to believe that the Aztecs were beginning to develop principles of general city planning in order to achieve an efficient urban organization. I consider this possibility based on the words of a well-known Mexican historian: "When a site was chosen to build a town, two crossing lines were drawn, one pointing north to south and the other from east to west. Where these lines crossed, a quadrangular space was reserved, and was enclosed by walls, leaving four gateways at each of the four cardinal points. Each of the four principal streets led up to these gateways. These streets were laid out in as straight a line as possible." He later added, "In the center of the court a truncated pyramid was constructed, its western side reserved for the principal stairway" (Alcocer, 1935).

Motolinia has left us a detailed description of Indian cities: "These temples are called teocallis, and we find all over this land, that in the best part of town, they made a large, square courtyard; in the large towns there is an arrow's shot from corner to corner, and in smaller towns the courtyards are smaller. They enclosed this court with a wall, and many of these were topped with merlons; their doors opened on to the principal streets and thoroughfares which were made to end at the courtyard. To further honor their temples, they laid out their roads in a very straight line, from one to two leagues, which was impressive to see from the height of the main temple, since from all the smaller settlements and districts, these very straight roads came up to the court of the teocallis." Later he says, "In the large teocallis they had two altars, and in the others, only one, and every altar had its offerings. . . . In front of these altars they left a large space, where they performed their sacrifices. . . . " After referring to the height of the teocallis in Mexico and Tezcuco (Texcoco), Motolinia explains the characteristics of the secondary commercial centers of the big cities. "In the same courtyards of the principal towns were twelve or fifteen other very large teocallis, some bigger than others, but not too near the principal one. Some had their fronts and steps facing others, some faced east, others south, and in each of these was only one altar with its chapel. Each one had its chambers or apartments for those Tlamacazques or ministers, who were many, and for those who served to bring water and firewood; because in front of all these altars were braziers which burned all night long, and there were also fires in the chambers. They kept all those teocallis very white, burnished and clean, and in some there were little gardens with flowers and trees" (Motolinia, 1941).

The Aztec capital was not the only one which deserved to be called a city. Even by today's standards, Texcoco, Cholula, Coyoacán and many others would be considered true cities. They had the physical characteristics, sufficient size and population and were, for their time and place, active centers for processing raw materials and markets of influence and attraction. Carlos I of Spain was told: "And they call this city Tezcuco (Texcoco), and it must have at least thirty thousand *vecinos*. They have here, My Lord, marvelous houses and mosques, and large well-built chapels. There are very big markets. . . ." (Cortés, 1961). If we interpret thirty thousand *vecinos* to mean that number of heads of families, Texcoco may have had about a hundred and fifty thousand inhabitants in 1520.

A few kilometers away, as Cortés relates, were the cities of Acurumán and Otumpa with three to four thousand *vecinos* each, or between fifteen and twenty thousand inhabitants. These cities were not unique. The chronicler Herrera attributes six thousand houses to Coyoacán, five thousand to Hiucilopuchco, and four thousand to Mexicaltcingo (Herrera, 1945). Next to the lake was Ixtapalapa, governed by a brother of Moctezuma II, a city of between twelve and fifteen thousand *vecinos* or some sixty or seventy-five thousand inhabitants who lived "half of them on water and the other half on dry land" (Cortés, 1961). Considering its location, we can assume that *chinampa* districts with their rectilinear systems of canals and streets existed in this city as well as in the other riparian towns.

Cortés considered Tlaxcala, the capital of his allies, as being larger, more powerful and having a greater population than Granada at the time of its conquest by the Catholic Kings in 1492, and having a market where "every day there are thirty thousand souls or more buying and selling" (Cortés, 1961).

On entering Cholula, the Spaniards found streets and rooftops filled with people anxious to see the "men like us" and the horses (Díaz del Castillo, 1955).

Herrera says of Cholula, "It was a very populous city in a beautiful plain, with twenty thousand Houses, and an equal number outside, in what they called farms, with many Towers on the Temples, which were beautiful to see, and according to what they say, these were as many as the Year has Days" (Herrera, 1945).

Cortés' reports, Díaz del Castillo's chronicles and the writings of the first chroniclers and historians of the Indies abound with phrases of admiration for the quality of the houses, the size of the temples, the well laid out buildings, the variety and order in the markets, the cleanliness of the streets, abundance of foodstuffs, and the excellence of services. All these are praises to a disciplined, responsible society which gradually enacted programs and laws to achieve an efficient urban arrangement. Aztec architects probably drew up their ideas and schematic designs in a presentation similar to the one we see in the maguey paper plan, using clay models to show ornamental details. We can be almost certain that they at least had a hand in planning and directing the construction of their cities.

A complex of buildings with the magnitude and proportion of the one the Spaniards encountered in the center of Tenochtitlán is not the result of chance. The street, "wide, straight and very beautiful, with Houses along both sides of the one by which the Spaniards entered" (Herrera, 1945), could only be part of a preconceived urban plan, at least in its general outlines. But, it is difficult to judge the degree of perfection the Aztecs reached in urban planning. We would have to study the chroniclers and the codices in much greater detail and verify descriptions of other Indian cities which kept their original appearance for a longer period than did the capital. . . .

The Markets of Tenochtitlán

Descriptions of Tlatelolco's market[5] left by Cortés and Díaz del Castillo point out some fundamental characteristics of Aztec society.[6] They give the impression that not only for its population, size, density, plan, and architecture was the Aztec capital a great city, but also for its economy, services and the specialization of its inhabitants.

The tourist who visits Mexico City today is invariably drawn to its markets. Some of these are famous enough to attract organized tours. Depending on the city, the tradition of its market and its zone of influence, these popular gatherings take place every day, or on special days of the week, today as they did four hundred and fifty years ago.

Unlike the cities, few smaller towns can organize a daily market. Even today, a significant percentage of Mexicans live off the land and maintain a self-sufficient familial economy, coming to market only to exchange their surplus products for articles they do not produce themselves. An exclusively agricultural population cannot support a daily market. If the market has enough patrons to warrant increasing its days of operation, a large enough sector of the population must be earning its livelihood from nonagricultural activities to serve as consumers of the market's produce.

A city, on the other hand, is characterized by its daily markets where employees, artisans and other specialized groups come to fill their needs. Tenochtitlán, Tlatelolco, Texcoco, Cholula, and the main cities of the Aztec federation fall into this category. A large portion of the population depended for its foodstuffs on the agricultural production from the areas bordering each city. The *chinampas*, forming some of the peripheral districts of Tenochtitlán and of the lake shore cities, supplied only a fraction of the daily consumption. The rest came from the rural villages.

For its time and place, Tenochtitlán was a specialized center with a sizeable concentration of artisan activity. Raw materials were brought to the markets of Tenochtitlán-Tlatelolco to be transformed by their craftsmen into articles of worth: crude gold, silver, copper, shell, and hard stones for the jewelers; wood for carving; brilliant feathers for Aztec artists; lime, adobe and stone for the masons; and medicinal herbs for the herbist to classify. Each day hairdressers came to market looking for clients, and set up their stalls "where they wash and trim heads." Here, too, were apothecaries who "sell prepared medicines, drinkable as well as unguents and poultices"; porters hoping to be hired; proprietors of houses "where they serve food and drink for a price"; those who "sell colors for painters," or "many kinds of cotton yarn of all colors, in their skeins," or "deer hides with and without hair, white and dyed different colors." The land's various products were assigned places in organized streets and sectors so that the vendors were easily found by the buyers and the market inspector's work was facilitated. Game was located in one street; fruit and vegetables in another; fish which was sold both "fresh and salted, raw and cooked in another; and further away were cooked eggs." There was sugar-cane syrup and bee's honey, mats for all purposes, clay braziers, pottery, earthenware jars, charcoal, and wood. Corn was sold as grain or in dough and cakes prepared with fish or fowl. "They sell everything by count and measure," says Cortés. Payment was by barter or in cacao beans after consulting price lists hung in conspicuous places. To arbitrate disputes and administer justice "in this great plaza, there is a very good house like a tribunal. Ten or twelve persons sit here, acting as judges and passing sentence on all cases and things which happen in this market, and ordering wrongdoers to be punished. In this market, there are persons who continually go about among the people looking at what is sold and the means used to measure it, and a false measure has been known to be broken" (Cortés, 1961).

Tlatelolco's market was the largest and best supplied in the city as well as in the whole Aztec empire.[7] It was not the only one in the city, nor was it the only one operating daily. Next to Tenochtitlán's Great Teocalli was another important market, situated in the enclosure of the city's main plaza, surrounded by the palaces of the nobles. The Colonial plaza later occupied the same space, and today, with altered proportions, it is called Plaza de la Constitución. There may have been other markets which served the people living in the various neighborhoods (Sanders, 1952), perhaps set up in the plazas adjoining the temples of each ward.

Like an Arabian bazaar or a Medieval fair, Tlatelolco's market provided the Aztecs with diversion and exchange of news. It was a place where they could amuse themselves for hours watching the thousands of passers-by, taking in the colors, noises, and odors of one of the most amazing human spectacles of Indian America.

The Center of Tenochtitlán

At the intersection of the two causeways, or main axes, stood the Great Teocalli, marking the center of the city. Thanks to the efforts and patient research of the Mexican architect Ignacio Marquina, it has been possible to construct a good-sized model of the Templo Mayor and study the urban and architectural characteristics of its composition as it was when the Spaniards arrived.[8]

The Templo Mayor of the Aztec capital was made up of a group of structures which occupied a square area of about four hundred and twenty meters, surrounded by a wall two and one-half meters high. This wall, or *coatepantli*, also called the "Serpent Wall" for its exterior decoration featuring hundreds of plumed serpents, outlined the Sacred Precinct (Figure 4.1). The Precinct had three gateways which marked the starting points of the principal causeways. Only the eastern wall was completely closed.[9] Inside the Precinct stood eighteen single structures and principal complexes as well as other smaller ones. The Great Pyramid stood out above all the rest. On its upper platform, at a height of some 30 meters, sat the twin temples consecrated to Huitzilopochtli, god of war and deity most venerated by the Aztecs, and to Tlaloc, the rain god.[10] All the rest of the structural complex revolved around the Great Pyramid.

From a study of the model, we see a complex of monumental proportions with an axis of symmetry which was not always respected in detail. This east-west axis was determined by the main façade of the Templo Mayor. Each of the single buildings or complexes had its own individual axis. Only one of the smaller, but important, structures—the platform, or table, of Huitzilopochtli—seems to have had two axes.

Between the structures and their bases were pedestrian areas where the public could walk, or linger to witness the ceremonies performed in the temples on the uppermost platforms of the pyramids, high above the level of the Plaza. We cannot know whether these open areas constituted thoroughfares or plazas. They were broad, quite similar to each other, and served to set off the individual architecture of each building as well as to permit traffic around the structures that filled the Sacred Precinct. With the exception of the street that connected the north and south gates of the Great Teocalli, running in front of the Great Temple-Pyramid, the other spaces were undefined and broken up by platforms supporting and elevating the larger structures.

Temples topped pyramidal structures on square or rectangular foundations. The Temple of Quetzalcóatl was an exception, having the circular foundation common in buildings dedicated to this god. Other structures might be described as adjuncts, such as the *calmecac*, or school, the ball court, or *tlachtli*, and the buildings around the Temple of the Sun. These were of one story and regular shape, supported by their respective platforms. The bases, gigantic pedestals for the pyra-

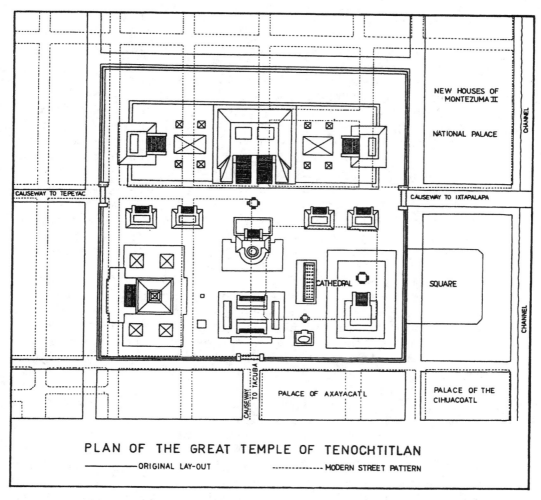

PLAN OF THE GREAT TEMPLE OF TENOCHTITLAN
———— ORIGINAL LAY-OUT   -------- MODERN STREET PATTERN

FIGURE 4.1 *Plan of the Templo Mayor of Tenochtitlán drawn up by Marquina for his reconstruction. Today's block-shaped outline of this central sector of Mexico City is indicated by fine lines. Numbers 1 and 2 point to the twin temples topping the Templo Mayor; number 8 is the Temple of Quetzalcóatl, 18 is the calmecac, 13 is the ball court. Numbers 23, 24, and 25 mark the three access gateways to the Templo Mayor. The Temple of the Sun is number 15, and 7 is the table of Huitzilopochtli. (Credit: Marquina, Ignacio: "Arquitectura prehispánica," I.N.A.H., Mexico, 1951.)*

mids and special buildings, were always painted white, their colored friezes standing out in contrast.

Trees and all other vegetation were excluded from the Sacred Precinct with the exception of the *Tentlalpán,* a small fenced grove of maguey and other plants which was the site of an annual ceremony simulating a hunt; the tree of *Xocotl-Huetzi,* a branchless timber planted yearly during the festivals of the tenth month;

and the *Tozpalatl,* a small temple of great importance to the Aztecs since it had been built around the spring which existed on the site where the first temple had been founded. These were kept for their symbolic rather than landscaping value (Marquina, 1960).

The people of Tenochtitlán, as well as visitors from other cities, freely entered the Sacred Precinct to witness religious ceremonies which they watched standing, or to participate in processions. The Great Teocalli did not attract crowds because of its renown as a civic or commercial center, but rather because the Aztec religious calendar was so full of ceremonies, many of which lasted several days or even weeks, that a large number of people must have passed through its gates every day, and at all hours, to gather before one of its altars.

Priests, novices, and servants of the various temples lived within the Precinct. Some lived in the *calmecac* in rooms arranged around a square central court about forty-five meters on each side or around four smaller courts each about eighteen meters wide. Others may have lived inside the precinct of the Temple of the Sun, in rooms to the north, south and west of the platform that served as a base for this complex. And we can not discard the possibility that, at least temporarily, a number of priests and servants of a particular cult lived in some of the temples.

Let me reconstruct the sensations experienced by a person arriving for a ceremony through the northern gateway and finding himself standing in front of the Templo Mayor.[11] Walking along the Tepeyac causeway, he would have seen from afar the twin temples of the Great Pyramid rising above the flat rooftops of the houses on either side of him, Tlaloc's blue temple in the foreground and behind it the sanctuary of Huitzilopochtli, painted red. To the right of these rose the conical straw roof of Quetzalcóatl's Temple and the tops of some lesser temples. Looking far away to the south, he might notice the jagged, snow-covered peaks and volcanos that encircle the central Valley of Mexico. At the end of the causeway, the visitor would encounter the canal which surrounded the Sacred Precinct.

The northern gateway was marked by an entrance hall, a kind of vestibule formed by a double row of eight columns, giving a feeling of transition between the city and the Precinct.[12] On each side of the door stretched the smooth merlon-topped wall, the heads of intertwined feathered serpents decorating its base. Once inside, the visitor's glance would fall on the polished surface of a perfectly level paved floor from which rose the simple, geometric shapes of temples and platforms. The ceremony he had come to see was about to take place right in front of him, a few hundred steps away, and some people had already arrived. The impassive silhouettes were outlined against the back of the opposite gateway, the *cuauhquiahuc* or "Eagle Gate," to the south, formed by a double colonnade marked by two solid pillars supporting a simple entablature decorated in its center and frieze with emblems of the military Orders of the Eagle and Jaguar Knights.

There were only 200 meters between the northern gate and the axis of the Great Temple-Pyramid. The visitor would cross over on a street bordered on his immediate left by the Great Pyramid's platform and on the right by two pyramids, each of which had two bodies and supported similar rectangular temples. The first of these, the *coateocalli,* was dedicated to the gods of the conquered countries. The second was the Temple of Cihuacóatl, goddess of the Xochimilco tribe. Walking past the long platform of the Great Pyramid toward the opposite gateway, the visitor might think he was seeing the same sight over again when he looked at two other pyramids supporting two more temples with rectangular bases. The first of these was dedicated to Chicomocóatl, goddess of vegetation, the second, to Xochiquetzalli, goddess of painters and weavers. Once past all four of these temples, the visitor would have crossed most of the Sacred Precinct.

Past the *coateocalii* and the Temple of Cihuacóatl, the street widened in front of the Templo Mayor. Here stood the Temple of Quetzalcóatl, with its circular foundation and conical crest. This was one of the most unusual structures in the Sacred Precinct, if not in the entire city. It was supported by a broad base and consisted of four stepped bodies. The rectangular pyramidal base was not, in itself, extraordinary. What captured the visitor's attention was the temple on the upper platform, circular in form with a straw roof, conch-shaped merlons, and an impressive entrance marked by the gaping fangs of a gigantic serpent.[12] From this temple, at sunrise and sunset of each day, a priest on the upper platform beat "an enormous drum which was heard all over the city and which was the signal to begin and end all business and work of the day" (Alcocer, 1935).

On the axis of the Great Pyramid and Quetzalcóatl's Temple, also the main axis of the entire ceremonial group, the visitor would notice a small platform on a square base with four symmetrically placed stairways. This was the table of Huitzilopochtli. Standing around it were a group of people staring up at the top of the double stairway of the Templo Mayor. There, on the terrace, some thirty meters high, lay a man, his body arched over a stone, arms and legs immobilized by four priests, ready to be sacrificed to the Aztec god.

Coming in by the western gate on the causeway from Tacuba was quite different. The visitor faced the Great Pyramid on its axis before even coming into the Sacred Precinct, and as he walked toward the complex of buildings, it seemed to open up as he drew nearer. He passed through a gateway structurally similar to the other two, with a pair of feathered serpent heads sculpted in stone on each of the side pillars, and found himself in front of the colonnaded entrance to a single-story construction. This was the *tlachtli*, or ball court, a structure completely closed on two sides. On the south end, the colonnade concealed a long narrow court from which a stairway of twenty steps led to the upper platform of the ball court. A similar stairway on the northern side permitted direct access from the level of the plaza.

The ball court and the Temple of Quetzalcóatl blocked the visitor's way to the Great Pyramid. On the left, the serene façade of the *calmecac* would steer him toward the base of the pyramid, passing quickly by the *Tentlalpán,* or grove, then by a symmetrical platform with steps on four sides and then a second grove. As he walked, the visitor noticed the imposing circular pyramid and temple of Quetzalcóatl with its elegant conical roof. At last he entered the north-south street and, crossing the line of temples, he came up to the foot of the Great Pyramid's stairway where he joined the other people who had already arrived to witness the ceremony.

In the southwest corner of the Precinct stood four structures. One of these, a well-proportioned pyramid of four bodies, was the second tallest in the entire complex. This pyramid was part of a group dedicated to the Sun, one of the most important cults in the Aztec religion. It was in front of the access stairway to the temple that one of the most curious customs of this people took place—the gladiatorial sacrifice.

The Great Pyramid was the most important structure in the Sacred Precinct. The line along its front and long platform-base, as well as two other symmetrically placed temples, follows the street line of today's Calle República de Argentina and its prolongation, Seminario. The pyramid's axis, also the east-west axis of the Sacred Precinct itself, lay a few meters north of the modern street, República de Guatemala.

The Great Pyramid, as the Spaniards saw it, had been completed during the reign of Ahuízotl, but four smaller structures had previously stood on the same site. According to calculations, the Great Pyramid's base measured 100 meters in the north-south direction and 80 east to west. The base rested on an immense platform about five meters high which supported two other twin pyramids of four sections each, topped with similar temples, one of these dedicated to Tezcatlicopa, the universal god. These temples, symmetrically placed on the Great Pyramid, were reached by a pair of forecourts. In the Great Pyramid we find proportions and shapes similar to those in earlier constructions in such other cities as Texcoco and Tlatelolco, the Pyramid of Tenayuca apparently having served as a model for them all. In the Great Teocalli of Tenochtitlán, certain architectural principles were also repeated, such as the double stairway flanked by ramps, the break in the ramps at a certain height, construction in stepped bodies—four in the pyramid of the Aztec capital—and the masterful use of stone.

Tenochtitlán was, in synthesis, one of the most truly urban of all the cities of pre-Columbian America's civilizations. It was the religious and cultural capital of a great people, the political center of a developing state and the military center of an army which undertook and successfully carried out many daring conquests. Furthermore, Tenochtitlán was a commercial center which developed the most important markets in Mesoamerica at that time. Attracted by the goods made by skillful artisans and the prospect of a large concentration of potential customers, merchants from distant regions flocked to these markets.

Tenochtitlán's growth was vertiginous. I can think of no city in the preindustrial world which reached such a vast size and population in so short a time as did the Aztec capital. A hundred years after its founding, already well into the fifteenth century, it was still a group of miserable huts inhabited by mercenaries. Less than a century later, after a cycle in which tribute and direct conquest gave it a prestige and wealth unequaled in Mesoamerica, Tenochtitlán had already been destroyed and replaced by a new urban concept which the conquered Aztec people themselves were forced to construct.

Why did Tenochtitlán fall and why did the Aztec state collapse? Not from lack of courage, certainly, nor lack of faith in their way of life and religion. We will undoubtedly never know. I believe that the Aztec weakness lay in the complexity of its government and in the demands of its religion. The arrival of the Spaniards elicited a variety of reactions among the subjugated peoples as well as among the Aztec's enemies. Some favored the Aztecs, but more often they did not. Cortés had only to exploit the resentments of whole groups and lead them against the common enemy.

Tenochtitlán was the capital of a nation which was approaching its territorial peak, although it is difficult to speculate how much farther it might have gone. I am inclined to think that not even its rulers knew. Perhaps the capital might have followed the evolution of the state: new inhabitants would have required new *chinampas*, the old *chinampa* districts would have become more urbanized, new temples would have replaced old ones and others would have sprung up in the new neighborhoods.

There were few regions of any economic or strategic importance left for the Aztecs to conquer. They could only tighten their control over the already conquered territory and increase its productivity. Perhaps their next move would have been to devote time and effort to technology, which could have moved the Mesoamerican peoples out of the years of stagnation following the Classic centuries. They might have pondered on the dangers of a religion which called for the sacrifice of their best subjects, or they might have revised the form of absolute government adopted by their last kings. But could the Aztecs have accomplished this? Or did they, as is suspected of the Maya, unknowingly carry within their very culture the seeds of its own destruction? Would there have been another barbarian invasion in central Mexico, another interregnum during which the cities would have been places of savagery and disorder? We will never know; we can only speculate.

For good or bad, the arrival of the Spaniards introduced a new concept of things. On the altar of a new religion, Mesoamerica's temples were destroyed; in the interest of a new culture, Indian books and documents were burned; in honor of a new form of government, the Aztec leaders were slaughtered.

Notes

1. The Aztecs of Tenochtitlán conquered Tlatelolco in 1478, destroying its Great Temple. A generation later, they began to rebuild it, and it was finished a few years before the arrival of the Spaniards (Peterson, 1959).

2. The causeway from Ixtapalapa had two lateral canals eight to ten meters wide. Its highest point rose 1.30 meters above lake level, and its width varied between fifteen and twenty meters. The causeway was not paved; its surface was made with a mixture of volcanic material and tamped earth (González Rul and Mooser, 1962).

3. See figure No. 1 in Callnek, 1969.

4. The measurements which Bernal Díaz del Castillo mentions are notably smaller than those cited by González Rul and Mooser (see note 2). On the other hand, Galindo y Villa gives larger measurements: thirty *varas* wide and two *varas* high above water level (25.98 by 1.72 meters) (Galindo y Villa, 1955).

5. The pre-Hispanic market was located where the Plaza de Santiago stands today. The church of Santiago is built on the site of Tlatelolco's temple.

6. Padden suggests that Díaz del Castillo described the view of the city from atop the pyramid of Tenochtitlán and not of Tlatelolco. See his note 3 in chapter IX (Padden, 1970).

7. When Tlatelolco was captured in 1473 by Tenochtitlán a heavy sales tax was imposed on all transactions that took place there.

8. The model is exhibited in the Mexican Museum of Ethnography which is situated precisely over one of the corners of the Great Pyramid of Tenochtitlán.

9. Some authors mention a fourth gateway located at the east side, which must have been much smaller than the other three. Alcocer calls it the Huitznahuac Gateway (Alcocer, 1935).

10. The height of the upper platform has been calculated by the number of steps in the central stairway. In general, the chroniclers give a figure which varies between 113 (Torquemada) and 120 or 130 steps (Durán), but all agree that there were more than 100. It is generally accepted that the two temples had a height of seventeen to eighteen meters. Therefore, the Great Pyramid must have had a total height of forty-seven to forty-eight meters.

11. I have made this reconstruction based on the reports from the time of the Conquest and on general data, but mostly on the excellent reconstructions of Marquina and the analysis of his model of the Templo Mayor.

12. The historian López de Gomara described it as follows: "And among them (the temples) was one round one; the entrance of which was through a doorway made like the mouth of a serpent, and diabolically painted."

References

Alcocer, Ignacio. *Apuentes sobre la Antigua Mexico-Tenochtitlán.* Tacubaya, Mexico: I.P.G.H., 1935.

Callnek, Edward. *Subsistence Agriculture and the Urban Development of Tenochtitlán.* Paper Presented at the 69th Annual Meeting of the American Anthropological Association, Boston, 1969.

Cortés, Hernan. *Cartas de relacion de la Conquista de Mexico.* Buenos Aires: Espasa-Calpe Argentina, Coleccion Austral, No. 547, 1961.

Díaz del Castillo, Bernal. *Historia verdadera de la conquista de la Nueva España.* Buenos Aires: Espasa-Calpe Argentina, Coleccion Austral, No. 1274, 1955.

Galindo y Villa, J. *Historia sumaria de la ciudad de Mexico.* Mexico Editora Nacional, 1955.

Gonzalez Rul, F., Mooser, F. "La calzada de Iztapalapa." *Anales del I.N.A.H.,* XIV-43, Mexico, 1962.

Herrera, Antonio de. *Historia de las Indias.* Buenos Aires: Editorial Guarania, 1945.

Marquina, Ignacio. *El Templo Mayor de Mexico.* Mexico: I.N.A.H., 1960.

Motolinia (Fray Toribio de Benavente). *Historia de los Indios de la Nueva España.* Mexico: Editorial Salvador Chavez Hayhoe, 1941.

Padden, R. *The Hummingbird and the Hawk: Conquest and Sovereignty in the Valley of Mexico.* New York: Harper and Row, 1970.

Peterson, F. *Ancient Mexico.* London: George Allen and Unwin Ltd., 1959.

Saunders, William T. "El mercado de Tlatelolco: un estudio en economia urban." *Tlatoani* I-1 (Mexico, 1952) p. 14.

5

The Emergence of Civilization in China

Kwang-chih Chang

Content and Style of the Shang Civilization

The earliest strata of the Shang civilization known at present in the form of the Erh-li-t'ou phase of western Honan are not adequately known, but it is already clear that by this time (ca. 1850 B.C.) the Neolithic economy had begun to give way to the formation of settlement groups as self-contained units. Bronze metallurgy was already well started, and at some sites one sees the beginning of a highly intensified and sophisticated aristocratic complex.

By the time the city wall was constructed at Cheng-chou, perhaps around 1650 B.C., there can no longer be any doubt that Chinese urbanization was mature and that a Shang style of Chinese art and culture is manifest in the archaeological record. Because the term *urbanization* is somewhat arbitrarily defined in the archaeological literature,[1] we must carefully characterize the nature of city life of the Shang dynasty in North China. The foremost feature of the Shang sites is that individual villages were organized into intervillage networks in economy, administration, and religion. Each group depended upon others for specialized services and offered services in return. There was a political and ceremonial center (a walled enclosure in the case of Cheng-chou), where the royal family and the nobles resided. It apparently served as the nucleus of the group and, when the capital of the dynasty was located there, as the center of political and economic control of the whole kingdom. Surrounding and centripetal to this nucleus were industrial quarters with high degrees of specalization, and farming villages. Goods apparently circulated among the various villages, with the administrative center serving also as the center for redistribution. The population of the entire settlement group was considerable, as indicated by the spatial dimensions and by the quantity and complexity of the cultural remains, and the social stratification and industrial specialization of the populace were highly intensified. We find in Shang China no physical counterparts to such large population and architectural configurations as Ur of Mesopotamia, Mohenjo-Daro on the Indus, and Teotihuacan of Mexico, yet the Shang capital sites performed all the essential functions of a city, indicating a definite break from the Neolithic community pattern. This basic Shang city pattern continued on into later historic periods. During the Eastern Chou period the capital sites grew into large commercial and political urban centers. . . .

Purely from an archaeological perspective, the populace of a Shang city seems to have been divided into three major groups: the aristocracy, the craftsmen, and the farmers.

The aristocracy. Archaeological excavations, oracle-bone inscriptions, and historic records have jointly established the fact that the Shang capitals at Cheng-chou and An-yang were seats of a powerful centralized government in control of a number of settlement groups scattered over a part of North China. At one or a few of the sites within a same settlement group, an aristocratic complex of artifacts and architecture can easily be recognized. In architecture, this includes ceremonial altars, rectangular house structures with stamped earth floors, stone pillar foundations, and in some cases, stone sculptures used as pillar bases. Such sites have a complex system of graves, including tombs of gigantic dimensions and sophisticated structure, evidence of human sacrifice and accompanying burials of animal victims and horse-drawn chariots. This aristocratic complex is often associated with a sophisticated ritual complex, manifested by human sacrifice, animal sacrifice, scapulimancy, and ceremonial vessels of pottery (e.g., white pottery) and bronze. Horse and chariot fittings and other apparatuses for ritual use help to mark the distinctions of status, along with such artifacts as prepared and inscribed oracle bones, white, hard, glazed pottery, elaborately carved bone hairpins, jade weapons, and bronze ceremonial and household utensils. Groups of bronze and pottery vessels for use in wine drinking and serving occurred in the Shang burials for the first time. Remains of cowrie shells, probably used as a medium of exchange, may also be significant. Writing is mainly associated with the aristocracy, as are highly developed decorative arts like the *t'ao-t'ieh* style, mosaic designs, and stone and bone sculptures and engravings. Discovery of such artifacts points to a strongly consolidated aristocracy that was definitely absent prior to the Shang.

From the oracle inscriptions and the historic records, a little is known about the Royal House, the rule of succession to the throne, and the political relationships between the various settlement groups. Mythological sources relate that the Royal

House of the Shang dynasty was a grand lineage by the name of Tzu, attributed to a divine birth in Ssu-ma Ch'ien's *Shih chi*, volume 3:

> The mother of Ch'i, founder of the Yin dynasty, was called Chien Ti, a daughter of the tribe Yu Jung and second consort of Emperor K'u. Basking with two companions, Chien Ti saw an egg fall from a black bird and swallowed it. She then became pregnant and gave birth to Ch'i.

The grand lineage occupied a central position in the state's political, economic, and ceremonial structures, which were expressed and maintained with elaborate and solemn ancestor-worship rites. There is little question about the relationship between the ancestor-worship rites performed by and for the grand lineages and the origin myths of the descent of these lineages. According to the ancestor-cult calendar worked out from the oracle inscriptions, Li Hsüeh-ch'in has been able to generalize that among thirty-five kings of the Shang dynasty, whose rules of succession are relatively clear, the throne was assumed by sons for eighteen generations, and for seven generations (ten kings) it was taken over by brothers.[2]

The settlement groups that were not under the direct rule of the monarch were administered by lords appointed by the central government. The lords were relatives of the monarch (sometimes junior sons), high officials who made great contributions to the cause of the Royal House, and the de facto rulers of regions that paid tribute to the central government but were out of the reach of the royal forces, and whose administrative status had to be recognized.[3]

The central government and the local governments thus formed a tightly organized hierarchy, with the king at the top, assisted by officials of a royal court and priests. Communications between the various settlement groups and the central administration were possible with the aid of a highly developed system of writing and a standardized currency. Raids and warfare between states were frequent, as judged by the war records in the inscriptions, the abundant remains of weapons, the sacrificial use of what were apparently war captives, and the chariots. The centralized power of government is most clearly indicated by the control of manpower. In addition, public works began to appear to a significant extent. The *hang-t'u* structures at Hsiao-t'un and Cheng-chou, such as the walled enclosure and the temples and altars, were probably built by large groups of people, organized and directed by administrative agencies. The construction of the large royal tombs at Hsi-pei-kang, An-yang, is of particular interest in this connection.

The social institutions that governed the aristocracy and its auxiliary groups, as indicated by the archaeological evidence and the oracle bone inscriptions, were as follows: Marriage in the royal family was as a rule monogamous. The families of the Royal House, the nobility, and some of the craftsmen were of the extended family type, probably patrilineal. Beyond the family, unilinear lineages may have been prevalent among the nobility and some of the craftsmen; these were possibly segmentary lineages based on patrilineality and primogeniture. The lineage system may have been related to a part of the class structure. The kinship terminology of the royal family was possibly of the generation type.

The organization of the royal family is relatively clear. According to the Shang calendar of rituals, as recorded in the oracle-bone inscriptions, each king had one particular spouse.

> *P'i* [grandmothers and female ancestors] were partnered to *tsu* [grandfathers and male ancestors], *mu* [mothers] partnered to *fu* [fathers], and *fu* [daughters-in-law] partnered to *tzu* [sons]. Each man usually had only one official spouse. Among all the fathers, one, and one only, had an especially supreme status, and his spouse also had supreme status. The family descent and the calendar of rituals were both based on patrilineality.[4]

The families of the nobility seem to be of the extended type. Their domiciles can be represented by the foundation A4 at Hsiao-t'un, which is 28.4 meters long and 8 meters wide and is divided into two large halls and eleven small rooms, all connected by doors.[5]

There is little question that lineages existed during the Shang dynasty. In Shang times the principle of primogeniture played an important role, and the order of seniority of birth was duly symbolized in the order of rituals and the classification of temples and altars into grand and lesser lines.[6] It is therefore possible that the so-called *tsung-fa* system of kinship, well known to be characteristic of the Chou dynasty, had already started in the Shang stage. This system is characterized above all by the close correlation of political status with kinship descent; i.e., an individual's rank within the clan is determined by his consanguineous proximity to the alleged main line of descent.

The highly organized ceremonial patterns of the Shang dynasty essentially carried on the Neolithic heritage, as indicated by an institutionalized ancestor worship, the practice of scapulimancy, and the elaboration of ceremonial objects, especially vessels. But by Shang times, the ceremonial structure of society had been very much intensified and was unmistakably tied up with the aristocracy. Priests, whose main duty was probably to divine and foretell events, served the royal court; the elaborate and sophisticated ceremonial bronze vessels were apparently used for rituals performed for the Royal House according to an annual calendar, mainly rituals of ancestor worship; the ceremonial center of the An-yang settlement group was spatially identified with the administrative center (Hsiao-t'un); and large-scale human and animal sacrifice was offered for the royal family.

In this manner the ceremonial structure was possibly correlated with the kinship structure on the one hand and with the economic system on the other. Ancestral worship was stressed and the calendar of ancestral worship rituals was carefully scheduled, as a reminder and reinforcement of the rules of primogeniture, the supremacy of the grand lineages, and the ramification of the lesser lineages, which became more and more degraded with each succeeding generation. The king, at the top of the hierarchal clan, as the supreme ruler of the kingdom and of the clan and also the focus of attention for all rituals. The relationship among the various settlement groups of the Shang kingdom was thus not only economically based (concentration and redistribution) but also accounted for in terms of kinship, and sanctioned and reinforced by rituals.

The craftsmen. At the Shang cities, craftsmen were physically identified with both farmers and the aristocracy, since the industrial quarters were distributed among the farming villages in the suburbs as well as near the palatial nuclei. Our knowledge about these men is rather limited, but we know that industry was a minutely specialized affair, that each settlement group had a number of industrial centers at the service of the aristocracy to provide for the whole settlement, that the craftsmen probably enjoyed a higher status than the farmers by virtue of their special skill and knowledge, and that various handicrafts may have been tied to kin groups. It is mentioned in the "Chronicle of the Fourth Year of Ting Kung" (of Lu state in the Spring-Autumn period) in *Tso chuan* that "after Wu Wang [of the Chou] conquered the Shang, Ch'eng Wang established the regime and selected men of wisdom and virtue and made them feudal lords to protect the royal Chou." To each of the lords Ch'eng Wang is said to have given a number of *tsu* (thought to be equivalent to minimal lineage), and the names of the *tsu* mentioned here included words for a drinking utensil, pottery, flag, and pots and pans. This passage shows that during the Shang dynasty, handicraft was possibly a kin-group affair. Some of the lineages specialized in particular branches of handicrafts either as a supplement to agriculture or full time. The Cheng-chou potters, as mentioned above, seem to have devoted full time to a special kind of pottery, whereas other kinds of ceramics probably were the business of other groups. The skills and special technical knowledge were probably passed down within the kin groups and because of this, the members of the group may have enjoyed certain privileges that the farmers did not have. At Cheng-chou the bronzesmiths and potters lived in above-ground, stamped-earth houses which were usually associated with the nobility. The bronzesmiths' dwellings found in the region north of Tzu-thing-shan in Cheng-chou consist of four houses:

> Each house is partitioned by a wall into two rooms. The two rooms are connected by a door. The two rooms may both have had a door to communicate with the outside, or only one of them may have had. Each room has an earth platform by the door, and a fireplace.[7]

Furthermore, these four houses are arranged according to a definite plan, and each is separated from the next by a distance of 10 or 11 meters. These facts may indicate that the bronzesmiths' families were of the extended type, and that their households belonged to the same patrilineage, a conclusion in complete agreement with the historic records concerning the lineage-occupation linkage.

Ground houses have also been uncovered at An-yang in association with the bronze technology. In 1959 and 1960 at the site of Miao-p'u-pei-ti, southeast of Hsiao-t'un, a number of ground-house floors were located, many of which were associated with clay molds. A large floor (more than 8 meters long and 4 meters wide), partitioned into two rooms, was built on a layer of *hang-t'u*; and the walls were also constructed by the *hang-t'u* technique. Posts were based on rocks here in the same manner as in the Hsiao-t'un palaces and temples. In the house, near the entrance, is a gourd-shaped pit, probably a hearth. Surrounding the floor were many piece molds of clay and fragments of crucibles, indicating a close connection with bronze work.[8]

From the large number of piece molds as well as the remains of clay models, crucible fragments, and the bronze artifacts themselves, the techniques of bronze making are well understood. Flat bronze implements such as knives and *ko* halberds were probably manufactured with the aid of a single mold or a two-piece mold into which molten copper and tin were poured. Hollow implements of plain form, such as axes, were also relatively simply made, with an outer mold and an inner core. The complicated vessels, especially large ones and those with cast decorative designs (a square *ting* from An-yang is 137 centimeters high, 110 centimeters long, 77 centimeters wide, and 700 kilograms in weight), involved a more complex process.

> A bronze casting is simply a replica in bronze of a model created in another medium. In the Western tradition this model has typically been made of wax on a clay core, then sheathed in a solid clay outer mold, melted out and replaced with molten bronze [the so-called lost-wax method]. In ancient China, on the contrary, it appears that the model was made of *clay* (and perhaps of other infusible materials such as wood) around a clay core and that the outer mold was not solid and continuous but segmented. This segmentation (making the outer mold a "piece mold") was necessitated by the fact that the baked clay model, unlike its wax counterpart, could not be melted out but had to be removed bodily. Thus when the mold segments have received the imprint of the model they are detached from it, the model is broken or scraped away from the core, and the mold segments are reassembled around the core ready to receive the molten bronze in the now hollow interstice between the two.[9]

This multiple piece-mold process of the Shang is what has convinced Noel Barnard that bronze metallurgy emerged independently in China,[10] but Wilma Fairbank goes so far as to see it as a far more complex application of the rudimentary bronze metallurgical principles for processing ores and alloying, heating, and pouring the metal, made possible by the superior ceramic craftsmanship of the Chinese.[11]

Perhaps the high social status apparently enjoyed by the bronzesmiths resulted from the association of bronze artifacts with the upper class. During the Yin phase of the Shang civilization at least, the bronze artifacts were made for the most part for exclusive purposes like ceremonies, warfare, and hunting. On the other hand, practically all the tools and implements for such basic subsistence purposes as agriculture and domestic utility continued to be made of wood, stone, clay, or bone. In all likelihood the industrial specialization at this time was tightly correlated with status differentiation.

Archaeologically substantiated handicrafts (whose "workshops" have been discovered) include manufacture of bronzes, pottery, and stone and bone artifacts, and possibly wine making. Other professions that can be inferred from archaeological remains or have been mentioned in the oracle bone inscriptions include carpentry, sculpture, earth construction, masonry, manufacture of drinking utensils, chariots, and weapons, tailoring, fabric making, and flag making.[12] Their extent of specialization seems to vary, and they had clienteles of differing social status.

The farmers. Shang subsistence was based on agriculture and supplemented by hunting and fishing. Remains of crops of the Shang period have been found at Cheng-chou, An-yang, and Hsing-t'ai, but have not been specified. From the oracle-bone inscriptions it can be determined that millet (probably both *Setaria* and *Panicum*), rice, and wheat were planted.[13] Little is known about the cultivation techniques except that stone hoes, spades, and sickles were used, as well as a kind of large wooden digging stick which may have been pushed by men or pulled by cattle and dogs and was possibly a prototype of the plow.[14] Two crops of millet and rice were harvested each year, and irrigation was probably employed,[15] although it has not been satisfactorily demonstrated that the water ditches discovered at An-yang and Cheng-chou are connected with irrigation. Those at Hsiao-t'un, at least, are not likely to have been related to irrigation. Fertilizers may have been used, but this again is by no means certain.[16] An elaborate agricultural calendar was developed.[17] Other archaeological finds connected with farming include pestles and mortars. Among the cultivated materials for fabrics were hemp[18] and silk.[19] In the domestication of animals the Shang carried on the Neolithic heritage (pigs, dogs, cattle, sheep, horses, and chickens), with some additions (water buffalo) and modifications (such as the use of dogs, cattle, and sheep for sacrifice and horses for chariot warfare).[20]

Fishing is indicated by fishbones,[21] fishhooks, and the scripts for fishnets and fishhooks. Hunting is indicated by the large quantity of wild-animal bone remains (tiger, leopard, bear, rhinoceros, deer, water deer, hare, etc.), by the remains of stone and bronze arrowheads, by the hunting records in the oracle-bone inscriptions, and by the animal designs in the decorative art. However, the part played in the basic subsistence by hunting may not have been very significant. According to Li Chi, the "game huntings mentioned in the ancient inscriptions were evidently pursued for pleasure and excitement rather than for economic necessity. . . . Such, pursuits were the monopolies of a privileged class."[22]

There is no question that agriculture was the basis of Shang subsistence, or that the techniques were highly developed and the yield considerable. In the suburbs of Cheng-chou and An-yang, the many residential hamlets were presumably occupied by farmers who tilled the fields in the neighborhood. One controversial point among Shang specialists is whether the direct participants in agricultural production were free farmers or slaves. It is known that slaves suffering from malnutrition, possibly war captives,[23] were sacrificed in the construction of palaces, temples, and royal tombs, were buried dead or alive with the royal body in the royal tomb, and that their bones were used for the manufacture of artifacts. But whether slaves were the sole laborers in the farming fields is not known. Amano suggests that during the Yin dynasty there were two kinds of fields: the royal field, cultivated by slaves under centralized management, and the clan fields cultivated by the lower classes of clan members.[24]

Created and sustained by people of all these categories, in concert if not in harmony, the Shang civilization by the Yin period at the latest achieved both distinction and greatness, placing it among the civilized giants of the ancient world. It can best be recognized through its art and religion—those complexes of culture through which the Shang expressed their minds about the world around them and indicated to us how the various aspects of their lives could be articulated.

Notes

1. V. G. Childe, *Town Planning Review* 21 (Liverpool, 1950), 3–17. Sec also R. J. Braidwood and G. R. Willey, eds., *Courses Toward Urban Life*, Viking Fund Publications in Anthropology, no. 32, 1962.

2. Li Hsüeh-ch'in, *Wen-shih-chê* 1957 (2), 21–37. For a new hypothesis on the rules of royal succession in the context of the kinship system, see Chang Kwang-chih, *BIE* 15 (1963), 65–94. *BIE* 35 (1973), 111–27.

3. Hu Hou-hsüan, *Chia-ku-hsüeh Shang-shih lun ts'ung*, vol. 1, Ch'i-lu Univ., 1944.

4. Li Hsüeh-ch'in, *Wen-shih-chê* 1957 (2), 36.

5. Shih Chang-ju, *Annals Acad. Sinica* 1 (1954), 267–80.

6. Hu Hou-hsüan, *Chia-ku-hsüeh Shang-shih lun ts'ung* 1, 16.

7. Liao Yüng-min, *WWTKTL* 1957 (6), 73.

8. An Chih-min et al., *KK* 1961 (2), 67.

9. Wilma Fairbank, *Archives of the Chinese Art Society of America* 16 (1962), 9. For detailed analyses of the bronze metallurgy of the Shang, see Noel Barnard, *Bronze Casting and Bronze Alloys in Ancient China*, Tokyo, Monumenta Serica Monograph no. 16 (1961); Shih Chang-ju, *BIHP* 26 (1955), 95–129.

10. Barnard, *op. cit.*, pp. 59–62.

11. Fairbank, *op. cit.*, pp. 10–11.

12. Li Chi, *The Beginnings of Chinese Civilization*. Li Ya-nung, *Yin-tai shê-hui sheng-huo*, Shanghai, Jenmin Press, 1955. Amano Motonosuke, *Tōhōgakuhō* 23 (1953). Shih Chang-ju, *BIHP* 26 (1955). Li Chi, *BIHP* 23 (1951), 523–619. Hsia Nai, *China Reconstructs* 1957 (12). Li Chi, *Hsiao-t'un t'ao-ch'i*. Yü Yü, *WWTKTL* 1958 (10), 26–28.

13. Hu Hou-hsüan, *Chia-ku-hsüeh Shang-shih lun ts'ung* 2 (1945), 134. Yü Hsing-wu, *Tung-pei ta-hsüeh jen-wen hsüeh pao* 1 (1957), 81–107.

14. Hu, *Chia-ku-hsüeh* 2 (1945), 134.

15. *Ibid.*

16. Hu Hou-hsüan, *Li-shih yen-chin* 1955 (1). *WW* 1963 (5), 27–31, 41.

17. Tung Tso-pin, *Yin li p'u*, Institute of History and Philology, Academia Sinica, Li-chuang, 1945

18. Li Chi, *An-yang fa-chüeh pao-kao* 3 (1931), 466. Iwama, *Manshu gakuhō* 4 (1936), 1–7.

19. Amano Motonosuke, *Tōhōgakuhō* 1 (1955). Vivi Sylwan, *BMFEA* 9 (1937), 119–26. Hu Hou-hsüan, *WW* 1972 (11), 2–7, 36.

20. Shih Chang-ju, *Bull. College of Arts, Nat'l. Taiwan Univ.*, no. 5 (1953), 1–14.

21. Chao Ch'üan-ku et al., *KKHP* 1957 (1), 63. Wu Hsien-wen, *Chung-kuo kao-k'u hsüeh pao* 4 (1949), 139–43.

22. Li Chi, *Bull. Dept. Archaeol. and Anthropol.*, Nat'l. Taiwan Univ., no. 9/10 (1957), 12.

23. Mao Hsieh-chün and Yen Yen, *VP* 3 (1959), 79–80. For human sacrifice, see Hu Hou-hsüan, *WW* 1974 (7), 74–84; 1974 (8), 56–72.

24. Amano Motonosuke, *Shigaku Kenkyu* 62 (1956), 11. See also Chang Cheng-lang, in *KKHP* 1973 (1).

6

The Polis

Jacob Burckhardt and Oswyn Murray

The *polis* was the definitive Greek form of the State; it was a small independent state controlling a certain area of land in which scarcely another fortified position and certainly no secondary independent citizenship were tolerated. This state was never thought of as having come into being gradually, but always suddenly, as the result of a momentary and deliberate decision. The Greek imagination was full of such instantaneous foundings of cities, and as from the beginning nothing happened of itself, the whole life of the *polis* was governed by necessity.

The small-state form was an invariable. Even when whole populations were expelled from their homes, they took with them on their wanderings the primary assumption that they had been dwellers in separate small states. The Achaeans, forced out of the southern Peloponnese, could certainly have formed a unified state in their new home in Achaea on the Gulf of Corinth, indeed it would have suited them well had it been in their nature; instead, in the twelve districts where Ionians had lived till then in villages, they founded the same number of *poleis,* and what they had in common amounted to little more than periodic sacrifices and festivals, probably at the Hamarion, in the grove of Zeus near Aegae.[1] And the Ionians, who had retreated before them and went, under Athenian leadership, to the west coast of Asia Minor, proceeded as a matter of course to set up a series of *poleis* numbering twelve as before.

As we shall see, the small state with a fortified town was very much aware that it needed to be limited in size and easily manageable. To control more extensive areas, in such a way that its individual settlements would not become centres of subversion, would have demanded either Spartan brutality or a quite exceptional natural disposition like that of the people of Attica. Attempts to form larger groups through alliances were only briefly successful, in time of war, but never in the long run. The hegemonies of Sparta and Athens were more and more hated the longer they went on, and the study of the *polis* will soon convince us that it was quite incapable of exercising even the minimal fairness towards weaker allies which would have served its own interest. The repeated attempts to make Boeotia a federal state were responsible for all the misfortunes of Boeotian history. Every alliance between Greeks seems characterized by the determination of the abler party to exploit and dominate. The traces of an early antiquity that was never fully understood, like the temple leagues or *amphictyoniai,* may safely be ignored in the period when the *polis* had come to full consciousness.

The feverish vital impulse which created the *polis* usually took the form of *synoecism,* the bringing of earlier village communities to settle together in a fortress town, if possible on the coast. The prevailing blend of piracy and commerce, features such as mountain foothills and bays, were perhaps the less essential influences; the chief consideration was to establish a strong political entity and to be prepared to resist neighbouring *poleis* in which the same process was at work. If the aim had been merely trade, material prosperity and so forth, the result would have been just a town or a city, but the *polis* was more than that.

However, the compulsive external incentive for its foundation was without doubt, in many cases, the movement known as the Dorian migration. The migrants themselves, as well as those who successfully resisted them, were seeking a system which would promise greater strength both in defence and attack, and be its own *raison d'être.* . . . For Achaea, the transition from village communities to urban life was explicitly connected with the Dorian migration; what we learn of that process from the accounts we have must have been repeated many times.

The period when people lived "village-style" (*komedon*) or sometimes in districts of seven or eight villages, was certainly one of greater innocence, however unruly the tribes may have been; they had needed to defend themselves against brigands and pirates, but they lived as peasants, cultivating the land; now each *polis* confronted another, competing for existence and political power. And there is no doubt that in the earlier period cultivation had been much better attended to, for as the population withdrew to the cities the remoter parts of their agricultural land must have become neglected. *Synoecism* may have been the first phase of aridification in Greece.[2] The fact that Athenian citizens would go, in time of peace, to live on their estates all over Attica does not mean that the same was true elsewhere.

The process became the norm and was perpetuated. Whenever political power was to be concentrated, this drawing together of a population in a union of citizens took place, all having equal burdens, duties and rights, and within a locality usually already settled, but not previously fully fortified; however, it was not unusual for a completely new site to be chosen. The political imagination which developed later was fond of embroidering on the model of the most famous example, handed down from mythical times: this was the *synoecism* of the people of Attica achieved by Theseus.[3] In the twelve districts in which Cecrops had formerly settled all the inhabitants together for their safety, it was Theseus who first abolished all their separate *prytaneis* (councillors) and *archontes* (chief administrators) and allowed only one council (*bouleuterion*) and one *prytaneion* in Athens to serve everybody. They might go on living outside the city on their own land, but they were to have only one *polis*, with everyone working together; it could be passed on to posterity as a great and powerful one. This was the arrangement generally desired everywhere, and progression towards this final system of the *polis* was an inherent tendency in Greece as a whole. Without it the full development of Greek culture would not have been conceivable.

From the clearly recorded examples of the historical period, however, we learn of the sacrifices this *synoecism* might cost: violent resettlements of resisting populations or their extermination. What can only be guessed at is the misery of the many who complied, but were forced to leave their familiar villages, districts and small towns, or could continue to live in them and work the land only with much less security and prosperity. To be taken far away from the places where their forefathers were buried was itself a misfortune for the Greeks; they were obliged to give up the cult of the dead, or found it very hard to continue; in any case they missed the daily sight of their family graves. In the whole course of history there is hardly another such accumulation of bitter grief as in this Greek *polis*, where the people with the strongest sense of place, and reverence for it, were forced out of their own places by violent arbitrary decrees. These measures must usually have been carried out by powerful tyrannical minorities. In turbulent later times, the only way of escaping ruthless oppression must often have been to form a *polis*.

A telling symbol of the vitality of the *polis* and its struggle for birth is the story of the dragon's teeth sown by Cadmus. The Spartoi, a troop of armed men, sprang up where the teeth were planted, and when Cadmus threw a stone in their midst they fought until only five of them were left alive. From this remaining quintessence were descended the Cadmean families of what became Thebes. The idea of decreeing capital punishment for anyone who made fun of the city's defences was also typical. Underlying it was the thought that it is easy to jeer, and hard to give practical help, and that beginnings have to be made in a small way. It was because he failed to understand this that Toxeus was killed by his father Oeneus of Calydon for jumping over the trench, exactly as Romulus killed his brother for the same offence.

There are many tales of the founding of cities: Mantinea in the Peloponnese, mentioned in Homer, became a *polis* through the union of five rural communities—*demoi* as the local expression was, instead of *komai*. Tegea arose from nine communities, as did Heraea too, Aegion from seven or eight, Patras from seven, Dyme from eight. Elis was formed into a city, from many surrounding villages, only after the end of the Persian Wars.[4] During the Peloponnesian War, the Mytileneans wanted to force all the people of Lesbos to live in their city, but the Methymneans complained of the matter in Athens and the plan was abandoned.[5] In the year 408 Lindos, Ialysos and Cameiros voluntarily combined to found the fine city of Rhodes, which was to have a brilliant future; but the feelings of the majority who had to leave their ancient towns can only be imagined.[6] At the time of the Peloponnesian War, Perdiccas II of Macedonia persuaded the inhabitants of the peninsula Chalcidice to leave their coastal towns and settle in the city of Olynthos, which entailed deserting the Athenian hegemony.[7] The city of Argos was particularly infamous for its violent enforcement of *synoecism* on the pretext of defending itself against Sparta. Not only were Hysiae, Orneae, Midea and other lesser places obliged to obey, but famous old cities like Mycenae and Tiryns were reduced to ruins, and if the inhabitants preferred to travel far away rather than become Argives this must have been because it was impossible to detain them. Against such an enemy as Sparta even Epaminondas had to resort to persuading a large number of Arcadian country towns to give up their identity and move to a "great city," Megalopolis. The Trapezuntians refused, and those who were not slaughtered fled to the new Trapezus on the Black Sea. After the Battle of Mantinea many tried to leave Megalopolis again, but their fellow citizens, using extreme brutality and helped by the Athenians, forced them to return.[8] Some of the abandoned dwelling places were later left completely deserted, and some became "villages" belonging to the Megalopolitans, that is, they still had a few residents, and their land was cultivated.[9]

Why were such cities not simply allowed to exist as country towns, perhaps sending elected representatives to the council of the *polis?* It was because they would never have remained compliant in the long run, but would have used all their energies to become independent and regain their status as *poleis.* Moreover, as we shall see, the mere delegation of representatives never satisfied the Greeks, because they would not tolerate any condition of things in which their popular assembly could not interfere at a moment's notice.

The entirely new city of Messene was perhaps the only one founded in a mood of completely undisputed enthusiasm, in 369 B.C. Epaminondas had no need, here, to bring in people expelled from their neighbouring lands; the new capital was built by Messenians who had fled long before to places all over the Greek world and were now reassembled in their native region. Those who had lost their homeland several generations or even centuries earlier, now regained it. In contrast, countless cities were founded by tyrants and powerful princes using the most brutal methods. The tyrants of Sicily, even the best of them, set about ruthlessly mixing the inhabitants of existing *poleis,* because they felt sure of being obeyed by them only when half or more of the population had been removed and replaced by strangers or mercenaries. Gelon, who in other ways was a good ruler, deported the upper classes of Camarina, Gela, Megara Hyblaea and other towns and concentrated them in Syracuse, while the common people were sold abroad as unwanted, since the *demos* was the least desirable element in the community. His brother Hieron transported the townspeople of Catana to Leontini, and settled five thousand Syracusans and the same number of Peloponnesians within the deserted walls, partly to ensure that Catana, with its excellent defensive position,[10] would be permanently garrisoned, and partly to perpetuate his own name in a heroic cult, as founder of this fine *polis,* something Gelon had already achieved (Diodorus 11.49). So that it would be reckoned a new foundation, the city was given the name of Etna, but soon after Hieron's death, when his decrees were rescinded, it again took its old name, and is still known as Catania.

The sole pretext the rulers gave was, always, that without these measures the cities would raise countertyrants against them and go over to the Carthaginians. King Mausolus, too, forcibly crammed together in his own Halicarnassus the people of six cities, that is three quarters of the eight Lelegian cities, whether they liked it or not.[11] In the history of the *diadochoi* the new foundations of towns in the East and in Egypt are given a great deal of attention, but since Asia Minor had long been Hellenized these must have involved violent deportations and mergings as well as the imposition of new names on cities that were old and famous. It is often maintained that only populations willing to move could be led in this fashion, but this does not stand up to the proof; more than once, when a new ruler allowed it, the people went away again.[12]

Of all the foundations of cities, the most likely to have been based on visible advantage to the population are those of Cassander of Macedonia. They may remind us of those of the thirteenth-century Counts of Zähring in Bavaria. Their purpose was to provide the safety of walled towns for their subjects, who were loyal and lived in freedom. Another parallel case of a decision by general consent, like the earlier Greek *synoecism,* occurred towards the end of the twelfth century, when Milan headed the Guelf party against the predominantly Ghibelline dynastic rulers, especially the Piedmontese, and prompted peasant communities to unite in constructing strongholds. At least this was the origin of Chivasso and Coni; then of Savigliano, built by peasants who had rejected the rule of the Marquisate of Saluzzo—though here Milanese help is not referred to; Alessandria, which had only just been created by the whole Lombard Alliance, assisted in building the new peasant-towns of Nizza di Monferrato, Fossano, and Montevico. Facing hostile Asti, between Tanaro and Stura, the town of Clarasco was being built, and many inhabitants of Alba were already moving there; indeed it seemed for a time as if Alba would consent to be demolished so as to be absorbed in Clarasco.[13] Many features of this period resemble those of life in ancient Greece. For instance the Emperor Frederick I, having conquered Milan, drove its people out of their city, which he was about to destroy, and directed them to four villages; in so doing he was following the example of antiquity, when it was called *dioikizein* (sending to separate districts); then too a victorious enemy would usually take revenge by dissolving a *polis* and forcing the inhabitants to return to their former village life. This was how King Agesipolis treated defeated Mantinea, and similarly the victors in the Holy War laid waste all the cities of Phocis except Abae, and sent their inhabitants away to live in the country.[14]

The making of a *polis* was the great, decisive experience in the whole existence of a population. Their way of life, even if they continued to cultivate the fields, became predominantly urban; formerly "countrymen," they now lived side by side and became "political," *polis*-beings. The importance of this experience was reflected in legends of the city's foundation, and of being saved from great dangers in the past. The city was conscious of its origin and gradual growth, of sacrifice and divine omens, all providing justification for its future. Even the drinking water, which was the very prerequisite of a foundation, perhaps the one pure spring in a large area round about, had had to be fought for and won from a sinister adversary;

Cadmus slew the dragon of Ares, which guarded the spring at the site of Thebes. In many cities, on the agora, in the precincts of a temple or on some other notable spot, was the grave of someone who, in ancient, perhaps mythical times, had given his life, or hers, voluntarily or involuntarily, for the birth or the preservation of the city, usually because of an oracle. For whatever flourished on earth had to pay the dark powers their due. In Thespiae it was known that formerly a youth had been annually chosen by lot and given to a dragon which threatened the town (Pausanias 9.26.5). At the centre of the inner Cerameicos in Athens was the Leocorion, the area sacred to Leon's three daughters whom he offered up as a sacrifice when the Delphic oracle pronounced this the only way to save the city.[15] A monument in the Italian city of Croton recalled the following legend: Heracles, driving his cattle through Italy, had killed Croton as an enemy in the darkness, though he was only trying to help; Heracles, recognizing his mistake, promised to build round the gravestone a city that would bear his name.[16] If it was not a monument, the remembrance might be linked with a spring. At Haliartos in Boeotia the river Lophis flowed from the blood of a boy who had beaten his own father to death, because in a time of total drought the Pythia commanded him to kill the first living thing he met (Pausanias 9.33.3). Once, at Celaenae in Phrygia, the ground opened and swallowed up many houses and people. The oracle said they must throw the most precious thing they had into the abyss; when gold and silver proved useless, the heir to the Phrygian King leapt in on horseback, and the crack closed up again.[17] In some cases animals showed more mercy than men and gods. An expedition sailing out to found Lesbos was told by an oracle that when they were passing the cliff of Mesogeion they must throw a bull into the sea as a sacrifice to Poseidon, and a living girl as a gift to Amphitrite and the Nereids. The girl was chosen by lot from the daughters of the seven leaders, and, richly bejewelled, was lowered into the water; but her lover jumped in after her and embraced her, and both were rescued by dolphins.[18] There are some examples of the foundation of a city being secured when the bones of someone who had died in mythical times were brought to the spot, for instance at the formal foundation of Amphipolis by the Athenians under Hagnon, when he secretly sent men to the field of Troy and had the remains of Rhesus fetched from his grave-mound (Polyaenus 6.53); or human sacrifice might be replaced by more innocent procedures, the so-called *telesmai*, or burial of mysterious objects. The precedent was the lock of Medea's hair which Athena gave to Cepheus for the foundation of the city of Tegea to ensure its impregnability (Pausanias 8.47.4). However, the horrible old rites were repeated even in later centuries when the foundation was to be a very solemn one. Seleucus, in other ways perhaps the noblest of Alexander's *diadochoi*, initiated the building of his great cities in Syria by sacrificing innocent maidens, and then put up bronze statues to them, by which the murdered girl was transfigured into the *Tyche* or fortune of the city, with her own cult in perpetuity.[19] In Laodiceia the unfortunate child was one Agave, and in Antioch on the Orontes the name of the one chosen has come down to us. She was immortalized in the famous bronze *Tyche* of which the little marble copy is now in the Vatican; in the centre of the planned city, at sunrise on the preordained day, the high priest sacrificed the beautiful Aimathe. On this occasion we are not told that the deed was urged by oracular decree, just that the destiny of the city was to be magically protected as a precaution.

In the agora there were also less fearful monuments to the dead: in Thurii the great Herodotus was buried in the agora,[20] and indeed later a perfect forest of statues of the famous, and of altars, rendered many squares in Greek cities almost impassable, but the monument to the sad memory of a sacrificial victim was seldom lacking.[21] Among other peoples a similar legend is sometimes connected with the building of a castle; when the Serbs composed the impressive song of the foundation of Skadar, they may well have been influenced by a Greek tradition.[22]

In truth this single human sacrifice seems a symbol of the many greater sacrifices demanded by the institution of nearly every *polis*, of the abandonment of the cultivated fields in a wide region, of the destruction or brutality inflicted on smaller inhabited places for the sake of the new settlement. It is no wonder that the life process of such a *polis* is characterized by violence.

We would know much more of these things but for the destruction of all the relevant sources apart from a few scattered fragments. A special branch of narrative in poetry and prose was devoted to the history or mythology of city-foundations; exalted names like that of Mimnermus of Smyrna, Cadmus of Miletus, and Xenophanes of Colophon are among the tellers of such local legends, and the last named also recounted the bold wanderings of the fleeing Phocians up to the founding of Elea (Diogenes Laertius 9.20). These are the true beginnings of what later became Greek historiography.

The external features by which a *polis* was distinguished from the village, and from the cities of other peoples, become plain from a negative description. Pausanias (10.4.1) says: "Panopeus is a city of the Phocians, if one can speak of a city where there is no official building, no gymnasium, no theatre, no agora and no water running together to a fountain." In fact the Panopeans lived in caves over a stream in a ravine. The "official building" means primarily the house where the council daily sat, that is the *prytaneion*: "the symbol of a city, for the villages have no such thing." There would also have been the magistrates' court and the chamber for the greater council, the *bouleuterion*, where one existed. At a later date the gymnasium was found wherever Greek culture spread; the theatres however were not universal until the time when the political power of the State was in decline.[23] Particularly in the complete overview they gave of the city population, and as the scene of the popular assembly, they were of immense value, and must have astonished any non-Greek. But the true focus of a *polis* was the agora, the public square.

In small old-fashioned cities this was all-important; here were the *prytaneion*, the *bouleuterion*, the court of justice and one or more temples; it was also used for public meetings and games. But even in towns where other, grander arrangements existed for these purposes, the agora was the chief vital organ of the city. "Marketplace" is a very inadequate translation, and every nation which had towns must certainly have had marketplaces. "Agora" by contrast comes from the verb *ageirein* to assemble, and indeed often means the assembly without reference to the place; Aristotle helps us to a clear distinction (*Politics* 7.10 f.). He thinks there should be an agora of free citizens, where nothing is on sale and where no workman or peasant may come unless summoned by the authorities; and another separate agora for the needs of buying and selling. Even the Achaean camp before Troy had its agora with altars to the gods, where justice was meted out.[24] In seaports the square must have been near the harbour, at least it was so among the Phaeacians, whose whole existence was arranged in the best possible way (*Odyssey* VIII.4). Here, in full view of the ships, surrounded by as many temples, civic buildings, monuments, shops and moneychangers' stalls as there was room for, the Greeks could occupy themselves with *agorazein,* that activity no northerner can render in a single word. Dictionaries give: "go about on the marketplace, shopping, chatting, consulting etc.," but can never convey the delightful leisurely mixture of doing business, conversing, standing and strolling about together. It is enough to know that the morning hours were generally described by it: the time when everybody is in the agora. Naturally it was only to be thoroughly enjoyed on the square of one's hometown, and those Persians who pursued Democedes home to Croton after he had given them the slip found him there very easily, *agorazonta*—"being in the agora"—(Herodotus 3.137). Even in barbarian lands the Greeks were recognized by this habit; the Samian Syloson promenaded at Memphis in his scarlet cloak (Herodotus 3.139), and barbarians who had become fond of Greek customs liked to frequent the agora in Greek cities. Skyles, king of Scythia, whenever he brought his army to the city of Olbia on the Borysthenes (in southern Russia), would leave his troops outside the walls, change his Scythian dress for the Greek tunic, and enjoy a walk in the agora with no bodyguard or retinue—until his Hellenic tastes proved unlucky for him (Herodotus 4.78).

When an urban proletariat developed in the cities, it was inevitably centred on the public square, and, thinking of the many activities in the Greek agora, Cyrus the Elder is said to have told a Spartan messenger. "I am not afraid of a people who have a place in the middle of their cities where they meet to deceive each other with false oaths."[25] In an institution of national life, such as the agora, there is an inextricable mixture of great and small, good and bad; but from the point of view of history it is certain that the intellectual development of the Greeks cannot be imagined without conversation, and that this is true of them to a greater extent than it is of other nations; the agora and the symposium were the two vital settings for conversation.

If it could be said of any people that they were greater than their dwelling place, then it was true of the Greeks. The living *polis,* the community of citizens, was very much more than all its walls, harbours and splendid edifices.[26] Aristotle says that man is by nature a *polis*-being. In an eloquent passage in Book 7 of *Politics* he then compares the Greek with the two kinds of barbarians, the northern savage and the civilized Asiatic, and acknowledges the best qualities of each—the valour of the one and the intelligence of the other—as attributes of the Greek, who is therefore not only capable of being free, and of developing the best political institutions, but also—as soon as he is able to form a state—fit to rule over all other peoples.

Above all, the *polis* existed before there was any theory about it. Odysseus encounters nations everywhere who already have a *polis*; the Laestrygonians have their Telepylos, even the Cimmerians have theirs, enveloped in mist and gloom (*Odyssey* XI.14). The founding of cities became a continuous process in Greece itself and in hundreds of places on barbarian shores. But the underlying desire was that each Greek race should have a *polis* of its own, and thus Bias could advise the Ionian citizens threatened by Persian power to emigrate to Sardinia and found an Ionian city there. Herodotus (1.170) says that if they had followed this advice they would have been the most fortunate of the Greeks. Even in comedy the theme is taken up, and Peisthetaerus' most important task is to impress on the birds that there is to be only one Bird-*polis* (Aristophanes, *Birds* 550).

The notion of the rights of man did not exist anywhere in antiquity, not even in Aristotle. The *polis,* for him, is a community only of the free; the metics and the numerous slaves are not citizens, and whether, apart from that, they are human beings is not discussed (*Politics* 3.4). The demands that are made upon the citizen are in fact, as will be seen, not for all and sundry, and it would be impossible to make them applicable to everybody. Those living outside may, if they can defend and assert themselves, live like the Cyclops, without an agora and without laws, each man ruling over his own family (*Odyssey* IX.112); in the *polis* things are different.

Quality is the most important consideration here, and quantity must, it is felt, be subject to limitations. Children born misshapen or deformed should not, according to Aristotle, be reared, and this is comprehensible when we think what an unhappy existence a cripple had among the Greeks (*Politics* 7.14.10). To limit the population, however (Aristotle continues) it is preferable not to practise exposure but to abort the child before it has independent life and consciousness; the dividing line between the permissible and the criminal is where life and consciousness begin. As is well known, though, large numbers of children always were exposed if only because their parents could not or would not support them.

The measure of population which a *polis* should contain is given in the word *autarkeia,* "what is sufficient to itself." To our understanding this is a very obscure expression, but it was easily grasped by the Greeks. An area of land capable of yielding the essential supplies, commerce and industry to provide for all other needs in moderation, and a hoplite army at least as strong as that of the nearest, usually hostile, *polis*—these were the elements of "sufficiency." Aristotle is as clear as could be wished on this; an overpopulated *polis* cannot really go on living according to the laws (*Politics* 7.4). It is the number of those who are fully citizens that makes a city great, not a preponderance of artisans with a small number of hoplites. Beauty consists, here as elsewhere, in moderation and proportion. A ship a handspan long is not a ship, nor is one that measures two furlongs. A city with too few people is not self-sufficient; one that has too many can of course suffice for its own needs, but more as a mass than as a city, for it can have no true constitution, no *politeia.* What general could lead such a mass? What herald could serve, unless he were [Homer's] Stentor? To administer justice and to allot the offices to the deserving, the citizens must all know each other and each man's quality. Ideally the city should be as large as the needs of life dictate, while still remaining manageable. And it seems that a city of 10,000 adult citizens was considered to approximate to the desirable size;[27] Heraclea Trachinia [in central Greece] had this number, and so did Catana [in Sicily] on its refoundation under the name of Etna. Then there was the popular assembly of the Ten Thousand in Arcadia, and, since even the utopias of the philosophers can throw so much light on the Greek state and Greek customs, we may mention that according to Hippodamus of Miletus the ideal state was to contain the same number.[28]

What the *polis* was, desired, was capable of or might be permitted, can best be deduced from its historical behaviour. All the city-republics of Western Europe in the Middle Ages, though they often strongly remind us of the *polis*, were fundamentally different; they were separate parts of previously existing larger realms and had broken away to become more or less independent. Even among the Italian city-states, only Venice possessed that absolute degree of autonomy that the *polis* enjoyed. Besides, the Church was a common bond, above and beyond all cities and kingdoms, and that was completely absent in Greece. But apart from these differences the *polis* in itself was a creation of quite another kind; it is as though, this one time in history, there emerged, fully developed in strength and single-mindedness, a will which had been waiting impatiently for its day on earth.

In modern times (philosophical and other idealistic programmes aside) it is essentially the single individual who postulates the State in the way he needs it. He demands of it only the security in which he will be able to develop his own powers; and in return he is willing to offer it carefully calculated sacrifices, but his sense of gratitude is in inverse proportion to the extent to which the State concerns itself with the rest of his activities. The Greek *polis*, by contrast, starts from the whole, which is conceived of as chronologically prior to the part, whether the individual household or the individual person. An inner logic allows us to add that this whole will also survive the part. It is not only the general taking precedence over the particular, but also the eternal over the momentary and the transient. Not only on the battlefield and in emergencies was the individual expected to give all that he had and was; it was equally so at all times, for he owed everything to the whole; and, in the first place, that security of his very existence which was enjoyed only by the citizen, and then only within his own city or as far as its influence reached. The *polis* was a higher product of Nature; it had come into being to make life possible, but continued to exist in order that life might be lived properly, happily, nobly and, as far as might be, in accordance with the standard of excellence. Anyone who had a part in ruling and being ruled was a citizen; the "ruling" was more precisely defined as sharing in the judicial and other public offices. Only the citizen realized all his opacities and virtues in and for the State; the whole spirit of the Greeks and their culture was closely bound up with the *polis*, and, in the golden age, by far the highest achievements in poetry and the arts belonged to public life, not to the realm of private pleasures.

The expression of all this is often sublime, and we find it in the poets of the golden age and sometimes in the philosophers and orators of the fourth century, who no longer record these ideas as actuality, but as an ideal.

A man's native city (*patris*) was therefore not just the homeland where he felt happiest or for which he would be homesick, not just the city in which he took pride despite its shortcomings, but a higher, divinely powerful being.[29] Above all it was death in battle that he owed the city, and if he died thus he was only repaying "the cost of his nurture."[30] Even Homer gives the Trojans, especially Hector, the most ardent expressions of patriotism, and the lyric poets sound the same note in the few fragments of their work that survive. Aeschylus is the most authoritative witness of all. His *Seven Against Thebes,* a tragedy "filled with the spirit of the war-god," combines, in the speeches of Eteocles, the most exalted view of the citizen's duty to sacrifice himself for his native soil with the ardour of the king and the defender. In his own epitaph the poet speaks not of his poetry but of his valour: "let the grove of Marathon tell of it, and the long-haired Mede, who has encountered it."[31]

However, the great deeds really belonged not to the individual but to the native city; it was the city, not Miltiades or Themistocles, that was victorious at Marathon and Salamis, and Demosthenes [in the next century] considers it a symptom of decadence that many have begun to say "Timotheus took Corcyra" or "Chabrias defeated the enemy at Naxos." Even the most meritorious citizen always owed more to his native city than the city did to him.[32] Pythagoras taught that anyone who has been treated unjustly by his native city should confront her as he would his mother in a similar case.

Apart from the duty to fight for victory without thought of self, there is in the great poets an ecstatic sentiment that is brought to the motherland like an offering. In particular, the Greek way of thinking permits of prayers for the prosperity of an individual city; Christianity could not do so, since as a world religion it must be mindful of mankind as a whole. In *Suppliants,* the magnificent choral ode of the Danaids (624 ff.) heaps every conceivable blessing in profusion on hospitable Argos, but Aeschylus reserves the best of all for his native city in the last great chorus of *Eumenides* with its interjections by Athena. Only in one text of the ancient world are such notes sounded with greater power, Aeschylus voices wishes and prayers, but Isaiah in his vision of the New Jerusalem (chapter 60) is both prophesying and seeing the fulfilment of his prophecy.

The *polis* was, further, an educative force; not only "the best of nurses, who when you were at play on the soft earth faithfully nourished and cherished you and found no care too tedious"—but continuing to educate the citizen throughout his life. She kept no school, though she promoted the traditional instruction in music and gymnastics. We need not detail here the many opportunities for spiritual development available to all citizens in the choral odes at the festivals, in the splendid cult rituals, buildings and works of art, and in the drama and recitations by the poets. It was the very fact of living in the *polis,* the ruling and being ruled, which was valued as a continuous education. In the better times the *polis* gave her people very strong guidance through the honours she could confer on individuals, until here too abuses set in, and wiser men preferred to forgo their claim to crowns, heralds' proclamations and so forth. In sum, the whole previous history of a famous city seemed one of the strongest encouragements to excellence: nowhere but in Athens, says Xenophon (*Memorabilia* 3.5.3), could men tell so many glorious stories of the deeds of their ancestors, and many citizens, first inspired by this, then sought to dedicate themselves to virtue and to become strong.

So the *polis,* with its vitality much more developed than that of the Phoenician city-republic, was a creation unique in the history of the world. It was the expression of a common will of the most extraordinary vigour and capability; indeed the *polis* succeeded in rising above mere village life thanks only to its deeds, the power it exercised, its passion. This was why the strictest criteria were needed for the definition of a full citizen, who after all was to form a part of this power. These *poleis* underwent quite a different order of good and bad fortune from the cities of other peoples and other epochs, and even in the liveliest of the mediaeval republics, such an intensity of living and suffering was only occasionally attained.

Hence too their violence. Externally the *polis* was in general isolated, despite all treaties and alliances, and was frequently competing with its nearest neighbours for its very life. In time of war, martial laws were in force with all their terrors.

Internally, the *polis* was implacable towards any individual who ceased to be totally absorbed in it. Its sanctions, often put into practice, were death, loss of civic rights, and exile. And we must bear in mind that there was no appeal to any external tribunal, except when cases were referred to be heard in the courts of Athens from cities in her empire. The *polis* was completely inescapable, for any desire to escape entailed the loss of all personal security. The absence of individual freedom went hand in hand with the omnipotence of the State in every context. Religion, the sacral calendar, the myths—all these were nationalized, so that the State was at the same time a church, empowered to try charges of impiety, and against this dual power the individual was totally helpless. His body was in bond for military service in Athens and Sparta till the end of his life, in Rome until his forty-sixth year; and his possessions were entirely in the power of the city, which could even determine the value of many of them. In short, there could be no guarantees of life or property that ran counter to the *polis* and its interests. Although this enslavement of the individual to the State existed under all constitutions, it must have been at its most oppressive under democracy, where the most villainous men, ridden by ambition, identified themselves with the *polis* and its interests and could therefore interpret in their own way the maxim *salus reipublicae suprema lex esto* ("let the safety of the Republic be the highest law"). Thus the *polis* got the maximum price for the small amount of security it afforded.

Yet since, in good times, all that was highest and noblest in the life of the Greeks was centred upon the *polis,* then fundamentally the *polis* was their religion. The worship of the gods found its strongest support against alien religions, philosophies and other undermining forces in its importance for the particular city, which had to maintain this worship exactly and in full, and the main cults were mainly the direct concern of the State. So while the *polis* was itself a religion, it contained the rest of religion within itself as well, and the communal nature of the sacrifices and festivals formed a very strong bond among the citizens, quite apart from the laws, the constitution and the public life they shared.

> Because all this is offered by the State and only by the State, it is perfectly clear why the Greek needs no church, why, in order to show piety in his own way, he need only be a good citizen; why there is no question of hierarchic rivalries, why the highest cult official in Athens, the *archon basileus,* is a State official, and why, finally, it is an offence not only against the duties of a citizen, but also against loyalty to the faith, to worship the gods in any rites but those recognized by the State.[33]

When the *polis* began to decline, the cult of the gods no longer sufficed, not even that of the "gods (and heroes) who protect the city," and the *polis* deified itself as Tyche (Fortune) with her crown of walls. This transition becomes very clear in some lines of Pindar's. Tyche is one of the personifications of Moira, or Fate, and it is in this general character that Pindar addresses her, asking her favour for one particular city: "I beg you, daughter of Zeus the Deliverer, to protect strong Himera, Tyche our saviour! At sea you command the swift ships, and on land the fierce battling armies and the wise counsels of the agora."[34] But the cult of the single city, idealized as Tyche, had probably begun in various places by the fifth century, with special temples and sometimes a colossal statue. The usual earlier representations of Tyche, like that set up by Bupalos for the Smyrnians, showed her with her wand and cornucopia;[35] now her attributes were the crown of walls and some feature of the particular city. Some superb figures were made for the purpose, for instance the row of bronzes Pausanias speaks of (1.18.6) fronting the columns of Hadrian's Olympieion in Athens, representing the *Tychai* of the Athenian colonies.

Later on Tyche herself was not enough, when the democracies who had taken power in most cities rubbed salt in the wounds of their defeated opponents by idealizing themselves as Demos. This, too, often took the form of colossal statues, like the one in the agora at Sparta,[36] which must have been put up at the lowest point in the fortunes of the city. As this Demos was usually shown in the likeness of the so-called "good daimon," it could become the object of a real cult. The point of all these deifications could only be the certainty of continuing prosperity; there is no record of the way people viewed such statues when everything lay in ruins.

There was also another sense and another form in which the *polis* regarded itself as an ideal whole, and that was in its *nomos,* a word used to embrace the laws and with them the constitution. *Nomos* is the higher objective power, supreme over all individual existence or will, not satisfied merely to protect the citizen in return for taxes and military service, as in modern times, but aspiring to be the very soul of the whole *polis.* Law and the constitution are hymned in the most sublime phrases as the invention and gift of the gods, as the city's personality, as the guardians and preservers of all virtue. They are the "rulers of the cities," and Demaratus the Spartan seeks to explain to Xerxes that his people fear King Law (*despotes nomos*) more than the Persians fear their Great King.[37] The officials in particular are, as Plato puts it, to be the slaves of the law. The lawgiver therefore appeared as a superhuman being, and the glory of Lycurgus, Solon, Zaleucus and Charondas sheds a reflected light on much later men, so that for instance, as late as about 400 B.C. the Syracusan law reformer Diocles received heroic honours and even a temple after his death (Diodorus 13.35).

Above all, *nomos* must not pander to the transitory interests and caprices of the individual or of those who happen to be in the majority. It was strongly felt, at least in theory, that old laws should be retained; indeed, customs and manners which were even older than laws, and had perhaps been in force from the very foundation of a city, were recognized as having a vigour of which the laws were only the outward expression.[38] And even inadequate laws, as long as they were strictly observed, seemed a better guarantee of stability than change would be.[39] Alcibiades said as much in the conclusion of his great speech in favour of the expedition to Sicily.[40] In certain states boys had to learn the laws by heart, set to a tune or cadence, not just to fix them in the memory but to ensure that they became unalterable.[41] (The Greek word *nomos* has the double meaning of law and of melody.)

None the less we learn from old sources, not merely late anecdotes, that even Solon, when he left the country for ten years after completing his legislative programme, had to bind the Athenians by solemn vows to alter nothing in his laws while he was away.[42] Soon afterwards they underwent a severe political crisis and finally [after nearly a century] changed his constitution into a fully democratic one. It was much the same story in many other Greek *poleis*; and even most of the colonies, in spite of all the initial lawgiving, had a restless, even stormy history. In its full development, democracy had a passion for revision; the letter of the constitution might be loudly praised and honoured while at the same time being altered and completely undermined by the endless promotion of popular decrees (*psephismata*). That was the state of affairs in which, in Aristotle's words (*Politics* 4.4.3) it was not the law, but the masses (*plethos*) who ruled.

For, as we shall see, the Greek idea of the State, with its total subordination of the individual to the general, had at the same time developed a strong tendency to encourage individuality. These tremendous individual forces ought in theory to have evolved entirely in the general interest, to have become its most vital expression; freedom and subordination ought to have been harmoniously fused into a unity. But in fact the Greek idea of freedom is qualified from the start, because, as we have said, the *polis* was inescapable; the individual could not even take refuge in religion, since this too belonged to the State, and in any case there was no assurance that the gods were kind and merciful. The highly gifted, obliged to stay on and endure, strove to gain power in the State. Individuals and parties ruled in the name of the *polis*. Whatever party happened to be in power behaved exactly as though it were the whole *polis* and had the right to exert its full authority.

In antiquity, anyone who believed he had the right to rule, or who merely wished to rule, at once resorted to extreme measures against his opponents and rivals, even to annihilating them. Occasionally in some unemphatic words of the poets this way of thinking slips out as the normal one. One need only study the speeches of the tutor in Euripides' *Ion,* where he urges Creusa to murder Xuthus and Ion.[43] Would it be possible, we wonder, for a criminal character in any modern drama to express himself so candidly in the name of power and authority? All political punishments in these city-states (some of them, it is true, for very serious offences) have the quality of revenge and of extermination. We shall see examples of punishment visited not only on the children of those exiled or executed but on their ancestors as well, when the family tombs were laid waste.[44] The Greeks thought they saw a clear alternative; either we destroy these people or they destroy us—and they acted accordingly with ruthless logic. The characteristic feature of this terrorism was its solemnity. The fact that tyrannicides, if they survived their deed, might receive the highest honours and be commemorated after death with monuments and rites, is too well known to give us pause. But one consequence was that obscure cutthroats were named as benefactors of society, granted citizenship, publicly crowned at the great Dionysian festival and so forth, because they happened to have murdered a man later found to have been a rogue and a traitor, like Phrynichus at Athens in 411 B.C., while their accomplices would at least have their names inscribed on the memorial column and be rewarded in other ways.[45]

The intention of the ruling party here was by no means just to intimidate and humiliate its remaining enemies, but chiefly to make their own triumph as striking as possible. Those who did the deed were honoured irrespective of their motives or their personal qualities.

Because the *polis* was the highest of all things for the Hellenes, in fact their religion, the struggles that surrounded it had all the horror of religious wars, and any break with the *polis* would cut off the individual from all normal conditions of life. Civil war was bewailed as the worst of all wars, the most appalling and most godless, loathsome to gods and men,[46] but this insight did not bring peace. In many cities the existing constitution, whatever it may have been, was the orthodoxy, and was defended by all the methods of terrorism. For generations, no-one dared to say openly that the fiction of the duties of citizenship as paramount had overstretched what human nature could bear, but there was no way of preventing the growth of secret, inner disaffection among intellectuals, and as time went on some came forward to declare it openly and defiantly. Philosophical ethics followed, gave up its earlier identification with the State and became the ethics of humanity in general. In the school of Epicurus, the *polis* is stripped of all its feverish divinization to become a mutual contract of security among all its members. The real *poleis*, however, convulsed as they were, continued on the path of violence. One thing they could not do was to surrender their autonomy to another city, a larger federal state or a ruler. Later the *polis* was to struggle for survival at any price amid terrible sufferings. "A single wicked man," says Isocrates (8.120) "may die before retribution overtakes him; but cities, since they cannot die, must suffer the vengeance of men and gods."

Notes

1. Herodotus 1.145, Strabo 8.7.4.

2. Strabo suggests that the people were more prosperous in the earlier period, e.g. in referring to Achaea, 8.7.5.

3. Despite all the pronouncements of Thucydides 2.15. He emphasizes that from the earliest times, the Athenians lived in the countryside more than other Greeks.

4. Strabo 8.3.2.

5. Thucydides 3.2 f.

6. According to Diodorus 13.75 they really did make the move. Cf. Strabo 14.2.

7. Diodorus 12.34, Xenophon, *Hellenica* 5.2.12.

8. Diodorus 15.94. Cf. Pausanias 8.27.1–15, 9.14.2.

9. Strabo, 8.8.1. dates the beginning of Arcadia's barrenness from this.

10. *Myriandros polis*. As we shall see, a population of 10,000 men fit to bear arms, or of full citizens, was considered the ideal medium size for a city.

11. Strabo 13.1.59.

12. Strabo 13.1.52., in connection with the Scepsians. Strabo also notes many cases of towns displaced; formerly a town was here and now it is there. This probably mostly occurred when a better site was found, but also perhaps when a number of the citizens left because of discontent, as those of Cos did (14.2.19). If the group were strong enough they could take the name with them.

13. Cf. Jacobus de Aquis, *Imago Mundi*, in *Historiae patriae monum. scriptt* Vol. 3 Col. 1569, 1605, 1614, in part very disorganized chronologically.

14. Pausanias 9.14.2 and 10.3.2. After the battle of Leuctra, Mantinea was re-established as a city.

15. Aelian, *Varia Historia* 12.28. For Thebes, Pausanias 9.17.1, the grave of Antipoenus' daughters.

16. Iamblichus, *Life of Pythagoras* c. 9.

17. Plutarch, *Parallela Minora* 306e–f.

18. Plutarch, *Moralia* 163a–d.

19. If Pausanias Damascenus (*FGH* 854 F.10) is to be trusted.

20. Suda, *sv. Herodotus*.

21. In many cities and especially colonies, the monument or at least the statue of the founder could be seen on the agora.

22. Talvj, *Serbian Folksongs* I. 78.

23. Herodotus' reference to the *theatron* in Sparta (6. 67) is to be understood as meaning a place for spectacle in general, not a theatre.

24. *Iliad* XI. 807. It was not far from the ships of Odysseus, which are said in line 5 f. to be in the middle of all the others.

25. Herodotus 4.153, which is informative in other ways too.

26. There are several statements which concur in this, including one in Lucian, *Enemies 20*, where Solon is the speaker.

27. Strabo, 14.5.19 mentions a city called Myriandros in Cilicia on the Gulf of Issicus. Perhaps it was founded with the intention that it should have 10,000 citizens.

28. Aristotle, *Politics* 2.5.

29. Much later, this attitude is seen in a fine little essay of Lucian's, *Patriae encomium*.

30. Not always voluntarily; most early statutes include the death penalty for evading military service.

31. Aeschylus II in Page, *Epigrammata Graeca* p. 42. Cf. the words Aristophanes gives to Aeschylus, *Frogs* 1004 ff.

32. However, compare the very sensible answer Themistocles gave to a man from Seriphos who told him he owed his renown not to himself but to Athens: "Yes indeed, but if I were a Seriphian I would not have become famous, and neither would you, if you had been an Athenian."

33. K. F. Nägelsbach, *Nachhomerische Theologie* (1857) p. 293.

34. Opening of *Olympian* XII.

35. Pausanias 4.30.3 f.

36. Pausanias 3.11.8.

37. Herodotus 1.104.

38. Simpler peoples contented themselves with this ancient unwritten morality; e.g. the Lycians.

39. Aristotle, *Politics* 4.6.3.

40. Thucydides 6.18.7.

41. E.g. in Crete: cf. Aelian, *Varia Historia* 2.39. Yet the states of Crete were notoriously some of the most politically corrupt.

42. Herodotus 1.29.

43. 846, 1040 ff. Ion too has a harsh speech: 1334.

44. Isocrates, *Oration* 16 Chap. 26. When Phocion, about to drink the hemlock, sends his son his command not to seek revenge on the Athenians, this may not be a sign of his noble character, but of his wish to save his son from further persecution.

45. Lysias, *Oration* 13.72 (*Against Agoratus*).

46. Xenophon, *History of Greece* 2.4. 22.

7

European Cities in the Middle Ages

Leonardo Benevolo

At the end of the tenth century Europe began to undergo an economic renaissance. The population increased (from approximately 22 million in 950 to some 55 million in 1350), agricultural output rose, and industry and commerce once more began to play an important economic role.

Historians have revealed a number of interrelated reasons for this phenomenon:

> the settlement of the last invaders, the Arabs, Vikings and Hungarians;
> new techniques in agriculture: the triennial rotation of fields, improved methods of yoking horses and oxen, the spread of water mills;
> the influence of the maritime cities (Venice, Genoa, Pisa, Amalfi), which had retained their international trading activities in the Mediterranean and now began to stimulate the development of other cities as commercial cities. . . .

1. The Development of the City-State

Some of the new population, unable to find work in the country, gathered in the cities, which explains the growth in the number of artisans and traders who lived on the fringes of the feudal organisation.

The fortified cities of the early Middle Ages, sometimes called burgs (from the medieval latin *burgus*), were too small to accommodate this increased population. As a result, new settlements sprang up outside the city gates, called suburbs, which soon became larger than the original urban nucleus. It became necessary, therefore, to build new walls to protect these suburbs and the other establishments (churches, abbeys, castles) that had grown up outside the old city, and this process of expansion often continued until some cities possessed several sets of walls.

The traders and artisans who inhabited these cities—the burgesses (*bourgeois*)—were in the majority from the very beginning. They therefore began to try and free themselves from the feudal political system and obtain conditions that would favour their own economic activities: freedom of the individual, judicial autonomy, administrative independence, and personal taxation proportionally related to income, the revenue from which could be used to finance works in the public interest (particularly defensive measures, such as walls and armaments).

This new movement, which originally started out as an association of private individuals, subsequently came into conflict with the bishops and feudal princes and grew into an organised political force. This was the origin of the Italian *comune*, a state with its own legislature, which had the power to overrule both groups and individuals, but which still respected their economic privileges.

The instruments of city government were as follows:

1. A main council, composed of representatives from the most important families;
2. A secondary council, which functioned as an executive body;
3. A certain number of magistrates, who were either elected or chosen by lot: in France they were called *jures*, in Italy *consoli*, in Flanders *échevins*.

These bodies were opposed by other associations that represented special sections of the community: the trade corporations, for example, known in England as guilds and in Italy and Germany as *arti* and *Zünfte* respectively, and the representatives of the soldiery, who elected their own magistrate, known in Italy as *il capitano del popolo*. In addition to the civil authorities, there were also the Church authorities, represented by the bishops and the monastic orders, who also had their seat in the city. In some parts of Italy there were also a chief magistrate, called the *podestà*, whose function was to arbitrate in case of political disagreement between the administration and the citizenry.

The medieval city-state depended on the countryside for its food supply and it always controlled a large area of land, the size of which varied according to the needs of the city. Unlike the Greek city, however, it did nor grant equal rights to its rural inhabitants; it remained a closed city, whose economic and political activities could equally well be on an international scale as on a national one, but whose politics were oriented to coincide with the restricted interests of the urban population. This population, however, was not a homogeneous one, which could take communal decisions like those taken in the democratic cities of Greece. The ruling class, represented in the councils, gradually expanded, but it never grew to include the manual workers, and when the latter attempted to seize power in Italy during the economic crisis in the second part of the fourteenth century, they were routed and the government fell into the hands of groups of aristocratic families, or sometimes a single family: the *comune,* a relatively democratic institution, had become a *signoria* (seigneury).

2. *The Colonisation of the Countryside*

The growth of the cities meant that the rural areas began to change at an ever increasing rate. The mercantile cities imported foodstuffs and raw materials, while at the same time exporting industrial and commercial goods, and the countryside, because of the reciprocal nature of this trade and because of the growth in population, was forced to raise its levels of agricultural production by putting new land under cultivation and by using the existent land more efficiently.

The old manorial system, based on the idea of economic self-sufficiency, was not able to cope with this new state of affairs and it began to disintegrate; until that time the villages had only produced enough food for themselves, as well as producing all their own equipment. The manorial villages now found themselves employing a growing number of freedmen, who came from outside the district, and the feudal lords began to establish new settlements for them on land that had not already been reclaimed for agricultural purposes.

Although these new towns were founded by the feudal lords, they were not organised along traditional lines: they guaranteed the individual freedom of the workers, they had self-government and were administered by a magistrate who was almost always elected by the inhabitants themselves. Also, despite the fact that they remained subject to feudal law, both politically and juridically, they copied the municipal organisation of the city-state.

Other new towns were founded on the fringes of Europe for a variety of economic and political reasons:

1. The *bastides* of southern France, erected by the English and French barons and kings during the Hundred Years War;
2. The *poblaciones* of Spain, built in the regions captured by the Christians from the Moors;
3. The settlements founded in eastern Germany in the areas captured from the Slavs by the Teutonic Knights.

The development of the city-state and the foundation of new towns in country areas was brought to a halt in the mid-fourteenth century by an abrupt decline in population levels, and by the resultant slowing down of economic activity. This drop in population was caused by the Black Death, and particularly by the Great Plague of 1348–9, whose effects were felt in every aspect of city life.

The very nature of medieval culture, which tended not to establish formal models like classical culture, means that it is impossible to generalise about the form taken by cities during the Middle Ages. Medieval towns and cities came in all shapes and sizes, adapting themselves freely to every geographical and economic circumstance, as has already been noted.

There are, however, universal characteristics, which can be related to the political and economic ones that have been mentioned previously.

1. Medieval towns had a street system that was only marginally less regular than that found in their Arab counterparts. Their streets were, however, laid out in such a way that people would always be able to tell approximately where they were, and also have a general idea of what the particular district or town was like. They varied considerably in size, ranging from full-scale streets to narrow alleyways, and the intervening squares were not just self-contained open spaces: they were closely integrated with the streets which ran into them. Only the lesser streets were intended to act purely as thoroughfares: all the other ones were designed to be used as places to stop, to conduct business or for holding meetings. The houses, almost always built on several floors, faced out on to the public area, and their façades were an important factor in determining the character of the street or square that they overlooked.

Thus the public and private areas did not form contiguous yet separate areas, as in the cities of antiquity: there was a single common public area, composed of many different elements, which spread throughout the city and provided the setting for all buildings, both public and private, together with whatever internal space they contained, whether courtyards or gardens.

This new balance between the two types of property was the result of a compromise between public law and private interests. In fact, the municipal statutes laid down comprehensive legislation concerning the relationship between the public and private domains and also concerning the areas in which the two sectors overlapped: the parts of a building projecting over a street, colonnades, or external staircases.

2. The public areas in the cities had a rather complex layout, due to the fact that they had to accommodate a number of different authorities: the local bishop, the municipal government, the religious orders and the trade guilds. As a result, any city of importance would have more than one centre: a religious centre (with a cathedral and an episcopal palace), a civil centre (with a town hall) and one or more commercial centres with arcades and guildhalls. These areas sometimes overlapped, but the contrast between civil and religious authority, which never existed in antiquity, was always fairly well defined.

Every city was divided into different quarters, each of which had its own character, its own emblem and often its own political organisation. During the thirteenth century, when the cities were growing at a very fast rate, a number of secondary centres sprang up on the outskirts: they were the establishments of the new religious orders—the Franciscans, the Dominicans, the Servites—together with their churches and surrounding squares.

3. Medieval cities were privileged political entities, with the city bourgeoisie representing only a small part of the total population, which grew rapidly and continuously from the beginning of the eleventh century up until the mid-fourteenth century. The laws were formulated for the benefit of the people concentrated within the city walls: the city centre, where the well-to-do people lived, was the most sought-after area, while the poorer sections of the community lived in the outer districts. The tallest structures were at the centre—the towers of the municipal palace, the campanile, the cathedral spire—and they represented the city's highest points, as well as providing an additional unifying and three-dimensional element.

Every city had to have a surrounding wall to defend it from the outside world, and each time it grew, its walls had to be correspondingly increased until a series of concentric circles of fortification had been constructed. These walls, which represented by far the largest item of public expenditure, almost always had an irregular and rounded outline, designed to encompass a given area of ground as economically as possible.

The construction of a new wall was always postponed until there was positively no room left for buildings within the existing walls, which accounts for the density of houses in medieval cities and also for the height of the buildings. Only the great walls built at the end of the thirteenth century and the beginning of the fourteenth century, in cities like Florence, Siena, Bologna, Padua and Ghent, proved to be too extensive during the mid-fourteenth century, when population levels remained static or actually dropped. They ended up by enclosing large areas of green, which were only built over during the nineteenth century.

4. The medieval cities that we know nowadays owe their present appearance to developments during the period between the fifteenth and seventeenth centuries, when their size and their architecture had already been firmly established.

8

Architecture and Urban Growth

Josef W. Konvitz

The Early Renaissance

Debates about the spatial, temporal, and conceptual boundaries of the Renaissance continue to animate scholarship, but broad agreement can be found for the proposition that cultural changes originating during the second half of the fifteenth century in Italy provoked some Europeans to explore their world in radically new ways. The Renaissance, like most great transformations, had its source in an earlier time and influenced later generations; and, like most, it can be stretched to cover too much. Nevertheless, particularly in terms of urban history, the intense and imaginative pursuit of knowledge which was grounded in the Renaissance stands apart.

Renaissance ideas about cities and architecture in Italy were both a reaction against medieval city-building patterns and directed toward possibilities in the medieval city which had never been perceived before. By any measure, Italy was the most advanced country of the fifteenth century: Its commercial systems were sophisticated and intensely developed; its civic life was concentrated in politically conscious, city-dominated provincial states; its culture was associated with Europe's oldest and most numerous universities. Italian city-states were small enough and sufficiently numerous to compose a political chessboard on which the balance of power could be pursued, securing small states against the designs of large ones, and distributing power among them as the condition of their collective independence.

This political system fostered a commitment on the part of the upper classes to sustain and enrich the city-state. Changes in economic and social conditions raised risks, costs, and anxieties in Italian affairs, in much the same way as they affected life across Europe, but with this difference: Because Italy was so urbanized, and because Italian culture and politics focused upon the city to an unusual degree, economic and social problems were perceived acutely in an urban dimension.

A desire for order and control found its finest expression in a new architecture. Two circumstances made changes in architecture more probable in Italy than elsewhere: First, Italians were less attached to medieval ideas and forms, and were more aware of ancient culture; second, the number of easily accessible cities, rivalry among patrons, and a reservoir of mobile artistic talent made it likely that fruitful experiments in building would take place, and could be replicated.

Artistic ideas provided the catalyst for architectural change. These ideas have long fascinated scholars, yet much will always remain a mystery about them because some of the most precious documents—drawings by Brunelleschi, for example—have been lost. Nevertheless, the essential story can be reconstructed. It begins in Florence in the 1420s, when Filippo Brunelleschi (1377?–1466) invented linear perspective in pictorial representation by placing all objects and figures within a spatial frame in relation to a geometrical, abstract superstructure dominated by a vanishing point.[1]

The theory which made linear perspective plausible stated that visually perceived space is ordered by an a priori, abstract system of linear coordinates. Linear perspective was not thought to be an artificial device to give the optical illusion of reality on two dimensions but a two-dimensional version of reality, a key to the spatial organization inherent in the world. It was believed that the real space before one's eyes can be understood in the mind and transferred onto canvas because it is structured according to divinely composed, geometrical laws of nature: There is truth in what one sees because God has constructed space according to true, natural laws.

This theoretical statement did not exist until Leon Battista Alberti (1404–1472), of whom more later, set the rules of linear perspective into print in the mid 1430s; but Brunelleschi's experiments must have been guided by some of these ideas, which were not particularly new or original. What was inventive was the artistic technique, which linear perspective provided, to give them precise visual form.

The composition of a painting based on linear perspective involved using a geometrical grid to determine the location and proportion of the details. Once the grid technique and linear perspective were linked, their use became generalized, with consequences for both architecture and city design. In the absence of linear perspective, a map or drawing of the spatial layout of a medieval city did not appear to have a logical structure which could be determined abstractly, but instead appeared as an agglomeration of parts whose internal connections did not require objective graphic description or verification to be understood.[2] Thus, artists who could not use linear perspective reproduced buildings from several different vantage points, notwithstanding the visual contradictions this produced in a two-dimensional work: Some buildings were shown from one vantage point, others from another; many buildings were rearranged in the same city, or combined with buildings from two or more cities.

Renaissance artists must have felt a tension between actual city space and theoretical notions about space as constructed according to eternal principles and divine laws. Brunelleschi demonstrated that the grid could be used to copy buildings to scale, and he incorporated it as well as a compositional element in some of his buildings; and Alberti used the grid to make more accurate city views. By the end of the fifteenth century, the grid had become the theoretical design model for city squares, and even more significantly for entire cities.

At first, buildings of a style we now identify as Renaissance were conceived by painters (Ghirlandaio, Pinturrichio, and Botticelli, among others) working from imagination, because no buildings had yet been erected which could have served them as models. The imaginary space in their paintings was composed of ideally shaped buildings, streets, colonnades, and the like, which were subordinated to the entire composition through symmetry, perspective, and proportion. The characters placed by artists into such settings were given a stage for moral, historic action which placed them outside ordinary living experience. The self-imposed task of the first great Renaissance builders was to transfer that setting from canvas to the real city. Artists became architects.

Between the end of the twelfth and thirteenth centuries, the population of Florence had at least quadrupled, with most new housing provided by building in open spaces and courtyards and by adding on stories to existing structures. Florence appeared as a "mass of tenements, towers protruding everywhere, . . . [with] little overall organization . . . and few points of focus to pull parts of it together visually."[3] Then the spirit of a new political order inspired Florentines to insist on a greater assertion of civic values against the centrifugal forces of a corporate society and to give more coherent shape to communal government.[4]

A fire in 1304 destroyed 1,700 buildings, a flood in 1333 everything along the Arno River; rebuilding gave Florentines an opportunity to start afresh. The cutting down of the towers of factious families, plans to enlarge the city and rebuild its walls, and legislation to give some order to urban expansion were "informed by a consciousness of public space and inspired by the desire to make a distinctive mark on it."[5] Uplifted by a sense of their uniqueness and superiority, Florentines developed a collective vision of their city which provided a civic context for public and private building.

The transformation of medieval into Renaissance Florence involved the construction of civic, ecclesiastical, and patrician buildings by artisans with little academic training.[6] Height and mass more than purely artistic features distinguished newer from older structures. So long as styles were traditional, architects encountered few problems in communicating their intentions to craftsmen, who in turn enjoyed some scope for their own talents. (Even after architectural style departed from tradition, architects were still paid at a foreman's rate for the amount of work they did, not for their ideas.)

Brunelleschi, the first to compose a painting according to linear perspective, was also the first to deal with the problem of designing a building according to the new aesthetic in an existing urban setting. A century before, Giotto had erected a campanile next to Florence's cathedral, but the dome over the cathedral still remained to be completed. Brunelleschi's design for the dome has been interpreted to symbolize the evolution of art since Giotto. Giulio Argan's discussion of Brunelleschi's dome brings out the protean consciousness of early Renaissance architectural design which conflated architectural form, urban space, and the universe and implied that a single, systematic, rational, homogenous order structured them all.[7] Argan makes clear that Brunelleschi's achievement represented the supremacy of the liberal (intellectual) over the mechanical (artisan) arts:

> From the point of view of the technical construction, the dome is a completely new thing which transformed not only traditional methods of work but the very social organization of the building trade as well. It is well known that before undertaking the technical problem of construction Brunelleschi went to Rome to study the fabric and proportions of the ancient city walls. However, it is clear that, although the dome of Santa Maria del Fiore implied a familiarity with ancient methods, it was not built in a traditional manner. It is thus a modern invention based on historical research. Evidently Brunelleschi thought that a new technique could not be derived from the past, but must come from a different cultural experience, from history. In this way he refuted the old "mechanical" technique and created a new "liberal" technique based on those typically individualistic actions which are historical research and inventiveness. He abolished the traditional hierarchical form of the mason's lodge where the head was the coordinator of the specialized work of the various groups of skilled workers who made up the lodge masters. Now there was only one planner or inventor; the others were merely manual laborers. When the master mason rose to the status of sole planner, whose activity was on a par with the other humanistic disciplines, the other members of the team of masons fell from the rank of *maestri* in charge of various aspects of the job to that of simple working men. This explains the impatience of the masons and their rebellion against the master mason who had become an "architect" or "engineer."
>
> The consequence of this—its importance also in the field of city planning—could be seen already in other works by Brunelleschi. He used the classical architectural morphology of equal, repetitive elements almost in series and eliminated the abundant Gothic decoration that had generally been carried out in the masons' workshop. Architectural elements such as columns, capitals, cornices, and so on, could now be constructed outside the shop and then put in place according to the architect's design, just as prefabricated elements are used today. This saved an enormous amount of time, both in the planning and in the execution. . . . Even with delays caused by unforeseen circumstances, the construction could be carried out according to the plan of the original architect; a great construction need no longer be the work of successive generations, but of a single artist. If it became possible in the Renaissance to think of the city as a unified form (in a utopian but not absurd manner), willed into being by a prince and created by his architect, this was due to the changes in the methods of planning and execution begun by Brunelleschi, which made it theoretically possible to construct a city within a man's lifetime.[8]

The key word in the last sentence is, of course, theoretically. Construction of private mansions and civic structures recycled wealth into art, generated demand for decorative arts of high quality, and stimulated the enjoyment of lovely things. Conspicuous consumption of this kind, however, did not generate new wealth. Given the deteriorating economic and social circumstances of late fifteenth- and sixteenth-century Italy, the demand for new construction could not be sustained long enough to transform the medieval city completely.[9]

Leon Battista Alberti (1404–1472) was the first to test the applicability of architectural design to city planning. Pope Nicholas V, having restored unity to the church and determined to safeguard its doctrines and institutions, elevated the Vatican as the seat of the Papacy, initiated the construction of St. Peter's, and adopted the arms of Peter as the papal seal. With Alberti's guidance, he also undertook to rebuild and restore the city of Rome to is rightful position as the greatest city of Christendom. This was no mere propaganda effort; the ideology behind midfifteenth-century plans for Rome was grounded in a vision of a city whose appearance would make manifest and visible the power, purpose, and primacy of the church. Alberti understood what Nicholas wanted.[10] He undertook to do two things: first, to formulate a theory to justify the reconstruction of Rome (published as *De re aedificatora,* in different editions between 1443 and 1452); second, to conceive of conspicuous architectural, spatial forms which could express the historical and contemporary significance of Rome, and to make a hierarchical order visible.

Alberti and Nicholas intended to design the entire district enclosed between the Vatican, the Castel Sant'Angelo, and the Tiber River, and a new piazza further along the Tiber; but their plans never advanced far enough for us to know what individual elements would have looked like. It took one century to complete St. Peter's, and another to integrate the Vatican into the structure of Rome; in the meantime, the city's demographic growth determined the shape and scale of most construction. Nevertheless, Alberti's conceptualization of a reconstructed Rome included all the features which characterized Renaissance city planning: the revision of existing urban space by opening it up with new streets and wide squares; the enlargement of a city by adding new, planned districts; the erection of monumental buildings whose presence and qualities would generate development around them.

Nicholas's plans exceeded the means available for their realization, but Alberti combined theoretical and practical considerations more satisfactorily in his other building ventures. More than anyone else, Alberti developed the idea, through his writings and designs, that a building's stylistic qualities, spatial form, and architectonic placement in the cityscape should integrate that building into the daily lives of the citizens. This dialectical approach toward the erection of churches, patrician palaces, and social welfare and public institutions—the kinds of buildings patrons of Renaissance architecture commissioned—emphasized respect for the total urban environment in all its manifestations as the setting for cultural, social, and political life.

Realizing that only a few buildings in the Renaissance style would be built in any city, Alberti did not require the destruction of large parts of existing cities as a precondition for rebuilding along fundamentally new lines. Rather, he wanted to maximize the visual and ideological impact of every project in the belief that a few Renaissance buildings, by their very presence, could revalue their surroundings and stimulate changes in the quality and meaning of urban life. This conservative, practical approach to construction, which preserved a balance between beauty (*voluptas*) and usefulness (*commoditas*), recognized that Renaissance styles were not appropriate for all kinds of buildings. It also contained within it an idea which, however, could not be restrained by utilitarian, quotidian considerations: that architecture, unifying all the arts with philosophical thought, could bring life to the medieval ideal of a community harmoniously integrating social order and moral action.

From this perspective, it appears that Renaissance architecture, for all its differences with medieval building, remained in the cultural mode to the extent that it emphasized the immediate and direct apprehension of space, and reaffirmed the power of spatial forms to influence people. In their attempts to make order in cities by promoting civic values that would engage people in socially responsible activities, Renaissance designers articulated a higher purpose for city building in the cultural mode. To clarify architecture's message and eliminate any ambiguity, complex and polyvalent spatial features which created many layers of meaning were cut.

The moral imperative of Renaissance architecture implied that the medieval urban world was morally corrupt and aesthetically inadequate, and hence could not provide the outlines of forms for a vision of the world as it ought to be. To penetrate the consciousness of city dwellers, Renaissance architects required styles which could symbolize, by directly embodying, the transcending reality behind appearances. Rudolph Wittkower has described how Renaissance artist-architects, starting with a revival of the Roman Vitruvius and an archeological search for classical buildings, produced a style in which proportion, harmony, and classical derivatives had unquestioned status as the most immediate and intuitive expressions of form and content. The result was a new humanistic, metaphoric architectural vocabulary which evoked a remote golden age in order to open up an imaginative vision of a future society immeasurably closer to divine and natural law than the present one.

Classically inspired ideals emphasized the city as the unit to be governed, produced the need for a new kind of public space as a forum for political action, and commanded architecture to visualize the secular and religious uses of power.[11] Although Renaissance architecture referred to a time sequence, it was nevertheless profoundly antihistorical, designed not so much to resemble antiquity as to point up the anachronisms in medieval urban culture. Renaissance artist-architects did not know, however, that their break with the past would inspire, and indeed compel, their successors to break with them. After all, they believed quite sincerely that their designs, which symbolized eternal values, would endure and would hasten the commencement of a new enlightened age for man.

In the 1490s the rise of genuine religious anguish and the destruction of the Italian city-state cut short the ambitions of artist-architects. Yet, they continued to pursue the visual representation of the ideal society without recognizing that their assumptions were illusory or impractical. Reaffirming their faith in imagination, and rejecting the real world as an unsatisfactory model for art, they persisted in the search for the perfect expression of truth, beauty, and goodness in architectural form. They did not reconcile themselves to the fact that their influence on cities was limited to the design of palaces, civic and ecclesiastical structures, fortifications, and public works, or to the fact that they often competed with traditional craftsmen even for these commissions.

Until the eighteenth century, vernacular, utilitarian construction evolved satisfactorily along established lines, enabling cities to grow and change with little direction from architects and planners. Traditional city-building methods thus preserved the latent adaptability of the urban environment to change, and thus kept the cost of providing and maintaining that environment low. For this reason, in that large part of the city that continued to evolve in the vernacular tradition, visible differences over time were much less striking than in that small part of the city affected by architecture, even though both parts might be rebuilt extensively in every century. Such change as took place usually did not affect the size and shape of the city but only land-use patterns and individual structures in ways that were easily assimilated into the city as a whole.

The role of vernacular, utilitarian construction in city building was largely lost on artist-architects, who continued to pursue their ideals. To the high-minded designers, for whom design was a principled intellectual activity, the coexistence of architectural masterpieces and ordinary dwellings, workshops, and public facilities was intolerable. The consequence of this situation for the history of the city was enormous: At a time of rapid urban development, those most able to speak, write, draw, and design ideas about and for cities were often unable to provide practical solutions to urban problems. Having placed theory before practice, artist-architects at the end of the fifteenth and the beginning of the sixteenth centuries contributed to a division in urban culture. This division separated those with ideas about urban affairs from those responsible for the everyday needs of ordinary people. There has been no turning back from the notion that architecture can restore order to society and dignity to man, but each generation from the sixteenth century to the present has recognized the failure of its predecessors to imagine architectural projects and city-planning schemes which successfully combine beauty with practicality and artistically designed structures with quotidian, vernacular ones.

Notes

1. Samuel Y. Edgerton, Jr., *The Renaissance Rediscovery of Linear Perspective* (New York: Harper and Row, 1975). Additional sources on the early Renaissance city include: Giovanni Fanelli, *Firenze, architettura e città*, 2 vols. (Florence: Vallecchi, 1973); Eugenio Garin, "La cité idéale de la Renaissance," in *Les Utopies à la Renaissance*, (Brussels: Presses universitaires de Bruxelles; Paris: Presses universitaires de France, 1963), 11–37; Pierre Francastel, "Imagination et réalité dans l'architecture civile du Quattro-cento," in *Hommage á Lucien Febvre: éventail de l'histoire vivante* (Paris: Armand Colin, 1953), 2:195–206; Wolfgang Lotz, *Studies in Italian Renaissance Architecture* (Cambridge, Mass.: MIT Press, 1977); Leopold D. Ettlinger, "The Emergence of the Italian Architect during the Fifteenth Century," in *The Architect: Chapters in the History of the Profession,* ed.

Spiro Kostof (New York: Oxford University Press, 1977), 96–123; Catherine Wilkinson, "The New Professionalism in the Renaissance," Ibid., 124–60.

2. Pierre Lavedan and Jeanne Hugueney, *La Représentation des villes dans l'art du moyen-âge* (Paris: Vanoest, 1954); John A. Pinto, "Origins and Development of the Ichnographic City Plan," *Journal of the Society of Architectural Historians* 35 (1976), and P. D. A. Harvey, *The History of Topographical Maps: Symbols, Pictures and Survey* (London: Thames and Hudson, 1980), 66–84.

3. Goldthwaite, *Building of Renaissance Florence,* 2.

4. Ibid., 4.

5. Ibid., 68; idem, "The Florentine Palace as Domestic Architecture," *American Historical Review* 77 (1972).

6. Idem, *Building of Renaissance Florence,* 15–16.

7. Ibid., 384, 392.

8. Giulio C. Argan, *The Renaissance City* (New York: George Braziller, 1969), 25–26.

9. Goldthwaite, *Building of Renaissance Florence,* 424–25.

10. Carroll William Westfall, *In This Most Perfect Paradise: Alberti, Nicholas V, and the Invention of Conscious Urban Planning in Rome, 1447–1555* (University Park, Pa.: Pennsylvania State University Press, 1974); Joan Gadol, *Leon Battista Alberti: Universal Man of the Early Renaissance* (Chicago: University of Chicago Press, 1969). Krautheimer describes overcrowded medieval Rome as a "labyrinth of houses large and small, tiny piazze, open or enclosed, courtyards with or without walls, narrow and dark passages. . . . " *Rome: Profile of a City,* 283.

11. Literary communication and artistic architectural representation are discussed by Rudolph Wittkower in *Architectural Principles in an Age of Humanism* (London: A. Tiranti, 1952) and *Studies in the Italian Baroque* (London: Thomas and Hudson, 1975). *See also* Denis Cosgrove, "The Myth and Stones of Venice: An Historical Geography of a Symbolic Landscape," *Journal of Historical Geography* 8 (1982).

Part II

The Industrial City

The city entered a new period during the Industrial Revolution. It was a period that ushered us into the modern industrial era by replacing the traditional ways of the preindustrial city. Cities grew and multiplied by drawing people to their mills and factories. Men, women, and children moved from every section of the land to industrial centers, eager to better themselves and to share in the rapid progress of a new way of living.

As cities mushroomed in number and size, rural and farm communities that had been relatively stable for centuries were depopulated and broken down. The stability of society was in jeopardy. The direction of the changes was unsettling and provoked new questions about modern society in general.

It is within this context that Part Two introduces classic works on the impact of the modern industrial city. These selections fall into two theoretical approaches—modernization and urban ecology.

Modernization is represented by six articles, brought together to emphasize the growing *depersonalization* and *secondarization of life*. The former refers to a condition in which individuals meld into a mass category due to the leveling effects of modern industrial society. The latter refers to the increasing replacement of primary and personal social bonds with more impersonal and contractual social relationships.

On Gemeinschaft and Gesellschaft, by Ferdinand Töennies, embodies a dichotomy of rural–urban differentials. *Gemeinschaft* is represented by a rural village characterized by emotional depth, homogeneity, and a sense of permanence. *Gesellschaft* is typified by a modern industrial city characterized by rationality, heterogeneity, impersonality, and impermanence. Töennies suggests that industrialization plays a crucial role in transforming rural communities into urbanized societies. Töennies had a pessimistic view of *gesellschaft-based* societies because of their tendencies to wipe out the simplicity, rhythm, and tranquility of rural life.

Emile Durkheim's essay, *On Mechanical Solidarity and Organic Solidarity*, exemplifies a parallel dichotomy. For Durkheim, *mechanical solidarity* involves a collective consciousness based on similarities and group will. However, as societies become more and more complex and differentiated, mechanical solidarity is replaced by *organic solidarity* which involves a collective consciousness based on the interdependence of social statuses and roles. Durkheim is optimistic about urban society's future. He anticipates the emergence of the modern industrial society as an outcome of the evolutionary process. This process occurs either through the adaptation of social structures to new needs and demands or the elimination of outmoded social structures.

The Nature of the City, by Max Weber, is a unique piece. Unlike Durkheim, Weber is pessimistic about the direction of the modern industrial city. Assuming a nonrigid and multidirectional development of history, he argues that the rational and bureaucratic processes underpinning modern capitalism appear to be complex and sophisticated but have actually produced less civilized, more crass, and more vulgar urban centers than the preindustrial cities of the Middle Ages. As such, he concludes that industrial cities do not articulate the possibility of the city as a culture.

The Great Towns, by Friedrich Engels, is another unique piece because it exposes and laments the conditions of the modern industrial city as the setting through which the ultimate profit motive of the **bourgeoisie** (capitalist class) exploits the labor of the **proletariat** (working class) and eventually leads to class conflict. Of course, Engels's idea of class conflict emanates from the theory of capitalist development and class struggle set forth by his friend Karl Marx.

In *The Metropolis and Mental Life* Georg Simmel recapitulates Weber's pessimism. Like Weber, he displays trepidation about the direction of modern industrial life, particularly its attendant effects on the individual personality. Simmel considers the rural–urban dichotomy as important because it demarcates the differences between the psyche of individuals from the country and individuals from the city. For him, the latter have become more and more calculating and blasé compared to their rural counterparts.

Louis Wirth's essay, *Urbanism as a Way of Life,* also strongly suggests the ideal dichotomies that Töennies and Durkheim constructed to stress the rural–urban differentials. For Wirth, the dichotomy helps explain the difference between *urbanization* and *urbanism*. Urbanization is a process, while urbanism is an outcome. For example, the process of migration from rural areas to cities (urbanization) necessarily results in a unique way of life, which Wirth refers to as *urbanism*. There are elements of both Simmel's pessimism and Durkheim's optimism in Wirth's idea of the city life. However, in general, he is somewhat hopeful because cities are not only susceptible to social disorganization but are also capable of creating new social arrangements.

The second theoretical approach that deals with the impact of the modern industrial city grew out of the University of Chicago in the 1920s and was pioneered by Robert Park and company (i.e., Ernest Burgess, Homer Hoyt, Chauncy Harris, and Edward Ullman). This **urban ecology** approach analyzes the growth of the modern industrial city within the context of capitalism and conducts its urban analysis from the basis that something new can be learned about human society by noting the features it shares with animal and plant societies. Thus, it explains how human populations spatially organized themselves in a natural and orderly sequence of urban change and development.

In *Human Ecology,* Robert Park illustrates the position that the modern industrial city is guided by the ecological processes of *competition, dominance,* and *succession.* Park considers competition as "conflicting, yet correlated interests" because it arises among potential land users, with victory eventually going to the most dominant user. He regards competition and dominance as the urban ecologist's control thesis and urban spatial patterns as dynamic expressions of that succession process.

The Nature of Cities, by Chauncy D. Harris and Edward L. Ullman, highlights the succession process by spelling out the three spatial models that characterize the modern industrial city—*concentric zone, sector,* and *multiple-nuclei.* The first model represents the ideal tendency of the city to expand in a ripple-like fashion from its central business district (CBD). The second model examines the radial expansion of cities as determined by a particular transportation axis. The third model addresses the deficiencies of the single-center based expansion by proposing a multi-centered expansion.

David Smith's essay, *The New Urban Sociology Meets the Old: Rereading Some Classical Human Ecology,* revisits the urban ecological perspective and its continued relevance to the contemporary urban setting.

9

On Gemeinschaft and Gesellschaft

Conclusions and Outlook

Ferdinand Töennies

1. Order—Law—Mores

There is a contrast between a social order which—being based upon consensus of wills—rests on harmony and is developed and ennobled by folkways, mores, and religion, and an order which—being based upon a union of rational wills—rests on convention and agreement, is safeguarded by political legislation, and finds its ideological justification in public opinion.

There is, further, in the first instance a common and binding system of positive law, of enforcible norms regulating the interrelation of wills. It has its roots in family life and is based on land ownership. Its forms are in the main determined by the code of the folkways and mores. Religion consecrates and glorifies these forms of the divine will, i.e., as interpreted by the will of wise and ruling men. This system of norms is in direct contrast to a similar positive law which upholds the separate identity of the individual rational wills in all their interrelations and entanglements. The latter derives from the conventional order of trade and similar relations but attains validity and binding force only through the sovereign will and power of the state. Thus, it becomes one of the most important instruments of policy; it sustains, impedes, or furthers social trends; it is defended or contested

"On Gemeinshaft and Gesellshaft: Conclusions and Outlooks" by Ferdinand Töennies from *Community and Society,* translated and edited by Charles P. Loomis (Michigan State University Press, 1957). Reprinted by permission.

publicly by doctrines and opinions and thus is changed, becoming more strict or more lenient.

There is, further, the dual concept of morality as a purely ideal or mental system of norms for community life. In the first case, it is mainly an expression and organ of religious beliefs and forces, by necessity intertwined with the conditions and realities of family spirit and the folkways and mores. In the second case, it is entirely a product and instrument of public opinion, which encompasses all relations arising out of contractual sociableness, contacts, and political intentions.

Order is natural law, law as such = positive law, mores = ideal law. Law as the meaning of what may or ought to be, of what is ordained or permitted, constitutes an object of social will. Even the natural law, in order to attain validity and reality, has to be recognized as positive and binding. But it is positive in a more general or less definite way. It is general in comparison with special laws. It is simple compared to complex and developed law.

2. Dissolution

The substance of the body social and the social will consists of concord, folkways, mores, and religion, the manifold forms of which develop under favorable conditions during its lifetime. Thus, each individual receives his share from this common center, which is manifest in his own sphere, i.e., in his sentiment, in his mind and heart, and in his conscience as well as in his environment, his possessions, and his activities. This is also true of each group. It is in this center that the individual's strength is rooted, and his rights derive, in the last instance, from the one original law which, in its divine and natural character, encompasses and sustains him, just as it made him and will carry him away. But under certain conditions and in some relationships, man appears as a free agent (person) in his self-determined activities and has to be conceived of as an independent person. The substance of the common spirit has become so weak or the link connecting him with the others worn so thin that it has to be excluded from consideration. In contrast to the family and co-operative relationship, this is true of all relations among separate individuals where there is no common understanding, and no time-honored custom or belief creates a common bond. This means war and the unrestricted freedom of all to destroy and subjugate one another, or, being aware of possible greater advantage, to conclude agreements and foster new ties. To the extent that such a relationship exists between closed groups or communities or between their individuals or between members and nonmembers of a community, it does not come within the scope of this study. In this connection we see a community organization and social conditions in which the individuals remain in isolation and veiled hostility toward each other so that only fear of clever retaliation restrains them from attacking one another, and, therefore, even peaceful and neighborly relations are in reality based upon a warlike situation. This is, according to our concepts, the condition of Gesellschaft-like civilization, in which peace and commerce are maintained through conventions and the underlying mutual fear. The state protects this civilization through legislation and politics. To a certain extent science and public opinion, attempting to conceive it as necessary and eternal, glorify it as progress toward perfection.

But it is in the organization and order of the Gemeinschaft that folk life and folk culture persist. The state, which represents and embodies Gesellschaft, is opposed to these in veiled hatred and contempt, the more so the further the state has moved away from and become estranged from these forms of community life. Thus, also in the social and historical life of mankind there is partly close interrelation, partly juxtaposition and opposition of natural and rational will.

3. *The People (Volkstum)* and the State (Staatstum)

In the same way as the individual natural will evolves into pure thinking and rational will, which tends to dissolve and subjugate its predecessors, the original collective forms of Gemeinschaft have developed into Gesellschaft and the rational will of the Gesellschaft. In the course of history, folk culture has given rise to the civilization of the state.

The main features of this process can be described in the following way. The anonymous mass of the people is the original and dominating power which creates the houses, the villages, and the towns of the country. From it, too, spring the powerful and self-determined individuals of many different kinds: princes, feudal lords, knights, as well as priests, artists, scholars. As long as their economic condition is determined by the people as a whole, all their social control is conditioned by the will and power of the people. Their union on a national scale, which alone could make them dominant as a group, is dependent on economic conditions. And their real and essential control is economic control, which before them and with them and partly against them the merchants attain by harnessing the labor force of the nation. Such economic control is achieved in many forms, the highest of which is planned capitalist production or large-scale industry. It is through the merchants that the technical conditions for the national union of independent individuals and for capitalistic production are created. This merchant class is by nature, and mostly also by origin, international as well as national and urban, i.e., it belongs to Gesellschaft, not Gemeinschaft. Later all social groups and dignitaries and, at least in tendency, the whole people acquire the characteristics of the Gesellschaft.

Men change their temperaments with the place and conditions of their daily life, which becomes hasty and changeable through restless striving. Simultaneously, along with this revolution in the social order, there takes place a gradual change of the law, in meaning as well as in form. The contract as such becomes the basis of the entire system, and rational will of Gesellschaft, formed by its interests, combines with authoritative will of the state to create, maintain and change the legal system. According to this conception, the law can and may completely change the Gesellschaft in line with its own discrimination and purpose; changes which, however, will be in the interest of the Gesellschaft, making for usefulness and efficiency. The state frees itself more and more from the traditions and customs of the past and the belief in their importance. Thus, the forms of law change from a product of the folkways and mores and the law of custom into a purely legalistic law, a product of policy. The state and its departments and the individuals are the only remaining agents, instead of numerous and manifold fellowships, communities, and commonwealths which have grown up organically. The characters of the people, which were influenced and determined by these previously existing institutions, undergo new changes in adaptation to new and arbitrary legal constructions. These earlier institutions lose the firm hold which folkways, mores, and the conviction of their infallibility gave to them.

Finally, as a consequence of these changes and in turn reacting upon them, a complete reversal of intellectual life takes place. While originally rooted entirely in the imagination, it now becomes dependent upon thinking. Previously, all was centered around the belief in invisible beings, spirits and gods; now it is focalized on the insight into visible nature. Religion, which is rooted in folk life or at least closely related to it, must cede supremacy to science, which derives from and corresponds to consciousness. Such consciousness is a product of learning and culture and, therefore, remote from the people. Religion has an immediate contact and is moral in its nature because it is most deeply related to the physical-spiritual link which connects the generations of men. Science receives its moral meaning only from an observation of the laws of social life, which leads it to derive rules for an arbitrary and reasonable order of social organization. The intellectual attitude of the individual becomes gradually less and less influenced by religion and more and more influenced by science. Utilizing the research findings accumulated by the preceding industrious generation, we shall investigate the tremendous contrasts which the opposite poles of this dichotomy and these fluctuations entail. For this presentation, however, the following few remarks may suffice to outline the underlying principles.

4. Types of Real Community Life

The exterior forms of community life as represented by natural will and Gemeinschaft were distinguished as house, village, and town. These are the lasting types of real and historical life. In a developed Gesellschaft, as in the earlier and middle stages, people live together in these different ways. The town is the highest, viz., the most complex, form of social life. Its local character, in common with that of the village, contrasts with the family character of the house. Both village and town retain many characteristics of the family; the village retains more, the town less. Only when the town develops into the city are these characteristics almost entirely lost. Individuals or families are separate identities, and their common locale is only an accidental or deliberately chosen place in which to live. But as the town lives on within the city, elements of life in the Gemeinschaft, as the only real form of life, persist within the Gesellschaft, although lingering and decaying. On the other hand, the more general the condition of Gesellschaft becomes in the nation or a group of nations, the more this entire "country" or the entire "world" begins to resemble one large city. However, in the city and therefore where general conditions characteristic of the Gesellschaft prevail, only the upper strata, the rich and the cultured, are really active and alive. They set up the standards to which the lower strata have to conform. These lower classes conform partly to supersede the others, partly in imitation of them in order to attain for themselves social power and independence. The city consists, for both groups (just as in the case of the "nation" and the "world"), of free persons who stand in contact with each other, exchange with each other and co-operate without any Gemeinschaft or will thereto developing among them except as such might develop sporadically or as a leftover from former conditions. On the contrary, these numerous external contacts, contracts, and contractual relations only cover up as many inner hostilities and antagonistic interests. This is especially true of the antagonism between the rich or the so-called cultured class and the poor or the servant class, which try to obstruct and destroy each other. It is this contrast which, according to Plato, gives the "city" its dual character and makes it divide in itself. This itself, according to our concept, constitutes the city, but the same contrast is also manifest in every large-scale relationship between capital and labor. The common town life remains within the Gemeinschaft of family and rural life; it is devoted to some agricultural pursuits but concerns itself especially with art and handicraft which evolve from these natural needs and habits. City life, however, is sharply distinguished from that; these basis activities are used only as means and tools for the special purposes of the city.

The city is typical of Gesellschaft in general. It is essentially a commercial town and, in so far as commerce dominates its productive labor, a factory town. Its wealth is capital wealth which, in the form of trade, usury, or industrial capital, is used and multiplies. Capital is the means for the appropriation of products of labor or for the exploitation of workers. The city is also the center of science and culture, which always go hand in hand with commerce and industry. Here the arts must make a living; they are exploited in a capitalistic way. Thoughts spread and change with astonishing rapidity. Speeches and books through mass distribution become stimuli of far-reaching importance.

The city is to be distinguished from the national capital, which, as residence of the court or center of government, manifests the features of the city in many respects although its population and other conditions have not yet reached that level. In the synthesis of city and capital, the highest form of this kind is achieved: the metropolis. It is the essence not only of a national Gesellschaft, but contains representatives from a whole group of nations, i.e., of the world. In the metropolis, money and capital are unlimited and almighty. It is able to produce and supply goods and science for the entire earth as well as laws and public opinion for all nations. It represents the world market and world traffic; in it world industries are concentrated. Its newspapers are world papers, its people come from all comers of the earth, being curious and hungry for money and pleasure.

5. *Counterpart of Gemeinschaft*

Family life is the general basis of life in the Gemeinschaft. It subsists in village and town life. The village community and the town themselves can be considered as large families, the various clans and houses representing the elementary organisms of its body; guilds, corporations, and offices, the tissues and organs of the town. Here original kinship and inherited status remain an essential, or at least the most important, condition of participating fully in common property and other rights. Strangers may be accepted and protected as serving-members or guests either temporarily or permanently. Thus, they can belong to the Gemeinschaft as objects, but not easily as agents and representatives of the Gemeinschaft. Children are, during minority, dependent members of the family, but according to Roman custom they are called free because it is anticipated that under possible and normal conditions they will certainly be masters, their own heirs. This is true neither of guests nor of servants, either in the house or in the community. But honored guests can approach the position of children. If they are adopted or civic rights are granted to them, they fully acquire this position with the right to inherit. Servants can be esteemed or treated as guests or even, because of the value of their functions, take part as members in the activities of the group. It also happens sometimes that they become natural or appointed heirs. In reality there are many gradations, lower or higher, which are not exactly met by legal formulas. All these relationships can, under special circumstances, be transformed into merely interested and dissolvable interchange between independent contracting parties. In the city such change, at least with regard to all relations of servitude, is only natural and becomes more and more widespread with its development. The difference between natives and strangers becomes irrelevant. Everyone is what he is, through his personal freedom, through his wealth and his contracts. He is a servant only in so far as he has granted certain services to someone else, master in so far as he receives such services. Wealth is, indeed, the only effective and original differentiating characteristic; whereas in Gemeinschaften property it is considered as participation in the common ownership and as a specific legal concept is entirely the consequence and result of freedom or ingenuity, either original or acquired. Therefore, wealth, to the extent that this is possible, corresponds to the degree of freedom possessed.

In the city as well as in the capital, and especially in the metropolis, family life is decaying. The more and the longer their influence prevails, the more the residuals of family life acquire a purely accidental character. For there are only few who will confine their energies within such a narrow circle; all are attracted outside by business, interests, and pleasures, and thus separated from one another. The great and mighty, feeling free and independent, have always felt a strong inclination to break through the barriers of the folkways and mores. They know that they can do as they please. They have the power to bring about changes in their favor, and this is positive proof of individual arbitrary power. The mechanism of money, under usual conditions and if working under high pressure, is means to overcome all resistance, to obtain everything wanted and desired, to eliminate all dangers and to cure all evil. This does not hold always. Even if all controls of the Gemeinschaft are eliminated, there are nevertheless controls in the Gesellschaft to which the free and independent individuals are subject. For Gesellschaft (in the narrower sense), convention takes to a large degree the place of the folkways, mores, and religion. It forbids much as detrimental to the common interest which the folkways, mores, and religion had condemned as evil in and of itself.

The will of the state plays the same role through law courts and police, although within narrower limits. The laws of the state apply equally to everyone; only children and lunatics are not held responsible to them. Convention maintains at least the appearance of morality; it is still related to the folkways, mores, and religious and aesthetic feeling, although this feeling tends to become arbitrary and formal. The state is hardly directly concerned with morality. It has only to suppress and punish hostile actions which are detrimental to the common weal or seemingly dangerous for itself and society. For as the state has to administer the common weal, it must be able to define this as it pleases. In the end it will probably realize that no increase in knowledge and culture alone will make people kinder, less egotistic, and more content and that dead folkways, mores, and religions cannot be revived by coercion and teaching. The state will then arrive at the conclusion that in order to create moral forces and moral beings it must prepare the ground and fulfill the necessary conditions, or at least it must eliminate counteracting forces. The state, as the reason of Gesellschaft, should decide to destroy Gesellschaft or at least to reform or renew it. The success of such attempts is highly improbable.

6. *The Real State*

Public opinion, which brings the morality of Gesellschaft into rules and formulas and can rise above the state, has nevertheless decided tendencies to urge the state to use its irresistible power to force everyone to do what is useful and to leave undone what is damaging. Extension of the penal code and the police power seems the right means to curb the evil impulses of the masses. Public opinion passes easily from the demand for freedom (for the upper classes) to that of despotism (against the lower classes). The makeshift, convention, has but little influence over the masses. In their striving for pleasure and entertainment they are limited only by the scarcity of the means which the capitalists furnish them as price for their labor, which condition is as general as it is natural in a world where the interests of the capitalists and merchants anticipate all possible needs and in mutual competition incite to the most varied expenditures of money. Only through fear of discovery and punishment, that is, through fear of the state, is a special and large group, which encompasses far more people than the professional criminals, restrained in its desire to obtain the key to all necessary and unnecessary pleasures. The state is their enemy. The state, to them, is an alien and unfriendly power; although seemingly authorized by them and embodying their own will, it is nevertheless opposed to all their needs and desires, protecting property which they do not possess, forcing them into military service for a country which offers them hearth and altar only in the form of a heated room on the upper floor or gives them, for native soil, city streets where they may stare at the glitter and luxury in lighted windows forever beyond their reach! Their own life is nothing but a constant alternative between work and leisure, which are both distorted into factory routine and the low pleasure of the saloons. City life and Gesellschaft down the common people to decay and death; in vain they struggle to attain power through their own multitude, and it seems to them that they can use their power only for a revolution if they want to free themselves from their fate. The masses become conscious of this social position through the education in schools and through newspapers. They proceed from class consciousness to class struggle. This class struggle may destroy society and the state which it is its purpose to reform. The entire culture has been transformed into a civilization of state and Gesellschaft, and this transformation means the doom of culture itself if none of its scattered seeds remain alive and again bring forth the essence and idea of Gemeinschaft, thus secretly fostering a new culture amidst the decaying one.

7. *The Periods*

To conclude our theory, two periods stand thus contrasted with each other in the history of the great systems of culture: a period of Gesellschaft follows a period of Gemeinschaft. The Gemeinschaft is characterized by the social will as concord, folkways, mores, and religion; the Gesellschaft by the social will as convention, legislation, and public opinion. The concepts correspond to the types of external social organization, which may be classed as follows:

A. Gemeinschaft

1. Family life = concord. Man participates in this with all his sentiments. Its real controlling agent is the people (*Volk*).
2. Rural village life = folkways and mores. Into this, man enters with all his mind and heart. Its real controlling agent is the commonwealth.
3. Town life = religion. In this, the human being takes part with his entire conscience. Its real controlling agent is the church.

B. Gesellschaft

1. City life = convention. This is determined by man's intentions. Its real controlling agent is Gesellschaft per se.
2. National life = legislation. This is determined by man's calculations. Its real controlling agent is the state.
3. Cosmopolitan life = public opinion. This is evolved by man's consciousness. Its real controlling agent is the republic of scholars.

10

On Mechanical Solidarity and Organic Solidarity

Emile Durkheim

Since negative solidarity does not produce any integration by itself, and since, moreover, there is nothing specific about it, we shall recognize only two kinds of positive solidarity which are distinguishable by the following qualities:

1. The first binds the individual directly to society without any intermediary. In the second, he depends upon society, because he depends upon the parts of which it is composed.

2. Society is not seen in the same aspect in the two cases. In the first, what we call society is a more or less organized totality of beliefs and sentiments common to all the members of the group: this is the collective type. On the other hand, the society in which we are solidary in the second instance is a system of different, special functions which definite relations unite. These two societies really make up only one. They are two aspects of one and the same reality, but none the less they must be distinguished.

3. From this second difference there arises another which helps us to characterize and name the two kinds of solidarity.

The first can be strong only if the ideas and tendencies common to all the members of the society are greater in number and intensity than those which pertain personally to each member. It is as much stronger as the excess is more considerable. But what makes our personality is how much of our own individual qualities we have, what distinguishes us from others. This solidarity can grow only in inverse ratio to personality. There are in each of us, as we have said, two consciences: one which is common to our group in its entirety, which, consequently, is not ourself, but society living and acting within us; the other, on the contrary, represents that in us which is personal and distinct, that which makes us an individual.[1] Solidarity which comes from likenesses is at its maximum when the collective conscience completely envelops our whole conscience and coincides in all points with it. But, at that moment, our individuality is nil. It can be born only if the community takes smaller toll of us. There are, here, two contrary forces, one centripetal, the other centrifugal, which cannot flourish at the same time. We cannot, at one and the same time, develop ourselves in two opposite senses. If we have a lively desire to think and act for ourselves, we cannot be strongly inclined to think and act as others do. If our ideal is to present a singular and personal appearance, we do not want to resemble everybody else. Moreover, at the moment when this solidarity exercises its force, our personality vanishes, as our definition permits us to say, for we are no longer ourselves, but the collective life.

The social molecules which can be coherent in this way can act together only in the measure that they have no actions of their own, as the molecules of inorganic bodies. That is why we propose to call this type of solidarity mechanical. The term does not signify that it is produced by mechanical and artificial means. We call it that only by analogy to the cohesion which unites the elements of an inanimate body, as opposed to that which makes a unity out of the elements of a living body. What justifies this term is that the link which thus unites the individual to society is wholly analogous to that which attaches a thing to a person. The individual conscience, considered in this light, is a simple dependent upon the collective type and follows all of its movements, as the possessed object follows those of its owner. In societies where this type of solidarity is highly developed, the individual does not appear, as we shall see later. Individuality is something which the society possesses. Thus, in these social types, personal rights are not yet distinguished from real rights.

It is quite otherwise with the solidarity which the division of labor produces. Whereas the previous type implies that individuals resemble each other, this type presumes their difference. The first is possible only in so far as the individual personality is absorbed into the collective personality; the second is possible only if each one has a sphere of action which is peculiar to him; that is, a personality. It is necessary, then, that the collective conscience leave open a part of the individual conscience in order that special functions may be established there, functions which it cannot regulate. The more this region is extended, the stronger is the cohesion which results from this solidarity. In effect, on the one hand, each one depends as much more strictly on society as labor is more divided; and, on the other, the activity of each is as much more personal as it is more specialized. Doubtless, as circumscribed as it is, it is never completely original. Even in the exercise of our occupation, we conform to usages, to practices which are common to our whole professional brotherhood. But, even in this instance, the yoke that we submit to is much less heavy than when society completely controls us, and it leaves much more place open for the free play of our initiative. Here, then, the individuality of all grows at the same time as that of its parts. Society becomes more capable of collective movement, at the same time that each of its elements has more freedom of movement. This solidarity resembles that which we observe among the higher animals. Each organ, in effect, has its special physiognomy, its autonomy. And, moreover, the unity of the organism is as great as the individuation of the parts is more marked. Because of this analogy, we propose to call the solidarity which is due to the division of labor, organic. . . .

In determining the principal cause of the progress of the division of labor, we have at the same time determined the essential factor of what is called civilization.

Civilization is itself the necessary consequence of the changes which are produced in the volume and in the density of societies. If science, art, and economic activity develop, it is in accordance with a necessity which is imposed upon men. It is because there is, for them, no other way of living in the new conditions in which they have been placed. From the time that the number of individuals among whom social relations are established begins to increase, they can maintain themselves only by greater specialization, harder work, and intensification of their faculties. From this general stimulation, there inevitably results a much higher degree of culture. From this point of view, civilization appears, not as an end which moves people by its attraction for them, not as a good foreseen and desired in advance, of which they seek to assure themselves the largest possible part, but as the effect of a cause, as the necessary resultant of a given state. It is not the pole towards which historic development is moving and to which men seek to get nearer in order to be happier or better, for neither happiness nor morality necessarily increases with the intensity of life. They move because they must move, and what determines the speed of this march is the more or less strong pressure which they exercise upon one another, according to their number.

This does not mean that civilization has no use, but that it is not the services that it renders that make it progress. It develops because it cannot fail to develop. Once effectuated, this development is found to be generally useful, or, at least, it is utilized. It responds to needs formed at the same time because they depend upon the same causes. But this is an adjustment after the fact. Yet, we must notice that the good it renders in this direction is not a positive enrichment, a growth in our stock of happiness, but only repairs the losses that it has itself caused. It is because this superactivity of general life fatigues and weakens our nervous system that it needs reparations proportionate to its expenditures, that is to say, more varied and complex satisfactions. In that, we see even better how false it is to make civilization the function of the division of labor; it is only a consequence of it. It can explain neither the existence nor the progress of the division of labor, since it has, of itself, no intrinsic or absolute value, but, on the contrary, has a reason for existing only in so far as the division of labor is itself found necessary.

We shall not be astonished by the importance attached to the numerical factor if we notice the very capital role it plays in the history of organisms. In effect, what defines a living being is the double property it has of nourishing itself and reproducing itself, and reproduction is itself only a consequence of nourishment. Therefore, the intensity of organic life is proportional, all things being equal, to the activity of nourishment, that is, to the number of elements that the organism is capable of incorporating. Hence, what has not only made possible, but even necessitated the appearance of complex organisms is that, under certain conditions, the more simple organisms remain grouped together in a way to form more voluminous aggregates. As the constitutive parts of the animal are more numerous, their relations are no longer the same, the conditions of social life are changed, and it is these changes which, in turn, determine both the division of labor, polymorphism, and the concentration of vital forces and their greater energy. The growth of organic substance is, then, the fact which dominates all zoological development. It is not surprising that social development is submitted to the same law.

Moreover, without recourse to arguments by analogy, it is easy to explain the fundamental role of this factor. All social life is made up of a system of facts which come from positive and durable relations established between a plurality of individuals. It is, thus, as much more intense as the reactions exchanged between the component units are themselves more frequent and more energetic. But, upon what does this frequency and this energy depend? Upon the nature of the elements present, upon their more or less great vitality? But we shall see in this very [reading] that individuals are much more a product of common life than they are determinants of it. If from each of them we take away everything due to social action, the residue that we obtain, besides being picayune, is not capable of presenting much variety. Without the diversity of social conditions upon which they depend, the differences which separate them would be inexplicable. It is not, then, in the unequal aptitudes of men that we must seek the cause for the unequal development of societies. Will it be in the unequal duration of these relations? But time, by itself, produces nothing. It is only necessary in bringing latent energies to light. There remains no other variable factor than the number of individuals in relation and their material and moral proximity, that is to say, the volume and density of society. The more numerous they are and the more they act upon one another, the more they react with force and rapidity; consequently, the more intense social life becomes. But it is this intensification which constitutes civilization.[2]

But, while being an effect of necessary causes, civilization can become an end, an object of desire, in short, an ideal. Indeed, at each moment of a society's history, there is a certain intensity of the collective life which is normal, given the number and distribution of the social units. Assuredly, if everything happens normally, this state will be realized of itself, but we cannot bring it to pass that things will happen normally. If health is in nature, so is sickness. Health is, indeed, in societies as in individual organisms, only an ideal type which is nowhere entirely realized. Each healthy individual has more or less numerous traits of it, but there is none that unites them all. Thus, it is an end worthy of pursuit to seek to bring society to this degree of perfection.

Moreover, the direction to follow in order to attain this end can be laid out. If, instead of letting causes engender their effects by chance and according to the energy in them, thought intervenes to direct the course, it can spare men many painful efforts. The development of the individual reproduces that of the species in abridged fashion; he does not pass through all the stages that it passed through; there are some he omits and others he passes through more quickly because the experiences of the race help him to accelerate them. But thought can produce analogous results, for it is equally a utilization of anterior experience, with a view to facilitating future experience. By thought, moreover, one must not understand exclusively scientific knowledge of means and ends. Sociology, in its present state, is hardly in a position to lead us efficaciously to the solution of these practical problems. But beyond these clear representations in the milieu in which the scholar moves, there are obscure ones to which tendencies are linked. For need to stimulate the will, it is not necessary that it be clarified by science. Obscure gropings are enough to teach men that there is something lacking, to awaken their aspirations and at the same time make them feel in what direction they ought to bend their efforts.

Hence, a mechanistic conception of society does not preclude ideals, and it is wrong to reproach it with reducing man to the status of an inactive witness of his own history. What is an ideal, really, if not an anticipated representation of a desired result whose realization is possible only thanks to this very anticipation? Because things happen in accordance with laws, it does not follow that we have nothing to do. We shall perhaps find such an objective mean, because, in sum, it is only a question of living in a state of health. But this is to forget that, for the cultivated man, health consists in regularly satisfying his most elevated needs as well as others, for the first are no less firmly rooted in his nature than the second. It is true that such an ideal is near, that the horizons it opens before us have nothing unlimited about them. In any event, it cannot consist in exalting the forces of society beyond measure, but only in developing them to the limit marked by the definite state of the social milieu. All excess is bad as well as all insufficiency. But what other ideal can we propose? To seek to realize a civilization superior to that demanded by the nature of surrounding conditions is to desire to turn illness loose in the very society of which we are part, for it is not possible to increase collective activity beyond the degree determined by the state of the social organism without compromising health. In fact, in every epoch there is a certain refinement of civilization whose sickly character is attested by the uneasiness and restlessness which accompanies it. But there is never anything desirable about sickness.

But if the ideal is always definite, it is never definitive. Since progress is a consequence of changes in the social milieu, there is no reason for supposing that it must ever end. For it to have a limit, it would be necessary for the milieu to become stationary at some given moment. But such an hypothesis is contrary to the most legitimate inductions. As long as there are distinct societies, the number of social units will necessarily be variable in each of them. Even supposing that the number of births ever becomes constant, there will always be movements of population from one country to another, through violent conquests or slow and unobtrusive infiltrations. Indeed, it is impossible for the strongest peoples not to tend to incorporate the feeblest, as the most dense overflow into the least dense. That is a mechanical law of social equilibrium not less necessary than that which governs the equilibrium of liquids. For it to be otherwise, it would be necessary for all human societies to have the same vital energy and the same density. What is irrepresentable would only be so because of the diversity of habitats.

It is true that this source of variations would be exhausted if all humanity formed one and the same society. But, besides our not knowing whether such an ideal is realizable, in order for progress to cease it would still be necessary for the relations between social units in the interior of this gigantic society to be themselves recalcitrant to all change. It would be necessary for them always to remain distributed in the same way, for not only the total aggregate but also each of the elementary aggregates of which it would be formed, to keep the same dimensions. But such a uniformity is impossible, solely because these partial groups do not all have the same extent nor the same vitality. Population cannot be concentrated in the same way at all points; it is inevitable that the greatest centres, those where life is most intense, exercise an attraction for the others proportionate to their importance. The migrations which are thus produced result in further concentrating social units in certain regions, and, consequently, in determining new advances there which irradiate little by little from the homes in which they were born into the rest of the country. Moreover, these changes call forth others, without it being possible to say where the repercussions stop. In fact, far from societies approaching a stationary position in proportion to their development, they become, on the contrary, more mobile and more plastic. . . .

With societies, individuals are transformed in accordance with the changes produced in the number of social units and their relations.

First, they are made more and more free of the yoke of the organism. An animal is almost completely under the influence of his physical environment; its biological constitution predetermines its existence. Man, on the contrary, is dependent upon social causes. Of course, animals also form societies, but, as they are very restricted, collective life is very simple. They are also stationary because the equilibrium of such small societies is necessarily stable. For these two reasons, it easily fixes itself in the organism. It not only has its roots in the organism, but it is entirely enveloped in it to such a point that it loses its own characteristics. It functions through a system of instincts, of reflexes which are not essentially distinct from those which assure the functioning of organic life. They present, it is true, the particular characteristic of adapting the individual to the social environment, not to the physical environment, and are caused by occurrences of the common life. They are not of different nature, however, from those which, in certain cases, determine without any previous education the necessary movements in locomotion. It is quite otherwise with man, because the societies he forms are much vaster. Even the smallest we know of are more extensive than the majority of animal societies. Being more complex, they also change more, and these two causes together see to it that social life with man is not congealed in a biological form. Even where it is most simple, it clings to its specificity. There are always beliefs and practices common to men which are not inscribed in their tissues. But this character is more manifest as the social mass and density grow. The more people there are in association, and the more they react upon one another, the more also does the product of these reactions pass beyond the bounds of the organism. Man thus finds himself placed under the sway of causes *sui generis* whose relative part in the constitution of human nature becomes ever more considerable.

Moreover, the influence of this factor increases not only in relative value, but also in absolute value. The same cause which increases the importance of the collective environment weakens the organic environment in such a manner as to make it accessible to the action of social causes and to subordinate it to them. Because there are more individuals living together, common life is richer and more varied, but for this variety to be possible, the organic type must be less definite to be able to diversify itself. We have seen, in effect, that the tendencies and aptitudes transmitted by heredity became ever more general and more indeterminate, more refractory consequently, to assuming the form of instincts. Thus, a phenomenon is produced which is exactly the inverse of that which we observe at the beginning of evolution. With animals, the organism assimilates social facts to it, and, stripping them of their special nature, transforms them into biological facts. Social life is materialized. In man, on the contrary, and particularly in higher societies, social causes substitute themselves for organic causes. The organism is spiritualized.

The individual is transformed in accordance with this change in dependence. Since this activity which calls forth the special action of social causes cannot be fixed in the organism, a new life, also *sui generis*, is superimposed upon that of the body. Freer, more complex, more independent of the organs which support it, its distinguishing characteristics become ever more apparent as it progresses and becomes solid. From this description we can recognize the essential traits of psychic life. To be sure, it would be exaggerating to say that psychic life begins only with societies, but certainly it becomes extensive only as societies develop. That is why, as has often been remarked, the progress of conscience is in inverse ratio to that of instinct. Whatever may be said of them, it is not the first which breaks up the second. Instinct, the product of the accumulated experience of generations, has a much greater resistive force to dissolution simply because it becomes conscious. Truly, conscience only invades the ground which instinct has ceased to occupy, or where instinct cannot be established. Conscience does not make instinct recede; it only fills the space instinct leaves free. Moreover, if instinct regresses rather than extends as general life extends, the greater importance of the social factor is the cause of this. Hence, the great difference which separates man from animals, that is, the greater development of his psychic life, comes from his greater sociability. To understand why psychic functions have been carried, from the very beginnings of the human species, to a degree of perfection unknown among animal species, one would first have to know why it is that men, instead of living in solitude or in small bands, were led to form more extensive societies. To put it in terms of the classical definition, if man is a reasonable animal, that is because he is a sociable animal, or at least infinitely more sociable than other animals.[3]

This is not all. In so far as societies do not reach certain dimensions nor a certain degree of concentration, the only psychic life which may be truly developed is that which is common to all the members of the group, which is found identical in each. But, as societies become more vast and, particularly, more condensed, a psychic life of a new sort appears. Individual diversities, at first lost and confused amidst the mass of social likenesses, become disengaged, become conspicuous, and multiply. A multitude of things which use to remain outside consciences because they did not affect the collective being become objects of representations. Whereas individuals use to act only by involving one another, except in cases where their conduct was determined by physical needs, each of them becomes a source of spontaneous activity. Particular personalities become constituted, take conscience of themselves. Moreover, this growth of psychic life in the individual does not obliterate the psychic life of society, but only transforms it. It becomes freer, more extensive, and as it has, after all, no other bases than individual consciences, these extend, become complex, and thus become flexible.

Hence, the cause which called forth the differences separating man from animals is also that which has forced him to elevate himself above himself. The ever growing distance between the savage and the civilized man has no other source. If the faculty of ideation is slowly disengaged from the confused feeling of its origin, if man has learned to formulate concepts and laws, if his spirit has embraced more and more extensive portions of space and time, if, not content with clinging to the past, he has trespassed upon the future, if his emotions and his tendencies, at first simple and not very numerous, have multiplied and diversified, that is because the social milieu has changed without interruption. In effect, unless these transformations were born from nothing, they can have had for causes only the corresponding transformations of surrounding milieux. But, man depends only upon three sorts of milieux: the organism, the external world, society. If one leaves aside the accidental variations due to combinations of heredity,—and their role in human progress is certainly not very considerable,—the organism is not automatically modified; it is necessary that it be impelled by some external cause. As for the physical world, since the beginning of history it has remained sensibly the same, at least if one does not take account of novelties which are of social origin.[4] Consequently, there is only society which has changed enough to be able to explain the parallel changes in individual nature.

It is not, then, audacious to affirm that, from now on, whatever progress is made in psycho-physiology will never represent more than a fraction of psychology, since the major part of psychic phenomena does not come from organic causes. This is what spiritualist philosophers have learned, and the great service that they have rendered science has been to combat the doctrines which reduce psychic life merely to an efflorescence of physical life. They have very justly felt that the first, in its highest manifestations, is much too free and complex to be merely a prolongation of the second. Because it is partly independent of the organism, however, it does not follow that it depends upon no natural cause, and that it must be put outside nature. But all these facts whose explanation we cannot find in the constitution of tissues derive from properties of the social milieu. This hypothesis assumes, at least, very great probability from what has preceded. But the social realm is not less natural than the organic realm. Consequently, because there is a vast region of conscience whose genesis is unintelligible through psycho-physiology alone, we must not conclude that it has been formed of itself and that it is, accordingly, refractory to scientific investigation, but only that it derives from some other positive science which can be called socio-psychology. The phenomena which would constitute its matter are, in effect, of a mixed nature. They have the same essential characters as other psychic facts, but they arise from social causes.

Notes

1. However, these two consciences are not in regions geographically distinct from us, but penetrate from all sides.
2. We do not here have to look to see if the fact which determines the progress of the division of labor and civilization, growth in social mass and density, explains itself automatically; if it is a necessary product of efficient causes, or else an imagined means in view of a desired end or of a very great foreseen good. We content ourselves with stating this law of gravitation in the social world without going any farther. It does not seem, however, that there is a greater demand here than elsewhere for a teleological explanation. The walls which separate different parts of society are torn down by the force of things, through a sort of natural usury, whose effect can be further enforced by the action of violent causes. The movements of population thus become more numerous and rapid and the passage-lines through which these movements are effected—the means of communication—deepen. They are more particularly active at points where several of these lines cross; these are cities. Thus social density grows. As for the growth in volume, it is due to causes of the same kind. The barriers which separate peoples are analogous to those which separate the different cells of the same society and they disappear in the same way.
3. The definition of de Quatrefages which makes man a religious animal is a particular instance of the preceding, for man's religiosity is a consequence of his eminent sociability. . . .
4. Transformations of the soil, of streams, through the art of husbandry, engineers, etc.

11

The Nature of the City

Max Weber

Economically defined, the city is a settlement the inhabitants of which live primarily off trade and commerce rather than agriculture. However, it is not altogether proper to call all localities "cities" which are dominated by trade and commerce. This would include in the concept "city" colonies made up of family members and maintaining a single, practically hereditary trade establishment such as the "trade villages" of Asia and Russia. It is necessary to add a certain "versatility" of practiced trades to the characteristics of the city. However, this in itself does not appear suitable as the single distinguishing characteristic of the city either.

Economic versatility can be established in at least two ways: by the presence of a feudal estate or a market. The economic and political needs of a feudal or princely estate can encourage specialization in trade products in providing a demand for which work is performed and goods are bartered. However, even though the *oikos* of a lord or prince is as large as a city, a colony of artisans and small merchants bound to villein services is not customarily called a "city" even though historically a large proportion of important "cities" originated in such settlements.[1] In cities of such origin the products for a prince's court often remained a highly important, even chief, source of income for the settlers.

The other method of establishing economic versatility is more generally important for the "city"; this is the existence in the place of settlement of a regular rather than an occasional exchange of goods. The market becomes an essential component in the livelihood of the settlers. To be sure, not every "market" converted the locality in which it was found into a city. The periodic fairs and yearly foreign-trade markets at which traveling merchants met at fixed times to sell their goods in wholesale or retail lots to each other or to consumers often occurred in places which we would call "villages."

Thus, we wish to speak of a "city" only in cases where the local inhabitants satisfy an economically substantial part of their daily wants in the local market, and to an essential extent by products which the local population and that of the immediate hinterland produced for sale in the market or acquired in other ways. In the meaning employed here the "city" is a market place. The local market forms the economic center of the colony in which, due to the specialization in economic products, both the non-urban population and urbanites satisfy their wants for articles of trade and commerce. Wherever it appeared as a configuration different from the country it was normal for the city to be both a lordly or princely residence as well as a market place. It simultaneously possessed centers of both kinds, *oikos* and market and frequently in addition to the regular market it also served as periodic foreign markets of traveling merchants. In the meaning of the word here, the city is a "market settlement."

Often the existence of a market rests upon the concessions and guarantees of protection by a lord or prince. They were often interested in such things as a regular supply of foreign commercial articles and trade products, in tolls, in moneys for escorts and other protection fees, in market tariffs and taxes from law suits. However, the lord or prince might also hope to profit from the local settlement of tradesmen and merchants capable of paying taxes and, as soon as the market settlement arose around the market, from land rents arising therefrom. Such opportunities were of especial importance to the lord or prince since they represented chances for monetary revenues and the increase in his treasure of precious metal.

However, the city could lack any attachment, physical or otherwise, to a lordly or princely residence. This was the case when it originated as a pure market settlement at a suitable intersection point (*Umschlageplatz*)[2] where the means of transportation were changed by virtue of concession to non-resident lords or princes or usurpation by the interested parties themselves. This could assume the form of concessions to entrepreneurs—permitting them to lay out a market and recruit settlers for it. Such capitalistic establishment of cities was especially frequent in medieval frontier areas, particularly in East, North, and Central Europe. Historically, though not as a rule, the practice has appeared throughout the world.

Without any attachment to the court of a prince or without princely concessions, the city could arise through the association of foreign invaders, naval warriors, or commercial settlers or, finally, native parties interested in the carrying trade. This occurred frequently in the early Middle Ages. The resultant city could be a pure market place. However, it is more usual to find large princely or patrimonial households and a market conjoined. In this case the eminent household as one contact point of the city could satisfy its want either primarily by means of a natural economy (that is by villein service or natural service or taxes placed upon the artisans and merchants dependent on it) or it could supply itself more or less secondarily by barter in the local market as that market's most important buyer. The more pronounced the latter relation the more distinct the market foundation of the city looms and the city ceases by degrees to be a mere appendaged market settlement alongside the *oikos*. Despite attachment to the large household it then became a market city. As a rule the quantitative expansion of the original princely city and its economic importance go hand in hand with an increase in the satisfaction of wants in the market by the princely household and other large urban households attached to that of the prince as courts of vassals or major officials.

Types of Consumer and Producer City

Similar to the city of the prince, the inhabitants of which are economically dependent upon the purchasing power of noble households are cities in which the purchasing power of other larger consumers, such as rentiers, determines the economic opportunities of resident tradesmen and merchants. In terms of the kind and source of their incomes such larger consumers may be of quite varied types. They may be officials who spend their legal and illegal income in the city or lords or other political power holders who spend their non-urban land rents or politically determined incomes there. In either of these cases the city closely approximates the princely city for it depends upon patrimonial and political incomes which supply the purchasing power of large consumers. Peking was a city of officials; Moscow, before suspension of serfdom, was a land-rent city.

Different in principle are the superficially similar cities in which urban land-rents are determined by traffic monopolies of landed property. Such cities originate in the trade and commerce consolidated in the hands of an urban aristocracy. This type of development has always been widespread: it appeared in Antiquity; in the Near East until the Byzantine Empire; and in the Middle Ages. The city that emerges is not economically of a rentier type but is, rather, a merchant or trade city the rents of which represent a tribute of acquisitors to the owners of houses. The conceptual differentiation of this case from the one in which rents are not determined by tributary obligations to monopolists but by non-urban sources, should not obscure the interrelation in the past of both forms. The large consumers can be rentiers spending their business incomes (today mainly interest on bonds, dividends or shares) in the city. Whereupon purchasing power rests on capitalistically conditioned monetary rentier sources as in the city of Arnheim. Or purchasing power can depend upon state pensions or other state rents as appears in a "pensionopolis" like Wiesbaden. In all similar cases one may describe the urban form as a consumer city, for the presence in residence of large consumers of special economic character is of decisive economic importance for the local tradesmen and merchants.

A contrasting form is presented by the producer city. The increase in population and purchasing power in the city may be due, as for example in Essen or Bochum, to the location there of factories, manufactures, or home-work industries supplying outside territories—thus representing the modern type. Or, again, the crafts and trades of the locality may ship their goods away as in cities of Asiatic, Ancient, and Medieval types. In either case the consumers for the local market are made up of large consumers if they are residents and/or entrepreneurs, workers and craftsmen who form the great mass, and merchants and benefactors of land-rent supported indirectly by the workers and craftsmen.

The trade city and merchant city are confronted by the consumer city in which the purchasing power of its larger consumers rests on the retail for profit of foreign products on the local market (for example, the woolen drapers in the Middle Ages), the foreign sale for profit of local products or goods obtained by native producers (for example, the herring of the Hansa) or the purchase of foreign products and their sale with or without storage at the place to the outside (intermediate commercial cities). Very frequently a combination of all these economic activities occurred: the *commenda* and *societas maris* implied that a *tractator* (travelling merchant) journied to Levantine markets with products purchased with capital entrusted to him by resident capitalists.[3] Often the *tractator* traveled entirely in ballast. He sold these products in the East and with the proceeds he purchased oriental articles brought back for sale in the local market. The profits of the undertaking were then divided between *tractator* and capitalist according to pre-arranged formulas.

The purchasing power and tax ability of the commercial city rested on the local economic establishment as was also the case for the producers' city in contrast to the consumers' city. The economic opportunities of the shipping and transport trade and of numerous secondary wholesale and retail activities were at the disposal of the merchants. However the economic activity of these establishments was not entirely executed for the local retail trade but in substantial measure for external trade. In principle, this state of affairs was similar to that of the modern city, which is the location of national and international financiers or large banks (London, Paris, Berlin) or of joint stock companies or cartels (Duesseldorf). It follows that today more than ever before a predominant part of the earnings of firms flow to localities other than the place of earning. Moreover, a growing part of business proceeds are not consumed by their rightful receivers at the metropolitan location of the business but in suburban villas, rural resorts or international hotels. Parallel with these developments "city-towns" or city-districts consisting almost exclusively of business establishments are arising.

There is no intention here of advancing the further casuistic distinctions required by a purely economic theory of the city. Moreover, it hardly needs to be mentioned that actual cities nearly always represent mixed types. Thus, if cities are to be economically classified at all, it must be in terms of their prevailing economic component.

Relation of the City to Agriculture

The relation of the city to agriculture has not been clear cut. There were and are "semi-rural cities" (*Ackerburgerstaedte*) localities which while serving as places of market traffic and centers of typically urban trade, are sharply separated from the average city by the presence of a broad stratum of resident burghers satisfying a large part of their food needs through cultivation and even producing food for sale. Normally the larger the city the less the opportunity for urban residents to dispose of acreage in relation to their food needs at the same time without controlling a self-sufficient pasture and wood lot in the manner of the village. Cologne, the largest German city in the Middle Ages, almost completely lacked the *Allmende* (commons) from the beginning though the commons was not absent from any normal village of the time. Other German and foreign medieval cities at least placed considerable pastures and woods at the disposal of their burghers.

The presence of large acreages accessible to the urbanite is found more frequently as one turns attention to the south or back toward antiquity. While today we justly regard the typical "urbanite" as a man who does not supply his own food need on his own land, originally the contrary was the case for the majority of typical ancient cities. In contrast to the medieval situation, the ancient urbanite was quite legitimately characterized by the fact that a *kleros, fundus* (In Israel: *chelek*) which he called his own, was a parcel of land which fed him.[4] The full urbanite of antiquity was a semi-peasant.

In the Medieval period, as in Antiquity, agricultural property was retained in the hands of merchant strata. This was more frequently the case in the south than in the north of Europe. In both medieval and ancient city states agricultural properties, occasionally of quite exorbitant size, were found widely scattered, either being politically dominated by municipal authorities of powerful cities or in the possession of eminent individual citizen landlords. Examples are supplied by the Cheronesic domination of the Miltiades or the political or lordly estates of medieval aristocratic families, such as the Genoese Grimaldi, in the provinces or overseas.

As a general rule inter-local estates and the sovereign rights of individual citizens were not the objects of an urban economic policy. However, mixed conditions at times arose such that according to the circumstances estates were guaranteed to individuals by the city. In the nature of the case this only occurred when the individuals whose estates were guaranteed by the city belonged to the most powerful patricians. In such cases the estate was acquired and maintained through indirect help of civic power which in turn might share in its economic and political usufruct. This was frequently the case in the past.

The relation of the city as agent of trade and commerce to the land as producer of food comprises one aspect of the "urban economy" and forms a special "economic stage" between the "household economy" on the one hand and the "national economy" on the other.[5] When the city is visualized in this manner, however, politico-economic aspects are conceptually fused with pure economic aspects and conceived as forming one whole. The mere fact that merchants and tradesmen live crowded together carrying on a regular satisfaction of daily needs in the market does not exhaust the concept of the "city." Where only the satisfaction of agricultural needs occurs within closed settlements and where—what is not identical with it—agricultural production appears in relation to non-agricultural acquisition, and when the presence or absence of markets constitutes the difference, we speak of trade and commercial localities and of small market-towns, but not of cities. There were, thus, hidden non-economic dimensions in the phenomena brought under review in the previous sections. It is time to expand the concept of the "city" to include extra-economic factors.

The Politico-Administrative Concept of the City

Beside possessing an accumulation of abodes the city also has an economic association with its own landed property and a budget of receipts and expenditure. Such an economic association may also appear in the village no matter how great the quantitative differences. Moreover, it was not peculiar to the city alone, at least in the past, that it was both an economic and a regulatory association. Trespass restrictions, pasture regulations, the prohibition of the export of wood and straw, and similar regulations are known to the village, constituting an economic policy of the association as such.

The cities of the past were differentiated only by the kinds of regulations which appeared. Only the objects of political economic regulation on behalf of the association and the range of characteristic measures embraced by them were peculiar. It goes without saying that measures of the "urban economic policy" took substantial account of the fact that under the transportation conditions of the time the majority of all inland cities were dependent upon the agricultural resources of the immediate hinterland. As shown by the grain policies of Athens and Rome this was true for maritime cities. In a majority, not all, of urban trades areas, opportunity was provided for the natural "play of the market." The urban market supplied the normal, not the sole, place for the exchange of products, especially food.

Account also must be taken of the fact that production for trade was predominantly in the form of artisan technology organized in specialized small establishments. Such production operated without or with little capital and with strictly limited numbers of journeymen who were trained in long apprenticeship. Such production was economically in the form of wage worker as price work for customers. Sale to the local retailers was largely a sale to customers.

The market conditions of the time were the kind that would naturally emerge, given the above facts. The so-called "urban economic policy" was basically characterized by its attempt to stabilize the conditions of the local urban economy by means of economic regulations in the interest of permanently and cheaply feeding the masses and standardizing the economic opportunities of tradesmen and merchants. However, as we shall see, economic regulation was not the sole object of the urban economic policy nor, when it historically appears, was it fully developed. It emerges only under the political regime of the guild. Finally it can not be proved to be simply a transitional stage in the development of all cities. In any case, the urban economic policy does not represent a universal stage in economic evolution.

On the basis of customer relations and specialized small establishments operating without capital, the local urban market with its exchange between agricultural and non-agricultural producers and resident merchants, represents a kind of economic counterpart to barter as against systematically divided performances in terms of work and taxes of a specialized dependent economy in connection with the *oikos*, having its basis in the accumulation and integration of work in the manner, without exchange occurring inside. Following out the parallel: the *regulation* (urban economic policy) of the exchange and production conditions in the city represent the counterpart to the *organization* (traditional and feudal-contractual) of activities united in the economy of the *oikos*.

The very fact that in drawing these distinctions we are led to use the concepts of an "urban economic area" and "urban area," and "urban authority," already indicates that the concept of the "city" can and must be examined in terms of a series of concepts other than the purely economic categories so far employed.

The additional concepts required for analysis of the city are political. This already appears in the fact that the urban economic policy itself may be the work of a prince to whom political dominion of the city with its inhabitants belongs. In this case when there is an urban economic policy it is determined *for* the inhabitants of the city not *by* them. However even when this is the case the city must still be considered to be a partially autonomous association, a "community" with special political and administrative arrangements.

The economic concept previously discussed must be entirely separated from the political-administrative concept of the city. Only in the latter sense may a special *area* belong to the city. A locale can be held to be a city in a political-administrative sense though it would not qualify as a city economically. In the Middle Ages there were areas legally defined as "cities" in which the inhabitants derived ninety percent or more of their livelihood from agriculture, representing a far larger fraction of their income than that of the inhabitants of many localities legally defined as "villages."

Naturally, the transition from such semi-rural cities to consumers', producers' or commercial cities is quite fluid. In those settlements which differ administratively from the village and are thus dealt with as cities only one thing, namely, the kind of regulations of land-owning, is customarily different from rural land-owning forms. Economically such cities are differentiated by a special kind of rent situation presented in urban real estate which consists in house ownership to which land ownership is accessory. The position of urban real estate is connected administratively with special taxation principles. It is bound even more closely to a further element decisive for the political-administrative concept of the city and standing entirely outside the purely economic analysis, namely, the fortress.

Fortress and Garrison

It is very significant that the city in the past, in Antiquity and the Middle Ages, outside as well as within Europe, was also a special fortress or garrison. At present this property of the city has been entirely lost, but it was not universal even in the past. In Japan, for example, it was not the rule. Administratively one may, with Rathgen,[6] doubt the existence of cities at all. In contrast to Japan, in China every city was surrounded with a gigantic ring of walls. However, it is also true that many economically rural localities which were not cities in the administrative sense, possessed walls at all times. In China such places were not the seat of state authorities.

In many Mediterranean areas such as Sicily a man living outside the urban walls as a rural worker and country resident is almost unknown. This is a product of century-long insecurity. By contrast in old Hellas the Spartan polis sparkled by the absence of walls, yet the property of being a "garrison-town" was met. Sparta despised walls for the very reason that it was a permanent open military camp.

Though there is still dispute as to how long Athens was without walls, like all Hellenic cities except Sparta it contained in the Acropolis a castle built on rock in the same manner as Ekbantama and Persepolis which were royal castles with surrounding settlements. The castle or wall belonged normally to Oriental as well as to ancient Mediterranean and ordinary medieval cities.

The city was neither the sole nor oldest fortress. In disputed frontier territory and during chronic states of war, every village fortified itself. Under the constant danger of attack in the area of the Elbe and Oder Rivers Slavic settlements were fortified, the national form of the rural village seems early to have been standardized in the form of the "hedge-enclosed" circular area with a single entrance which could be locked and through which at night cattle were driven to the central protection of the village area. Similarly, walled hill retreats were diffused throughout the world from Israelite East Jordan to Germanic territories. Unarmed persons and cattle took refuge within in times of danger. The so-called "cities" of Henry I in the German East were merely systematically established fortresses of this sort.

In England during the Anglo-Saxon period a "burgh" (borough) belonged to each shire whose name it took. Guard and garrison duty as the oldest specifically "civic" obligations were attached to certain persons or pieces of land. When in normal times such fortresses were occupied, guards or vassals were maintained as a permanent garrison and paid in salaries or in land. There were fluid transitions from the permanently garrisoned fortress to the Anglo-Saxon burgh, the "garrison-city," in the sense of Maitland's theory, with a "burgess" as inhabitants. The burgess received its name from its political position which like the legal nature of its civic land and house property was determined by the duty of maintaining and guarding the fortress.

However, historically neither the palisaded village nor the emergency fortification are the primary fore-runners of the city fortress, which was, rather, the manorial castle. The manorial castle was a fortress occupied by the lord and warriors subordinated to him as officials or as a personal following, together with their families and servants.

Military castle construction is very old, doubtlessly older than the chariot and military use of the horse. Like the war chariot the importance of the castle was determined by the development of knightly and royal warfare. In old China of the classic songs, in India of the Vedas, in Egypt and Mesopotamia, in Canaan, in Israel at the time of the Song of Deborah, in Greece during the period of the Homeric epics, and among the Etruscans, Celts, and Irish, the building of castles and the castle-principality were diffused universally. Old Egyptian sources speak of castles and their commanders and it may be assumed that they originally accommodated just as many small princes. From old documents it can be inferred that in Mesopotamia the development of the provincial kingships was preceded by a castle-dwelling princedom such as existed in Western India at the time of the Vedas and such as was probable in Iran at the time of the oldest *Gathas*. The castle was certainly universally dominant in Northern India on the Ganges during the time of political disintegration. In this last instance, the old Kshatriyas whom the sources show to be peculiarly sandwiched between the king and nobility, were obviously princes.

In the period of Christianization, castle construction was pressed in Russia. It appears also during the dynasty of Thutmose in Syria at the time of the Israelite confederation (Abmilech). Old Chinese literature also provides irrefutable evidence of its original occurrence. The Hellenic and Asia Minor sea-castle was as universally diffused as piracy. There must have been an interim period of especially deep pacification to allow the Cretan unfortified palaces to arise in the place of the castle. In this area later castles like the Decelia,[7] so important in the Peloponnesian Wars, were originally fortresses of noble families.

The medieval development of a politically independent gentry opened with the *castelli* in Italy. In Northern Europe the independence of the vassals was also bound up with enormous castle construction as established by Below.[8] Even in modern times individual deputyship in Germany has been dependent upon possession by the family of a castle, even if only the meager ruins of one. Disposal of a castle originally signified military dominion over the country. The only question was: In whose hands? It could be in the hands of the individual lords, or confederations of knights, or of a ruler who could depend on the trustworthiness of his vassals, ministers, or officers.

The City as the Fusion of Fortress and Market

In the first stage of its development into a special political form the fortified city was incorporated in or dependent upon a castle, the fortress of a King, noblemen, or association of knights. Such nobles either resided in the fortress themselves or maintained a garrison of mercenaries, vassals, or servants therein. In Anglo-Saxon England the right to possess a "haw," a fortified house in a "burgh," was bestowed as a privilege on certain land owners of the surrounding countryside. In Antiquity and Medieval Italy the cityhouse of the nobleman was held in addition to his rural castle. The inhabitants or residents adjoining the castle, sometimes all, sometimes special strata, were bound as citizens (burgess) to the performance of certain military duties such as building and repair of the walls, guard duty, defense service and, at times, other military services such as communication and supply for the urban military noble. In this instance the burgher is a member of his estate because, and insofar as, he participates in the military association of the city.

Maitland[9] has worked this out with especial clarity for England. The houses of the "burgh" were in the possession of people having the duty of maintaining the fortification. This contrasts with the village. Alongside royal or aristocratically guaranteed market peace appears military jurisdiction. The politically oriented castle and economically oriented market with the market area of the towns at times simultaneously serving both functions, again drill field and assembly area of the army and the place of pacific economic exchange on the other, often stand in plastic dualism beside one another.

The military drill field and economic market are not everywhere spatially separated. The Attic *pnyx* was a much later development than the *agora* which originally served the economic traffic as well as political and religious activities. On the other hand in Rome from ancient times the *comitium* and *campus martius* were separated from the economic *fora* as in the Middle Ages the *piazza del campo* at Siena (a tournament place still used today as a place for holding races between the wards of the city), as the front of the municipal place, is distinct from the *mercato* at the rear. Analogously in Islamic cities the *kasbeh*, the fortified camp of the warriors, was spatially separate from the *bazaar*. In Southern India the political city of notable men appears separately alongside the economic city.

The relation between the garrison of the political fortress and the civil economic population is complicated but always decisively important for the composition of the city. Wherever a castle existed artisans came or were settled for the satisfaction of manorial wants and the needs of the warriors. The consumption power of a prince's military household and the protection it guaranteed attracted the merchants. Moreover the lord was interested in attracting these classes since he was in position to procure money revenues through them either by taxing commerce or trade or participating in it through capital advances. At times the lord engaged in commerce on his own, even monopolizing it. In maritime castles as ship owner or ruler of the port the lord was in a position to procure a share in piratical or peacefully won sea-borne profits. His followers and vassals resident in the place were also in position to profit whether he voluntarily gave them permission or, being dependent on their good will, was forced to do so.

The evidences of the participation of the ancient city lords in commercial activities are many. Vases from old Hellenic cities like Cyrene picture the king weighing goods (*silphion*). In Egypt at the beginning of historical time a commercial fleet of the Lower-Egyptian Pharaoh is reported. Widely diffused over the world, but especially in maritime "cities" where the carrying trade was easily controlled, the economic interest of resident military families flourished beside the monopoly of the castle chieftain, as a result of their own participation in commercial profits. Their capacity to participate in the civic economy often shattered the monopoly (if it existed) of the prince. When this occurred the prince was considered only to be *primus inter pares* in the ruling circle or even simply as equal. The ruling circle comprised the urban sibs domiciled through landed property and deriving capital from some form of peaceful commerce, especially the *commenda* capital in the Middle Ages, or from personal participation in piracy or sea war. Often the prince was elected for short times and in any case he was decisively limited in power. In ancient maritime cities since Homer's time yearly municipal councils gradually appeared. Quite similar formations often occur in the early Middle Ages. In Venice they formed a counter balance to the doges though with very different leadership positions depending on whether a royal count or vicomte or bishop or someone else was lord of the city. Equivalent developments also appear in other typical commercial cities.

Thus in early Antiquity and in the Middle Ages the urban commercial capitalists, the financiers of commerce, the specific notable persons of the city, have to be separated in principle from the domiciled holders of commercial "establish-ments," the merchants proper. To be sure the strata often blended into each other. However, with this we already anticipate later explanations.

In the hinterland, shipping points, terminals, crossings of rivers and caravan routes (for example, Babylon) could become locations of similar developments. At times competition arose between the priest of the temple, and priestly lord of the city, for temple districts of famous gods offered sacred protection to inter-ethnic elements. Such areas could provide locations for politically unprotected commerce. Thus a city-like settlement, economically supplied by temple revenues, could attach itself to the temple district in a manner similar to the princely city with its tributes to the prince.

Individual cases varied depending on the extent to which the prince's interest in monetary revenues predominated in the granting of privileges for merchandis-ing and manufacturing independent of the lordly household and taxed by the lord. On the other hand, the lord could be interested in satisfying his own needs hence in acting in ways strengthening his own powers and monopolizing trade in his own hands. When attracting foreigners by offering special privileges the lord also had to take into consideration the interests and "established" ability (which was also important for himself) of those already resident, who were dependent on his political protection or manorial supplies.

To this variety of possible development must be added the effects of the political-militaristic structure of the dominating group within which the founding of the city or its development occurred. We must consider the main antitheses in city development arising therefrom.

Associational and Status Peculiarities of the Occidental City

Neither the "city," in the economic sense, nor the garrison, the inhabitants of which are accoutred with special political-administrative structures, necessarily consti-tute a "community." An urban "community," in the full meaning of the word, ap-pears as a general phenomenon only in the Occident. Exceptions occasionally were to be found in the Near East (in Syria, Phoenicia, and Mesopotamia) but only occa-sionally and in rudiments. To constitute a full urban community a settlement must display a relative predominance of trade-commercial relations with the settlement as a whole displaying the following features: 1. a fortification; 2. a market; 3. a court of its own and at least partially autonomous law; 4. a related form of association; and 5. at least partial autonomy and autocephaly, thus also an administration by authorities in the election of whom the burghers participated.

In the past, rights such as those which define the urban community were normally privileges of the estates. The peculiar political properties of the urban community appeared only with the presence of a special stratum, a distinct new estate. Measured by this rule the "cities" of the Occidental Middle Ages only qual-ify in part as true cities; even the cities of the eighteenth century were genuine urban communities only in minor degree. Finally measured by this rule, with possible isolated exceptions, the cities of Asia were not urban communities at all even though they all had markets and were fortresses.

All large seats of trade and commerce in China and most of the small ones were fortified. This was true also for Egyptian, Near Eastern, and Indian centers of commerce and trade. Not infrequently the large centers of trade and commerce of those countries were also separate jurisdictional districts. In China, Egypt, the Near East, and India the large commercial centers have also been seats of large political associations—a phenomenon not characteristic of Medieval Occidental cities, especially those of the North. Thus, many, but not all of the essential elements of the true urban community were at hand. However, the possession by the urbanites of a special substantive or trial law or of courts autonomously nominated by them were unknown to Asiatic cities. Only to the extent that guilds or castes (in India) were located in cities did they develop courts and a special law. Urban location of these associations was legally incidental. Autonomous administration was unknown or only vestigial.

If anything, even more important than the relative absence of autonomous administration, the appearance in the city of an association of urbanites in contradiction to the countryman was also found only in rudiments. The Chinese urban dweller legally belonged to his family and native village in which the temple of his ancestors stood and to which he conscientiously maintained affiliation. This is similar to the Russian village-comrade, earning his livelihood in the city but legally remaining a peasant. The Indian urban dweller remained a member of the caste. As a rule urban dwellers were also members of local professional associations, such as crafts and guilds of specific urban location. Finally they belonged to administrative districts such as the city wards and street districts into which the city was divided by the magisterial police.

Within the administrative units of the city, wards and street districts, urban dwellers had definite duties and even, at times, rights as well. In the attempt to secure peace, city or street districts could be made liturgically responsible collectively for the security of persons or other police purposes. It was possible thus for them to be formed into communities with elected officials or hereditary elders. This occurred in Japan where one or more civil-administrative body (*Machi-Bugyo*) was established as superior to self-administered street communities. However, a city law similar to that of Antiquity or the Middle Ages was absent. The city as corporate *per se* was unknown. Of course, eventually the city as a whole formed a separate administrative district as in the Merovingian and Carolingian Empires, but as was still the case in the Medieval and Ancient Occident, the autonomy and participation of the inhabitants in local administration were out of the question. As a matter of fact, local individual participation in self-administration was often more strongly developed in the country than in the relatively large commercially organized city.

In the village, for example, in China, in many affairs the confederation of elders was practically all-powerful and the Pao-Chia[10] was dependent on them, even though this was not legally expressed. Also in India the village community had nearly complete autonomy in most significant circumstances. In Russia the mir enjoyed nearly complete autonomy until bureaucratization under Alexander III. In the whole of the Near Eastern world the "elders" (in Israel, *sekenim*)[11] originally of the family and later chiefs of noble clans were representatives and administrators of localities and the local court. This could not occur in the Asiatic city because it was usually the seat of a high official or prince and thus under the direct supervision of their bodyguards. However, the city was a princely fortress and administered by royal officials (in Israel, *sarim*)[12] who retained judicial power.

In Israel the dualism of officials and elders can be traced in the royal period. Royal officials everywhere triumphed in bureaucratic kingdoms. Such royal bureaucrats were not all-powerful but subject to public opinion often to an astonishing degree. As a rule the Chinese official was quite powerless against local associations such as the clans and professional associations when they united in a particular case. At every serious united opposition of the clans and local associations the Chinese Official lost his position. Obstruction, boycott, closing of shops, and strikes of artisans and merchants in response to oppression were a daily occurrence, setting limits on the power of officials. However, such limits on official power were of a completely indeterminate kind.

In China and India the guilds and other professional associations had competencies with which the officials had to reckon. The chairman of the local associations often exercised extensive coercive powers even against third parties. However all their powers involved only special competencies of particular association in particular questions of concrete group interest. Moreover, there was ordinarily no joint association representing a community of city burghers *per se,* even the concept of such a possibility is completely lacking. Citizenship as a specific status quality of the urbanite is missing. In China, Japan, and India neither urban community nor citizenry can be found and only traces of them appear in the Near East.

In Japan the organization of estates was purely feudal. The *samurai* (mounted) and *kasi* (unmounted) ministerial officials confronted the peasant (*no*) and the merchants and tradesmen who were partly united in professional associations. However, here too, the concepts of a "citizenry" and an "urban community" are absent. This was also true in China during the feudal period. After the feudal period in China a bureaucratic administration of literati qualified for office in terms of examinations leading to academic degrees confronted the illiterate strata among whom appeared economically privileged guilds of merchants and professional associations. But in this period in China, too, the ideas of an "urban citizenry" and "urban community" are missing. This was true even though in China as well as in Japan the professional associations were self-administered. Moreover while the villages were self-administered the cities were not. In China the city was a fortress and official seat of imperial authorities in a sense completely unknown in Japan.

The cities of India were royal seats or official centers of royal administration as well as fortresses and market places. Guilds of merchants and castes largely coinciding with professional associations were present, enjoying considerable autonomy especially with respect to their own legal competence and justice. Nevertheless, the hereditary caste system of Indian society with its ritualistic segregation of the professions, excluded the emergence of a citizenry and urban community. And though there were numerous castes and sub-castes of traders and artisans they cannot be taken together and equated with the Occidental burgher strata. Nor was it possible for the commercial and artisan castes of India to unite in a form corresponding to the medieval urban corporations for caste estrangement hindered all inter-caste fraternization.

To be sure in India during the period of the great salvation religions, guilds appeared with hereditary elders (*schreschths*) uniting in many cities into an association. As residues from this period there are, at present, some cities (Allahabad) with a mutual urban *schreschth* (elder) corresponding to the occidental mayor. Moreover, in the period before the great bureaucratic kingdoms there were some politically autonomous cities in India ruled by a patriciate recruited from families supplying elephants to the army. Later this phenomenon almost completely disappeared. The triumph of ritualistic caste estrangement shattered the guild associations and royal bureaucracies in alliance with the Brahmans swept away, except for vestiges, such trends toward a citizenry and urban community in Northwestern India.

In Near Eastern Egyptian antiquity the cities were fortresses and official administrative centers with royal market privileges. However, in the period of the dominion of the great kingdom they lacked autonomy, community organizations, and a privileged citizen estate. In Egypt during the Middle Empire office feudalism existed; in the New Empire a bureaucratic administration of clerks appeared "Civic privileges" were bestowed on feudal or prebendal office holders in localities comparable to the privileges of bishops in old Germany. However, civic rights were not bestowed on an autonomous citizenry and even the beginnings of a "city patriciate" have not been found.

In contrast to the complete absence of a citizenry in ancient Egypt were the phenomena in Mesopotamia, Syria and especially Phoenicia, where at an early period typical city-kingdoms emerged at intersection points of sea and caravan traffic. Such civic kingdoms were of intensified sacred-secular character. They were also typified by the rising power of patrician families in the "city-house" (*bitu* in the Tel-el-Amarna tablets) in the period of charioteering.[13] In the Canaanite city an association of chariot-fighting knights possessing urban residences appeared. This knighthood kept the peasant farmers in a state of debt servitude and clientship as in the case of the early Hellenic polis. It was obviously similar in Mesopotamia where the "patrician" as a land-owning full burgher economically qualified for war service is separated from the peasant. Immunities and privileges of this stratum were chartered by the king. However, with the mounting military power of the government this also disappeared. Politically autonomous cities and a burgher stratum of Occidental type are as little to be found in Mesopotamia as is a special urban law alongside royal law.

Only in Phoenicia did the landed patriciate engaging in commerce with its capital manage to maintain its dominion over the city-state. However, the coins of the time *am Sôr* and *am Karthadast* in Tyre and Carthage hardly indicate the presence of a ruling "demos" and if such was ever the case it was only at a later time. Thus a true citizenry only partly developed. In Israel, Juda became a city-state but the elders (*sekenim*) who in the early period governed the administration as chieftains of patrician sibs were thrust into the background by the royal administration. The *gibborim* (knights) became royal attendants and soldiers. In contrast to the countryside, the royal *sarim* (officials) ruled in the large cities. Only after the exile did the community (*kahal*) or fellowship (*cheber*) appear as an institution on a confessional basis under the rule of priestly families.[14]

Nevertheless, all these phenomena indicate that here on the coasts of the Mediterranean Sea and on the Euphrates appeared the first real analogies of a civic development equivalent to that of Rome at the time of the reception of the Gens Claudia. The city is ruled by a patriciate resident in the city with powers resting on monetary wealth primarily won in commerce and secondarily invested in landed property, debt slaves and war slaves.[15] The military power of the urban patriciate was a product of its training for knightly warfare, a training often spent in feuds against one another. The patricians were inter-locally diffused and united with the king or *schofeten* or *sekenim* as *primus inter pares*. Such a patriciate like the Roman nobility with consuls was threatened by the tyranny of the charismatic war king relying upon recruited bodyguards (Abimelech, Jepthah, David). Prior to the Hellenic period this stage of urban development was nowhere permanently surpassed.

Obviously such a patriciate also dominated in cities of the Arabian coast during the period of Mohammed, remaining in existence in those Islamic cities where the autonomy of the city and its patriciate was not completely destroyed as in the larger state. Under Islamic rule ancient oriental conditions were often preserved, whereupon a labile ratio of autonomy between urban families and princely officials appears. Resident city families enjoyed a position of power resting on wealth from urban economic opportunities and invested in land and slaves. Without formal legal recognition the princes and their officials had to take account of the power of the patriciate in the same manner that the Chinese Pao Chia had to take account of the obstruction of clan elders of the villages and merchant and professional associations. However, the city was not thereby necessarily formed into an independent association. Often the contrary occurred, as may be exemplified.

Arabian cities like Mecca were settlements of clans such as remained typical in the Middle Ages to the threshold of the present. Snouck Hurgronje[16] has proven that the city of Mecca was surrounded by the *bilad* representing lordly property of an individual *dewis* of sibs descending from Ali—such were the *hasnaidic* and other noble sibs. The *bilad* was occupied by peasants, clients, and protected Bedouins. *Bilads* were often intermixed. A *dewis* was any sib one ancestor of which was once a sherif. Since 1200 the sherif himself belonged without exception to the Alidic family *Katadahs*. Legally the sherif should have been installed by the governor of the caliph (who was often unfree and once, under Harun al Rashid, was a Berber slave). However in reality the sherif was chosen from the qualified family by election of the chieftains of the *dewis* who were resident in Mecca. For this reason as well as the fact that residence in Mecca offered opportunities to exploit pilgrims, the heads of the class (*emirs*) lived in the city. Between them at times alliances obtained with agreements for preserving the peace and establishing quotas for dividing chances for gain. Such alliances were terminable at any time, dissolution signaling the start of a feud inside and outside the city. Slave troops were employed in such feuds and the defeated group was exiled from the city. However, despite defeat the community of interest between hostile families as against outsiders led to observance of the courtesy of sparing the goods and lives of members of the families and clientele of the exiles. Such courtesies were observed under the threat of general mutiny of one's own partisans.

In modern times the city of Mecca recognizes the following official authorities: 1. On paper the collegiate administrative council (*Medschlis*) installed by the Turks appears as the authority; 2. In fact the Turkish governor is the effective authority, occupying the position of protector (in former times usually the ruler of Egypt); 3. authority is shared by the four *cadis* of the orthodox rights who are always noble men of Mecca, the most eminent (schafitic) for centuries being nominated from one family by the sherif or proposed by the protector; 4. The sherif simultaneously is head of the urban corporation of nobles; 5. The guilds, especially the cicerones, followed by the butchers, corn merchants and others. 6. The city ward with its elders is partly autonomous. These authorities competed with each other in many ways without fixed competences. A party to a legal suit selected the authority appearing most favorable or whose power against the accused seemed to be most strong. The governor was unable to prevent an appeal to the *cadi* who competed with him in all matters of ecclesiastical law. The sherif was held to be the proper authority of the natives especially in all matters concerning the Bedouins and caravans of pilgrims. The governor was dependent on the willingness of the sherif to cooperate. Finally, here as in other Arabic areas, particularly in the cities, the cooperation of the nobility was decisive for the effectiveness of authority.

In the ninth century a development reminiscent of Occidental circumstances occurred when with the flight of the Tuluniden and Deschafariden, in Mecca the position of the richest guilds, that of the butchers and corn merchants, held the balance of power. However, it was still unconditionally true at the time of Mohammed that only the noble *koreischitic* families were militarily and politically important, thus, a government by guilds never arose. Slave troups sustained by profit-shares of resident urban families continually sustained their power. In a similar manner, in medieval Italian cities power continually tended to glide into the hands of the knightly families as wielders of military power.

The idea of an association which could unite the city into a corporate unit was missing in Mecca. This furnished its characteristic difference from the ancient polis and the early medieval Italian commune. However, when all is said and done, this Arabic condition—of course omitting specific Islamic traits or replacing them by Christian counterparts—may be taken to typify the period before the emergence of the urban community association. It is also typical for Occidental commercial sea cities.

So far as sound information extends, in Asiatic and Oriental settlements of an urban economic character, normally only extended families and professional associations were vehicles of communal actions. Communal action was not the product of an urban burgher stratum as such. Transitions, of course, are fluid but precisely the largest settlements at times embracing hundreds of thousands even millions of inhabitants display this very phenomenon. In medieval Byzantine Constantinople the representatives of urban districts were leaders of party divisions who financed circus races (as is still the case for the horse race of Siena.) The Nika revolt under Justinian was a product of such local cleavages of the city. Also in Constantinople, from the time of the Islamic Middle Ages until the sixteenth century, only merchants, corporations, and guilds appear as representatives of the interests of the burghers beside purely military associations such as the *Janitscharen* and *Sipahis* and the religious organizations of the *Ulemas* and *Dervishes*. However, in sixteenth century Constantinople there is still no city representation. Similarly in late Byzantine Alexandria, beside the power of the patricians, relying upon the support of very sturdy monks, and the competitive power of the governor relying on a small garrison there was no militia of particular city districts. Within the districts of the city only the circus parties of rival "greens" and "blues" represented the leading organizations.

Notes

1. For the place of the household or oikos-economy cf. Max Weber, *General Economic History*, trans. Frank H. Knight (Glencoe: The Free Press, 1950) pp. 48, 58, 124 ff., 131, 146, 162 and Johannes Hase Broek, *Griechische Wirtschafts-geschichte* (Tübingen: J. C. B. Mohr, 1931) pp. 15, 24, 27, 29, 38, 46, 69, 284.

2. Charles H. Cooley's theory of transportation took the break in communication either physical or economic as the most critical of all factors for the formation of the city.

3. Weber, *General Economic History*, pp. 205, 206 and W. Silberschmidt, *Die Commenda in ihrer Frühesten Entwicklung* (1884).

4. Pöhlmann, *Aus Altertum und Gegenwart*, p. 124 ff.; Weber, *General Economic History*, p. 328; Weber, *Ancient Judaism* (Glencoe: The Free Press, 1952), p. 465.

5. Weber has in mind distinctions introduced by Gustave Schmoller.

6. Karl Rathgen, "Gemeindefinanzen" in *Verein für Sozialpolitik* (Leipzig: Duncker & Humblot, 1908–10) and *Allgemeine Verfassungs und Verwaltungsgeschichte* (Leipzig: Huebner, 1911).

7. Hill commanding the pass between Pentelicus and Poenes, occupied by the Spartans in 413.

8. Georg Below, *Der deutsche Staat des Mittelalters* (Leipzig: Zuelle & Meyer, 1914); *Territorium und Stadt* (München: R. Oldenberg, 1900).

9. Frederic William Maitland, *The Charters of the Borough of Cambridge* (Cambridge: University Press, 1901) and *The Court Law* (London: Quaritsch, 1891).

10. Even until recent times every ten families constituted a "pao" formally under a headman. A hundred families constituted a "Chia" under a "Pao Chia" also called "Ti Pao." We read Pao-Chia for Taotai.

11. Weber, *Ancient Judaism*, p. 16.

12. *Ibid.*, p. 18.

13. Weber, *Ancient Judaism*, p. 14 f.

14. *Ibid.*, p. 385 f.

15. In all these areas in the early period enslavement for debt appears and debt slaves are found alongside slaves captured in battles—battles at times being actually slave raids.

16. Snouck Hurgronje, *Mekka in the Latter Part of the 19th Century* (London: Luzac, 1931).

12

The Great Towns

Friedrich Engels

Manchester lies at the foot of the southern slope of a range of hills, which stretch hither from Oldham, their last peak, Kersalmoor, being at once the racecourse and the Mons Sacer of Manchester. Manchester proper lies on the left bank of the Irwell, between that stream and the two smaller ones, the Irk and the Medlock, which here empty into the Irwell. On the right bank of the Irwell, bounded by a sharp curve of the river, lies Salford, and farther westward Pendleton; northward from the Irwell lie Upper and Lower Broughton; northward of the Irk, Cheetham Hill; south of the Medlock lies Hulme; farther east Chorlton on Medlock; still farther, pretty well to the east of Manchester, Ardwick. The whole assemblage of buildings is commonly called Manchester, and contains about 400,000 inhabitants, rather more than less. The town itself is peculiarly built, so that a person may live in it for years, and go in and out daily without coming into contact with a working people's quarter or even with workers, that is, so long as he confines himself to his business or to pleasure walks. This arises chiefly from the fact, that by unconscious tacit agreement, as well as with outspoken conscious determination, the working people's quarters are sharply separated from the sections of the city reserved for the middle class; or, if this does not succeed, they are concealed with the cloak of charity. Manchester contains, at its heart, a rather extended commercial district, perhaps half a mile long and about as broad, and consisting almost wholly of offices and warehouses. Nearly the whole district is abandoned by dwellers, and is lonely and deserted at night; only watchmen and policemen traverse its narrow lanes with their dark lanterns. This district is cut through by certain main thoroughfares upon which the vast traffic concentrates, and in which the ground level is lined with brilliant shops. In these streets the upper floors are occupied, here and there, and there is a good deal of life upon them until late at night. With the exception of this commercial district, all Manchester proper, all Salford and Hulme, a great part of Pendleton and Chorlton, two-thirds of Ardwick, and single stretches of Cheetham Hill and Broughton are all unmixed working people's quarters, stretching like a girdle, averaging a mile and a half in breadth, around the commercial district. Outside, beyond this girdle, lives the upper and middle bourgeoisie, the middle bourgeoisie in regularly laid out streets in the vicinity of the working quarters, especially in Chorlton and the lower lying portions of Cheetham Hill; the upper bourgeoisie in remoter villas with gardens in Chorlton and Ardwick, or on the breezy heights of Cheetham Hill, Broughton, and Pendleton, in free, wholesome country air, in fine, comfortable homes, passed once every half or quarter hour by omnibuses going into the city. And the finest part of the arrangements is this, that the members of this money aristocracy can take the shortest road through the middle of all the labouring districts to their places of business, without ever seeing that they are in the midst of the grimy misery that lurks to the right and the left. For the thoroughfares leading from the Exchange in all directions out of the city are lined, on both sides, with an almost unbroken series of shops, and are so kept in the hands of the middle and lower bourgeoisie, which, out of self-interest, cares for a decent and cleanly external appearance and *can* care for it. True, these shops bear some relation to the districts which lie behind them, and are more elegant in the commercial and residential quarters than when they hide grimy working men's dwellings; but they suffice to conceal from the eyes of the wealthy men and women of strong stomachs and weak nerves the misery and grime which form the complement to their wealth. So, for instance, Deansgate, which leads from the Old Church directly southward, is lined first with mills and warehouses, then with second-rate shops and alehouses; farther south, when it leaves the commercial district, with less inviting shops, which grow dirtier and more interrupted by beerhouses and gin palaces the farther one goes, until at the southern end the appearance of the shops leaves no doubt that workers and workers only are their customers. So Market Street running south-east from the Exchange; at first brilliant shops of the best sort, with counting-houses or warehouses above; in the continuation, Piccadilly, immense hotels and warehouses; in the farther continuation, London Road, in the neighbourhood of the Medlock, factories, beerhouses, shops for the humbler bourgeoisie and the working population; and from this point onward, large gardens and villas of the wealthier merchants and manufacturers. In this way anyone who knows Manchester can infer the adjoining districts, from the appearance of the thoroughfare, but one is seldom in a position to catch from the street a glimpse of the real labouring districts. I know very well that this hypocritical plan is more or less common to all great cities; I know, too, that the retail dealers are forced by the nature of their business to take possession of the great highways; I know that there are more good buildings than bad ones upon such streets everywhere, and that the value of land is greater near them than in remoter districts; but at the same time I have never seen so systematic a shutting out of the working class from the thoroughfares, so tender a concealment of everything which might affront the eye and the nerves of the bourgeoisie, as in Manchester. And yet, in other respects, Manchester is less built according to a plan, after official regulations, is more an outgrowth of accident, than any other city; and when I consider in this connection the eager assurances of the middle class, that the working class is doing famously,

I cannot help feeling that the liberal manufacturers, the bigwigs of Manchester, are not so innocent after all, in the matter of this sensitive method of construction.

I may mention just here that the mills almost all adjoin the rivers or the different canals that ramify throughout the city, before I proceed at once to describe the labouring quarters. First of all, there is the Old Town of Manchester, which lies between the northern boundary of the commercial district and the Irk. Here the streets, even the better ones, are narrow and winding, like Todd Street, Long Millgate, Withy Grove, and Shude Hill, the houses dirty, old, and tumble-down, and the construction of the side streets utterly horrible. Going from the Old Church to Long Millgate, the stroller has at once a row of old-fashioned houses on the right, of which not one has kept its original level; these are remnants of the old pre-manufacturing Manchester, whose former inhabitants have removed with their descendants into better-built districts, and have left the houses, which were not good enough for them, to a working-class population strongly mixed with Irish blood. Here one is in an almost undisguised working men's quarter, for even the shops and beerhouses hardly take the trouble to exhibit a trifling degree of cleanliness. But all this is nothing in comparison with the courts and lanes which lie behind, to which access can be gained only through covered passages, in which no two human beings can pass at the same time. Of the irregular cramming together of dwellings in ways which defy all rational plan, of the tangle in which they are crowded literally one upon the other, it is impossible to convey an idea. And it is not the buildings surviving from the old times of Manchester which are to blame for this; the confusion has only recently reached its height when every scrap of space left by the old way of building has been filled up and patched over until not a foot of land is left to be further occupied.

To confirm my statement I have drawn here a small section of the plan of Manchester—not the worst spot and not one-tenth of the whole Old Town.

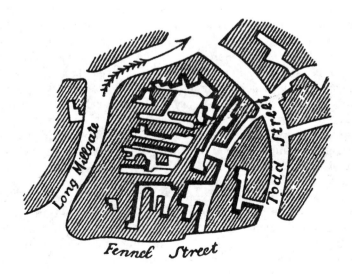

This drawing will suffice to characterize the irrational manner in which the entire district was built, particularly the part near the Irk.

The south bank of the Irk is here very steep and between fifteen and thirty feet high. On this abrupt slope there are planted three rows of houses, of which the lowest rise directly out of the river, while the front walls of the highest stand on the crest of the rise in Long Millgate. Among them are mills on the river, in short, the method of construction is as crowded and disorderly here as in the lower part of Long Millgate. Right and left a multitude of covered passages lead from the main street into numerous courts, and he who turns in thither gets into filth and disgusting grime, the equal of which is not to be found—especially in the courts which lead down to the Irk, and which contain unqualifiedly the most horrible dwellings which I have yet beheld. In one of these courts there stands directly at the entrance, at the end of the covered passage, a privy without a door, so dirty that the inhabitants can pass into and out of the court only by passing through foul pools of stagnant urine and excrement. This is the first court on the Irk above Ducie Bridge—in case any one should care to look into it. Below it on the river there are several tanneries which fill the whole neighbourhood with the stench of animal putrefaction. Below Ducie Bridge the only entrance to most of the houses is by means of narrow, dirty stairs and over heaps of refuse and filth. The first court below Ducie Bridge, known as Allen's Court, was in such a state at the time of the cholera that the sanitary police ordered it evacuated, swept, and disinfected with chloride of lime. Dr Kay gives a terrible description of the state of this court at the time.[1] Since then, it seems to have been partially torn down and rebuilt; at least looking down from Ducie Bridge, the passer-by sees several ruined walls and heaps of débris with some newer houses. The view from this bridge, mercifully concealed from mortals of small stature by a parapet as high as a man, is characteristic for the whole district. At the bottom flows, or rather stagnates, the Irk, a narrow, coal-black, foul-smelling stream, full of debris and refuse, which it deposits on the lower right bank. In dry weather, a long string of the most disgusting blackish-green slime pools are left standing on this bank, from the depths of which bubbles of miasmatic gas constantly arise and give forth a stench unendurable even on the bridge forty or fifty feet above the surface of the stream. But besides this, the stream itself is checked every few paces by high weirs, behind which slime and refuse accumulate and rot in thick masses. Above the bridge are tanneries, bonemills, and gasworks, from which all drains and refuse find their way into the Irk, which receives further the contents of all the neighbouring sewers and privies. It may be easily imagined, therefore, what sort of residue the stream deposits. Below the bridge you look upon the piles of débris, the refuse, filth, and offal from the courts on the steep left bank; here each house is packed close behind its neighbour and a bit of each is visible, all black, smoky, crumbling, ancient, with broken panes and window-frames. The background is furnished by old barrack-like factory buildings. On the lower right bank stands a long row of houses and mills, the second row being a ruin without a roof, piled with débris; the third stands so low that the lowest floor is uninhabitable, and therefore without windows or doors. Here the background embraces the pauper burial-ground, the station of the Liverpool and Leeds railway, and, in the rear of this, the Workhouse, the "Poor-Law Bastille" of Manchester, which, like a citadel, looks threateningly down from behind its high walls and parapets on the hilltop, upon the working people's quarter below.

Above Ducie Bridge, the left bank grows more flat and the right bank steeper, but the condition of the dwellings on both banks grows worse rather than better. Whoever turns to the left here from the main street, Long Millgate, is lost; he wanders from one court to another, turns countless corners, passes nothing but narrow, filthy nooks and alleys, until after a few minutes he has lost all clue, and knows not whither to turn. Everywhere half or wholly ruined buildings, some of them actually uninhabited, which means a great deal here; rarely a wooden or stone floor to be seen in the houses, almost uniformly broken, ill-fitting windows and doors, and a state of filth! Everywhere heaps of débris, refuse, and offal; standing pools for gutters, and a stench which alone would make it impossible for a human being in any degree civilized to live in such a district. The newly-built extension of the Leeds railway, which crosses the Irk here, has swept away some of these courts and lanes, laying others completely open to view. Immediately under the railway bridge there stands a court, the filth and horrors of which surpass all the others by far, just because it was hitherto so shut off, so secluded that the way to it could not be found without a good deal of trouble. I should never have discovered it myself, without the breaks made by the railway, though I thought I knew this whole region thoroughly. Passing along a rough bank, among stakes and washing-lines, one penetrates into this chaos of small one-storeyed, one-roomed hovels, in most of which there is no artificial floor; kitchen, living and sleeping-room all in one. In such a hole, scarcely five feet long by six broad, I found two beds—and such bedsteads and beds!—which, with a staircase and chimney-place, entirely filled the room. In several others I found absolutely nothing, while the door stood open, and the inhabitants leaned against it. Everywhere before the doors refuse and offal; that any sort of pavement lay underneath could not be seen but only felt, here and there, with the feet. This whole collection of cattle-sheds for human beings was surrounded on two sides by houses and a factory, and on the third by the river, and besides the narrow stair up the bank, a narrow doorway alone led out into another almost equally ill-built, ill-kept labyrinth of dwellings.

Enough! The whole side of the Irk is built in this way, a planless, knotted chaos of houses, more or less on the verge of uninhabitableness, whose unclean interiors fully correspond with their filthy external surroundings. And how could the people be clean with no proper opportunity for satisfying the most natural and ordinary wants? Privies are so rare here that they are either filled up every day, or are too remote for most of the inhabitants to use. How can people wash when they have only the dirty Irk water at hand, while pumps and water pipes can be found in decent parts of the city alone? In truth, it cannot be charged to the account of these helots of modern society if their dwellings are not more clean than the pig-sties which are here and there to be seen among them. The landlords are not ashamed to let dwellings like the six or seven cellars on the quay directly below Scotland Bridge, the floors of which stand at least two feet below the low-water level of the Irk that flows not six feet away from them; or like the upper floor of the corner-house on the opposite shore directly above the bridge, where the ground-floor, utterly uninhabitable, stands deprived of all fittings for doors and windows, a case by no means rare in this region, when an open ground-floor is used as a privy by the whole neighbourbood for want of other facilities!

If we leave the Irk and penetrate once more on the opposite side from Long Millgate into the midst of the working men's dwellings, we shall come into a somewhat newer quarter, which stretches from St Michael's Church to Withy Grove and Shude Hill. Here there is somewhat better order. In place of the chaos of buildings, we find at least long straight lanes and alleys or courts, built according to a plan and usually square. But if, in the former case, every house was built according to caprice, here each lane and court is so built, without reference to the situation of the adjoining ones. The lanes run now in this direction, now in that, while every two minutes the wanderer gets into a blind alley, or, on turning a comer, finds himself back where he started from; certainly no one who has not lived a considerable time in this labyrinth can find his way through it.

If I may use the word at all in speaking of this district, the ventilation of these streets and courts is, in consequence of this confusion, quite as imperfect as in the Irk region; and if this quarter may, nevertheless, be said to have some advantage over that of the Irk, the houses being newer and the streets occasionally having gutters, nearly every house has, on the other hand, a cellar dwelling, which is rarely found in the Irk district, by reason of the greater age and more careless construction of the houses. As for the rest, the filth, débris, and offal heaps, and the pools in the streets are common to both quarters, and in the district now under discussion, another feature most injurious to the cleanliness of the inhabitants is the multitude of pigs walking about in all the alleys, rooting into the offal heaps, or kept imprisoned in small pens. Here, as in most of the working men's quarters of Manchester, the pork-raisers rent the courts and build pigpens in them. In almost every court one or even several such pens may be found, where the inhabitants of the court throw all refuse and offal, on which the swine grow fat; and the atmosphere, confined on all four sides, is utterly corrupted by putrefying animal and vegetable substances. Through this quarter, a broad and measurably decent street has been cut, Millers Street, and the background has been pretty successfully concealed. But if anyone should be led by curiosity to pass through one of the numerous passages which lead into the courts, he will find a piggery repeated at every twenty paces.

Such is the Old Town of Manchester, and on re-reading my description, I am forced to admit that instead of being exaggerated, it is far from black enough to convey a true impression of the filth, ruin, and uninhabitableness, the defiance of all considerations of cleanliness, ventilation, and health which characterize the construction of this single district, containing at least twenty to thirty thousand inhabitants. And such a district exists in the heart of the second city of England, the first manufacturing city of the world. If anyone wishes to see in how little space a human being can move, how little air—and *such* air!—he can breathe, how little of civilization he may share and yet live, it is only necessary to travel hither. True, this is the *Old* Town, and the people of Manchester emphasize the fact whenever anyone mentions to them the frightful condition of this hell upon earth; but what does that prove? Everything which here arouses horror and indignation is of recent origin, belongs to the *industrial epoch*. The couple of hundred houses which belong to Old Manchester have been long since abandoned by their original inhabitants; the industrial epoch alone has crammed into them the swarms of workers whom they now shelter; the industrial epoch alone has built up every spot between these old houses to make a covering for the masses whom it has conjured hither from the agricultural districts and from Ireland; the industrial epoch alone enables the owners of these cattlesheds to rent them for high prices to human beings, to plunder the poverty of the workers, to undermine the health of thousands, in order that they only, the owners, may grow rich. In the industrial epoch alone has it become possible that the worker scarcely freed from feudal servitude can be used as mere material, a mere chattel; that he must let himself be crowded into a dwelling too bad for every other, which he for his hard-earned wages buys the right to let go utterly to ruin. This is what manufacture has achieved, and, without these workers and their poverty, this slavery would have been impossible. True, the original construction of this quarter was bad, little good could have been made out of it; but, have the land-owners, has the municipality done anything to improve it when rebuilding? On the contrary, wherever a nook, or corner was free, a house has been run up; where a superfluous passage remained, it has been built on; the value of land rose with the blossoming out of manufacture, and the more it rose, the more madly was the work of building carried on, without reference to the health or comfort of the inhabitants, with sole reference to the highest possible profit, on the principle that *no hole is so bad but that some poor creature must take it who can pay for nothing better.*

To sum up briefly the facts thus far cited. The great towns are chiefly inhabited by working people, since in the best case there is one of better class for two workers, often for three, here and there for four; these workers have no property whatsoever of their own, and live wholly upon wages, which usually go from hand to mouth. Society, composed wholly of atoms, does not trouble itself about them; leaves them to care for themselves and their families, yet supplies them no means of doing this in an efficient and permanent manner. Every working man, even the best, is therefore constantly exposed to loss of work and food, that is to death by starvation, and many perish in this way. The dwellings of the workers are everywhere badly planned, badly built, and kept in the worst condition, badly ventilated, damp, and unwholesome. The inhabitants are confined to the smallest possible space, and at least one family usually sleeps in each room. The interior arrangement of the dwellings is poverty-stricken in various degrees, down to the utter absence of even the most necessary furniture. The clothing of the workers, too, is generally scanty, and that of great multitudes is in rags. The food is, in general, bad; often almost unfit for use, and in many cases, at least at times, insufficient in quantity, so that, in extreme cases, death by starvation results. Thus the working class of the great cities offers a graduated scale of conditions in life, in the best cases a temporarily endurable existence for hard work and good wages, good and endurable, that is, from the worker's standpoint; in the worst cases, bitter want, reaching even homelessness and death by starvation. The average is much nearer the worst case than the best. And this series does not fall into fixed classes, so that one might say, this fraction of the working class is well off, has always been so, and remains so. If that is the case here and there, if single branches of work have in general an advantage over others, yet the condition of the workers in each branch is subject to such great fluctuations that a single working man may be so placed as to pass through the whole range from comparative comfort to the extremest need, even to death by starvation, while almost every English working man can tell a tale of marked changes of fortune.

Note

1. James Ph. Kay, M.D., *The Moral and Physical Condition of the Working Class Employed in the Cotton Manufacture in Manchester,* 2nd edn, 1832. Dr Kay confuses the working class in general with the factory workers, otherwise an excellent pamphlet.

13

The Metropolis and Mental Life

Georg Simmel

The deepest problems of modern life derive from the claim of the individual to preserve the autonomy and individuality of his existence in the face of overwhelming social forces, of historical heritage, of external culture, and of the technique of life. The fight with nature which primitive man has to wage for his *bodily* existence attains in this modern form its latest transformation. The eighteenth century called upon man to free himself of all the historical bonds in the state and in religion, in morals and in economics. Man's nature, originally good and common to all, should develop unhampered. In addition to more liberty, the nineteenth century demanded the functional specialization of man and his work; this specialization makes one individual incomparable to another, and each of them indispensable to highest possible extent. However, this specialization makes each man the more directly dependent upon the supplementary activities of all others. Nietzsche sees the full development of the individual conditioned by the most ruthless struggle of individuals; socialism believes in the suppression of all competition for the same reason. Be that as it may, in all these positions the same basic motive is at work: the person resists to being leveled down and worn out by a social-technological mechanism. An inquiry into the inner meaning of specifically modern life and its products, into the soul of the cultural body, so to speak, must seek to solve the equation which structures like the metropolis set up between the individual and the super-individual contents of life. Such an inquiry must answer the question of how the personality accommodates itself in the adjustments to external forces. This will be my task today.

The psychological basis of the metropolitan type of individuality consists in the *intensification of nervous stimulation* which results from the swift and uninterrupted change of outer and inner stimuli. Man is a differentiating creature. His mind is stimulated by the difference between a momentary impression and the one which preceded it. Lasting impressions, impressions which differ only slightly from one another, impressions which take a regular and habitual course and show regular and habitual contrasts—all these use up, so to speak, less consciousness than does the rapid crowding of changing images, the sharp discontinuity in the grasp of a single glance, and the unexpectedness of onrushing impressions. These are the psychological conditions which the metropolis creates. With each crossing of the street, with the tempo and multiplicity of economic, occupational and social life, the city sets up a deep contrast with small town and rural life with reference to the sensory foundations of psychic life. The metropolis exacts from man as a discriminating creature a different amount of consciousness than does rural life. Here the rhythm of life and sensory mental imagery flows more slowly, more habitually, and more evenly. Precisely in this connection the sophisticated character of metropolitan psychic life becomes understandable—as over against small town life which rests more upon deeply felt and emotional relationships. These latter are rooted in the more unconscious layers of the psyche and grow most readily in the steady rhythm of uninterrupted habituations. The intellect, however, has its locus in the transparent, conscious, higher layers of the psyche; it is the most adaptable of our inner forces. In order to accommodate to change and to the contrast of phenomena, the intellect does not require any shocks and inner upheavals; it is only through such upheavals that the more conservative mind could accommodate to the metropolitan rhythm of events. Thus the metropolitan type of man—which, of course, exists in a thousand individual variants—develops an organ protecting him against the threatening currents and discrepancies of his external environment which would uproot him. He reacts with his head instead of his heart. In this an increased awareness assumes the psychic prerogative. Metropolitan life, thus, underlies a heightened awareness and a predominance of intelligence in metropolitan man. The reaction to metropolitan phenomena is shifted to that organ which is least sensitive and quite remote from the depth of the personality. Intellectuality is thus seen to preserve subjective life against the overwhelming power of metropolitan life, and intellectuality branches out in many directions and is integrated with numerous discrete phenomena.

The metropolis has always been the seat of the money economy. Here the multiplicity and concentration of economic exchange gives an importance to the means of exchange which the scantiness of rural commerce would not have allowed. Money economy and the dominance of the intellect are intrinsically connected. They share a matter-of-fact attitude in dealing with men and with things; and, in this attitude, a formal justice is often coupled with an inconsiderate hardness. The intellectually sophisticated person is indifferent to all genuine individuality, because relationships and reactions result from it which cannot be exhausted with logical operations. In the same manner, the individuality of phenomena is not commensurate with the pecuniary principle. Money is concerned only with what is common to all: it asks for the exchange value, it reduces all quality and individuality to the question: How much? All intimate emotional relations between persons are founded in their individuality, whereas in rational relations man is reckoned with like a number, like an element which is in itself indifferent. Only the objective measurable achievement is of interest. Thus metropolitan man reckons with his merchants and customers, his domestic servants and often even with persons with whom he is obliged to have social intercourse. These features of intellectuality contrast with the nature of the small circle in which the inevitable knowledge of individuality as inevitably produces a warmer tone of behavior, a behavior which is beyond a mere objective balancing of service and return. In the sphere of the economic psychology of the small group it is of importance that under primitive conditions production serves the customer who orders the good, so that the producer and the consumer are acquainted. The modern metropolis, however, is supplied almost entirely by production for the market, that is, for entirely unknown purchasers who never personally enter the producer's actual field of vision. Through this anonymity the interests of each party acquire an unmerciful matter-of-factness; and the intellectually calculating economic egoism of both parties need not fear any deflection because of the imponderables of personal relationships. The money economy dominates the metropolis; it has displaced the last survivals of domestic production and the direct barter of goods; it minimizes, from day to day, the amount of work ordered by customers. The matter-of-fact attitude is obviously so intimately interrelated with the money economy, which is dominant in the metropolis, that nobody can say whether the intellectualistic mentality first promoted the money economy or whether the latter determined the former. The metropolitan way of life is certainly the most fertile soil for this reciprocity, a point which I shall document merely by citing the dictum of the most eminent English constitutional historian: throughout the whole course of English history, London has never acted as England's heart but often as England's intellect and always as her moneybag!

In certain seemingly insignificant traits, which lie upon the surface of life, the same psychic currents characteristically unite. Modern mind has become more and more calculating. The calculative exactness of practical life which the money economy has brought about corresponds to the ideal of natural science: to transform the world into an arithmetic problem, to fix every part of the world by mathematical formulas. Only money economy has filled the days of so many people with weighing, calculating, with numerical determinations, with a reduction of qualitative values to quantitative ones. Through the calculative nature of money a new precision, a certainty in the definition of identities and differences, an unambiguousness in agreements and arrangements has been brought about in the relations of life-elements—just as externally this precision has been effected by the universal diffusion of pocket watches. However, the conditions of metropolitan life are at once cause and effect of this trait. The relationships and affairs of the typical metropolitan usually are so varied and complex that without the strictest punctuality in promises and services the whole structure would break down into

an inextricable chaos. Above all, this necessity is brought about by the aggregation of so many people with such differentiated interests, who must integrate their
relations and activities into a highly complex organism. If all clocks and watches
in Berlin would suddenly go wrong in different ways, even if only by one hour, all
economic life and communication of the city would be disrupted for a long time. In
addition an apparently mere external factor: long distances, would make all waiting and broken appointments result in an ill-afforded waste of time. Thus, the technique of metropolitan life is unimaginable without the most punctual integration
of all activities and mutual relations into a stable and impersonal time schedule.
Here again the general conclusions of this entire task of reflection become obvious,
namely, that from each point on the surface of existence—however closely attached
to the surface alone—one may drop a sounding into the depth of the psyche so that
all the most banal externalities of life finally are connected with the ultimate decisions concerning the meaning and style of life. Punctuality, calculability, exactness
are forced upon life by the complexity and extension of metropolitan existence
and are not only most intimately connected with its money economy and intellectualistic character. These traits must also color the contents of life and favor the
exclusion of those irrational, instinctive, sovereign traits and impulses which aim
at determining the mode of life from within, instead of receiving the general and
precisely schematized form of life from without. Even though sovereign types of
personality, characterized by irrational impulses, are by no means impossible in
the city, they are, nevertheless, opposed to typical city life. The passionate hatred
of men like Ruskin and Nietzsche for the metropolis is understandable in these
terms. Their natures discovered the value of life alone in the unschematized existence which cannot be defined with precision for all alike. From the same source
of this hatred of the metropolis surged their hatred of money economy and of the
intellectualism of modern existence.

The same factors which have thus coalesced into the exactness and minute
precision of the form of life have coalesced into a structure of the highest impersonality; on the other hand, they have promoted a highly personal subjectivity. There
is perhaps no psychic phenomenon which has been so unconditionally reserved
to the metropolis as has the blasé attitude, The blasé attitude results first from the
rapidly changing and closely compressed contrasting stimulations of the nerves.
From this, the enhancement of metropolitan intellectuality, also, seems originally
to stem. Therefore, stupid people who are not intellectually alive in the first place
usually are not exactly blasé. A life in boundless pursuit of pleasure makes one
blasé because it agitates the nerves to their strongest reactivity for such a long
time that they finally cease to react at all. In the same way, through the rapidity and contradictoriness of their changes, more harmless impressions force such
violent responses, tearing the nerves so brutally hither and thither that their last
reserves of strength are spent; and if one remains in the same milieu they have no
time to gather new strength. An incapacity thus emerges to react to new sensations with the appropriate energy. This constitutes that blasé attitude which, in fact,
every metropolitan child shows when compared with children of quieter and less
changeable milieus.

This physiological source of the metropolitan blasé attitude is joined by another source which flows from the money economy: The essence of the blasé attitude consists in the blunting of discrimination. This does not mean that the objects are not perceived, as is the case with the half-wit, but rather that the meaning and differing values of things, and thereby the things themselves, are experienced as insubstantial. They appear to the blasé person in an evenly flat and gray tone; no one object deserves preference over any other. This mood is the faithful subjective reflection of the completely internalized money economy. By being the equivalent to all the manifold things in one and the same way, money becomes the most frightful leveler. For money expresses all qualitative differences of things in terms of "how much?" Money, with all its colorlessness and indifference, becomes the common denominator of all values; irreparably it hollows out the core of things, their individuality, their specific value, and their incomparability. All things float with equal specific gravity in the constantly moving stream of money. All things lie on the same level and differ from one another only in the size of the area which they cover. In the individual case this coloration, or rather discoloration, of things through their money equivalence may be unnoticeably minute. However, through the relations of the rich to the objects to be had for money, perhaps even through the total character which the mentality of the contemporary public everywhere imparts to these objects, the exclusively pecuniary evaluation of objects has become quite considerable. The large cities, the main seats of the money exchange, bring the purchasability of things to the fore much more impressively than do smaller localities. That is why cities are also the genuine locale of the blasé attitude. In the blasé attitude the concentration of men and things stimulate the nervous system of the individual to its highest achievement so that it attains its peak. Through the mere quantitative intensification of the same conditioning factors this achievement is transformed into its opposite and appears in the peculiar adjustment of the blasé attitude. In this phenomenon the nerves find in the refusal to react to their stimulation the last possibility of accommodating to the contents and forms of metropolitan life. The self-preservation of certain personalities is brought at the price of devaluating the whole objective world, a devaluation which in the end unavoidably drags one's own personality down into a feeling of the same worthlessness.

Whereas the subject of this form of existence has to come to terms with it entirely for himself, his self-preservation in the face of the large city demands from him a no less negative behavior of a social nature. This mental attitude of metropolitans toward one another we may designate, from a formal point of view, as reserve. If so many inner reactions were responses to the continuous external contacts with innumerable people as are those in the small town, where one knows almost everybody one meets and where one has a positive relation to almost everyone, one would be completely atomized internally and come to an unimaginable psychic state. Partly this psychological fact, partly the right to distrust which men have in the face of the touch-and-go elements of metropolitan life, necessitates our reserve. As a result of this reserve we frequently do not even know by sight those who have been our neighbors for years. And it is this reserve which in the eyes of the small-town people makes us appear to be cold and heartless. Indeed, if I do not deceive myself, the inner aspect of this outer reserve is not only indifference but, more often than we are aware, it is a slight aversion, a mutual strangeness and repulsion, which will break into hatred and fight at the moment of a closer contact, however caused. The whole inner organization of such an extensive communicative life rests upon an extremely varied hierarchy of sympathies, indifferences, and aversions of the briefest as well as of the most permanent nature. The sphere of indifference in this hierarchy is not as large as might appear on the surface. Our psychic activity still responds to almost every impression of somebody else with a somewhat distinct feeling. The unconscious, fluid and changing character of this impression seems to result in a state of indifference. Actually this indifference would be just as unnatural as the diffusion of indiscriminate mutual suggestion would be unbearable. From both these typical dangers of the metropolis, indifference and indiscriminate suggestibility, antipathy protects us. A latent antipathy and the preparatory stage of practical antagonism effect the distances and aversions without which this mode of life could not at all be led. The extent and the mixture of this style of life, the rhythm of its emergence and disappearance, the forms in which it is satisfied—all these, with the unifying motives in the narrower sense, form the inseparable whole of the metropolitan style of life. What appears in the metropolitan style of life directly as dissociation is in reality only one of its elemental forms of socialization.

This reserve with its overtone of hidden aversion appears in turn as the form or the cloak of a more general mental phenomenon of the metropolis: it grants to the individual a kind and an amount of personal freedom which has no analogy whatsoever under other conditions. The metropolis goes back to one of the large developmental tendencies of social life as such, to one of the few tendencies for which an approximately universal formula can be discovered. The earliest phase of social formations found in historical as well as in contemporary social structures is this: a relatively small circle firmly closed against neighboring, strange, or in some way antagonistic circles. However, this circle is closely coherent and allows its individual members only a narrow field for the development of unique qualities and free, self-responsible movements. Political and kinship groups, parties and religious associations begin in this way. The self-preservation of very young associations requires the establishment of strict boundaries and a centripetal unity. Therefore they cannot allow the individual freedom and unique inner and outer development. From this stage social development proceeds at once in two different, yet corresponding, directions. To the extent to which the group grows—numerically, spatially, in significance and in content of life—to the same degree the group's direct, inner unity loosens, and the rigidity of the original demarcation against others is softened through mutual relations and connections. At the same time, the individual gains freedom of movement, far beyond the first jealous delimitation. The individual also gains a specific individuality to which the division of labor in the enlarged group gives both occasion and necessity. The state and Christianity, guilds and political parties, and innumerable other groups have developed according to this formula, however much, of course, the special conditions and forces of the respective groups have modified the general scheme. This scheme seems to me distinctly recognizable also in the evolution of individuality within urban life. The small-town life in Antiquity and in the Middle Ages set barriers against movement and relations of the individual toward the outside, and it set up barriers against individual independence and differentiation within the individual self. These barriers were such that under them modern man could not have breathed. Even today a metropolitan man who is placed in a small town feels a restriction similar, at least, in kind. The smaller the circle which forms our milieu is, and the more restricted those relations to others are which dissolve the boundaries of the individual, the more anxiously the circle guards the achievements, the conduct of life, and the outlook of the individual, and the more readily a quantitative and qualitative specialization would break up the framework of the whole little circle.

The ancient *polis* in this respect seems to have had the very character of a small town. The constant threat to its existence at the hands of enemies from near and afar effected strict coherence in political and military respects, a supervision of the citizen by the citizen, a jealousy of the whole against the individual whose particular life was suppressed to such a degree that he could compensate only by acting as a despot in his own household. The tremendous agitation and excitement, the unique colorfulness of Athenian life, can perhaps be understood in terms of the fact that a people of incomparably individualized personalities struggled against the constant inner and outer pressure of a de-individualizing small town. This produced a tense atmosphere in which the weaker individuals were suppressed and those of stronger natures were incited to prove themselves in the most passionate manner. This is precisely why it was that there blossomed in Athens what must be called, without defining it exactly, "the general human character" in the intellectual development of our species. For we maintain factual as well as historical validity for the following connection: the most extensive and the most general contents and forms of life are most intimately connected with the most individual ones. They have a preparatory stage in common, that is, they find their enemy in narrow formations and groupings the maintenance of which places both of them into a state of defense against expanse and generality lying without and the freely moving individuality within. Just as in the feudal age, the "free" man was the one who stood under the law of the land, that is, under the law of the largest social orbit, and the unfree man was the one who derived his right merely from the narrow circle of a feudal association and was excluded from the larger social orbit—so today metropolitan man is "free" in a spiritualized and refined sense, in contrast to the pettiness and prejudices which hem in the small-town man. For the reciprocal reserve grid and indifference and the intellectual life conditions of large circles are never felt more strongly by the individual in their impact upon his independence than in the thickest crowd of the big city. This is because the bodily proximity and narrowness of space makes the mental distance only the more visible. It is obviously only the obverse of this freedom if, under certain circumstances, one nowhere feels as lonely and lost as in the metropolitan crowd. For here as elsewhere it is by no means necessary that the freedom of man be reflected in his emotional life as comfort.

It is not only the immediate size of the area and the number of persons which, because of the universal historical correlation between the enlargement of the circle and the personal inner and outer freedom, has made the metropolis the locale of freedom. It is rather in transcending this visible expanse that any given city becomes the seat of cosmopolitanism. The horizon of the city expands in a manner comparable to the way in which wealth develops; a certain amount of property increases in a quasi-automatical way in ever more rapid progression. As soon as a certain limit has been passed, the economic, personal, and intellectual relations of the citizenry, the sphere of intellectual predominance of the city over its hinterland, grow as in geometrical progression. Every gain in dynamic extension becomes a step, not for an equal, but for a new and larger extension. From every thread spinning out of the city, ever new threads grow as if by themselves, just as within the city the unearned increment of ground rent, through the mere increase in communication, brings the owner automatically increasing profits. At this point, the quantitative aspect of life is transformed directly into qualitative traits of character. The sphere of life of the small town is, in the main, self-contained and autarchic. For it is the decisive nature of the metropolis that its inner life overflows by waves into a far-flung national or international area. Weimar is not an example to the contrary, since its significance was hinged upon individual personalities and died with them; whereas the metropolis is indeed characterized by its essential independence even from the most eminent individual personalities. This is the counterpart to the independence, and it is the price the individual pays for the independence, which he enjoys in the metropolis. The most significant characteristic of the metropolis is this functional extension beyond its physical boundaries. And this efficacy reacts in turn and gives weight, importance, and responsibility to metropolitan life. Man does not end with the limits of his body or the area comprising his immediate activity. Rather is the range of the person constituted by the sum of effects emanating from him temporally and spatially. In the same way, a city consists of its total effects which extend beyond its immediate confines. Only this range is the city's actual extent in which its existence is expressed. This fact makes it obvious that individual freedom, the logical and historical complement of such extension, is not to be understood only in the negative sense of mere freedom of mobility and elimination of prejudices and petty philistinism. The essential point is that the particularity and incomparability, which ultimately every human being possesses, be somehow expressed in the working-out of a way of life. That we follow the laws of our own nature—and this after all is freedom—becomes obvious and convincing to ourselves and to others only if the expressions of this nature differ from the expressions of others. Only our unmistakability proves that our way of life has not been superimposed by others.

Cities are, first of all, seats of the highest economic division of labor. They produce thereby such extreme phenomena as in Paris the renumerative occupation of the *quatorzième*. They are persons who identify themselves by signs on their residences and who are ready at the dinner hour in correct attire, so that they can be quickly called upon if a dinner party should consist of thirteen persons. In the measure of its expansion, the city offers more and more the decisive conditions of the division of labor. It offers a circle which through its size can absorb a highly diverse variety of services. At the same time, the concentration of individuals and their struggle for customers compel the individual to specialize in a function from which he cannot be readily displaced by another. It is decisive that city life has transformed the struggle with nature for livelihood into an inter-human struggle for gain, which here is not granted by nature but by other men. For specialization does not flow only from the competition for gain but also from the underlying fact that the seller must always seek to call forth new and differentiated needs of the lured customer. In order to find a source of income which is not yet exhausted, and to find a function which cannot readily be displaced, it is necessary to specialize in one's services. This process promotes differentiation, refinement, and the enrichment of the public's needs, which obviously must lead to growing personal differences within this public.

All this forms the transition to the individualization of mental and psychic traits which the city occasions in proportion to its size. There is a whole series of obvious causes underlying this process. First, one must meet the difficulty of asserting his own peronality within the dimensions of metropolitan life. Where the quantitative increase in importance and the expense of energy reach their limits, one seizes upon qualitative differentiation in order somehow to attract the attention of the social circle by playing upon its sensitivity for differences. Finally, man is tempted to adopt the most tendentious peculiarities, that is, the specifically metropolitan extravagances of mannerism, caprice, and preciousness. Now, the meaning of these extravagances does not at all lie in the contents of such behavior, but rather in its form of "being different," of standing out in a striking manner and thereby attracting attention. For many character types, ultimately the only means of saving for themselves some modicum of self-esteem and the sense of filling a position is indirect, through the awareness of others. In the same sense a seemingly insignificant factor is operating, the cumulative effects of which are, however, still noticeable. I refer to the brevity and scarcity of the inter-human contacts granted to the metropolitan man, as compared with social intercourse in the small town. The temptation to appear "to the point," to appear concentrated and strikingly characteristic, lies much closer to the individual in brief metropolitan contacts than in an atmosphere in which frequent and prolonged association assures the personality of an unambiguous image of himself in the eyes of the other.

The most profound reason, however, why the metropolis conduces to the urge for the most individual personal existence—no matter whether justified and successful—appears to me to be the following: the development of modern culture is characterized by the preponderance of what one may call the "objective spirit" over the "subjective spirit." This is to say, in language as well as in law, in the technique of production as well as in art, in science as well as in the objects of the domestic environment, embodied a sum of spirit. The individual in his intellectual development follows the growth of this spirit very imperfectly and at an ever increasing distance. If, for instance, we view the immense culture which for the last hundred years has been embodied in things and in knowledge, in institutions and in comforts, and if we compare all this with the cultural progress of the individual during the same period—at least in high status groups—a frightful disproportion in growth between the two becomes evident. Indeed, at some points we notice a retrogression in the culture of the individual with reference to spirituality, delicacy, and idealism. This discrepancy results essentially from the growing division of labor. For the division of labor demands from the individual an ever more one-sided accomplishment, and the greatest advance in a one-sided pursuit only too frequently means dearth to the personality of the individual. In any case, he can cope less and less with the overgrowth of objective culture. The individual is reduced to a negligible quantity, perhaps less in his consciousness than in his practice and in the totality of his obscure emotional states that are derived from this practice. The individual has become a mere cog in an enormous organization of things and powers which tear from his hands all progress, spirituality, and value in order to transform them from their subjective form into the form of a purely objective life. It needs merely to be pointed out that the metropolis is the genuine arena of this culture which outgrows all personal life. Here in buildings and educational institutions, in the wonders and comforts of space-conquering technology, in the formations of community life, and in the visible institutions of the state, is offered such an overwhelming fullness of crystallized and impersonalized spirit that the personality, so to speak, cannot maintain itself under its impact. On the one hand, life is made infinitely easy for the personality in that stimulations, interests, uses of time and consciousness are offered to it from all sides. They carry the person as if in a stream, and one needs hardly to swim for oneself. On the other hand, however, life is composed more and more of these impersonal contents and offerings which tend to displace the genuine personal colorations and incomparabilities. This results in the individual's summoning the utmost in uniqueness and particularization, in order to preserve his most personal core. He has to exaggerate this personal element in order to remain audible even to himself. The atrophy of individual culture through the hypertrophy of objective culture is one reason for the bitter hatred which the preachers of the most extreme individualism, above all Nietzsche, harbor against the metropolis. But it is, indeed, also a reason why these preachers are so passionately loved in the metropolis and why they appear to the metropolitan man as the prophets and saviors of his most unsatisfied yearnings.

If one asks for the historical position of these two forms of individualism which are nourished by the quantitative relation of the metropolis, namely, individual independence and the elaboration of individuality itself, then the metropolis assumes an entirely new rank order in the world history of the spirit. The eighteenth century found the individual in oppressive bonds which had become meaningless—bonds of a political, agrarian, guild, and religious character. They were restraints which, so to speak, forced upon man an unnatural form and outmoded, unjust inequalities. In this situation the cry for liberty and equality arose, the belief in the individual's full freedom of movement in all social and intellectual relationships. Freedom would at once permit the noble substance common to all to come to the fore, a substance which nature had deposited in every man and which society and history had only deformed. Besides this eighteenth-century ideal of liberalism, in the nineteenth century, through Goethe and Romanticism, on the one hand, and through the economic division of labor, on the other hand, another ideal arose: individuals liberated from historical bonds now wished to distinguish themselves from one another. The carrier of man's values is no longer the "general human being" in every individual, but rather man's qualitative uniqueness and irreplaceability. The external and internal history of our time takes its course within the struggle and in the changing entanglements of these two ways of defining the individual's role in the whole of society. It is the function of the metropolis to provide the arena for this struggle and its reconciliation. For the metropolis presents the peculiar conditions which are revealed to us as the opportunities and the stimuli for the development of both these ways of allocating roles to men. Therewith these conditions gain a unique place, pregnant with inestimable meanings for the development of psychic existence. The metropolis reveals itself as one of those great historical formations in which opposing streams which enclose life unfold, as well as join one another with equal right. However, in this process the currents of life, whether their individual phenomena touch us sympathetically or antipathetically, entirely transcend the sphere for which the judge's attitude is appropriate. Since such forces of life have grown into the roots and into the crown of the whole of the historical life in which we, in our fleeting existence, as a cell, belong only as a part, it is not our task either to accuse or to pardon, but only to understand.[1]

Note

1. The content of this [reading] by its very nature does not derive from a citable literature. Argument and elaboration of its major cultural-historical ideas are contained in my *Philosophie des Geldes* [The Philosophy of Money: München und Leipzig: Duncker and Humblot, 1900].

14

Urbanism as a Way of Life

Louis Wirth

I. The City and Contemporary Civilization

Just as the beginning of Western civilization is marked by the permanent settlement of formerly nomadic peoples in the Mediterranean basin, so the beginning of what is distinctively modern in our civilization is best signalized by the growth of great cities. Nowhere has mankind been farther removed from organic nature than under the conditions of life characteristic of great cities. The contemporary world no longer presents a picture of small isolated groups of human beings scattered over a vast territory, as Sumner described primitive society.[1] The distinctive feature of the mode of living of man in the modern age is his concentration into gigantic aggregations around which cluster lesser centers and from which radiate the ideas and practices that we call civilization.

The degree to which the contemporary world may be said to be "urban" is not fully or accurately measured by the proportion of the total population living in cities. The influences which cities exert upon the social life of man are greater than the ratio of the urban population would indicate, for the city is not only in ever larger degrees the dwelling-place and the workshop of modern man, but it is the initiating and controlling center of economic, political, and cultural life that has drawn the most remote parts of the world into its orbit and woven diverse areas, peoples, and activities into a cosmos.

The growth of cities and the urbanization of the world is one of the most impressive facts of modern times. Although it is impossible to state precisely what

"Urbanism as a Way of Life" by Louis Wirth from *American Journal of Sociology*, Vol. 44, July 1938, pp. 1–24. Reprinted by permission of The University of Chicago Press.

proportion of the estimated total world-population of approximately 1,800,000,000 is urban, 69.2 per cent of the total population of those countries that do distinguish between urban and rural areas is urban.[2] Considering the fact, moreover, that the world's population is very unevenly distributed and that the growth of cities is not very far advanced in some of the countries that have only recently been touched by industrialism, this average understates the extent to which urban concentration has proceeded in those countries where the impact of the industrial revolution has been more forceful and of less recent date. This shift from a rural to a predominantly urban society, which has taken place within the span of a single generation in such industrialized areas as the United States and Japan, has been accompanied by profound changes in virtually every phase of social life. It is these changes and their ramifications that invite the attention of the sociologist to the study of the differences between the rural and the urban mode of living. The pursuit of this interest is an indispensable prerequisite for the comprehension and possible mastery of some of the most crucial contemporary problems of social life since it is likely to furnish one of the most revealing perspectives for the understanding of the ongoing changes in human nature and the social order.[3]

Since the city is the product of growth rather than of instantaneous creation, it is to be expected that the influences which it exerts upon the modes of life should not be able to wipe out completely the previously dominant modes of human association. To a greater or lesser degree, therefore, our social life bears the imprint of an earlier folk society, the characteristic modes of settlement of which were the farm, the manor, and the village. This historic influence is reinforced by the circumstance that the population of the city itself is in large measure recruited from the countryside, where a mode of life reminiscent of this earlier form of existence persists. Hence we should not expect to find abrupt and discontinuous variation between urban and rural types of personality. The city and the country may be regarded as two poles in reference to one or the other of which all human settlements tend to arrange themselves. In viewing urban-industrial and rural-folk society as ideal types of communities, we may obtain a perspective for the analysis of the basic models of human association as they appear in contemporary civilization.

II. A Sociological Definition of the City

Despite the preponderant significance of the city in our civilization, however, our knowledge of the nature of urbanism and the process of urbanization is meager. Many attempts have indeed been made to isolate the distinguishing characteristics of urban life. Geographers, historians, economists, and political scientists have incorporated the points of view of their respective disciplines into diverse definitions of the city. While in no sense intended to supersede these, the formulation of a sociological approach to the city may incidentally serve to call attention to the interrelations between them by emphasizing the peculiar characteristics of the city as a particular form of human association. A sociologically significant definition of the city seeks to select those elements of urbanism which mark it as a distinctive mode of human group life.

The characterization of a community as urban on the basis of size alone is obviously arbitrary. It is difficult to defend the present census definition which designates a community of 2,500 and above as urban and all others as rural. The situation would be the same if the criterion were 4,000, 8,000, 10,000, 25,000, or 100,000 population, for although in the latter case we might feel that we were more nearly dealing with an urban aggregate than would be the case in communities of lesser size, no definition of urbanism can hope to be completely satisfying as long as numbers are regarded as the sole criterion. Moreover, it is not difficult to demonstrate that communities of less than the arbitrarily set number of inhabitants lying within the range of influence of metropolitan centers have greater claim to recognition as urban communities than do larger ones leading a more isolated existence in a predominantly rural area. Finally, it should be recognized that census definitions are unduly influenced by the fact that the city, statistically speaking, is always an administrative concept in that the corporate limits play a decisive role in delineating the urban area. Nowhere is this more clearly apparent than in the concentrations of population on the peripheries of great metropolitan centers which cross arbitrary administrative boundaries of city, county, state, and nation.

As long as we identify urbanism with the physical entity of the city, viewing it merely as rigidly delimited in space, and proceed as if urban attributes abruptly ceased to be manifested beyond an arbitrary boundary line, we are not likely to arrive at any adequate conception of urbanism as a mode of life. The technological developments in transportation and communication which virtually mark a new epoch in human history have accentuated the role of cities as dominant elements in our civilization and have enormously extended the urban mode of living beyond the confines of the city itself. The dominance of the city, especially of the great city, may be regarded as a consequence of the concentration in cities of industrial and commercial, financial and administrative facilities and activities, transportation and communication lines, and cultural and recreational equipment such as the press, radio stations, theaters, libraries, museums, concert halls, operas, hospitals, higher educational institutions, research and publishing centers, professional organizations, and religious and welfare institutions. Were it not for the attraction and suggestions that the city exerts through these instrumentalities upon the rural population, the differences between the rural and the urban modes of life would be even greater than they are. Urbanization no longer denotes merely the process by which persons are attracted to a place called the city and incorporated into its system of life. It refers also to that cumulative accentuation of the characteristics distinctive of the mode of life which is associated with the growth of cities, and finally to the changes in the direction of modes of life recognized as urban which are apparent among people, wherever they may be, who have come under the spell of the influences which the city exerts by virtue of the power of its institutions and personalities operating through the means of communication and transportation.

The shortcomings which attach to number of inhabitants as a criterion of urbanism apply for the most part to density of population as well. Whether we accept the density of 10,000 persons per square mile as Mark Jefferson[4] proposed, or 1,000, which Willcox[5] preferred to regard as the criterion of urban settlements, it is clear that unless density is correlated with significant social characteristics it can furnish only an arbitrary basis for differentiating urban from rural communities. Since our census enumerates the night rather than the day population of an area, the locale of the most intensive urban life—the city center—generally has low population density, and the industrial and commercial areas of the city, which contain the most characteristic economic activities underlying urban society, would scarcely anywhere be truly urban if density were literally interpreted as a mark of urbanism. Nevertheless, the fact that the urban community is distinguished by a large aggregation and relatively dense concentration of population can scarcely be left out of account in a definition of the city. But these criteria must be seen as relative to the general cultural context in which cities arise and exist and are sociologically relevant only in so far as they operate as conditioning factors in social life.

The same criticisms apply to such criteria as the occupation of the inhabitants, the existence of certain physical facilities, institutions, and forms of political organization. The question is not whether cities in our civilization or in others do exhibit these distinctive traits, but how potent they are in molding the character of social life into its specifically urban form. Nor in formulating a fertile definition can we afford to overlook the great variations between cities. By means of a typology of cities based upon size, location, age, and function, such as we have undertaken to establish in our recent report to the National Resources Committee,[6] we have found it feasible to array and classify urban communities ranging from struggling small towns to thriving world-metropolitan centers; from isolated trading-centers in the midst of agricultural regions to thriving world-ports and commercial and industrial conurbations. Such differences as these appear crucial because the social characteristics and influences of these different "cities" vary widely.

A serviceable definition of urbanism should not only denote the essential characteristics which all cities—at least those in our culture—have in common, but should lend itself to the discovery of their variations. An industrial city will differ significantly in social respects from a commercial, mining, fishing, resort, university, and capital city. A one-industry city will present different sets of social characteristics from a multi-industry city, as will an industrially balanced from an imbalanced city, a suburb from a satellite, a residential suburb from an industrial suburb, a city within a metropolitan region from one lying outside, an old city from a new one, southern city from a New England, a middle-western from a Pacific Coast city, a growing from a stable and from a dying city.

A sociological definition must obviously be inclusive enough to comprise whatever essential characteristics these different types of cities have in common as social entities, but it obviously cannot be so detailed as to take account of all the variations implicit in the manifold classes sketched above. Presumably some of the characteristics of cities are more significant in conditioning the nature of urban life than others, and we may expect the outstanding features of the urban-social scene to vary in accordance with size, density, and differences in the functional type of cities. Moreover, we may infer that rural life will bear the imprint of urbanism in the measure that through contact and communication it comes under the influence of cities. It may contribute to the clarity of the statements that follow to repeat that while the locus of urbanism as a mode of life is, of course, to be found characteristically in places which fulfil the requirements we shall set up as a definition of the city, urbanism is not confined to such localities but is manifest in varying degrees wherever the influences of the city reach.

While urbanism, or that complex of traits which makes up the characteristic mode of life in cities, and urbanization, which denotes the development and extensions of these factors, are thus not exclusively found in settlements which are cities in the physical and demographic sense, they do, nevertheless, find their most pronounced expression in such areas, especially in metropolitan cities. In formulating a definition of the city it is necessary to exercise caution in order to avoid identifying urbanism as a way of life with any specific locally or historically conditioned cultural influences which, while they may significantly affect the specific character of the community, are not the essential determinants of its character as a city.

It is particularly important to call attention to the danger of confusing urbanism with industrialism and modern capitalism. The rise of cities in the modern world is undoubtedly not independent of the emergence of modern power-driven machine technology, mass production, and capitalistic enterprise. But different as the cities of earlier epochs may have been by virtue of their development in a preindustrial and precapitalistic order from the great cities of today, they were, nevertheless, cities.

For sociological purposes a city may be defined as a relatively large, dense, and permanent settlement of socially heterogeneous individuals. On the basis of the postulates which this minimal definition suggests, a theory of urbanism may be formulated in the light of existing knowledge concerning social groups.

III. A Theory of Urbanism

In the rich literature on the city we look in vain for a theory of urbanism presenting in a systematic fashion the available knowledge concerning the city as a social entity. We do indeed have excellent formulations of theories on such special problems as the growth of the city viewed as a historical trend and as a recurrent process,[7] and we have a wealth of literature presenting insights of sociological relevance and empirical studies offering detailed information on a variety of particular aspects of urban life. But despite the multiplication of research and textbooks on the city, we do not as yet have a comprehensive body of compendent hypotheses which may be derived from a set of postulates implicitly contained in a sociological definition of the city, and from our general sociological knowledge which may be substantiated through empirical research. The closest approximations to a systematic theory of urbanism that we have are to be found in a penetrating essay, "Die Stadt," by Max Weber,[8] and a memorable paper by Robert E. Park on "The City: Suggestions for the Investigation of Human Behavior in the Urban Environment."[9]

But even these excellent contributions are far from constituting an ordered and coherent framework of theory upon which research might profitably proceed.

In the pages that follow we shall seek to set forth a limited number of identifying characteristics of the city. Given these characteristics we shall then indicate what consequences or further characteristics follow from them in the light of general sociological theory and empirical research. We hope in this manner to arrive at the essential propositions comprising a theory of urbanism. Some of these propositions can be supported by a considerable body of already available research materials; others may be accepted as hypotheses for which a certain amount of presumptive evidence exists, but for which more ample and exact verification would be required. At least such a procedure will, it is hoped, show what in the way of systematic knowledge of the city we now have and what are the crucial and fruitful hypotheses for future research.

The central problem of the sociologist of the city is to discover the forms of social action and organization that typically emerge in relatively permanent, compact settlements of large numbers of heterogeneous individuals. We must also infer that urbanism will assume its most characteristic and extreme form in the measure in which the conditions with which it is congruent are present. Thus the larger, the more densely populated, and the more heterogeneous a community, the more accentuated the characteristics associated with urbanism will be. It should be recognized, however, that in the social world institutions and practices may be accepted and continued for reasons other than those that originally brought them into existence, and that accordingly the urban mode of life may be perpetuated under conditions quite foreign to those necessary for its origin.

Some justification may be in order for the choice of the principal terms comprising our definition of the city. The attempt has been made to make it as inclusive and at the same time as denotative as possible without loading it with unnecessary assumptions. To say that large numbers are necessary to constitute a city means, of course, large numbers in relation to a restricted area or high density of settlement. There are, nevertheless, good reasons for treating large numbers and density as separate factors, since each may be connected with significantly different social consequences. Similarly the need for adding heterogeneity to numbers of population as a necessary and distinct criterion of urbanism might be questioned, since we should expect the range of differences to increase with numbers. In defense, it may be said that the city shows a kind and degree of heterogeneity of population which cannot be wholly accounted for by the law of large numbers or adequately represented by means of a normal distribution curve. Since the population of the city does not reproduce itself, it must recruit its migrants from other cities, the countryside, and—in this country until recently—from other countries. The city has thus historically been the melting-pot of races, peoples, and cultures, and a most favorable breeding-ground of new biological and cultural hybrids. It has not only tolerated but rewarded individual differences. It has brought together people from the ends of the earth *because* they are different and thus useful to one another, rather than because they are homogeneous and like-minded.[10]

There are a number of sociological propositions concerning the relationship between (*a*) numbers of population, (*b*) density of settlement, (*c*) heterogeneity of inhabitants and group life, which can be formulated on the basis of observation and research.

Size of the Population Aggregate

Ever since Aristotle's *Politics*,[11] it has been recognized that increasing the number of inhabitants in a settlement beyond a certain limit will affect the relationships between them and the character of the city. Large numbers involve, as has been pointed out, a greater range of individual variation. Furthermore, the greater the number of individuals participating in a process of interaction, the greater is the *potential* differentiation between them. The personal traits, the occupations, the cultural life, and the ideas of the members of an urban community may, therefore, be expected to range between more widely separated poles than those of rural inhabitants.

That such variations should give rise to the spatial segregation of individuals according to color, ethnic heritage, economic and social status, tastes and preferences, may readily be inferred. The bonds of kinship, of neighborliness, and the sentiments arising out of living together for generations under a common folk tradition are likely to be absent or, at best, relatively weak in an aggregate the members of which have such diverse origins and backgrounds. Under such circumstances competition and formal control mechanisms furnish the substitutes for the bonds of solidarity that are relied upon to hold a folk society together.

Increase in the number of inhabitants of a community beyond a few hundred is bound to limit the possibility of each member of the community knowing all the others personally. Max Weber, in recognizing the social significance of this fact, pointed out that from a sociological point of view large numbers of inhabitants and density of settlement mean that the personal mutual acquaintanceship between the inhabitants which ordinarily inheres in a neighborhood is lacking.[12] The increase in numbers thus involves a changed character of the social relationships. As Simmel points out:

> [If] the unceasing external contact of numbers of persons in the city should be met by the same number of inner reactions as in the small town, in which one knows almost every person he meets and to each of whom he has a positive relationship, one would be completely atomized internally and would fall into an unthinkable mental condition.[13]

The multiplication of persons in a state of interaction under conditions which make their contact as full personalities impossible produces that segmentalization of human relationships which has sometimes been seized upon by students of the mental life of the cities as an explanation for the "schizoid" character of urban personality. This is not to say that the urban inhabitants have fewer acquaintances than rural inhabitants, for the reverse may actually be true; it means rather that in relation to the number of people whom they see and with whom they rub elbows in the course of daily life, they know a smaller proportion, and of these they have less intensive knowledge.

Characteristically, urbanites meet one another in highly segmental roles. They are, to be sure, dependent upon more people for the satisfactions of their life-needs than are rural people and thus are associated with a greater number of organized groups, but they are less dependent upon particular persons, and their dependence upon others is confined to a highly fractionalized aspect of the other's round of activity. This is essentially what is meant by saying that the city is characterized by secondary rather than primary contacts. The contacts of the city may indeed be face to face, but they are nevertheless impersonal, superficial, transitory, and segmental. The reserve, the indifference, and the blasé outlook which urbanites manifest in their relationships may thus be regarded as devices for immunizing themselves against the personal claims and expectations of others.

The superficiality, the anonymity, and the transitory character of urban-social relations make intelligible, also, the sophistication and the rationality generally ascribed to city-dwellers. Our acquaintances tend to stand in a relationship of utility to us in the sense that the role which each one plays in our life is overwhelmingly regarded as a means for the achievement of our own ends. Whereas, therefore, the individual gains, on the one hand, a certain degree of emancipation or freedom from the personal and emotional controls of intimate groups, he loses, on the other hand, the spontaneous self-expression, the morale, and the sense of participation that comes with living in an integrated society. This constitutes essentially the state of *anomie* or the social void to which Durkheim alludes in attempting to account for the various forms of social disorganization in technological society.

The segmental character and utilitarian accent of interpersonal relations in the city find their institutional expression in the proliferation of specialized tasks which we see in their most developed form in the professions. The operations of the pecuniary nexus leads to predatory relationships, which tend to obstruct the efficient functioning of the social order unless checked by professional codes and occupational etiquette. The premium put upon utility and efficiency suggests the adaptability of the corporate device for the organization of enterprises in which individuals can engage only in groups. The advantage that the corporation has over the individual entrepreneur and the partnership in the urban-industrial world derives not only from the possibility it affords of centralizing the resources of thousands of individuals or from the legal privilege of limited liability and perpetual succession, but from the fact that the corporation has no soul.

The specialization of individuals, particularly in their occupations, can proceed only, as Adam Smith pointed out, upon the basis of an enlarged market, which in turn accentuates the division of labor. This enlarged market is only in part supplied by the city's hinterland; in large measure it is found among the large numbers that the city itself contains. The dominance of the city over the surrounding hinterland becomes explicable in terms of the division of labor which urban life occasions and promotes. The extreme degree of interdependence and the unstable equilibrium of urban life are closely associated with the division of labor and the specialization of occupations. This interdependence and instability is increased by the tendency of each city to specialize in those functions in which it has the greatest advantage.

In a community composed of a larger number of individuals than can know one another intimately and can be assembled in one spot, it becomes necessary to communicate through indirect mediums and to articulate individual interests by a process of delegation. Typically in the city, interests are made effective through representation. The individual counts for little, but the voice of the representative is heard with a deference roughly proportional to the numbers for whom he speaks.

While this characterization of urbanism, in so far as it derives from large numbers, does not by any means exhaust the sociological inferences that might be drawn from our knowledge of the relationship of the size of a group to the characteristic behavior of the members, for the sake of brevity the assertions made may serve to exemplify the sort of propositions that might be developed.

Density

As in the case of numbers, so in the case of concentration in limited space, certain consequences of relevance in sociological analysis of the city emerge. Of these only a few can be indicated.

As Darwin pointed out for flora and fauna and as Durkheim[14] noted in the case of human societies, an increase in numbers when area is held constant (i.e., an increase in density) tends to produce differentiation and specialization, since only in this way can the area support increased numbers. Density thus reinforces the effect of numbers in diversifying men and their activities and in increasing the complexity of the social structure.

On the subjective side, as Simmel has suggested, the close physical contact of numerous individuals necessarily produces a shift in the mediums through which we orient ourselves to the urban milieu, especially to our fellow-men. Typically, our physical contacts are close but our social contacts are distant. The urban world puts a premium on visual recognition. We see the uniform which denotes the role of the functionaries and are oblivious to the personal eccentricities that are hidden behind the uniform. We tend to acquire and develop a sensitivity to a world of artefacts and become progressively farther removed from the world of nature.

We are exposed to glaring contrasts between splendor and squalor, between riches and poverty, intelligence and ignorance, order and chaos. The competition for space is great, so that each area generally tends to be put to the use which yields the greatest economic return. Place of work tends to become dissociated from place of residence, for the proximity of industrial and commercial establishments makes an area both economically and socially undesirable for residential purposes.

Density, land values, rentals, accessibility, healthfulness, prestige, aesthetic consideration, absence of nuisances such as noise, smoke, and dirt determine the desirability of various areas of the city as places of settlement for different sections of the population. Place and nature of work, income, racial and ethnic characteristics, social status, custom, habit, taste, preference, and prejudice are among the significant factors in accordance with which the urban population is selected and distributed into more or less distinct settlements. Diverse population elements inhabiting a compact settlement thus tend to become segregated from one another in the degree in which their requirements and modes of life are incompatible with one another and in the measure in which they are antagonistic to one another. Similarly, persons of homogeneous status and needs unwittingly drift into, consciously select, or are forced by circumstances into, the same area. The different parts of the city thus acquire specialized functions. The city consequently tends to resemble a mosaic of social worlds in which the transition from one to the other is abrupt. The juxtaposition of divergent personalities and modes of life tends to produce a relativistic perspective and a sense of toleration of differences which may be regarded as prerequisites for rationality and which lead toward the secularization of life.[15]

The close living together and working together of individuals who have no sentimental and emotional ties foster a spirit of competition, aggrandizement, and mutual exploitation. To counteract irresponsibility and potential disorder, formal controls tend to be resorted to. Without rigid adherence to predictable routines a large compact society would scarcely be able to maintain itself. The clock and the traffic signal are symbolic of the basis of our social order in the urban world. Frequent close physical contact, coupled with great social distance, accentuates the reserve of unattached individuals toward one another and, unless compensated for by other opportunities for response, gives rise to loneliness. The necessary frequent movement of great numbers of individuals in a congested habitat gives occasion to friction and irritation. Nervous tensions which derive from such personal frustrations are accentuated by the rapid tempo and the complicated technology under which life in dense areas must be lived.

Heterogeneity

The social interaction among such a variety of personality types in the urban milieu tends to break down the rigidity of caste lines and to complicate the class structure, and thus induces a more ramified and differentiated framework of social stratification than is found in more integrated societies. The heightened mobility of the individual, which brings him within the range of stimulation by a great number of diverse individuals and subjects him to fluctuating status in the differentiated social groups that compose the social structure of the city, tends toward the acceptance of instability and insecurity in the world at large as a norm. This fact helps to account, too, for the sophistication and cosmopolitanism of the urbanite. No single group has the undivided allegiance of the individual. The groups with which he is affiliated do not lend themselves readily to a simple hierarchical arrangement. By virtue of his different interests arising out of different aspects of social life, the individual acquires membership in widely divergent groups, each of which functions only with reference to a single segment of his personality. Nor do these groups easily permit of a concentric arrangement so that the narrower ones fall within the circumference of the more inclusive ones, as is more likely to be the case in the rural community or in primitive societies. Rather the groups with which the person typically is affiliated are tangential to each other or intersect in highly variable fashion.

Partly as a result of the physical footlooseness of the population and partly as a result of their social mobility, the turnover in group membership generally is rapid. Place of residence, place and character of employment, income and interests fluctuate, and the task of holding organizations together and maintaining and promoting intimate and lasting acquaintanceship between the members is difficult. This applies strikingly to the local areas within the city into which persons become segregated more by virtue of differences in race, language, income, and social status, than through choice or positive attraction to people like themselves. Overwhelmingly the city-dweller is not a home-owner, and since a transitory habitat does not generate binding traditions and sentiments, only rarely is he truly a neighbor. There is little opportunity for the individual to obtain a conception of the city as a whole or to survey his place in the total scheme. Consequently he finds it difficult to determine what is to his own "best interests" and to decide between the issues and leaders presented to him by the agencies of mass suggestion. Individuals who are thus detached from the organized bodies which integrate society comprise the fluid masses that make collective behavior in the urban community so unpredictable and hence so problematical.

Although the city, through the recruitment of variant types to perform its diverse tasks and the accentuation of their uniqueness through competition and the premium upon eccentricity, novelty, efficient performance, and inventiveness, produces a highly differentiated population, it also exercises a leveling influence. Wherever large numbers of differently constituted individuals congregate, the process of depersonalization also enters. This leveling tendency inheres in part in the economic basis of the city. The development of large cities, at least in the modern age, was largely dependent upon the concentrative force of steam. The rise of the factory made possible mass production for an impersonal market. The fullest exploitation of the possibilities of the division of labor and mass production, however, is possible only with standardization of processes and products. A money economy goes hand in hand with such a system of production. Progressively as cities have developed upon a background of this system of production, the pecuniary nexus which implies the purchasability of services and things has displaced personal relations as the basis of association. Individuality under these circumstances must be replaced by categories. When large numbers have to make common use of facilities and institutions, an arrangement must be made to adjust the facilities and institutions to the needs of the average person rather than to those of particular individuals. The services of the public utilities, of the recreational, educational, and cultural institutions must be adjusted to mass requirements. Similarly, the cultural institutions, such as the schools, the movies, the radio, and the newspapers, by virtue of their mass clientele, must necessarily operate as leveling influences. The political process as it appears in urban life could not be understood without taking account of the mass appeals made through modern propaganda techniques. If the individual would participate at all in the social, political, and economic life of the city, he must subordinate some of his individuality to the demands of the larger community and in that measure immerse himself in mass movements.

IV. The Relation between a Theory of Urbanism and Sociological Research

By means of a body of theory such as that illustratively sketched above, the complicated and many-sided phenomena of urbanism may be analyzed in terms of a limited number of basic categories. The sociological approach to the city thus acquires an essential unity and coherence enabling the empirical investigator not merely to focus more distinctly upon the problems and processes that properly fall in his province but also to treat his subject matter in a more integrated and systematic fashion. A few typical findings of empirical research in the field of urbanism, with special reference to the United States, may be indicated to substantiate the theoretical propositions set forth in the preceding pages, and some of the crucial problems for further study may be outlined.

On the basis of the three variables, number, density of settlement, and degree of heterogeneity, of the urban population, it appears possible to explain the characteristics of urban life and to account for the differences between cities of various sizes and types.

Urbanism as a characteristic mode of life may be approached empirically from three interrelated perspectives: (1) as a physical structure comprising a population base, a technology, and an ecological order; (2) as a system of social organization involving a characteristic social structure, a series of social institutions, and a typical pattern of social relationships; and (3) as a set of attitudes and ideas, and a constellation of personalities engaging in typical forms of collective behavior and subject to characteristic mechanisms of social control.

Urbanism in Ecological Perspective

Since in the case of physical structure and ecological processes we are able to operate with fairly objective indices, it becomes possible to arrive at quite precise and generally quantitative results. The dominance of the city over its hinterland becomes explicable through the functional characteristics of the city which derive in large measure from the effect of numbers and density. Many of the technical facilities and the skills and organizations to which urban life gives rise can grow and prosper only in cities where the demand is sufficiently great. The nature and scope of the services rendered by these organizations and institutions and the advantage which they enjoy over the less developed facilities of smaller towns enhances the dominance of the city and the dependence of ever wider regions upon the central metropolis.

The urban-population composition shows the operation of selective and differentiating factors. Cities contain a larger proportion of persons in the prime of life than rural areas which contain more old and very young people. In this, as in so many other respects, the larger the city the more this specific characteristic of urbanism is apparent. With the exception of the largest cities, which have attracted the bulk of the foreign-born males, and a few other special types of cities, women predominate numerically over men. The heterogeneity of the urban population is further indicated along racial and ethnic lines. The foreign born and their children constitute nearly two-thirds of all the inhabitants of cities of one million and over. Their proportion in the urban population declines as the size of the city decreases, until in the rural areas they comprise only about one-sixth of the total population. The larger cities similarly have attracted more Negroes and other racial groups than have the smaller communities. Considering that age, sex, race, and ethnic origin are associated with other factors such as occupation and interest, it becomes clear that one major characteristic of the urban-dweller is his dissimilarity from his fellows. Never before have such large masses of people of diverse traits as we find in our cities been thrown together into such close physical contact as in the great cities of America. Cities generally, and American cities in particular, comprise a motley of peoples and cultures, of highly differentiated modes of life between which there often is only the faintest communication, the greatest indifference and the broadest tolerance, occasionally bitter strife, but always the sharpest contrast.

The failure of the urban population to reproduce itself appears to be a biological consequence of a combination of factors in the complex of urban life, and the decline in the birth-rate generally may be regarded as one of the most significant signs of the urbanization of the Western world. While the proportion of deaths in cities is slightly greater than in the country, the outstanding difference between the failure of present-day cities to maintain their population and that of cities of the past is that in former times it was due to the exceedingly high death-rates in cities, whereas today, since cities have become more livable from a health standpoint, it is due to low birth-rates. These biological characteristics of the urban population are significant sociologically, not merely because they reflect the urban mode of existence but also because they condition the growth and future dominance of cities and their basic social organization. Since cities are the consumers rather than the producers of men, the value of human life and the social estimation of the personality will not be unaffected by the balance between births and deaths. The pattern of land use, of land values, rentals, and ownership, the nature and functioning of the physical structures, of housing, of transportation and communication facilities, of public utilities—these and many other phases of the physical mechanism of the city are not isolated phenomena unrelated to the city as a social entity, but are affected by and affect the urban mode of life.

Urbanism as a Form of Social Organization

The distinctive features of the urban mode of life have often been described sociologically as consisting of the substitution of secondary for primary contacts, the weakening of bonds of kinship, and the declining social significance of the family, the disappearance of the neighborhood, and the undermining of the traditional basis of social solidarity. All these phenomena can be substantially verified through objective indices. Thus, for instance, the low and declining urban-reproduction rates suggest that the city is not conducive to the traditional type of family life, including the rearing of children and the maintenance of the home as the locus of a whole round of vital activities. The transfer of industrial, educational, and recreational activities to specialized institutions outside the home has deprived the family of some of its most characteristic historical functions. In cities mothers are more likely to be employed, lodgers are more frequently part of the household, marriage tends to be postponed, and the proportion of single and unattached people is greater. Families are smaller and more frequently without children than in the country. The family as a unit of social life is emancipated from the larger kinship group characteristic of the country, and the individual members pursue their own diverging interests in their vocational, educational, religious, recreational, and political life.

Such functions as the maintenance of health, the methods of alleviating the hardships associated with personal and social insecurity, the provisions for education, recreation, and cultural advancement have given rise to highly specialized institutions on a community-wide, statewide, or even national basis. The same factors which have brought about greater personal insecurity also underlie the wider contrasts between individuals to be found in the urban world. While the city has broken down the rigid caste lines of pre-industrial society, it has sharpened and differentiated income and status groups. Generally, a larger proportion of the adult-urban population is gainfully employed than is the case with the adult-rural population. The white-collar class, comprising those employed in trade, in clerical, and in professional work, are proportionately more numerous in large cities and in metropolitan centers and in smaller towns than in the country.

On the whole, the city discourages an economic life in which the individual in time of crisis has a basis of subsistence to fall back upon, and it discourages self-employment. While incomes of city people are on the average higher than those of country people, the cost of living seems to be higher in the larger cities. Home ownership involves greater burdens and is rarer. Rents are higher and absorb a larger proportion of the income. Although the urban-dweller has the benefit of many communal services, he spends a large proportion of his income for such items as recreation and advancement and a smaller proportion for food. What the communal services do not furnish the urbanite must purchase, and there is virtually no human need which has remained unexploited by commercialism. Catering to thrills and furnishing means of escape from drudgery, monotony, and routine thus become one of the major functions of urban recreation, which at its best furnishes means for creative self-expression and spontaneous group association, but which more typically in the urban world results in passive spectatorism on the one hand, or sensational record-smashing feats on the other.

Being reduced to a stage of virtual impotence as an individual, the urbanite is bound to exert himself by joining with others of similar interest into organized groups to obtain his ends. This results in the enormous multiplication of voluntary organizations directed toward as great a variety of objectives as there are human needs and interests. While on the one hand the traditional ties of human association are weakened, urban existence involves a much greater degree of interdependence between man and man and a more complicated, fragile, and volatile form of mutual interrelations over many phases of which the individual as such can exert scarcely any control. Frequently there is only the most tenuous relationship between the economic position or other basic factors that determine the individual's existence in the urban world and the voluntary groups with which he is affiliated. While in a primitive and in a rural society it is generally possible to predict on the basis of a few known factors who will belong to what and who will associate with whom in almost every relationship of life, in the city we can only project the general pattern of group formation and affiliation, and this pattern will display many incongruities and contradictions.

Urban Personality and Collective Behavior

It is largely through the activities of the voluntary groups, be their objectives economic, political, educational, religious, recreational, or cultural, that the urbanite expresses and develops his personality, acquires status, and is able to carry on the round of activities that constitute his life-career. It may easily be inferred, however, that the organizational framework which these highly differentiated functions call into being does not of itself insure the consistency and integrity of the personalities whose interests it enlists. Personal disorganization, mental breakdown, suicide, delinquency, crime, corruption, and disorder might be expected under these circumstances to be more prevalent in the urban than in the rural community. This has been confirmed in so far as comparable indices are available; but the mechanisms underlying these phenomena require further analysis.

Since for most group purposes it is impossible in the city to appeal individually to the large number of discrete and differentiated individuals, and since it is only through the organizations to which men belong that their interests and resources can be enlisted for a collective cause, it may be inferred that social control in the city should typically proceed through formally organized groups. It follows, too, that the masses of men in the city are subject to manipulation by symbols and stereotypes managed by individuals working from afar or operating invisibly behind the scenes through their control of the instruments of communication. Self-government either in the economic, the political, or the cultural realm is under these circumstances reduced to a mere figure of speech or, at best, is subject to the unstable equilibrium of pressure groups. In view of the ineffectiveness of actual kinship ties we create fictional kinship groups. In the face of the disappearance of the territorial unit as a basis of social solidarity we create interest units. Meanwhile the city as a community resolves itself into a series of tenuous segmental relationships superimposed upon a territorial base with a definite center but without a definite periphery and upon a division of labor which far transcends the immediate locality and is world-wide in scope. The larger the number of persons in a state of interaction with one another the lower is the level of communication and the greater is the tendency for communication to proceed on an elementary level, i.e., on the basis of those things which are assumed to be common or to be of interest to all.

It is obviously, therefore, to the emerging trends in the communication system and to the production and distribution technology that has come into existence with modern civilization that we must look for the symptoms which will indicate the probable future development of urbanism as a mode of social life. The direction of the ongoing changes in urbanism will for good or ill transform not only the city but the world. Some of the more basic of these factors and processes and the possibilities of their direction and control invite further detailed study.

It is only in so far as the sociologist has a clear conception of the city as a social entity and a workable theory of urbanism that he can hope to develop a unified body of reliable knowledge, which what passes as "urban sociology" is certainly not at the present time. By taking his point of departure from a theory of urbanism such as that sketched in the foregoing pages to be elaborated, tested, and revised in the light of further analysis and empirical research, it is to be hoped that the criteria of relevance and validity of factual data can be determined. The miscellaneous assortment of disconnected information which has hitherto found its way into sociological treatises on the city may thus be sifted and incorporated into a coherent body of knowledge. Incidentally, only by means of some such theory will the sociologist escape the futile practice of voicing in the name of sociological science a variety of often unsupportable judgments concerning such problems as poverty, housing, city-planning, sanitation, municipal administration, policing, marketing, transportation, and other technical issues. While the sociologist cannot solve any of these practical problems—at least not by himself—he may, if he discovers his proper function, have an important contribution to make to their comprehension and solution. The prospects for doing this are brightest through a general, theoretical, rather than through an *ad hoc* approach.

Notes

1. William Graham Sumner, *Folkways* (Boston, 1906), p. 12.

2. S. V. Pearson, *The Growth and Distribution of Population* (New York, 1935), p. 211.

3. Whereas rural life in the United States has for a long time been a subject of considerable interest on the part of governmental bureaus, the most notable case of a comprehensive report being that submitted by the Country Life Commission to President Theodore Roosevelt in 1909, it is worthy of note that no equally comprehensive official inquiry into urban life was undertaken until the establishment of a Research Committee on Urbanism of the National Resources Committee. (Cf. *Our Cities: Their Role in the National Economy* [Washington: Government Printing office, 1937].)

4. "The Anthropogeography of Some Great Cities," *Bull. American Geographical Society*, XLI (1909), 537–66.

5. Walter F. Willcox, "A Definition of 'City' in Terms of Density," in E. W. Burgess, *The Urban Community* (Chicago, 1926), p. 119.

6. *Op. cit.*, p. 8.

7. See Robert E. Park, Ernest W. Burgess, et al., *The City* (Chicago, 1925), esp. chaps. ii and iii; Werner Sombart, "Städtische Siedlung, Stadt," *Handwörterbuch der Soziogie*, ed. Alfred Vierkandt (Stuttgart, 1931). . . .

8. *Wirlschaft und Gesllschaft* (Tübingen, 1925), Part II, chap. viii, pp. 514–601.

9. Park, Burgess, *et al., op. cit.*, chap. i.

10. The justification for including the term "permanent" in the definition may appear necessary. Our failure to give an extensive justification for this qualifying mark of the urban rests on the obvious fact that unless human settlements take a fairly permanent root in a locality the

characteristics of urban life cannot arise, and conversely the living together of large numbers of heterogeneous individuals under dense conditions is not possible without the development of a more or less technological structure.

11. See esp. vii. 4. 4–14. Translated by B. Jowett, from which the following may be quoted:

"To the size of states there is a limit, as there is to other things, plants, animals, implements; for none of these retain their natural power when they are too large or too small, but they either wholly lose their nature, or are spoiled. . . . [A] state when composed of too few is not as a state ought to be, self-sufficing; when of too many, though self-sufficing in all mere necessaries, it is a nation and not a state, being almost incapable of constitutional government. For who can be the general of such a vast multitude, or who the herald, unless he have the voice of a Stentor?

"A state then only begins to exist when it has attained a population sufficient for a good life in the political community: it may indeed somewhat exceed this number. But, as I was saying, there must be a limit. What should be the limit will be easily ascertained by experience. For both governors and governed have duties to perform; the special functions of a governor are to command and to judge. But if the citizens of a state are to judge and to distribute offices according to merit, then they must know each other's characters; where they do not possess this knowledge, both the election to offices and the decision of lawsuits will go wrong. When the population is very large they are manifestly settled at haphazard, which clearly ought not to be. Besides, in an overpopulous state foreigners and metics will readily acquire the rights of citizens, for who will find them out? Clearly, then, the best limit of the population of a state is the largest number which suffices for the purposes of life, and can be taken in at a single view. Enough concerning the size of a city."

12. *Op. cit.*, p. 514.

13. Georg Simmel, "Die Grossstädte und das Geistesleben," *Die Grossstadt*, ed. Theodor Petermann (Dresden, 1903), pp. 187–206.

14. E. Durkheim, *De la division du travail social* (Paris, 1932), p. 248.

15. The extent to which the segregation of the population into distinct ecological and cultural areas and the resulting social attitude of tolerance, rationality, and secular mentality are functions of density as distinguished from heterogeneity is difficult to determine. Most likely we are dealing here with phenomena which are consequences of the simultaneous operation of both factors.

15

Human Ecology

Robert Ezra Park

I. The Web of Life

Naturalists of the last century were greatly intrigued by their observation of the interrelations and co-ordinations, within the realm of animate nature, of the numerous, divergent, and widely scattered species. Their successors, the botanists, and zoölogists of the present day, have turned their attention to more specific inquiries, and the "realm of nature," like the concept of evolution, has come to be for them a notion remote and speculative.

The "web of life," in which all living organisms, plants and animals alike, are bound together in a vast system of interlinked and interdependent lives, is nevertheless, as J. Arthur Thompson puts it, "one of the fundamental biological concepts" and is "as characteristically Darwinian as the struggle for existence."[1]

Darwin's famous instance of the cats and the clover is the classic illustration of this interdependence. He found, he explains, that humblebees were almost indispensable to the fertilization of the heartsease, since other bees do not visit this flower. The same thing is true with some kinds of clover. Humblebees alone visit red clover, as other bees cannot reach the nectar. The inference is that if the humblebees became extinct or very rare in England, the heartsease and red clover would become very rare, or wholly disappear. However, the number of humblebees in any district depends in a great measure on the number of field mice, which destroy their combs and nests. It is estimated that more than two-thirds of them are thus destroyed all over England. Near villages and small towns the nests of humblebees are more numerous than elsewhere and this is attributed to the number of cats that destroy the mice.[2] Thus next year's crop of purple clover in certain parts of Eng-

"Human Ecology" by Robert Ezra Park from *American Journal of Sociology*, Vol. 42, July 1936, pp. 1–15. Reprinted by permission of The University of Chicago Press.

land depends on the number of humblebees in the district; the number of humble-bees depends upon the number of field mice, the number of field mice upon the number and the enterprise of the cats, and the number of cats—as someone has added—depends on the number of old maids and others in neighboring villages who keep cats.

These large food chains, as they are called, each link of which eats the other, have as their logical prototype the familiar nursery rhyme, "The House that Jack Built." You recall:

> *The cow with the crumpled horn,*
> *That tossed the dog,*
> *That worried the cat,*
> *That killed the rat,*
> *That ate the malt*
> *That lay in the house that Jack built.*

Darwin and the naturalists of his day were particularly interested in observing and recording these curious illustrations of the mutual adaptation and correlation of plants and animals, because they seemed to throw light on the origin of the species. Both the species and their mutual interdependence, within a common habitat, seem to be a product of the same Darwinian struggle for existence.

It is interesting to note that it was the application to organic life of a sociological principle—the principle, namely, of "competitive co-operation"—that gave Darwin the first clue to the formulation of his theory of evolution.

"He projected on organic life," says Thompson, "a sociological idea," and "thus vindicated the relevancy and utility of a sociological idea within the biological realm."[3]

The active principle in the ordering and regulating of life within the realm of animate nature is, as Darwin described it, "the struggle for existence." By this means the numbers of living organisms are regulated, their distribution controlled, and the balance of nature maintained. Finally, it is by means of this elementary form of competition that the existing species, the survivors in the struggle, find their niches in the physical environment and in the existing correlation or division of labor between the different species. J. Arthur Thompson makes an impressive statement of the matter in his *System of Animate Nature*. He says:

> The hosts of living organisms are not . . . isolated creatures, for every thread of life is intertwined with others in a complex web. . . . Flowers and insects are fitted to one another as hand to glove. Cats have to do with the plague in India as well as with the clover crop at home. . . . *Just as there is a correlation of organs in the body, so there is a correlation of organisms in the world of life.* When we learn something of the intricate give and take, supply and demand, action and reaction between plants and animals, between flowers and insects, between herbivores and carnivores, and between other conflicting yet correlated interests, we begin to get a glimpse of a vast self-regulating organization.

These manifestations of a living, changing, but persistent order among competing organisms—organisms embodying "conflicting yet correlated interests"—seem to be the basis for the conception of a social order transcending the individual species, and of a society based on a biotic rather than a cultural basis, a conception later developed by the plant and animal ecologists.

In recent years the plant geographers have been the first to revive something of the earlier field naturalists' interest in the interrelations of species. Haeckel, in 1878, was the first to give to these studies a name, "ecology," and by so doing gave them the character of a distinct and separate science, a science which Thompson describes as "the new natural history."[4]

The interrelation and interdependence of the species are naturally more obvious and more intimate within the common habitat than elsewhere. Furthermore, as correlations have multiplied and competition has decreased, in consequence of mutual adaptations of the competing species, the habitat and habitants have tended to assume the character of a more or less completely closed system.

Within the limits of this system the individual units of the population are involved in a process of competitive co-operation, which has given to their interrelations the character of a natural economy. To such a habitat and its inhabitants—whether plant, animal, or human—the ecologists have applied the term "community."

The essential characteristics of a community, so conceived, are those of: (1) a population, territorially organized, (2) more or less completely rooted in the soil it occupies, (3) its individual units living in a relationship of mutual interdependence that is symbiotic rather than societal, in the sense in which that term applies to human beings.

These symbiotic societies are not merely unorganized assemblages of plants and animals which happen to live together in the same habitat. On the contrary, they are interrelated in the most complex manner. Every community has something of the character of an organic unit. It has a more or less definite structure and it has "a life history in which juvenile, adult and senile phases can be observed."[5] If it is an organism, it is one of the organs which are other organisms. It is, to use Spencer's phrase, a superorganism.

What more than anything else gives the symbiotic community the character of an organism is the fact that it possesses a mechanism (competition) for (1) regulating the numbers, and (2) preserving the balance between the competing species of which it is composed. It is by maintaining this biotic balance that the community preserves its identity and integrity as an individual unit through the changes and the vicissitudes to which it is subject in the course of its progress from the earlier to the later phases of its existence.

II. The Balance of Nature

The balance of nature, as plant and animal ecologists have conceived it, seems to be largely a question of numbers. When the pressure of population upon the natural resources of the habitat reaches a certain degree of intensity, something invariably happens. In the one case the population may swarm and relieve the pressure of population by migration. In another, where the disequilibrium between population and natural resources is the result of some change, sudden or gradual, in the conditions of life, the pre-existing correlation of the species may be totally destroyed.

Change may be brought about by a famine, an epidemic, or an invasion of the habitat by some alien species. Such an invasion may result in a rapid increase of the invading population and a sudden decline in the numbers if not the destruction of the original population. Change of some sort is continuous, although the rate and pace of change sometimes vary greatly. Charles Elton says:

> The impression of anyone who has studied animal numbers in the field is that the "balance of nature" hardly exists, except in the minds of scientists. It seems that animal numbers are always tending to settle down into a smooth and harmonious working mechanism, but something always happens before this happy state is reached.[6]

Under ordinary circumstances, such minor fluctuations in the biotic balance as occur are mediated and absorbed without profoundly disturbing the existing equilibrium and routine of life. When, on the other hand, some sudden and catastrophic change occurs—it may be a war, a famine, or pestilence—it upsets the biotic balance, breaks "the cake of custom," and releases energies up to that time held in check. A series of rapid and even violent changes may ensue which profoundly alter the existing organization of communal life and give a new direction to the future course of events.

The advent of the boll weevil in the southern cotton fields is a minor instance but illustrates the principle. The boll weevil crossed the Rio Grande at Brownsville in the summer of 1892. By 1894 the pest had spread to a dozen counties in Texas, bringing destruction to the cotton and great losses to the planters. From that point it advanced, with every recurring season, until by 1928 it had covered practically all the cotton producing area in the United States. Its progress took the form of a territorial succession. The consequences to agriculture were catastrophic but not wholly for the worse, since they served to give an impulse to changes in the organization of the industry long overdue. It also hastened the northward migration of the Negro tenant farmer.

The case of the boll weevil is typical. In this mobile modern world, where space and time have been measurably abolished, not men only but all the minor organisms (including the microbes) seem to be, as never before, in motion. Commerce, in progressively destroying the isolation upon which the ancient order of nature rested, has intensified the struggle for existence over an ever widening area of the habitable world. Out of this struggle a new equilibrium and a new system of animate nature, the new biotic basis of the new world-society, is emerging.

It is, as Elton remarks, the "fluctuation of numbers" and "the failure" from time to time "of the regulatory mechanism of animal increase" which ordinarily interrupts the established routine, and in so doing releases a new cycle of change. In regard to these fluctuations in numbers Elton says:

These failures of the regulating mechanism of animal increase—are they caused by (1) internal changes, after the manner of an alarm clock which suddenly goes off, or the boilers of an engine blowing up, or are they caused by some factors in the outer environment—weather, vegetation, or something like that?[7]

and he adds:

It appears that they are due to both but that the latter (external factor) is the more important of the two, and usually plays the leading rôle.

The conditions which affect and control the movements and numbers of populations are more complex in human societies than in plant and animal communities, but they exhibit extraordinary similarities.

The boll weevil, moving out of its ancient habitat in the central Mexican plateau and into the virgin territory of the southern cotton plantations, incidentally multiplying its population to the limit of the territories and resources, is not unlike the Boers of Cape Colony, South Africa, trekking out into the high veldt of the central South African plateau and filling it, within a period of one hundred years, with a population of their own descendants.

Competition operates in the human (as it does in the plant and animal) community to bring about and restore the communal equilibrium, when, either by the advent of some intrusive factor from without or in the normal course of its life-history, that equilibrium is disturbed.

Thus every crisis that initiates a period of rapid change, during which competition is intensified, moves over finally into a period of more or less stable equilibrium and a new division of labor. In this manner competition brings about a condition in which competition is superseded by co-operation.

It is when, and to the extent that, competition declines that the kind of order which we call society may be said to exist. In short, society, from the ecological point of view, and in so far as it is a territorial unit, is just the area within which biotic competition has declined and the struggle for existence has assumed higher and more sublimated forms.

III. Competition, Dominance and Succession

There are other and less obvious ways in which competition exercises control over the relations of individuals and species within the communal habitat. The two ecological principles, dominance and succession, which operate to establish and maintain such communal order as here described are functions of, and dependent upon, competition.

In every life-community there is always one or more dominant species. In a plant community this dominance is ordinarily the result of struggle among the different species for light. In a climate which supports a forest the dominant species will invariably be trees. On the prairie and steppes they will be grasses.

Light being the main necessity of plants, the dominant plant of a community is the tallest member, which can spread its green energy-trap above the heads of the others. What marginal exploitation there is to be done is an exploitation of the dimmer light below this canopy. So it comes about in every life-community on land, in the cornfield just as in the forest, that there are layers of vegetation, each adapted to exist in a lesser intensity of light than the one above. Usually there are but two or three such layers; in an oak-wood for example there will be a layer of moss, above this herbs or low bushes, and then nothing more to the leafy roof; in the wheat-field the dominating form is the wheat, with lower weeds among its stalks. But in tropical forests the whole space from floor to roof may be zoned and populated.[8]

But the principle of dominance operates in the human as well as in the plant and animal communities. The so-called natural or functional areas of a metropolitan community—for example, the slum, the rooming-house area, the central shopping section and the banking center—each and all owe their existence directly to the factor of dominance, and indirectly to competition.

The struggle of industries and commercial institutions for a strategic location determines in the long run the main outlines of the urban community. The distribution of population, as well as the location and limits of the residential areas which they occupy, are determined by another similar but subordinate system of forces.

The area of dominance in any community is usually the area of highest land values. Ordinarily there are in every large city two such positions of highest land value—one in the central shopping district, the other in the central banking area. From these points land values decline at first precipitantly and then more gradually toward the periphery of the urban community. It is these land values that determine the location of social institutions and business enterprises. Both the one and the other are bound up in a kind of territorial complex within which they are at once competing and interdependent units.

As the metropolitan community expands into the suburbs the pressure of professions, business enterprises, and social institutions of various sorts destined to serve the whole metropolitan region steadily increases the demand for space at the center. Thus not merely the growth of the suburban area, but any change in the method of transportation which makes the central business area of the city more accessible, tends to increase the pressure at the center. From thence this pressure is transmitted and diffused, as the profile of land values discloses, to every other part of the city.

Thus the principle of dominance, operating within the limits imposed by the terrain and other natural features of the location, tends to determine the general ecological pattern of the city and the functional relation of each of the different areas of the city to all others.

Dominance is, furthermore, in so far as it tends to stabilize either the biotic or the cultural community, indirectly responsible for the phenomenon of succession.

The term "succession" is used by ecologists to describe and designate that orderly sequence of changes through which a biotic community passes in the course of its development from a primary and relatively unstable to a relatively permanent or climax stage. The main point is that not merely do the individual plants and animals within the communal habitat grow but the community itself, i.e., the system of relations between the species, is likewise involved in an orderly process of change and development.

The fact that, in the course of this development, the community moves through a series of more or less clearly defined stages is the fact that gives this development the serial character which the term "succession" suggests.

The explanation of the serial character of the changes involved in succession is the fact that at every stage in the process a more or less stable equilibrium is achieved, which in due course, and as a result of progressive changes in life-conditions, possibly due to growth and decay, the equilibrium achieved in the earlier stages is eventually undermined. In such case the energies previously held in balance will be released, competition will be intensified, and change will continue at a relatively rapid rate until a new equilibrium is achieved.

The climax phase of community development corresponds with the adult phase of an individual's life.

> In the developing single organism, each phase is its own executioner, and itself brings a new phase into existence, as when the tadpole grows the thyroid gland which is destined to make the tadpole state pass away in favour of the miniature frog. And in the developing community of organisms, the same thing happens— each stage alters its own environment, for it changes and almost invariably enriches the soil in which it lives; and thus it eventually brings itself to an end, by making it possible for new kinds of plants with greater demands in the way of mineral salts or other riches of the soil to flourish there. Accordingly bigger and more exigent plants gradually supplant the early pioneers, until a final balance is reached, the ultimate possibility for that climate.[9]

The cultural community develops in comparable ways to that of the biotic, but the process is more complicated. Inventions, as well as sudden or catastrophic changes, seem to play a more important part in bringing about serial changes in the cultural than in the biotic community. But the principle involved seems to be substantially the same. In any case, all or most of the fundamental processes seem to be functionally related and dependent upon competition.

Competition, which on the biotic level functions to control and regulate the interrelations of organisms, tends to assume on the social level the form of conflict. The intimate relation between competition and conflict is indicated by the fact that wars frequently, if not always, have, or seem to have, their source and origin in economic competition which, in that case, assumes the more sublimated form of a struggle for power and prestige. The social function of war, on the other hand, seems to be to extend the area over which it is possible to maintain peace.

IV. Biological Economics

If population pressure, on the one hand, co-operates with changes in local and environmental conditions to disturb at once the biotic balance and social equilibrium, it tends at the same time to intensify competition. In so doing it functions, indirectly, to bring about a new, more minute and, at the same time, territorially extensive division of labor.

Under the influence of an intensified competition, and the increased activity which competition involves, every individual and every species, each for itself, tends to discover the particular niche in the physical and living environment where it can survive and flourish with the greatest possible expansiveness consistent with its necessary dependence upon its neighbors.

It is in this way that a territorial organization and a biological division of labor, within the communal habitat, is established and maintained. This explains, in part at least, the fact that the biotic community has been conceived at one time as a kind of superorganism and at another as a kind of economic organization for the exploitation of the natural resources of its habitat.

In their interesting survey, *The Science of Life,* H. G. Wells and his collaborators, Julian Huxley and G. P. Wells, have described ecology as "biological economics," and as such very largely concerned with "the balances and mutual pressures of species living in the same habitat."[10]

"Ecology," as they put it, is "an extension of Economics to the whole of life." On the other hand the science of economics as traditionally conceived, though it is a whole century older, is merely a branch of a more general science of ecology which includes man with all other living creatures. Under the circumstances what has been traditionally described as economics and conceived as restricted to human affairs, might very properly be described as Barrows some years ago described geography, namely as human ecology. It is in this sense that Wells and his collaborators would use the term.

> The science of economic—at first it was called Political Economy—is a whole century older than ecology. It was and is the science of social subsistence, of needs and their satisfactions, of work and wealth. It tries to elucidate the relations of producer, dealer, and consumer in the human community and show how the whole system carries on. Ecology broadens out this inquiry into a general study of the give and take, the effort, accumulation and consumption in every province of life. Economics, therefore, is merely Human Ecology, it is the narrow and special study of the ecology of the very extraordinary community in which we live. It might have been a better and brighter science if it had begun biologically.[11]

Since human ecology cannot be at the same time both geography and economics, one may adopt, as a working hypothesis, the notion that it is neither one nor the other but something independent of both. Even so the motives for identifying ecology with geography on the one hand, and economics on the other, are fairly obvious.

From the point of view of geography, the plant, animal, and human population, including their habitations and other evidence of man's occupation of the soil, are merely part of the landscape, of which the geographer is seeking a detailed description and picture.

On the other hand ecology (biologic economics), even when it involves some sort of unconscious co-operation and a natural, spontaneous, and non-rational division of labor, is something different from the economics of commerce; something

quite apart from the bargaining of the market place. Commerce, as Simmel somewhere remarks, is one of the latest and most complicated of all the social relationships into which human beings have entered. Man is the only animal that trades
and traffics.

Ecology, and human ecology, if it is not identical with economics on the distinctively human and cultural level is, nevertheless, something more than and
different from the static order which the human geographer discovers when he
surveys the cultural landscape.

The community of the geographer is not, for one thing, like that of the ecologist, a closed system, and the web of communication which man has spread over
the earth is something different from the "web of life" which binds living creatures
all over the world in a vital nexus.

V. Symbiosis and Society

Human ecology, if it is neither economics on one hand nor geography on the other,
but just ecology, differs, nevertheless, in important respects from plant and animal
ecology. The interrelations of human beings and interactions of man and his habitat are comparable but not identical with interrelations of other forms of life that
live together and carry on a kind of "biological economy" within the limits of a
common habitat.

For one thing man is not so immediately dependent upon his physical environment as other animals. As a result of the existing world-wide division of labor,
man's relation to his physical environment has been mediated through the intervention of other men. The exchange of goods and services have co-operated to
emancipate him from dependence upon his local habitat.

Furthermore man has, by means of inventions and technical devices of the
most diverse sorts, enormously increased his capacity for reacting upon and re-
making, not only his habitat but his world. Finally, man has erected upon the basis
of the biotic community an institutional structure rooted in custom and tradition.

Structure, where it exists, tends to resist change, at least change coming from
without; while it possibly facilitates the cumulation of change within.[12] In plant
and animal communities structure is biologically determined, and so far as any
division of labor exists at all it has a physiological and instinctive basis. The social
insects afford a conspicuous example of this fact, and one interest in studying their
habits, as Wheeler points out, is that they show the extent to which social organization can be developed on a purely physiological and instinctive basis, as is the
case among human beings in the natural as distinguished from the institutional
family.[13]

In a society of human beings, however, this communal structure is reinforced
by custom and assumes an institutional character. In human as contrasted with
animal societies, competition and the freedom of the individual is limited on every
level above the biotic by custom and consensus.

The incidence of this more or less arbitrary control which custom and consensus imposes upon the natural social order complicates the social process but does not fundamentally alter it—or, if it does, the effects of biotic competition will still be manifest in the succeeding social order and the subsequent course of events.

The fact seems to be, then, that human society, as distinguished from plant and animal society, is organized on two levels, the biotic and the cultural. There is a symbiotic society based on competition and a cultural society based on communication and consensus. As a matter of fact the two societies are merely different aspects of one society, which, in the vicissitudes and changes to which they are subject remain, nevertheless, in some sort of mutual dependence each upon the other. The cultural superstructure rests on the basis of the symbiotic substructure, and the emergent energies that manifest themselves on the biotic level in movements and actions reveal themselves on the higher social level in more subtle and sublimated forms.

However, the interrelations of human beings are more diverse and complicated than this dichotomy, symbiotic and cultural, indicates. This fact is attested by the divergent systems of human interrelations which have been the subject of the special social sciences. Thus human society, certainly in its mature and more rational expression, exhibits not merely an ecological, but an economic, a political, and a moral order. The social sciences include not merely human geography and ecology, but economics, political science, and cultural anthropology.

It is interesting also that these divergent social orders seem to arrange themselves in a kind of hierarchy. In fact they may be said to form a pyramid of which the ecological order constitutes the base and the moral order the apex. Upon each succeeding one of these levels, the ecological, economic, political, and moral, the individual finds himself more completely incorporated into and subordinated to the social order of which he is a part than upon the preceding.

Society is everywhere a control organization. Its function is to organize, integrate, and direct the energies resident in the individuals of which it is composed. One might, perhaps, say that the function of society was everywhere to restrict competition and by so doing bring about a more effective co-operation of the organic units of which society is composed.

Competition, on the biotic level, as we observe it in the plant and animal communities, seems to be relatively unrestricted. Society, so far as it exists, is anarchic and free. On the cultural level, this freedom of the individual to compete is restricted by conventions, understandings, and law. The individual is more free upon the economic level than upon the political, more free on the political than the moral.

As society matures control is extended and intensified and free commerce of individuals restricted, if not by law then by what Gilbert Murray refers to as "the normal expectation of mankind." The mores are merely what men, in a situation that is defined, have come to expect.

Human ecology, in so far as it is concerned with a social order that is based on competition rather than consensus, is identical, in principle at least, with plant and animal ecology. The problems with which plant and animal ecology have been traditionally concerned are fundamentally population problems. Society, as ecologists have conceived it, is a population settled and limited to its habitat. The ties that unite its individual units are those of a free and natural economy, based on a natural division of labor. Such a society is territorially organized and the ties which hold it together are physical and vital rather than customary and moral.

Human ecology has, however, to reckon with the fact that in human society competition is limited by custom and culture. The cultural superstructure imposes itself as an instrument of direction and control upon the biotic substructure.

Reduced to its elements the human community, so conceived, may be said to consist of a population and a culture, including in the term culture (1) a body of customs and beliefs and (2) a corresponding body of artifacts and technological devices.

To these three elements or factors—(1) population, (2) artifact (technicological culture), (3) custom and beliefs (non-material culture)—into which the social complex resolves itself, one should, perhaps, add a fourth, namely, the natural resources of the habitat.

It is the interaction of these four factors—(1) population, (2) artifacts (technicological culture), (3) custom and beliefs (non-material culture), and (4) the natural resources that maintain at once the biotic balance and the social equilibrium, when and where they exist.

The changes in which ecology is interested are the movements of population and of artifacts (commodities) and changes in location and occupation—any sort of change, in fact, which affects an existing division of labor or the relation of the population to the soil.

Human ecology is, fundamentally, an attempt to investigate the processes by which the biotic balance and the social equilibrium (1) are maintained once they are achieved and (2) the processes by which, when the biotic balance and the social equilibrium are disturbed, the transition is made from one relatively stable order to another.

Notes

1. *The System of Animate Nature* (Gifford Lectures, 1915–16), II (New York, 1920), 58.
2. J. Arthur Thompson, *Darwinism and Human Life* (New York, 1911), pp. 52–53.
3. *Ibid.*, p. 72.
4. "Ecology," says Elton, "corresponds to the older terms Natural History and Bionomics, but is methods are now accurate and precise." See article, "Ecology," *Encyclopedia Britannica* (14th ed.).
5. Edward J. Salisbury, "Plants," *Encyclopaedia Britannica* (14th ed.).
6. "Animal Ecology," *ibid.*
7. *Ibid.*
8. H. G. Wells, Julian S. Huxley, and G. P. Wells, *The Science of Life* (New York, 1934), pp. 968–69.
9. *Ibid.*, pp. 977–78.
10. *Ibid.*
11. H. H. Barrows, "Geography as Human Ecology," *Annals Association American Geographers*, XIII (1923), 1–14. See H. G. Wells, *et al.*, *op. cit.*, pp. 961–62.

12. Here is, obviously, another evidence of that organic character of the interrelations of organisms in the biosphere to which J. Arthur Thompson and others have referred. It is an indication of the way in which competition mediates the influences from without by the adjustment and readjustment of relations within the community. In this case "within" coincides with the orbit of the competitive process, at least so far as the effects of that process are substantive and obvious. See Simmel's definition of society and the social group in time and space quoted in Park and Burgess, *Introduction to the Science of Sociology* (2d ed.), pp. 348–56.

13. William Morton Wheeler, *Social Life among the Insects* (Lowell Institute Lectures, March, 1922), pp. 3–18.

16

The Nature of Cities

Chauncy D. Harris and Edward L. Ullman

Cities are the focal points in the occupation and utilization of the earth by man. Both a product of and an influence on surrounding regions, they develop in definite patterns in response to economic and social needs.

Cities are also paradoxes. Their rapid growth and large size testify to their superiority as a technique for the exploitation of the earth, yet by their very success and consequent large size they often provide a poor local environment for man. The problem is to build the future city in such a manner that the advantages of urban concentration can be preserved for the benefit of man and the disadvantages minimized.

Each city is unique in detail but resembles others in function and pattern. What is learned about one helps in studying another. Location types and internal structure are repeated so often that broad and suggestive generalizations are valid, especially if limited to cities of similar size, function, and regional setting. This paper will be limited to a discussion of two basic aspects of the nature of cities—their support and their internal structure. Such important topics as the rise and extent of urbanism, urban sites, culture of cities, social and economic characteristics of the urban population, and critical problems will receive only passing mention.

The Support of Cities

As one approaches a city and notices its tall buildings rising above the surrounding land and as one continues into the city and observes the crowds of people hurry-

"The Nature of Cities" by Chauncy D. Harris and Edward L. Ullman from *The Annals of the American Academy of Political and Social Science*, Vol. 242, November 1945, pp. 7–17.

ing to and fro past stores, theaters, banks, and other establishments, one naturally is struck by the contrast with the rural countryside. What supports this phenomenon? What do the people of the city do for a living?

The support of a city depends on the services it performs not for itself but for a tributary area. Many activities serve merely the population of the city itself. Barbers, dry cleaners, shoe repairers, grocerymen, bakers, and movie operators serve others who are engaged in the principal activity of the city, which may be mining, manufacturing, trade, or some other activity.

The service by which the city earns its livelihood depends on the nature of the economy and of the hinterland. Cities are small or rare in areas either of primitive, self-sufficient economy or of meager resources. As Adam Smith stated, the land must produce a surplus in order to support cities. This does not mean that all cities must be surrounded by productive land, since strategic location with reference to cheap ocean highways may enable a city to support itself on the specialized surplus of distant lands. Nor does it mean that cities are parasites living off the land. Modern mechanization, transport, and a complex interdependent economy enable much of the economic activity of mankind to be centered in cities. Many of the people engaged even in food production are actually in cities in the manufacture of agricultural machinery.

The support of cities as suppliers of urban services for the earth can be summarized in three categories, each of which presents a factor of urban causation:[1]

1. Cities as central places performing comprehensive services for a surrounding area. Such cities tend to be evenly spaced throughout productive territory (Fig. 16.1). For the moment this may be considered the "norm" subject to variation primarily in response to the ensuing factors.

2. Transport cities performing break-of-bulk and allied services along transport routes, supported by areas which may be remote in distance but close in connection because of the city's strategic location on transport channels. Such cities tend to be arranged in linear patterns along rail lines or at coasts (Fig. 16.2).

3. Specialized-function cities performing one service such as mining, manufacturing, or recreation for large areas, including the general tributary areas of hosts of other cities. Since the principal localizing factor is often a particular resource such as coal, water power, or a beach, such cities may occur singly or in clusters (Fig. 16.3).

Most cities represent a combination of the three factors, the relative importance of each varying from city to city (Fig. 16.4).

Cities as Central Places

Cities as central places serve as trade and social centers for a tributary area. If the land base is homogeneous these centers are uniformly spaced, as in many parts of the agricultural Middle West (Fig. 16.1). In areas of uneven resource distribution, the distribution of cities is uneven. The centers are of varying sizes, ranging from

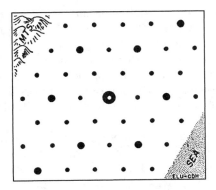

FIGURE 16.1 *Theoretical distribution of central places. In a homogeneous land, settlements are evenly spaced; largest city in center surrounded by 6 medium-sized centers which in turn are surrounded by 6 small centers. Tributary areas are hexagons, the closest geometrical shapes to circles which completely fill area with no unserved spaces.*

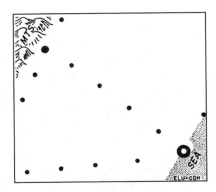

FIGURE 16.2 *Transport centers, aligned along railroads or at coast. Large center is port; next largest is railroad junction and engine-changing point where mountain and plain meet. Small centers perform break of bulk principally between rail and roads.*

FIGURE 16.3 *Specialized-function settlements. Large city is manufacturing and mining center surrounded by a cluster of smaller settlements located on a mineral deposit. Small centers on ocean and at edge of mountains are resorts.*

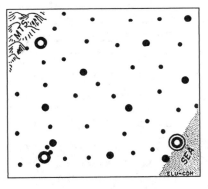

FIGURE 16.4 *Theoretical composite grouping. Port becomes the metropolis and, although off center, serves as central place for whole area. Manufacturing-mining and junction centers are next largest. Railroad alignment of many towns evident. Railroad route in upper left of Fig. 16.2 has been diverted to pass through manufacturing and mining cluster. Distribution of settlements in upper right follows central-place arrangement.*

small hamlets closely spaced with one or two stores serving a local tributary area, through larger villages, towns, and cities more widely spaced with more special services for larger tributary areas, up to the great metropolis such as New York or Chicago offering many specialized services for a large tributary area composed of a whole hierarchy of tributary areas of smaller places. Such a net of tributary areas and centers forms a pattern somewhat like a fish net spread over a beach, the network regular and symmetrical where the sand is smooth, but warped and distorted where the net is caught in rocks.

The central-place type of city or town is widespread throughout the world, particularly in nonindustrial regions. In the United States it is best represented by the numerous retail and wholesale trade centers of the agricultural Middle West, Southwest, and West. Such cities have imposing shopping centers or wholesale districts in proportion to their size; the stores are supported by the trade of the surrounding area. This contrasts with many cities of the industrial East, where the centers are so close together that each has little trade support beyond its own population.

Not only trade but social and religious functions may support central places. In some instances these other functions may be the main support of the town. In parts of Latin America, for example, where there is little trade, settlements are scattered at relatively uniform intervals through the land as social and religious centers. In contrast to most cities, their busiest day is Sunday, when the surrounding populace attend church and engage in holiday recreation, thus giving rise to the name "Sunday town."

Most large central cities and towns are also political centers. The county seat is an example. London and Paris are the political as well as trade centers of their countries. In the United States, however, Washington and many state capitals are specialized political centers. In many of these cases the political capital was initially chosen as a centrally located point in the political area and was deliberately separated from the major urban center.

Cities as Transport Foci and Break-of-Bulk Points

All cities are dependent on transportation in order to utilize the surplus of the land for their support. This dependence on transportation destroys the symmetry of the central-place arrangement, inasmuch as cities develop at foci or breaks of transportation, and transport routes are distributed unevenly over the land because of relief or other limitations (Fig. 16.2). City organizations recognize the importance of efficient transportation, as witness their constant concern with freight-rate regulation and with the construction of new highways, port facilities, airfields, and the like.

Mere focusing of transport routes does not produce a city, but according to Cooley, if break of bulk occurs, the focus becomes a good place to process goods. Where the form of transport changes, as transferring from water to rail, break of bulk is inevitable. Ports originating merely to transship cargo tend to develop auxiliary services such as repackaging, storing, and sorting. An example of simple break-of-bulk and storage ports is Port Arthur-Fort William, the twin port and wheat-storage cities at the head of Lake Superior; surrounded by unproductive land, they have arisen at the break-of-bulk points on the cheapest route from the wheat-producing Prairie Provinces to the markets of the East. Some ports develop as entrepôts, such as Hong Kong and Copenhagen, supported by transshipment of goods from small to large boats or vice versa. Servicing points or minor changes in transport tend to encourage growth of cities as establishment of division points for changing locomotives on American railroads.

Transport centers can be centrally located places or can serve as gateways between contrasting regions with contrasting needs. Kansas City, Omaha, and Minneapolis-St. Paul serve as gateways to the West, as well as central places for productive agricultural regions, and are important wholesale centers. The ports of New Orleans, Mobile, Savannah, Charleston, Norfolk, and others served as traditional gateways to the Cotton Belt with its specialized production. Likewise, northern border metropolises such as Baltimore, Washington, Cincinnati, and Louisville served as gateways to the South, with St. Louis a gateway to the Southwest. In recent years the South has been developing its own central places, supplanting some of the monopoly once held by the border gateways. Atlanta, Memphis, and Dallas are examples of the new southern central places and transport foci.

Changes in transportation are reflected in the pattern of city distribution. Thus the development of railroads resulted in a railroad alignment of cities which still persists. The rapid growth of automobiles and widespread development of highways in recent decades, however, has changed the trend toward a more even distribution of towns. Studies in such diverse localities as New York and Louisiana have shown a shift of centers away from exclusive alignment along rail routes. Airways may reinforce this trend or stimulate still different patterns of distribution for the future city.

Cities as Concentration Points for Specialized Services

A specialized city or cluster of cities performing a specialized function for a large area may develop at a highly localized resource (Fig. 16.3). The resort city of Miami, for example, developed in response to a favorable climate and beach. Scranton, Wilkes-Barre, and dozens of nearby towns are specialized coal-mining centers developed on anthracite coal deposits to serve a large segment of the northeastern United States. Pittsburgh and its suburbs and satellites form a nationally significant iron-and-steel manufacturing cluster favored by good location for the assembly of coal and iron ore and for the sale of steel to industries on the coal fields.

Equally important with physical resources in many cities are the advantages of mass production and ancillary services. Once started, a specialized city acts as a nucleus for similar or related activities, and functions tend to pyramid, whether the city is a seaside resort such as Miami or Atlantic City, or, more important, a manufacturing center such as Pittsburgh or Detroit. Concentration of industry in a city means that there will be a concentration of satellite services and industries—supply houses, machine shops, expert consultants, other industries using local industrial by-products or waste, still other industries making specialized parts for other plants in the city, marketing channels, specialized transport facilities, skilled labor, and a host of other facilities; either directly or indirectly, these benefit industry and cause it to expand in size and numbers in a concentrated place or district. Local personnel with the know-how in a given industry also may decide to start a new plant producing similar or like products in the same city. Furthermore, the advantages of mass production itself often tend to concentrate production in a few large factories and cities. Examples of localization of specific manufacturing industries are clothing in New York City, furniture in Grand Rapids, automobiles in the Detroit area, pottery in Stoke-on-Trent in England, and even such a specialty as tennis rackets in Pawtucket, Rhode Island.

Such concentration continues until opposing forces of high labor costs and congestion balance the concentrating forces. Labor costs may be lower in small towns and in industrially new districts; thus some factories are moving from the great metropolises to small towns; much of the cotton textile industry has moved from the old industrial areas of New England to the newer areas of the Carolinas in the South. The tremendous concentration of population and structures in large cities exacts a high cost in the form of congestion, high land costs, high taxes, and restrictive legislation.

Not all industries tend to concentrate in specialized industrial cities; many types of manufacturing partake more of central-place characteristics. These types are those that are tied to the market because the manufacturing process results in an increase in bulk or perishability. Bakeries, ice cream establishments, ice houses, breweries, soft-drink plants, and various types of assembly plants are examples. Even such industries, however, tend to be more developed in the manufacturing belt because the density of population and hence the market is greater there.

The greatest concentration of industrial cities in America is in the manufacturing belt of northeastern United States and contiguous Canada, north of the Ohio and east of the Mississippi. Some factors in this concentration are: large reserves of fuel and power (particularly coal), raw materials such as iron ore via the Great Lakes, cheap ocean transportation on the eastern seaboard, productive agriculture (particularly in the west), early settlement, later immigration concentrated in its cities, and an early start with consequent development of skilled labor, industrial know-how, transportation, facilities, and prestige.

The interdependent nature of most of the industries acts as a powerful force to maintain this area as the primary home of industrial cities in the United States. Before the war, the typical industrial city outside the main manufacturing belt had only a single industry of the raw-material type, such as lumber mills, food canneries, or smelters (Longview, Washington; San Jose, California; Anaconda, Montana). Because of the need for producing huge quantities of ships and airplanes for a two-ocean war, however, many cities along, the Gulf and Pacific coasts have grown rapidly during recent years as centers of industry.

Application of the Three Types of Urban Support

Although examples can be cited illustrating each of the three types of urban support, most American cities partake in varying proportions of all three types. New York City, for example, as the greatest American port is a break-of-bulk, point; as the principal center of wholesaling and retailing it is a central-place type; and as the major American center of manufacturing it is a specialized type. The actual distribution and, functional classification of cities in the United States, more complex than the simple sum of the three types (Fig. 16.4), has been mapped and described elsewhere in different terms.[2]

The three basic types therefore should not be considered as a rigid framework excluding all accidental establishment, although even fortuitous development of a city becomes part of the general urban-supporting environment. Nor should the urban setting be regarded as static; cities are constantly changing, and exhibit characteristic lag in adjusting to new conditions.

Ample opportunity exists for use of initiative in strengthening the supporting base of the future city, particularly if account is taken of the basic factors of urban support. Thus a city should examine: (1) its surrounding area to take advantage of changes such as newly discovered resources or crops, (2) its transport in order to adjust properly to new or changed facilities, and (3) its industries in order to benefit from technological advances.

Internal Structure of Cities

Any effective plans for the improvement or rearrangement of the future city must take account of the present pattern of land use within the city, of the factors which have produced this pattern, and of the facilities required by activities localized within particular districts.

Although the internal pattern of each city is unique in its particular combination of details, most American cities have business, industrial, and residential districts. The forces underlying the pattern of land use can be appreciated if attention is focused on three generalizations of arrangement—by concentric zones, sectors, and multiple nuclei.

Concentric Zones

According to the concentric-zone theory, the pattern of growth of the city can best be understood in terms of five concentric zones[3] (Fig. 16.5).

1. *The central business district.*—This is the focus of commercial, social, and civic life, and of transportation. In it is the downtown retail district with its department stores, smart shops, office buildings, clubs, banks, hotels, theaters, museums, and organization headquarters. Encircling the downtown retail district is the wholesale business district.

2. *The zone in transition.*—Encircling the downtown area is a zone of residential deterioration. Business and light manufacturing encroach on residential areas characterized particularly by rooming houses. In this zone are the principal slums, with their submerged regions of poverty, degradation, and disease, and their un-

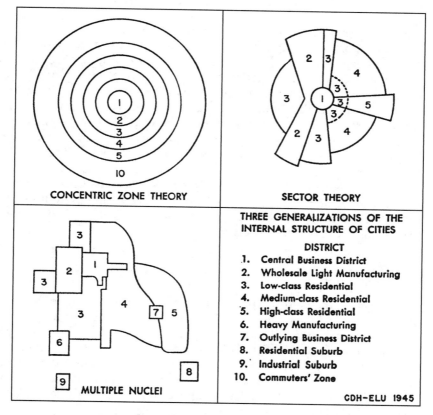

FIGURE 16.5   *Generalizations of internal structure of cities. The concentric-zone theory is a generalization for all cities. The arrangement of the sectors in the sector theory varies from city to city. The diagram for multiple nuclei represents one possible pattern among innumberable variations.*

derworlds of vice. In many American cities it has been inhabited largely by colonies of recent immigrants.

3. *The zone of independent working-men's homes.*—This is inhabited by industrial workers who have escaped from the zone in transition but who desire to live within easy access of their work. In many American cities second-generation immigrants are important segments of the population in this area.

4. *The zone of better residences.*—This is made up of single-family dwellings of exclusive "restricted districts," and of high-class apartment-buildings.

5. *The commuters' zone.*—Often beyond the city limits in suburban areas or in satellite cities, this is a zone of spotty development of high-class residences along lines of rapid travel.

Sectors

The theory of axial development, according to which growth takes place along main transportation routes or along lines of least resistance to form a star-shaped city, is refined by Homer Hoyt in his sector theory, which states that growth along particular axis of transportation usually consists of similar types of land use[4] (Fig. 16.5). The entire city is considered as a circle and the various areas as sectors radiating out from the center of that circle; similar types of land use originate near the center of the circle and migrate outward toward the periphery. Thus a high-rent residential area in the eastern quadrant of the city would tend to migrate outward, keeping always in the eastern quadrant. A low-quality housing area, if located in the southern quadrant, would tend to extend outward to the very margin of the city in that sector. The migration of high-class residential areas outward along established lines of travel is particularly pronounced on high ground, toward open country, to homes of community leaders, along lines of fastest transportation, and to existing nuclei of buildings or trading centers.

Multiple Nuclei

In many cities the land-use pattern is built not around a single center but around several discrete nuclei (Fig. 16.5). In some cities these nuclei have existed from the very origins of the city; in others they have developed as the growth of the city stimulated migration and specialization. An example of the first type is Metropolitan London, in which "The City" and Westminster originated as separate points separated by open country, one as the center of finance and commerce, the other as the center of political life. An example of the second type is Chicago, in which heavy industry, at first localized along the Chicago River in the heart of the city, migrated to the Calumet District, where it acted as a nucleus for extensive new urban development.

The initial nucleus of the city may be the retail district in a central-place city, the port or rail facilities in a break-of-bulk city, or the factory, mine, or beach in a specialized-function city.

The rise of separate nuclei and differentiated districts reflects a combination of the following four factors:

1. Certain activities require specialized facilities. The retail district, for example, is attached to the point of greatest intracity accessibility, the port district to suitable water front, manufacturing districts to large blocks of land and water or rail connection, and so on.

2. Certain like activities group together because they profit from cohesion.[5] The clustering of industrial cities has already been noted above under "Cities as concentration points for specialized services." Retail districts benefit from grouping which increases the concentration of potential customers and makes possible comparison shopping. Financial and office-building districts depend upon facility of

communication among offices within the district. The Merchandise Mart of Chicago is an example of wholesale clustering.

3. Certain unlike activities are detrimental to each other. The antagonism between factory development and high-class residential development is well known. The heavy concentrations of pedestrians, automobiles, and streetcars in the retail district are antagonistic both to the railroad facilities and the street loading required in the wholesale district and to the rail facilities and space needed by large industrial districts, and vice versa.

4. Certain activities are unable to afford the high rents of the most desirable sites. This factor works in conjunction with the foregoing. Examples are bulk wholesaling and storage activities requiring much room, or low-class housing unable to afford the luxury of high land with a view.

The number of nuclei which result from historical development and the operation of localization forces varies greatly from city to city. The larger the city, the more numerous and specialized are the nuclei. The following districts, however, have developed around nuclei in most large American cities.

The central business district.—This district is at the focus of intracity transportation facilities by sidewalk, private car, bus, streetcar, subway, and elevated. Because of asymmetrical growth of most large cities, it is generally not now in the areal center of the city but actually near one edge, as in the case of lake-front, riverside, or even inland cities; examples are Chicago, St. Louis, and Salt Lake City. Because established internal transportation lines converge on it, however, it is the point of most convenient access from all parts of the city, and the point of highest land values. The retail district, at the point of maximum accessibility, is attached to the sidewalk; only pedestrian or mass-transportation movement can concentrate the large numbers of customers necessary to support department stores, variety stores, and clothing shops, which are characteristic of the district. In small cities financial institutions and office buildings are intermingled with retail shops, but in large cities the financial district is separate, near but not at the point of greatest intracity facility. Its point of attachment is the elevator, which permits three-dimensional access among offices, whose most important locational factor is accessibility to other offices rather than to the city as a whole. Government buildings also are commonly near but not in the center of the retail district. In most cities a separate "automobile row" has arisen on the edge of the central business district, in cheaper rent areas along one or more major highways; its attachment is to the highway itself.

The wholesale and light-manufacturing district.—This district is conveniently within the city but near the focus of extra city transportation facilities. Wholesale houses, while deriving some support from the city itself, serve principally a tributary region reached by railroad and motor truck. They are, therefore, concentrated along railroad lines, usually adjacent to (but not surrounding) the central business district. Many types of light manufacturing which do not require specialized buildings are attracted by the facilities of this district or similar districts: good rail and road transportation, available loft buildings, and proximity to the markets and labor of the city itself.

The heavy industrial district.—This is near the present or former outer edge of the city. Heavy, industries require large tracts of space, often beyond any available in sections already subdivided into blocks and streets. They also require good transportation, either rail or water. With the development of belt lines and switching yards, sites on the edge of the city may have better transportation service than those near the center. In Chicago about a hundred industries are in a belt three miles long, adjacent to the Clearing freight yards on the southwestern edge of the city. Furthermore, the noise of boiler works, the odors of stockyards, the waste disposal problems of smelters and iron and steel mills, the fire hazards of petroleum refineries, and the space and transportation needs which interrupt streets and accessibility—all these favor the growth of heavy industry away from the main center of the large city. The Calumet District of Chicago, the New Jersey marshes near New York City, the Lea marshes near London, and the St. Denis district of Paris are examples of such districts. The stockyards of Chicago, in spite of their odors and size, have been engulfed by urban growth and are now far from the edge of the city. They form a nucleus of heavy industry within the city but not near the center, which has blighted the adjusted residential area, the "back-of-the-yards" district.

The residential district.—In general, the high-class districts are likely to be on well-drained, high land and away from nuisances such as noise, odors, smoke, and railroad lines. Low-class districts are likely to arise near factories and railroad districts, wherever located in the city. Because of the obsolescence of structures, the older inner margins of residential districts are fertile fields for invasion by groups unable to pay high rents. Residential neighborhoods have some measure of cohesiveness. Extreme cases are the ethnically segregated groups, which cluster together although including members in many economic groups; Harlem is an example.

Minor nuclei.—These include cultural centers, parks, outlying business districts, and small industrial centers. A university may form a nucleus for a quasi-independent community; examples are the University of Chicago, the University of California, and Harvard University. Parks and recreation areas occupying former wasteland too rugged or wet for housing may form nuclei for high-class residential areas; examples are Rock Creek Park in Washington and Hyde Park in London. Outlying business districts may in time become major centers. Many small institutions and individual light manufacturing plants, such as bakeries, dispersed throughout the city may never become nuclei of differentiated districts.

Suburb and satellite.—Suburbs, either residential or industrial, are characteristic of most of the larger American cities.[6] The rise of the automobile and the improvement of certain suburban commuter rail lines in a few of the largest cities have stimulated suburbanization. Satellites differ from suburbs in that they are separated from the central city by many miles and in general have little daily commuting to or from the central city, although economic activities of the satellite are closely geared to those of the central city. Thus Gary may be considered a suburb but Elgin and Joliet are satellites of Chicago.

Appraisal of Land-Use Patterns

Most cities exhibit not only a combination of the three types of urban support, but also aspects of the three generalizations of the land-use pattern. An understanding of both is useful in appraising the future prospects of the whole city and the arrangement of its parts.

As a general picture subject to modification because of topography, transportation, and previous land use, the concentric-zone aspect has merit. It is not a rigid pattern, inasmuch as growth or arrangement often reflects expansion within sectors or development around separate nuclei.

The sector aspect has been applied particularly to the outward movement of residential districts. Both the concentric-zone theory and the sector theory emphasize the general tendency of central residential areas to decline in value as new construction takes place on the outer edges; the sector theory is, however, more discriminating in its analysis of that movement.

Both the concentric zone, as a general pattern, and the sector aspect, as applied primarily to residential patterns, assume (although not explicitly) that there is but a single urban core around which land use is arranged symmetrically in either concentric or radial patterns. In broad theoretical terms such an assumption may be valid, inasmuch is the handicap of distance alone would favor as much concentration as possible in a small central core. Because of the actual physical impossibility of such concentration and the existence of separating factors, however, separate nuclei arise. The specific separating factors are not only high rent in the core, which can be afforded by few activities, but also the natural attachment of certain activities to extra-urban transport, space, or other facilities, and the advantages of the separation of unlike activities and the concentration of like functions.

The constantly changing pattern of land use poses many problems. Near the core, land is kept vacant or retained in antisocial slum structures in anticipation of expansion of higher-rent activities. The hidden costs of slums to the city in poor environment for future citizens and excessive police, fire, and sanitary protection underlie the argument for a subsidy to remove the blight. The transition zone is not everywhere a zone of deterioration with slums, however, as witness the rise of high-class apartment development near the urban core in the Gold Coast of Chicago or Park Avenue in New York City. On the fringe of the city, overambitious subdividing results in unused land to be crossed by urban services such as sewers and transportation. Separate political status of many suburbs results in a lack of civic responsibility for the problems and expenses of the city in which the suburbanites work.

Notes _____

1. For references, see Edward Ullman, "A Theory of Location for Cities," *American Journal of Sociology,* Vol. 46, No. 6 (May 1941), pp. 853–64.

2. Chauncy D. Harris, "A Functional Classification of Cities in the United States," *The Geographical Review,* Vol. 33, No. 1 (Jan. 1943), pp. 85–99.

3. Ernest W. Burgess, "The Growth of the City," in *The City,* ed. by Robert E. Park, Ernest W. Burgess, and Roderick D. McKenzie (Chicago: University of Chicago Press, 1925), pp. 47–62; and Ernest W. Burgess, "Urban Areas," in *Chicago, an Experiment in Social Science Research,* ed. by T. V. Smith and Leonard D. White (Chicago: University of Chicago Press, 1929), pp. 113–38.

4. Homer Hoyt, "City Growth and Mortgage Risk," *Insured Mortgage Portfolio,* Vol. 1, Nos. 6–10 (Dec. 1936–April 1937), *passim;* and U.S. Federal Housing Administration, *The Structure and Growth of Residential Neighborhoods in American Cities* by Homer Hoyt (Washington: Government Printing Office, 1939), *passim.*

5. Exceptions are service-type establishments such as some grocery stores, dry cleaners, and gasoline stations.

6. Chauncy D. Harris, "Suburbs," *American Journal of Sociology,* Vol. 49, No. 1 (July 1943), p. 6.

17

The New Urban Sociology Meets the Old

Rereading Some Classical Human Ecology

David A. Smith

A paradigm shift has taken place in urban sociology. A theoretical approach and research agenda have emerged over the past two decades that challenge the once dominant urban ecology approach. Despite resistance from those who rigidly defend the old orthodoxy (see, for instance, Kasarda and Crenshaw 1991), the *new urban sociology* is presenting a major theoretical challenge that is revitalizing research on cities (see Gottdeiner and Feagin 1988 for a programmatic statement). In contrast to conventional ecological theory, the alternative perspective pays more attention to social inequality and conflict while downplaying the primacy of technology and functional necessity as motors of cities and urbanization. Instead of developing as a unitary theory, the new urban sociology represents the confluence of a number of diverse conceptual and theoretical streams of urban studies variously labeled *critical theory, neo-Marxist sociology, urban political economy,* and *dependency/world-system analysis.*

The new urban sociologists interpret social change and urbanization in terms of the way societal processes and structures produce advantages for some groups and disadvantages for others. Their focus is often on the problematic "underside" of modern city life: urban poverty, housing segregation by race and social class, urban fiscal crises, deindustrialization, structured inequality in the built environment, and the massive level of human misery associated with the rapid growth of megacities in the Third World. In analyzing these problems, scholars emphasize such factors as the interests and actions of economic and political elites, influential urban institutions, the organizations, incentives, and disincentives that are built into the system (or systems) in which cities are situated, and relationships between cities and global forces.

Like urban ecologists, the new urban sociologists are concerned with systems of dominance and subordination operating across spatial boundaries. Unlike traditional human ecologists, the new urban sociologists view these hierarchies as driven by the actions (or inaction) of concrete social groups pursuing their particular perceived interests, sometimes with a vengeance. So the new urban sociologists are less interested in technological determinants or functional imperatives shaping urbanization and are more concerned with how political economic systems work, about which groups tend to monopolize power, and about who is likely to benefit, or suffer, from the status quo in cities.

This emerging paradigm offers many insights into cities and urban processes at a time when understanding urbanization is a particularly pressing social scientific and policy priority. In the late twentieth century, there has been unprecedented growth of cities in world regions that have always been predominantly rural, with the rapid growth of giant megacities in the Third World (Dogan and Kasarda 1988; United Nations 1991). Further, the unresolved problems of the urban areas of the advanced industrial nations have been thrown in sharp relief in recent years (the 1992 civil unrest in Los Angeles is one of the most recent, and most graphic, reminders).

Unfortunately, as Hutchinson (1993) argued in the introduction to the latest volume of *Research in Urban Sociology,* the new urban sociology is in crisis. The problem, simply put, is a classic "dialogue of the deaf." The older, more institutionally entrenched human ecological scholars have refused to "seriously engage the ideas presented by marxist scholars in the 1970s and by the new urban sociology of the 1980s" (Hutchinson 1993, 9). Evidence of this is found in the dismissive treatment of the new urban sociology in textbooks on the sociology of cities (examples include Choldin 1985; Schwab 1992) and in review articles in handbooks and annuals (see Frisbie and Kasarda 1988; Kasarda and Crenshaw 1991). On the other hand, proponents of the new urban sociology argue that their perspective is premised on a radical rejection of the basic assumptions of conventional mainstream sociological thinking about cities and urbanization derived from the human ecological perspective (see Gottdiener and Feagin 1988). The resulting "turf battles" and polarization of scholarship leads to needlessly fragmented, mutually uninformed research in contemporary urban sociology that inhibits understanding on all sides.

There is little doubt that the new urban sociology developed as a reaction to conventional ecological studies—to the basic assumptions about the "naturalness" of economic competition, technological change, and population dynamics and to the functionalist image of society's tendency toward collective adaptation. Proponents of contemporary urban ecology claim that these positions reflect basic tenets of traditional, or *classical,* human ecology (Berry and Kasarda 1977). In this article, a reexamination of some of the earlier texts on human ecology, however, leads to a different conclusion. Although the writings of Roderick McKenzie ([1921, 1924, 1926, 1933a, 1936] 1968, 1933b) and Amos Hawley (1950, 1968, 1979, 1984, 1986) mirror some of the conventional wisdom and biases of an earlier time, and although they tended to use language and a type of formal theorizing that may seem passé, I find some surprising affinities to the new urban sociology. It is a propitious time to reexamine (and, perhaps, even reclaim) some work associated with the older ecological paradigm.

Excavating of the *old* urban sociology and rediscovering it in light of the *new* is important for two reasons. First, there is the symbolic issue of intellectual patrimony and legitimation. Contemporary urban ecologists, like proponents of any scientific paradigm; defend their claims of theoretical, hegemony, in part, by positioning their theory as heir to a venerated tradition of scholarship. Unearthing work by classical ecological theorists that resonates with the new urban sociology undermines this argument and should serve as an impetus for dialogue and theoretical bridge building.

Second, and probably more critical, reexamining the old urban sociology may highlight some areas of theoretical overlap and continuity that are underappreciated and may offer real opportunities for the new urban sociologists to learn from urban ecology. Some of the variables that ecologists highlighted and began to understand really *are* important factors in city growth, urban life, and the urbanization processes. Rather than eschewing research into these factors (because they were central in the other paradigm), new urban sociologists can selectively learn from the old paradigm. Many of the ecological variables should remain central in any new sociology of cities: Changes in key technologies, dominant industries, and basic transportation systems *do* exert a profound influence on population distributions and the built environment. The challenge to urban sociologists today is to see these variables illuminated differently through the prism of the new paradigm.

This article begins with an abbreviated history and a summary of the new urban sociology. My vision of this perspective is a catholic one that is deliberately inclusive and avoids internecine squabbling and boundary drawing. The bulk of the article is devoted to revisiting two classical human ecology theorists, McKenzie and Hawley, in light of the basic premises of the new urban sociology. McKenzie's often ignored essays (written in the 1920s and 1930s) show that some of the key ideas of the new urban sociology about the global economy, economic exploitation, and uneven development were present in very early ecological formulations but were never fully explored by later ecologists. Hawley's sweeping theoretical statements, although perhaps overly abstract, provide a *formal* conceptual framework for analyzing some of the macro-level power relations and spatial arrangements that the political economists of the new-urban-sociology school describe.

Near the end of this discussion, I speculate about the potential contribution that Hawley's theory of social organization, technology, and population distributions, infused with new-urban-sociology assumptions about the specific content and nature of the contemporary capitalist global economy, might make to the beginnings of synthesized urban theory. The basic political-economic assumptions of the new urban sociology should allow scholars to recast and strengthen their understanding of how these processes play themselves out rather than lead scholars to ignore them. I suggest (albeit in a very preliminary way) that recent theoretical debates about *the new international division of labor, post-Fordism,* and *flexible production* (which have largely been borrowed from interdisciplinary urban and regional research and cognate fields such as geography) are very helpful here.

The Rise of the New Urban Sociology

There is little doubt that the new urban sociology received its initial impetus from critiques of conventional wisdom in the sociology of cities. On the one hand, it is a reaction to the inadequacies of mainstream approaches to U.S. cities, which have been dominated by the human ecology paradigm since the rise of the Chicago School in the 1920s and 1930s. On the other hand, the new urban sociology arose as a critical response to the *modernization theory,* or *developmentalist,* conceptualization of the rapid urbanization taking place in the less developed countries.

The New Urban Sociology and North American Cities

Probably the most important contributions leading to the emergence of the new urban sociology were two books about cities in advanced industrial societies published in the 1970s. In *Social Justice and the City*, Harvey (1973) argued that severe urban problems and social inequality in Baltimore were the direct, predictable results of the operation of capitalist markets in land and real estate. In a similar vein, in *The Urban Question,* Castells (1977) proposed a sweeping critique of the existing field of urban sociology, suggesting that it be supplanted by a more theoretically comprehensive Marxist approach to cities and urban life.

In the wake of these pioneering works, a variety of studies of urbanization in industrial core societies appeared during the late 1970s and the 1980s (examples of the early work are Harloe 1977; Tabb and Sawers 1978). This research is characterized by a rich, historically nuanced understanding of the growth of specific urban places. For instance, Feagin's (1988) case study of the rise of Houston from a sparsely populated swampland to one of the largest cities in the United States illustrates how the local economic elites and the *state* (in this case various levels of local, state, and national government) controlled and channeled urban and regional development even as the economic base of the area was transformed from timber and cotton production to local oil extraction and, finally, to corporate control over the global oil industry. Feagin convincingly argued that the supposedly quintessential free-enterprise city is less a product of free markets than it is a carefully molded result of collusion between government and business elites for the benefit of the few.

In another text, Feagin and Parker (1990, 2) claimed that U.S. cities generally are controlled by powerful circles of insiders composed of "industrial executives, developers, bankers, and their political allies." In other case studies, Soja (1987) identified business interests and the state as the driving forces behind the restructuring of Los Angeles, Glasberg (1989) emphasized the disproportionate power of banks in setting urban policy in Cleveland after the city went into default, and Gottdeiner (1977) highlighted the role land investors and speculators played in the suburbanization of New York's Long Island. Along with a better appreciation of the elite dominance of urban growth in United States has come an understanding that these places are enmeshed in an increasingly global economy. In landmark studies of New York (Sassen 1991), Detroit (Feagin and Hill 1987), and Buffalo (Perry 1987), scholars have emphasized this world-system link.

Perhaps the most systematic attempt to unite the themes of the new urban sociology in one study of U.S. urban dynamics appears in *Urban Fortunes: A Political Economy of Place* (Logan and Molotch 1987). Although the authors attempted to distance themselves from Marxist approaches, their central theme was the contradiction between *use value* and *exchange value* in North American communities and land markets. Particular pieces of land take on value to their residents because they are associated with neighborhoods and neighbors, schools, jobs, and all the psychological and symbolic values tied to the notions of *community* or *hometown*. However, the people who make up the *urban growth coalition* are primarily interested in this same real estate as a commodity that can be bought and sold. Instead of viewing cities and towns as places to live and work and enjoy various amenities, the growth elites primarily are interested in promoting a good business climate that will draw more migrants and investment and increase the market value or land. In addition to explaining how and why "banks and savings institutions, real estate brokers, and landlords" (p. 26) dominate local decision making over urban processes, Logan and Molotch also pointed to the way that U.S. localities are dependent players in the *transnational system* of the late twentieth century (pp. 248–96). Thus class structures and political systems dominated by narrow elite interests and the difficulties of dealing with issues like *international competitiveness* make the possibility of progressive popular control of urban and regional growth increasingly difficult.

Needless to say, this conceptualization of *the political economy of place* represents a coherent statement of a theoretical framework on urbanization that is breathtakingly different from the old ecological emphasis on how technological change allows populations aggregates to adapt to their environment through changes in social and spatial organization.

The New Urban Sociology and Comparative Urban Research

During the past 20 years, there has been a parallel paradigm shift in comparative social science. Throughout the 1970s, the dominant developmentalist approach was subject to scathing criticism, primarily from proponents of world-system and dependency theories (see Portes 1976 for a seminal statement). In the last decade, the political economy of the world-system assumptions have become widely accepted and the starting point for a plethora of studies on macrostructural change.

Despite this major theoretical-sea change and the world-system perspective's obvious relevance to cities, comparative urban sociology remains heavily influenced by the earlier developmentalist assumptions of modernization theory and human ecology. This is particularly true among area specialists and urban planners with expertise in non-Western societies (see Mills and Song 1979; Richardson 1980; Murphey 1988). This lingering developmentalism reflects an old, deeply ingrained heritage in urban studies. The basic assumptions of stages and phases of city growth were implicit in the classical sociological theories of the nineteenth century and explicitly formulated in the touchstone texts of early urban sociology, such as in Weber's ([1899] 1963) *The Growth of Cities in the Nineteenth Century*. The structural-functional and developmentalist assumptions were further codified by the founders of human ecology in the early decades of the twentieth century (Park 1916; Park and Burgess 1925; McKenzie 1933b). Later modernization theorists who researched city growth in the less developed countries continued this tradition. Following a European/North American model implied that city growth was integrally tied to industrialization and economic growth (Bose 1971; Ginsburg 1972; for a critique, see Roberts 1978, 10–11).

By the mid-1970s, the growing inequality and continued economic underdevelopment in much of the Third World, particularly manifest in the largest cities, led many comparative social scientists to reevaluate the conventional developmentalist assumptions of modernization theory and human ecology (Walton 1977). It had become obvious that Third World patterns and processes were not conforming to the models of urbanization and development borrowed from the Western experience, with its emphasis on generative cities and intersocietal convergence (Roberts 1978, 5–35). Evidence mounted that highlighted the diverse trajectories of urban growth *between* different Third World countries and regions.

In the last decade, the dependency/world-system perspective has proven to be a particularly powerful tool for analyzing macrostructural change. In the late 1970s, a number of pioneering efforts were made to apply the general logic of this international political-economy perspective to comparative research on cities and urban systems (Castells 1977; Walton 1977; Slater 1978; Roberts 1978). More recently, programmatic statements of a world-system perspective on urbanization have appeared, synthesizing the early formulations and a growing body of empirical research (Walton 1982; Chase-Dunn 1984; Timberlake 1987).

Timberlake (1985, 10) succinctly summarized the major premise of the world-system perspective:

> Urbanization must be studied holistically—part of the logic of a larger process of socioeconomic development that encompasses it, and that entails systematic unevenness across regions of the world. The dependence relation is an important theoretical construct used to pry into the ways in which the processes embodied

in the world-system produce various manifestations of this unevenness, including divergent patterns of urbanization.

Gugler and Flanagan (1977, 273) specified three potential types of unevenness, or inequality, related to urbanization (and prevalent in the Third World):

1. the imbalance between life chances in urban and rural sectors;
2. among cities, the concentration of limited resources in the capitals and/or primate cities;
3. within cities, the economic disparity between the masses and a small wealthy elite.

Researchers using a global perspective attempt to account for the extent of such unevenness by linking urbanization to the expansion and changing dynamics of the capitalist world-system. They emphasize the way cities were shaped by the historical impact of colonialism, as well as the contemporary effects of international trade and investment. The current mode of production operates at the global level, incorporating virtually the entire earth (including seemingly remote regions of underdeveloped countries) into a world-system of hierarchical social, economic, and political relationships. Therefore, they believe, city growth must be analyzed in this context. Structural similarity between nations or regions in the global hierarchy (core, semiperiphery, periphery) may lead to parallel patterns of urban growth. More generally, in the capitalist world-economy, the fundamental units of rational profit and loss calculation are usually extralocal (depending on the historical period: colonial empires, mercantile companies, multinational corporations). Therefore, the development needs of specific countries, cities, and communities are not likely to be very relevant to key decision makers at the globally important levels.

Although the global economy provides the backdrop for urbanization, this perspective moves politics to center stage. Cities are the outcome of decision-making processes influenced or directed by dominant classes and the state. Although some world-system analysts of urbanization and development continue to focus on the generic links between dependence/world-system position and types of urbanization (Evans and Timberlake 1980; Kentor 1981; London 1987; Smith and London 1990), authors of many recent studies are more concerned with specifying how socioeconomic processes operating at the global level interact with local processes, events, and structures pertinent to particular cities and urban systems (C. Smith 1985; Nemeth and Smith 1985; London 1985; Armstrong and McGee 1985; D. Smith 1987; Cooke 1989; King 1990; Sassen 1991).

Basic Assumptions of the New Urban Sociology

At this point, I would like to lay out what, in my view, are the underlying principles of the new urban sociology. The following five assumptions are, drawn and modified from the theoretical chapter in Feagin (1988, 14–42) and abstracted from a fuller discussion in Smith and Timberlake (1992):

1. *Cities are situated in a hierarchical global system.* Cities and urban life throughout the world are shaped, to a significant degree, by their specific location and involvement in the international system. The world-system's history is marked by unevenness, with some groups in core areas exploiting people and resources in other regions. Today, with the entire globe increasingly integrated into a single global political economy, patterns of urbanization have much to do with how a region fits into the international division of labor and with how local systems of class, racial/ethnic, and gender relations develop in connection with the operation of the world-system.

2. *The world-system is one of competitive capitalism.* Because the international system is driven by the competitive logic of capitalism, locally based actors (i.e., politicians and businesspeople) attempt to outbid one another for access to capital, cheap labor, and resources. This process transmits aspects of competitive capitalism to geographic space; therefore, as Feagin (1988, 23) explained, "it involves the creation and destruction of land and built environments we term 'cities.'" Moreover, this leads to concentrations and locational shifts of human populations, infrastructure, and buildings within the urban landscape (resulting in suburbs, neighborhoods, slums, etc.).

3. *Capital is easily moved; cities are locationally fixed.* Gain and loss is usually calculated within corporations, with owners and managers acting to maximize profitability. These actions include moving capital (in the form of factories, corporate offices, etc.) from one location to another, in an attempt to improve the "bottom line." Both investment and disinvestment profoundly affect communities, sometimes leading to local congestion and overdevelopment and in other cases, resulting in capital drain and deindustrialization in these places (see Bluestone and Harrison 1982).

4. *Politics and government matter.* Feagin (1988, 24) wrote that "the state in modern capitalist societies is linked, in historically shaped and fluctuating ways" to the economic processes that form cities. Contrary to the simplistic assumption that the lone driving force behind spatial patterns in capitalist economies is the invisible hand of the market, states are fundamental actors determining the flow of capital over the face of the earth, including from one city or region to another. The policies of different political jurisdictions (whether they are towns, counties, provinces, or nations) on matters like corporate taxes, road building, and the regulation of workplaces, shape local business climates, which strongly influence patterns of urban growth or decline.

5. *People and circumstances differ according to time and place, and these differences matter.* Cities are created by real flesh-and-blood people making decisions in particular situations (about things like taxes, roads, regulations, and investments). This may seem fairly obvious—but it can get lost in abstract social science explanations focusing on variables and social forces. People may cooperate with each

other in opposition to, or in support of, a variety of policies that determine the spatial and social character of cities. Although it is likely that historical changes can largely be explained by using general theories about how members of various classes or groups act under specified structural conditions, these processes are not deterministic and there is always room for contingency and *conjunctural causation* (see Ragin 1987). This assumption explains why many new urban sociologists prefer case studies.

Reexamining Classical Human Ecology

With the basic assumptions of the new urban sociology firmly in mind, I now turn to an excavation of the classical texts of two writers who are strongly identified with the human ecology tradition. Surprisingly, some of this work actually *foreshadows* new-urban-sociology premises and may help bridge some theoretical gaps. First, I will discuss some remarkable essays by McKenzie, written well over half a century ago, that presented images strikingly prescient of some of the basic insights of the new urban sociology about urbanization in the global system. Second, I examine the basic theoretical framework developed by Hawley—who, of course, wrote the book on human ecology (literally) in 1950. Hawley's highly abstract formulations are not so antithetical to new-urban-sociology ideas; they might even provide some basic scaffolding on which to build synthesized urban theory consistent with this approach.

McKenzie: Glimpses of the Capitalist World-System?

Along with Ernest Burgess and Robert Park, Roderick McKenzie was part of the founding trioka of the Chicago School of human ecology. Perhaps his most famous work is a definitive 1933 study of urbanization in the United States entitled *The Metropolitan Community* (McKenzie 1933b). This exhaustive study, commissioned by the President's Commission on Recent Social Trends, represented a then state-of-the-art demographic analysis of U.S. census data. It continues to be cited in urban sociology texts today (for example, Palen 1992). The book established McKenzie as a pioneer in the analysis of population statistics and census data.

There is another, relatively unexplored side to McKenzie's thinking buried in his less well-known work, however. Fortunately, his most famous student, Amos Hawley, compiled a collection of McKenzie's journal articles, book chapters, and even one previously unpublished essay in a book published in 1968. Most of this volume allows the reader to sketch the evolution of now standard ideas identified with the human ecological approach: the importance of technology, the friction of space, *zones of transition* in cities, *daily urban systems* for commuters, and the like. It is obvious that the rough-hewn building blocks of Hawley's own *Human Ecology* (1950) were scattered through these chapters. But for the reader versed in the new urban sociology there are some startlingly familiar conceptions here about cities and social change in the global system.

McKenzie shared the view of other ecological theorists that technological changes and quasi-natural competition are the driving forces shaping political and economic institutions, as well as the distribution of population in space. Yet, he also was an astute observer who saw basic changes in economic structure as critically important to understanding modern society. One of these trends was the increasing concentration of power and resources in very large economic institutions with growing international power. In different words and in a morally detached way, McKenzie described the rise of what later global political economy theorists call *monopoly capitalism* (and he was not shy about repeatedly asserting the importance of capital and its movement). Although it is a consistent theme throughout these essays—for example, he wrote that "centralization of economic control will undoubtedly be the trend in the future" ([1926] 1968, 139)—his clearest discussion of this issue and its impact on urbanization was in a 1936 essay, "The Ecology of Institutions" (McKenzie [1936] 1968). Here, he claimed that technological changes that improve transportation and communications lead to "a pronounced tendency toward fewer and larger units among all classes of institutions—industrial, commercial, financial, social—followed by increasing territorial concentrations of activities" (p. 107). Although this quote suggests that economic institutions are only one type undergoing change, he pointed out later (p. 110) that

> it is important in the study of any unit of settlement to differentiate those types of activities which furnish the economic base of the institutional hierarchy from those which relate to consumption and the cultural life of the community. The former we may characterize as the basic institutions. . . . The basic institutions play a predominant role in the life and character of the local community; in fact, they constitute the very foundation of the community's existence.

This discussion is a direct prelude to Hawley's formulation of the *key function* in a community, but it also bears an obvious affinity to Marx's materialist model of change. Later in the essay (p. 115), McKenzie wrote that the pattern of concentration has resulted in "greater efficiency," but "as our institutions have grown in size and range of function, competition has compelled them to consider their own interests above those of their employees and of the communities in which they happen to be located." Here, McKenzie was presaging one of the basic assumptions (number 3) of the new urban sociology listed earlier.

Even more striking are McKenzie's discussions of *industrial expansion* and *world dominance*. The previously discussed processes of centralization and concentration of economic power, he argued, must be placed in the context of the global expansion of the world market. In a chapter entitled "Industrial Expansion and the Interrelations of Peoples" (McKenzie [1933a] 1968, just over 40 years before Wallerstein [1974] published the first volume of *The Modern World-System*), he explained that

> the history of modern civilisation is largely the story of European expansion, which, slowly at first, then with increasing momentum, brought different regions and peoples within a common economic order and a common cultural milieu. While this development, extending over four centuries, is a single process, it is by no means a simple one. The rate of change has not been uniform; there have been periods

of rapid expansion followed by periods of relative stagnation. Different European peoples have taken the lead at different times. Frequent changes have occurred in the political and economic alignments of centers and peripheries. (p. 123)

In this remarkable essay, McKenzie described the cyclic nature of "uneven development" (p. 122), the phenomena of economic "penetration" of newly incorporated areas (p. 123), and three phases of Western expansion. He wrote that the first stage (fifteenth through early nineteenth centuries) witnessed "transoceanic rim-settlement," which occurred because "the attitude and practice of the different European powers throughout this period were predatory and exploitative" (p. 124). At this time, trade was the key, and McKenzie hinted that a process that Marxist scholars call *primitive accumulation* was the result: "The lucrative trade of plantation and Eastern products furnished certain European powers, notably England, with the capital reserves necessary for the subsequent development of manufacturing" (p. 125). During the next phase of "the rise of industrial cities" (from the mid-nineteenth century to World War I), an international division of labor emerged based on "the exchange of manufactured goods for food and other raw materials" (p. 126). The final phases of "cultural maturation and economic nationalism" was the post–World War I period that witnessed the "rise of the U.S. and Japan as centers of world expansion" (p. 128). This delineation of stages of global economic expansion, in both style and substance, is strikingly similar to period identifications provided by dependency/world-system writers in the late twentieth century. McKenzie's essay also included a discussion of "backward countries" that are under U.S. "economic dominance" and "political hegemony" that could have come right out of the Latin American *dependista* tradition. All the more so when McKenzie pointed out that the "regions specializing in the production of a single export product" (which he later identified as *monoexport*) faced "the most serious problems" (pp. 129–30).

In another essay, McKenzie ([1926] 1968) specified how the relatively new "Euro-American world dominance" (p. 136) and "the recent emergence of a world market" (p. 136) affects migration and settlement patterns. He was careful to make the causality explicit: "Under the dominance of the greater market, it is the movement of capital that determines the movement of people rather than the reverse" (p. 137). By McKenzie's time, this market had become a global one in which "the sweep of western capital into the remote corners of the world is of profound importance with reference to human migration" (p. 139). This general notion of the role of foreign investment in stimulating migration from underdeveloped countries and regions presages the more precise empirically grounded formulation of the relationship between the mobility of labor and capital by leading new-urban-sociology theorists in the late twentieth century (for instance, Sassen 1988). So, although contemporary ecologists/modernization proponents continue to emphasize internal factors endogenous to developing countries over external ones (see, for instance, Kasarda and Crenshaw 1991), McKenzie clearly identified himself with a view that would later be labeled a world-system perspective. Although he conceived of development as a "problem of equilibrium," he clearly argued that in a world of increasing economic interdependence, "regional prosperity or depression is determined largely by forces which operate in parts of the world over which the region itself has little or no control" (p. 138). McKenzie ended this essay by darkly suggesting that because "the West still treats the East as though it were a subordinate outpost" (p. 140), there is a real prospect that the non-Western masses might rise up and demand their fair share of global output (shades of Wallerstein's [1984, Part II] *antisystemic movements?*). There is no reason to doubt that this early progenitor of the ecological school would agree with the new urban sociologists that social change must be situated in a hierarchical global system (basic assumption number one listed earlier). McKenzie's essays should be required reading for all those who think that human ecology is intrinsically linked to modernization theory. A number of his notions (and, indeed, even some of the *specific terminology*) is much closer in spirit to Wallerstein (1984), Chase-Dunn (1984), or Sassen (1988, 1991) than to contemporary urban ecologists!

It is important to insert a caveat here. Although I have shown that it is possible to glean a surprisingly contemporary and sophisticated image of the global system and its role in social change from McKenzie's writing, it is important to acknowledge that there are other elements in these essays that are more consistent with evolutionary theory and developmentalism—for example, McKenzie wrote that "in the process of community growth there is a development from simple to complex, from general to specialized" ([1924] 1968, 12), and "cities constitute the engines which drive the expansion process" ([1933a] 1968, 132). There is also a heavy, arguably naive and illegitimate, emphasis in McKenzie's essays on biological analogies to social processes like urban growth (for example, comparing "primitive human communities" to simple life forms seems problematic). Of course, throughout these essays, written over a half century ago, McKenzie reported "current research results" that, with the benefit of hindsight, one now knows are simplistic or wrong and perpetuate inaccurate (or even offensive) racial, national, and gender stereotypes—for example, he wrote that "E. L. Thorndike says, 'old age, femaleness, and physical weakness' seem to favor 'the long familiar physical environment' while 'adolescence, maleness, and energy' seem to be combined with the roaming disposition" ([1921] 1968, 66). McKenzie's work *is* part of the Chicago School and reflects the interests and biases of the early-twentieth-century social science.

Still, there is something exhilarating and dazzling about McKenzie's 60-year-old insights into the nature of urbanization and socioeconomic change in the global system. Unfortunately, these parts of McKenzie's work read like lost manuscripts containing the wisdom of the ancients. They were ignored by later human ecologists and probably unknown to the founders of the new urban sociology. It is impossible not to be struck by the enormity of the lost opportunity. Why did later urban ecologists adopt views consistent with this theorist's ideas about technology and transport, urban dominance, and community but not those that focus on global markets and the effects of economic concentration? I suspect that there may be some ideological explanation. Perhaps ideas about equilibrium, competition, and collective adaptation fit better during the putative American Century than those about problems associated with the global reach of capital.

In a recent review article, contemporary urban ecologists Kasarda and Crenshaw (1991, 485) implied that modernization/ecology and new-urban-sociology approaches are fundamentally contradictory and efforts at finding common ground are futile because "such marriages of theoretical families may not be particularly happy." They proceeded to assert that ecologists reject the idea of core exploitation of the periphery and to claim that "most modernization/ecological theorists have trouble understanding the phrase 'uneven development'" (p. 485). McKenzie described core-periphery exploitation and would have had no difficulty with the concept of uneven development. He was quite comfortable with *combining* themes that resonate with world-system/dependency theory or the new urban sociology with his ecological approach. Although coming up with some type of synthesized urban sociology that integrates today's competing perspectives is an onerous task, it may not be impossible. Could it be that those who argue the most vociferously against theoretical accommodation may fear that it may not take place on their terms? It seems safe to say that at least one of the founders of human ecology would be leading efforts to bridge the paradigmatic gap.

Amos Hawley's Human Ecology

The research and writing of Amos Hawley have now covered almost half a century. He was a student of Roderick McKenzie; in turn, he has been the teacher of many of today's urban sociologists (including some who identify with the new urban sociology). His early work quickly established him as both a prominent social theorist and a skilled demographic researcher—a most rare combination. In his recent work, Hawley has returned to theory construction, and he grapples with some very sophisticated issues of ecological expansion and cumulative social change (Hawley 1979, 1986) and makes a serious attempt to understand the parallels and contrasts between human ecological and Marxian theories (Hawley 1984). The following is a brief, tentative look at how Hawley's human ecology might be relevant to the new urban sociology. It mainly draws on his most famous book and his short theoretical summary of human ecology in 1968.

Human Ecology: A Theory of Community Structure, which Hawley published in 1950, was dedicated to McKenzie and represented the student's attempt to codify and expand the theoretical system of his teacher. It became the so-called Green Bible of the ecological tradition. In it, Hawley described the relationship between biological ecology and human ecology, discussed the relationship between environment, population, and social organization, and outlined a theory of change and development. His goal was "to develop a full and coherent theory of human ecology" (p. v), establishing it as a nomothetic scientific subdiscipline. Even though the pages are filled with graphs, statistics, and detailed descriptions of particular places and processes, Hawley's intention was to develop an abstract, encompassing theory about social organization. In this regard, the volume is not so different from Parsons' *The Social System*, which appeared a year later. There are other similarities as well: Although rejecting the "culturalistic" approach of Parsons' *cybernetic hierarchy*, Hawley's human ecology is unabashedly functionalist. He focused on the community as a complete and self-sustaining whole that is interdependent and constantly adapting to its physical and social environment and that passes through various stages of equilibrium. There is also an evolutionary image of organizations, communities, and societies having a natural history in which they tend to move from a simple to an increasingly complex division of labor (Hawley 1968, 330–31).

However, human ecology is distinguished from other variants of evolutionary structural-functionalism in several ways. First, it is a materialistic approach, emphasizing the importance of how people gain sustenance from their environment. Second, population, its size, and its spatial distribution are seen as key factors in social organization (although Hawley [1968, 30] argued that in many instances, population is "better regarded as the dependent variable"). Third, technology, particularly as it shapes communication and transportation networks, is critically important to understanding social change. Finally, the emergence of dominance and hierarchy is a central issue in human ecology and is linked closely to a community's key function: "the activity that extracts the principal sustenance from local resources" (p. 332).

Scholars familiar with urban sociology in the United States over the past 40 years know that the ecological approach inspired by Hawley's formulation led to a plethora of empirical studies focusing on spatial arrangements, metropolitan dominance, and the relationships between the variables in the POET (population, organization, environment, and technology) complex; (see Duncan 1959). These were the studies that the new urban sociology's early practitioners were reacting against. But Hawley (1984, 914) has also been critical of the studies done in the name of human ecology that have a "preoccupation with spatial patterns and distribution" and has argued that even Marxists and human ecologists can learn from each other (1984, 914). So what can the new urban sociologists team from his perspective?

Before answering that question, it is necessary to mention that there are some elements of the original formulations that are not compatible with the basic understandings of the new urban sociology. The idea of communities as symbiotically engaged in adaptive upgrading was consistent with the functional themes of the 1950s and 1960s, but it obscures actors (both individual and collective) and agency in urban process. The comparative studies of urbanization and social change that debunked modernization theory cast doubt on developmentalist natural history conceptions of societal evolution. Indeed, the idea of a nomothetic theory of urbanization and societal growth is greeted with a healthy skepticism by new urban sociology researchers (see basic assumption 5 listed earlier). Hawley's notion that increased differentiation is linked to community size and changes in its key function is problematic in this regard. Also, this conception of differentiation and the formation of "categoric units" (Hawley 1968, 334) is overly abstract and indeterminate, sliding over the crucial issue of social class.

There are also some elements of Hawley's human ecology that overlap with the concerns of the new urban sociology and may offer opportunities for bridge building and synthesis. Certainly, this type of theoretical cross-fertilization is something he himself supports. Writing about human ecology and Marxian theory, Hawley (1984, 914) argued,

> Each theory could accommodate the problem with which the other is concerned. That is, greater sensitivity to environmental effects could have enriched Marxian theory, just as further development of the political-economic implications of its theory can raise the explanatory power of human ecology.

Some theoretical bridges are possible in places at which the ecological model provides an initial framework but needs revision and specification. One of these entry points involves the emphasis on hierarchical patterns of relationships and the idea of dominance. Here is a point at which the "further development of the political-economic implications" of the new urban sociology can strengthen and flesh out the abstract (almost skeletal!) image that ecology presents. Hawley (1984, 910) perceptively commented,

> A hierarchy is clearly a power gradient; power inherent in functions diminishes with degree of removal from the role at the apex, whether regarded as key function or as capitalist.

The problem with the conception of power and dominance in Hawley's classical statements (1950 and 1968) is the vague formulation of *differentiation* and the assumption of multiple *gradients* in the social hierarchies. This high level of generality is designed to produce nomothetic propositions that will fit virtually all empirical situations. So instead of discussing social classes as defined by people's roles as managers or workers in their economic system (which could be linked to the manner in which they derive sustenance, or their relationship to the key function), Hawley saw differentiation in modern societies creating many diverse categories of people. Occupational categories may be the most salient of these, but there is no privileged position for social class per se. In the 1984 essay, Hawley reiterated that for ecologists, "class is one of several species of categoric grouping in ecological thought" (p. 910). He proceeded to make a justifiable criticism of simplistic classical Marxist conceptions of class as inadequate in the more complex economy of the late twentieth century. The new urban sociology, however, uses more sophisticated images of classes under various forms of contemporary capitalism to pry into the political economy of urban processes. If one accepts the new-urban-sociology premise that there is a capitalist global economy in which class interests (sometimes mediated through political states) are likely to be particularly important in shaping macroprocesses like urbanization, it is possible to move to a set of better specified research hypotheses about power and dominance.

One type of dominance involves the idea of global power in the modern world-system. Here, Hawley was very clear in his critique of later ecologists, pointing to the relative neglect of interregional and international relationships "despite the early interest in imperialism shown by R. D. McKenzie and others" (1984, 913). In their very one-sided review of research on Third World urbanization, even Kasarda and Crenshaw (1991, 486) acknowledged that ecological studies have learned to be more "sensitive to international/economic contexts" as a result of new-urban-sociology research. So even the most dyed-in-the-wool urban ecologists accept the idea that cities must be understood in terms of their niches in the global system (see basic assumption number one). This is another point of theoretical convergence. In an adequate synthesized urban theory, the global embeddedness of urbanization would be an integral element, rather than the post hoc addendum of recent ecological writings. Yet, reviewing McKenzie's early attempts to understand world dominance reminds today's scholar that this is a forgotten insight of human ecology rather than a foreign one.

There are also elements of Hawley's human ecology that highlight factors that the new urban sociologists have neglected and need to consider more seriously. Among these are population and demography. The fact is that most urban political economists and comparative urban researchers who use world-system analysis are not particularly sensitive to, or knowledgeable about, population. (Demographers also tend to be poorly informed about recent theoretical developments in macrosociology.) This exposes new-urban-sociology research to criticism that size is not taken into account or that population growth is ignored (see Kasarda and Crenshaw 1991). In fact, there *have* been some serious attempts to explore the relationship between demographic dynamics and global political economy (Michaelson 1981; Seccombe 1983). These researchers debunk mainstream conceptions, for instance, by showing that it makes more sense to see fertility change and population growth as a *result* of social inequality or poverty rather than as a *cause* (consistent with Hawley's [1968] hunch that population is better conceived as a dependent variable). Most of the criticism directed at the new urban sociology about ignoring population is not particularly damaging, however, because the critics tend to misconstrue the arguments that are being made. Yet, more attention to the demographic process and variables would be desirable. By default, it may be up to researchers in the new urban sociology, perhaps drawing on work in cognate fields like geography, to develop a theory of demographic change under global capitalism.

Finally, and perhaps most important, there is the issue of technology. It is central to Hawley's theory, with the emphasis on the way changes in communication and transportation effect societal expansion and settlement patterns. Although Hawley rightly criticized Marx for offering "no explanation for technological change" (1984, 908), his own approach is problematic as well. He underscored the gradual accretion and combination of available information and assumed that technology evolves in a value-free manner as part of the process of adaptive upgrading, thus ignoring the fact that technology itself is a *social* product, often designed to fit the needs of the rich and powerful. Furthermore, the application and use of technology is also determined by political-economic processes. So configurations of communication and transportation infrastructure are shaped not only by the limits of existing scientific knowledge and engineering techniques but also by the interests of the powerful. Contrary to developmentalist/modernization/convergence theories, technology does not simply diffuse across space—or across states or societies either—except in the most superficial way.

In these approaches, this pattern of technological diffusion is assumed to lead to industrialization and economic growth in less developed regions. Today, even though FAX machines and computerized air traffic systems are found in the most isolated and destitute African countries, such technology has not led to developmental miracles. The key is not the *physical possession* of sophisticated equipment or system but the effective *control* of the know-how and organization to *produce* innovative science and technology. Third World countries plagued by technological dependence (see Ernst 1980; Gereffi 1983) and the difficult issues of technology transfer (Stewart 1977; Robinson 1988) highlight the extent to which technological and scientific change are embedded in their global context.

Current interdisciplinary debates about the relationship between technology and urban and regional development are closely tied to debates about the nature of global restructuring. Economic geographer Peter Dicken (1992, 97), in his influential book *Global Shift: The Internationalization of Economic Activity,* claimed that "technological change is the heart of the process of economic growth and economic development." Indeed, a number of conceptions of global economic realignment call attention to the technology/information dimension, claiming that the changes taking place represent the crossing of a new *industrial divide* (Piore and Sabel 1984) leading to the rise of *post-Fordist production* (Storper and Walker 1989) and *flexible production complexes* (Scott 1988). These views emphasize the advantages of location in tightly integrated and economically interdependent *industrial districts* that permits quick and flexible responses to the rapidly changing demands of the world market (Scott 1988; Porter 1990). The name of the game for urban, regional, and national development becomes *industrial upgrading* to move to a more advantageous position in worldwide production networks, variously described as *value chains* (Porter 1990), *production chains* (Dicken 1992), and *global commodity chains* (Gereffi, Korzeniewicz, and Korzeniewicz 1994). To succeed in this new post-Fordist world, firms need (1) access to information and innovation and (2) linkages to other firms (as suppliers, buyers, or production partners), research and development organizations, and marketing outlets. The competitive advantages of nations will be held by those who control key technologies and production/distribution networks (Porter 1990). "Flexible production complexes" in agglomerations of linked activities will "form the new growth centers of the world system" (Scott 1988, 178).

Although the new urban sociologists and other critics are right to be wary of the technological determinism of some contemporary ecological research, the recent debates about industrial districts and flexible accumulation really *do* move technological innovation back to the center of analysis. Technology (especially as it is produced via research and development) and infrastructure (particularly in terms of transportation and communications networks to integrate production/marketing complexes) are viewed as crucial shapers of urban, regional, and national development trajectories. From the new-urban-sociology perspective, however, these factors must be conceptualized in the context of both on-the-ground politics and class dynamics and the wider global capitalist economy. Most of the literature from regional science and geography and on post-Fordism and flexible accumulation asserts that this transformation of industrial economies is unlikely to solve basic problems of inequality and uneven development. But a few commentators argue that flexibility and *technolopolis* strategies are panaceas offering solutions to development problems for cities, regions, and nations. They recommend that cities and regions emulate specific industrial districts in Italy (Porter 1990) and encourage people to become highly skilled *symbolic analysts* (Reich 1991). In its more sanguine forms, this recent literature swerves perilously close to an old modernization/developmentalist view of *industrial society* (see Giddens 1985, 122–47) that downplays local and regional class inequality and ignores the reality of uneven development and exploitation on a global scale. McKenzie would remind scholars of the importance of taking both into account!

Toward Dialogue and Common Ground

In this rereading of some classical ecological theory in light of the assumptions of the new urban sociology, I had two goals. First, there was a problem in the realm of the history of ideas. By showing that two venerated ecological theorists presented images that fit as well (or better!) with the new urban sociology than with contemporary urban ecology, this article challenges one of the underpinnings of ecologists' claim to paradigmatic dominance. Second, by highlighting some of the areas of overlap (and, surprisingly, agreement) between the new urban sociology and classical ecology, I hope that this article will open constructive dialogue between the competing paradigms and, ultimately, point urban sociology in the direction of synthesized theory building, however limited and middle range.

I want to differentiate this strategy from one that argues for an eclectic approach that results in a conceptual stew. In particular, quantitative multivariate analyses of urbanization are prone to mixed results that often provide some evidence for competing theoretical perspectives, and sometimes neither is the clear "winner." The tendency then is to suggest that because some hypotheses of both the ecological and new-urban-sociology/political-economy approaches are correct, the best one can produce are explanations that include a little of this theory and a little of that theory. This is unsatisfactory. The goal of any scientific field should be to arrive at parsimonious explanations derived from careful development of theories. Obviously, one's conceptual apparati will rarely explain everything and are likely to be constantly under construction. But cobbling together explanations from competing theoretical traditions, without trying to grasp their underlying coherence, is a slippery slope that ultimately leads to pure description. This is particularly the case when two theoretical perspectives *share* as many basic assumptions about the nature of change and appropriate levels of analysis as the contending urban sociologies do.

This does not mean that urban sociology should seek one grand theory (à la either Karl Marx or Talcott Parsons) that will explain everything in a neat comprehensive way. This is hardly possible. More realistically, urban sociologists should strive to develop general orienting assumptions about cities and change that facilitate dialogue, discussion, and systematic accumulation of research among scholars.

Doubtlessly, it would take at least another article, and probably a book, to begin to develop this sort of urban sociological synthesis. But, preliminarily, I suggest that it would begin by acknowledging the importance of the global dynamics of capitalism. The various assumptions of the new urban sociology would be operant here, and the international context would set the parameters for national and local processes. Although this would move one away from some of the preoccupations of contemporary urban ecology, procrustean notions about hierarchy and dominance influenced by the writings of classical ecologists like McKenzie and Hawley could be reformulated and revised. A place would have to be found for population dynamics. Factors traditionally associated with human ecology (infrastructure provision, level of technology) are still likely to be the proximate cause of urban change. But these would be understood in the political economic context of national societies (including class dynamics, local mode of production [key function?], and the role of the state), which, in turn, are embedded in the world-system and various historically constrained logics of global restructuring. The true test of this theoretical apparatus would be its ability to generate research, accommodate discrepant findings, and be flexible enough to grow and change in sync with new evidence and ideas in urban studies and macrosociology. Even the attempt to build a synthesized urban theory of this type could lead to better understanding of the considerable conceptual convergence that already exists in urban sociology, build better dialogue between the adherents of competing paradigms, and redirect attention to sociological studies of cities and away from polemical defenses of intellectual turf.

References

Armstrong, w., and T. G. McGee. 1985. *Theatres of accumulation: Studies in Asian and Latin American urbanization.* London: Methuen.

Berry, B., and J. Kasarda. 1977. *Contemporary human ecology.* New York: Macmillan.

Bluestone, B., and B. Harrison. 1982. *The deindustrialization of America.* New York: Basic Books.

Bose, A. 1971. The urbanization process in Southeast Asia. In *Urbanization and national development,* edited by L. Jakobson and V. Prakash, 81–109. Beverly Hills, CA: Sage.

Castells, M. 1977. *The urban question: A Marxist approach.* Cambridge, MA: MIT.

Chase-Dunn, C. 1984. Urbanization in the world-system: New directions for research. In *Cities in transformation,* edited by M. Smith, 111–20. Beverly Hills, CA: Sage.

Choldin, H. 1985. *Cities and suburbs.* New York: McGraw-Hill.

Cooke, P., ed. 1989. *Localities: The changing face of Britain.* London: Unwin Hyman.

Dicken, P. 1992. *Global shift: The internationalization of economic activity.* 2d ed. New York: Guilford.

Dogan, M., and J. Kasarda, eds. 1988. *The metropolis era. Volume 2: Mega-cities.* Newbury Park, CA: Sage.

Duncan, O. D. 1959. Human ecology and population studies. In *The study of population: An inventory and appraisal,* edited by P. Hauser and O. Duncan, 678–716. Chicago: Univ. of Chicago Press.

Ernst, D. 1980. *The new international division of labor, technology and development.* Frankfurt, Germany: Campus Verlag.

Evans, P., and M. Timberlake. 1980. Dependence, inequality, and the growth of the tertiary: A comparative analysis of less developed countries. *American Sociological Review* 45 (4): 531–55.

Feagin, J. 1988. *The free enterprise city: Houston in political-economic perspective.* New Brunswick NJ: Rutgers Univ. Press.

Feagin, J., and R. Hill. 1987. Detroit and Houston: Two cities in global perspective. In *The capitalist city: Global restructuring and community politics,* edited by M. Smith and J. Feagin, 155–77. New York: Basil Blackwell.

Feagin, J., and R. Parker. 1990. *Building American cities: The urban real estate game.* Englewood Cliffs, NJ: Prentice-Hall.

Frisbie, W. P., and J. D. Kasarda. 1988. Spatial processes. In *The handbook of modern sociology,* edited by N. Smelser. Newbury Park, CA: Sage.

Gereffi, G. 1983. *The pharmaceutical industry and dependency in the Third World.* Princeton, NJ: Princeton Univ. Press.

Gereffi, G., M. Korzeniewicz, and R. Korzeniewicz. 1994. Introduction: Global commodity chains. In *Commodity chains and global capitalism,* edited by G. Gereffi and M. Korzeniewic, 1–14. Westport, CT: Praeger.

Giddens, A. 1985. The nation state and violence. In *A critique of historical materialism.* Vol. 2. Berkeley: Univ. of California Press.

Ginsburg, N. 1972. Planning the future of the Southeast Asian city. In *Focus on Southeast Asia,* edited by A. Taylor, 43–59. New York: Praeger.

Glasberg, D. 1989. *The power of collective purse strings: The effects of bank hegemony on corporations and the state.* Berkeley: Univ. of California Press.

Gottdiener, M. 1977. *Planned sprawl: Private and public interests in suburbia.* Beverly Hills, CA: Sage.

Gottdiener, M., and J. Feagin. 1988. The paradigm shift in urban sociology. *Urban Affairs Quarterly* 24 (2): 163–87.

Gugler, J., and W. Flanagan. 1977. Can the political economy of urbanization in the Third World: The case of West Africa. *International Journal of Urban and Regional Research* 1 (2): 272–92.

Harloe, M., ed 1977. *Captive cities: Studies in the political economy of cities and regions.* London: Wiley.

Harvey, D. 1973. *Social justice and the city.* London: Edward Arnold.

Hawley, A. 1950. *Human ecology: A theory of community structure.* New York: Ronald Press.

———. 1968. Human ecology. In *International encyclopedia of social sciences,* 328–37. New York: Macmillan.

———. 1979. Cumulative change in theory and in history. In *Societal growth: Processes and implications,* edited by A. Hawley. Boulder, CO: Westview.

———. 1984. Human ecological and Marxian theories. *American Journal of Sociology* 89 (4): 904–17.

———. 1986. *Human ecology: A theoretical essay.* Chicago: Univ. of Chicago Press.

Hutchinson, R. 1993. The crisis in urban sociology. In *Urban sociology in transition. Research in urban sociology, Vol. 3.,* edited by R. Hutchinson, 3–26. Greenwich, CT. JAI.

Kasarda, J., and E. Crenshaw. 1991. Third World urbanization: Dimensions, theories, and determinants. In *Annual Review of Sociology.* Vol. 17, edited by W. R. Scott and J. Blake, 467–501. Palo Alto, CA: Annual Reviews Inc.

Kentor, J. 1981. Structural determinants of peripheral urbanization: The effects of international dependence. *American Sociological Review* 46:201–11.

King, A. 1990. *Urbanism, colonialism, and the world-economy.* New York: Routledge.

Logan, J., and H. Molotch. 1987. *Urban fortunes: The political economy of place.* Berkeley: Univ. of California Press.

London, B. 1985. Thai city-hinterland relationships in an international context: Development as social control in Northern Thailand. In *Urbanization in the world-economy,* edited by M. Timberlake, 207–30. New York: Academic Press.

———. 1987. The structural determinants of Third World urban change: An ecological and political economic analysis. *American Sociological Review* 52:28–43.

McKenzie, R. [1921] 1968. The neighborhood: A study of local life in Columbus, Ohio. Reprinted in *Roderick McKenzie on human ecology,* edited by A. Hawley, 51–93. Chicago: Univ. of Chicago Press.

———. [1924] 1968. The ecological approach to the study of human community. Reprinted in *Roderick McKenzie on human ecology,* edited by A. Hawley, 3–18. Chicago: Univ, of Chicago Press.

———. [1926] 1968. Movement and the ability to live. Reprinted in *Roderick McKenzie on human ecology,* edited by A. Hawley, 134–40. Chicago: Univ. of Chicago Press.

———. [1933a] 1968. Industrial expansion and the interrelations of peoples. Reprinted in *Roderick McKenzie on human ecology,* edited by A. Hawley. Chicago: Univ. of Chicago press.

———. 1933b. *The metropolitan community.* New York: McGraw-Hill.

———. [1936] 1968. The ecology of institutions. Reprinted in *Roderick McKenzie on human ecology,* edited by A. Hawley. Chicago: Univ. of Chicago Press.

Michaelson, K., ed. 1981. *And the poor get children: Radical perspectives on populations dynamics.* New York: Monthly Review.

Mills, E., and B.-N. Song. 1979. *Studies in the modernization of the republic of Korea: 1945–1975, urbanization and urban problems.* Cambridge, MA: Harvard Univ Press.

Murphey, R. 1988. Modernization and urbanization in Asia: Plague or promise? Presidential Address, Association for Asian Studies. Reprinted in *Asian Studies Newsletter* (Spring): A–D.

Nemeth, R., and D. Smith. 1995. The political economy of contrasting urban hierarchies in South Korea and the Philippines. In *Urbanization in the world-economy,* edited by M. Timberlake, 183–206. New York: Academic Press.

Palen, J. J. 1992. *The urban world.* 4th ed. New York: McGraw-Hill.

Park, R. 1916. The city: Suggestions for the investigation of human behavior in an urban environment. *American Journal of Sociology* 20:577–612.

Park, R., and E. Burgess. 1925. *The city.* Chicago: Univ. of Chicago Press.

Perry, D. 1987. The politics of dependency in deindustrializing America: The case of Buffalo, New York. In *The capitalist city: Global restructuring and community politics,* edited by M. Smith and J. Feagin, 113–37. New York: Basil Blackwell.

Piore, M., and C. Sabel. 1984. *The second industrial divide: Possibilities for prosperity.* New York: Basic Books.

Porter, M. 1990. *The competitive advantages of nations.* New York: Free Press.

Portes, A. 1976. On the sociology of national development. *American Journal of Sociology* 82:3–38.

Ragin, C. 1987. *The comparative method.* Berkeley: Univ. of California Press.

Reich, R. 1991. *The work of nations: Preparing ourselves for 21st century capitalism.* New York: Alfred A. Knopf.

Richardson. H. 1980. Polarization reversal in developing countries. *Papers of the Regional Science Association* 45:67–85.

Roberts, B. 1978. *Cities of peasants.* Beverly Hills, CA: Sage.

Robinson, R. 1988. *The international transfer of technology: Theory, issues, and practice.* Cambridge, MA: Ballinger.

Sassen, S. 1988. *The mobility of labor and capital. A study in international investment and labor flow.* New York: Cambridge Univ. Press.

———. 1991. *The global city: New York London, Tokyo.* Princeton, NJ: Princeton Univ. Press.

Schwab, W. A. 1992. *Urban sociology: A human ecological perspective.* 2d ed. Reading, MA: Addison-Wesley.

Scott, A. 1988. Flexible production systems and regional development. *International Journal of Urban and Regional Research* 12:171–85.

Seccombe, W. 1983. Marxism and demography. *New Left Review* 137:22–47.

Slater, D. 1978. Towards a political economy of urbanization in peripheral capitalist societies. *International Journal of Urban and Regional Research* 2 (1): 26–52.

Smith, C. 1985. Class relations and urbanization in Guatemala: Toward an alternative theory of urban primacy. In *Urbanization in the world-economy,* edited by M. Timberlake, 121–67. New York: Academic Press.

Smith, D. 1987. Dependent urbanization in colonial America: The case of Charleston, South Carolina. *Social Forces* 66 (1): 1–28.

Smith, D., and B. London. 1990. Convergence in world urbanization? A quantitative assessment. *Urban Affairs Quarterly, 25* (4): 574–90.

Smith, D., and M. Timberlake. 1992. The new urban sociology. In *The urban world,* edited by J. Palen, 338–56. New York: McGraw-Hill.

Soja, E. 1987, Restructuring the internationalization of the Los Angeles region. In *The capitalist city: Global restructuring and community politics,* edited by M. Smith and J. Feagin, 178–98. New York: Basil Blackwell.

Stewart, F. 1977. *Technology and underdevelopment.* New York: Macmillan.

Storper, M., and R. Walker. 1989. *The capitalism imperative: Territory, technology, and industrial growth.* New York: Basil Blackwell.

Tabb, W., and L. Sawers. 1978. *Marxism and the metropolis: New perspectives in urban political economy.* New York: Oxford Univ. Press.

Timberlake, M. 1985. *Urbanization in the world-economy.* New York: Academic Press.

———. 1987. World-system theory and the study of comparative urbanization. In *The capitalist city: Global restructuring and community politics,* edited by M. Smith and J. Feagin, 37–65. New York: Basil Blackwell.

United Nations. 1991. *World urbanization prospects 1990: Estimates and projections of urban and rural populations and of urban agglomerations.* Population Studies no. 121. ST/ESA/SER.A/121. New York: Author.

Wallerstein, I. 1984. *The politics of the world-economy.* London: Cambridge Univ. Press.

Walton, J. 1977. Accumulation and comparative urban systems: Theory and some tentative contrasts of Latin America and Africa. *Comparative Urban Research* 5 (1): 5–18.

———. 1982. The international economy and peripheral urbanization. In *Urban policy under capitalism,* edited by N. Fainstein and S. Fainstein, 119–35. Beverly Hills, CA: Sage.

Weber, A. [1899] 1963. *The growth of cities in the nineteenth century.* Ithaca, NY: Cornell Univ. Press.

Part III

The Postindustrial City

Today, we have just entered the gate of the twenty-first century, a postindustrial century awash with change and marked by two dominant global trends—global production and marketing and global networking—animated by information and communication technology. **Global production and marketing** requires a footloose transnational urban space for the production, distribution, and consumption of economic goods and services. **Global networking,** on the other hand, creates the virtual reality of a networked global village. Nowhere is the logic of these global trends more evident than in the circulation of capital and labor on a global scale. As an Archer Daniels Midland Company (ADM) ad claims, "We are the supermarket to the world."

This is indeed a new era that represents a qualitative change in our urban experience. What happens then as capital and labor move around the world with relative ease? Primarily, it challenges the territorial prerogatives of nation-states. As business outmaneuvers both governments and labor unions in the regulation of transnational economic activity, it makes the latter extremely sensitive and vulnerable to the impact of international competition and market fluctuation. Such symptomatic expendability and lack of central control has a destabilizing effect in the relationships between business, government, and labor.

Does this mean that nation-states will become less and less capable of carrying the hopes and responding to the questions of the day? Does this mean that the postindustrial condition heralds the end of the nation-state? To ask these questions is to provoke what the historian Lactantius asked in the third century, "When Rome, the head of the world, shall have fallen, who can doubt that the end is come of human beings, aye, of the earth itself?" These questions raise many unsettling but critical issues, but whether nation-states decline or incline in their influence, one thing is certain, a new urban landscape is rising from the ashes of the old as world cities become almost autonomous centers of large national and global corporations.

It is therefore the task of Part Three to present selections examining the new urban landscape through which the postindustrial city must be understood. In particular, the readings were selected to shed light on the spatial, as well as aspatial, dimensions of the postindustrial city.

Peter Hall's essay, *The Industrialization of Information: San Francisco/Palo Alto/Berkeley 1950–1990*, examines the genesis and role of Silicon Valley in the development of the postindustrial landscape.

In *The Dependent Future*, John Logan and H. Molotch anticipate the emergence of a new urban era. They proposes five postindustrial typologies of American cities: headquarter city, innovation city, module city, third world entrepôt, and retirement city.

H. V. Savitch's essay on *Post-Industrial Cities* discusses how the economic transformation brought about by postindustrialism affects the political, physical, and personal configurations of three world cities—New York, London, and Paris.

Paul L. Knox's essay, *The Postmodern Urban Matrix*, explores the social ecology of Metropolitan Washington, D.C. as a postindustrial, postmodern setting articulated by new consumerism and lifestyles.

Saskia Sassen's essay, *The New Urban Economy: The Intersection of Global Processes and Place*, argues that the new urban economy must be understood within the context of the growth of global economy and the growth of service industry. She also argues that these two major processes result in the demise and replacement of the older industrial and manufacturing centers.

In *Social Change and Vulnerable Neighborhoods*, William Julius Wilson communicates the impact of deindustrialization through the disappearance of work in many inner-city neighborhoods in the United States.

Another Saskia Sassen essay, *The State and the Global City: Notes Toward a Conception of Place-Centered Governance*, highlights the declining significance of the nation-state in the global economy and the increasing function of cities as places for transnational economic transactions.

In *Planning the American Dream*, Todd Bressi offers a hopeful note. While he criticizes the modernist approach to urban development and its consequences, he proposes a postmodernist planning approach he calls **new urbanism** in order to reclaim and reconstruct the urban landscape through the principle of "regionalism via localism," that is, planning the metropolitan region through the development of neighborhoods incorporating pedestrian scale design and public space.

18

The Industrialization of Information

San Francisco/Palo Alto/ Berkeley 1950–1990

Peter Hall

The world knows it as Silicon Valley, a name coined in 1971 by the editor of a microelectronics newsletter; but on the Rand McNally Atlas it is the Santa Clara Valley, a 40-mile by 10-mile strip running from Palo Alto to the southern suburbs of San Jose, at the southern end of the San Francisco Bay Area. It constitutes just over one-third of the 1312-square-mile Santa Clara County.[1] In 1950 it was the prune capital of America. It had only 800 manufacturing workers, half of them working in canneries and food processing plants.

Today its fruit trees have long gone. It is "the birthplace of pocket calculators, video games, home computers, cordless telephones, laser technology, microprocessors, and digital watches. Just about everything that's new in electronics in recent years has come out of Silicon Valley."[2] It is the ninth-largest manufacturing centre in the USA, with sales of over $40 billion annually, and with 40,000 new jobs a year during the early 1980s; it also has over 6000 Ph.D.s, the biggest concentration in the United States. At that time it counted 2736 electronics manufacturing firms and an estimated 3000 firms in service activities like marketing, advertising, public relations, selling, consulting, headhunting, supplying, R and D, training, management, market research, design, venture capital, legal, and numerous other support services—plus at least another 2000 in other high-tech activities, a total of 8000. The electronics firms area extraordinarily small: 70 per cent have less than ten workers, 85 per cent have. less than fifty.[3]

This, the newest major industrial centre in America, has inevitably seen explosive urban growth. With a population of under 200,000 in 1940, in less than two decades it was transformed from an agricultural community into one of the fastest-growing urban centres in the United States. In the early 1950s a few fledgling electronics firms located here; by 1971, the area was already celebrated as Silicon Valley. The name was appropriate; for silicon, a chemical element, is the primary ingredient of the chips, or solid-state integrated circuits, that provide the basic components of all the area's electronic products. On the basis of that minuscule component, the county's population rose 121 per cent from 1950 to 1960 and another 66 per cent from 1960 to 1970; total employment nearly doubled in the 1940s, and more than doubled in the 1950s, adding 60,000 manufacturing jobs in twenty years; and each manufacturing job generated two or three additional jobs, representing a total of 400,000 new jobs in two decades.

Somewhat amazingly, this dizzy rate of growth continued from 1960 to 1975 employment grew 156 per cent, three times the national rate and more than double the California rate. As agriculture declined from 15 per cent to less than 1 per cent of total employment from 1940 to 1980, manufacturing rose from 15 per cent to 35 per cent. By 1970, five out of seven of the largest semiconductor firms in the United States were headquartered here, and clustered around them was the largest concentration of electronic communication, laser, microwave, computer, advanced instrument and equipment manufacturers in the world. As early as 1969 median family income was already the highest in California.[4]

And despite dire expert predictions in the late 1970s that the area's growth had peaked, in the 1980s it again went from strength to strength. In 1990, Silicon Valley was home to one-third of the 100 largest technology companies created in the United States since 1965; their market value increased by $25 billion between 1986 and 1990, dwarfing the $1 billion increase achieved by their competitors in the most nearly comparable area, Route 128 around Boston in Massachusetts; between 1975 and 1990 Silicon Valley created 150,000 technology-related jobs—triple the number on Highway 128.[5]

Why should this have happened? It represented a most remarkable geographical shift. For, as late as 1940, even 1950, there was little to suggest the explosive growth to come. The incipient American electronics industry had firmly established itself at the start of the twentieth century in the Boston–New York axis, and this concentration—lightly modified by outward deconcentration—persisted down to the 1940s. Bell Laboratories remained in New York City until it moved to Murray Hill in suburban New Jersey, in 1941, and here the transistor was invented at the end of 1947; RCA's research work was also in New York City, with an outlier at Princeton. IBM's headquarters in Endicott, New York State—about 140 miles north-west of New York City—was the location of one of its three original constituents, the International Time Recording Company, which had been established in 1900 in New Jersey and had found itself here after several mergers and acquisitions. In Greater Boston, a MIT research played a key role in the development of radar; work on the early development of the computer was shared among Eckert and Mauchly at the University of Pennsylvania, von Neumann at Princeton, Aiken at Harvard, and Forrester at MIT. Eckert and Mauchly had already left university life to set up Univac, the first computer company, in Philadelphia. In 1950, all the signs were that the next wave of advance in electronics would occur somewhere within this corridor, probably at a number of points along it. The sole significant exceptions were IBM at Endicott and General Electric at Schenectady, both essentially local out-movements from the corridor to smaller towns close by.[6]

Nor were the indications very different in the early and mid-1950s. Bell Labs undertook major development work for the American Department of Defense on the transistor, at a special facility at Whippany, New Jersey, not far from Murray Hill. IBM began to take a commanding lead in commercial production. Around MIT, a major electronics complex began to develop from the mid-1950s, perhaps because of MIT's willingness to take military contracts; the area's older firms, like Raytheon, which had already become heavily involved in this work during World War II, expanded; more importantly still, new start-up firms developed out of MIT—and, much more rarely, Harvard—research: Wang in 1951, Digital in 1957. Henceforward, a regular process of breakaway and firm swarming occurred: fifty-four firms were founded between 1955 and 1981, forty-five of them after 1965 as a few of them, principally Digital, identified a new product, the minicomputer. The whole process was underpinned by the region's huge supply of qualified workers, the availability of venture capital, and the development of agglomeration economies. The new firms were disproportionately located along Highway 128—the original beltway around the city of Boston, started in the 1930s but completed only in 1951, and linking no less than twenty different towns in the Greater Boston area—which thus became the first great electronics complex in the United States.[7]

Early Days

In the 1950s the Santa Clara Valley was still fundamentally rural, dotted with a line of small towns which Spanish explorers and missionaries had founded along the line of El Camino Real. The valley was extremely fertile and was blessed by an ideal climate, free from the cold bay fog. Almost untouched by the 1849 gold rush, from the first settlement by Spanish colonizers in the late 1770s it was occupied and cultivated by ranchers and farmers hoping to become gentlemen squires. In 1876 Leland Stanford, the great Californian railroad magnate, bought ranching land here and named it Palo Alto after a tall redwood tree first identified in 1769 by Captain Gaspar de Portolá, Spanish governor of the Californias. By 1940 it had some 100,000 acres of orchards and some 8000 acres of more traditional vegetable crops; it was ranked as one of the fifteen most productive agricultural counties in the entire country, producing one-third of California's annual crop of plums, cherries, pears and apricots.[8] It was the "Valley of the Heart's Delight," the subject of a lyrical poem of 1931 by Clara Louise Laurence. . . . [9]

The valley was traversed by the parallel lines of El Camino Real and the Southern Pacific Railroad, built in 1861–4 in anticipation that it would form the western end of the transcontinental railroad; a hope dashed when, in 1869, the Union Pacific made its terminus in the East Bay city of Oakland. They crossed a long, narrow bay plain which, at least until 1920, was given over almost entirely to large estates and farms. The few towns in the fifty-mile stretch between San Francisco and San Jose—Menlo Park, Redwood City, San Mateo and South San Francisco to the north, Mountain View and Santa Clara to the south—remained small, and efforts to promote new communities met with little or no success. Only a few trains a day ran down the Peninsula, linking it with San Francisco to the north or with the much smaller city of San Jose to the immediate south; fares were high in comparison with the frequent and cheap trans-bay ferries that plied every few minutes between San Francisco and Oakland; and, despite plans, the line was never electrified—even to this day.[10]

But there was one significant early development. These early settlers believed in education: the Jesuits founded Santa Clara University at the mission in 1851; San Jose State Normal School, later the State University, was founded in San Francisco in 1862 and moved south in 1870. Then, in 1891, a gift from Leland Stanford—by now a United States Senator—and his wife established a new university as a memorial to their son, who died just before college age—hence the name, Leland Stanford Junior University. Stanford endowed it with $20 million, at the time one of the largest philanthropic gifts ever made; it included his Palo Alto Stock Farm of 880 acres, still known by everyone on campus as "the Farm," thirty miles south of San Francisco. The East Coast establishment were unimpressed: the New York *Mail and Express* declared that "there is about as much need for a new university in California as for an asylum of decayed sea captains in Switzerland;" but, with an enrollment of 1700 students in 1911, the upstart university developed a strong sense of camaraderie among its alumni.[11]

The new university took an extraordinarily close interest in the birth of electronics. As early as 1899, a Marconi wireless in a lighthouse off the coast was able to relay the return of the troopship *Sherman* from the Spanish War. This set up a craze for amateur radio clubs in the Bay Area but above all at Stanford, among both students like Cy Elwell and James Muller, and also faculty like Fred Terman and Roland Marx. On graduating, Elwell worked for a San Francisco radio firm; in the fall of 1909 he demonstrated his wireless telephone to prospective backers and Stanford family members. Supported by money from the university's president David Starr Jordan and from faculty—who also acted as consultants—he set up Poulsen Wireless Telephone and Telegraph. Only two years later, in 1911, it changed its name to the Federal Telegraph Company and was already one of the largest wireless firms in the country. That year it hired Lee De Forest, who five years earlier had invented the electronic valve or vacuum tube, the basis of all radio until the development of the transistor; here in Palo Alto, in 1912, in a small house on Emerson Street, now demolished, he and two fellow-researchers discovered the use of his three-electrode audion as an amplifying device, another crucial development in the history of the fledgling radio industry. De Forest soon left to go east, but the area continued to be a flourishing centre for electronics, especially after the sinking of the *Titanic* and the 1913 radio law which required ship radio.[12]

Federal finally moved to New Jersey in 1932, and is now part of ITT. But that did not inhibit Stanford graduates from starting their own firms; indeed, it may have encouraged them. Charles Litton from San Francisco, who built his first ham radio at ten, graduated in 1924 and went into business as a glass-blower, being hired in 1928 by Federal Telegraph to direct the radio valve department and take on RCA; he did so by sidestepping their patent and producing a tube of such quality that it won a contract from the new ITT. When Federal Telegraph moved, Litton stayed and set up Litton Engineering Laboratories in Redwood City, later in San Carlos. The firm expanded hugely in World War II; by 1960, it was a billion-dollar operation. Litton was outstandingly successful, but there were scores of small firms linked to Stanford through a supply of graduates on one side, money and internships on the other.[13]

Throughout the 1920s, while other universities like Berkeley offered radio courses, Stanford retained its pre-eminence in electrical engineering. Most of its prestige was due to Dr. Harris Ryan, who supported radio and educated many electronics pioneers. Because of the reputation of the department, many graduates chose to remain, working for Federal Telegraph or starting their own firms. Ryan set up a radio communications lab in 1924, and selected Fred Terman to run it.[14]

Frederick Terman grew up on campus where his father, Louis Terman, was a well-known psychology professor and creator of the Stanford-Binet IQ test. The campus was then still "a minor league, country-club school," and indeed remained such until Terman fundamentally changed it thirty years later. A delicate child, Terman became intrigued with ham radio. After Palo Alto High School he enrolled in Stanford, winning his bachelor's in chemistry and—after a spell with Federal—his master's in electrical engineering. He then entered the doctoral programme at MIT under Vannevar Bush, an electrical engineering professor who later became dean and then vice-president of MIT. Bush, who believed in close university–industry relations and was one of the four founders of Raytheon, encouraged Terman to think of the university as an applied R and D centre rather than as an ivory tower.[15]

Completing his Ph.D., Terman accepted a faculty position at MIT. But, before this, he was stricken with tuberculosis while visiting his family and spent the year 1924 in bed; he stayed at Palo Alto for his health, and became a professor of "Radio Engineering" at Stanford. As two historians of Silicon Valley have commented, "Thus, but for the fickle fact of being struck with a serious illness, Fred Terman would probably have become the godfather of Boston's Route 128, instead of its counterpart in Santa Clara County. And, without Fred Terman, Silicon Valley might never have happened."[16] It is not an exaggerated verdict: his role as godfather to the incipient industry was crucial, and without it the rest of the story would probably never have taken place.

During his tenure as head of the communications laboratory (1924–45), it was the focal point of the college careers of many bright young scientific minds on campus (much as the computer lab is to "hackers" now). Because of this, until the end of the Second World War and Terman's promotion to dean, the Stanford communications lab was the heart of technological innovation on the West Coast. By the time Terman moved on, the ties between Stanford and the surrounding electronics industry were so strong that the university was all but guaranteed its present role of providing apprenticeship to each generation of high-tech leaders.[17]

By far the most significant early Terman students were David Packard and William R. Hewlett. Hewlett came from Ann Arbor, Packard from Pueblo, Colorado, both stemming from professional families; Hewlett's father became professor at Stanford's medical school. They met through Ed Porter, a ham radio enthusiast. Both took Terman's radio course; then Packard went to General Electric at Schenectady, while Hewlett spent a year in graduate school at Stanford, going on to MIT for his master's in 1936. Terman found a job for Hewlett and a fellowship for Packard; they worked with Terman and soon decided on partnership. They set up a workshop in a garage behind their boarding house and did odd electronics jobs. Terman helped them find these jobs; he was interested in negative feedback, then new, and out of this came Hewlett's master's thesis, to design and build a new model of a machine called a variable frequency oscillator, which enhanced the quality of sound reproduction. It was not only versatile, but cheap: it cost a little over one-tenth that of existing machines, $55 instead of $500. In 1938 Terman persuaded Hewlett to join Packard in a partnership to exploit its commercial possibilities, loaned them $538 and arranged a $1000 bank loan. They made sales of $5369 and profits of $1653 that year and then concentrated on the oscillator. The first big sale, of eight oscillators, was to Walt Disney studios for recording the sound on *Fantasia*. By 1940, the firm had expanded into half a cabinet shop on El Camino Real in Palo Alto; by 1941 it was a $100,000 a year firm; by 1942, the workforce was about a hundred and sales about $1 billion.[18]

Hewlett-Packard expanded hugely during the war in radio, radar, sonar, nautical and aviation instrumentation, with sales of $2 million and 200 workers in 1945, but then came slump. It did not again reach these employment and sales figures until 1950, though by then it made 70 different products, indicating the slow rate of change at that time. After the war Hewlett joined the new development division of the War Department's special staff where he made useful military and corporate contacts. Then began an astonishing rate of growth: 50 to 100 per cent a year through the 1950s. By the 1980s HP had 68,000 employees, manufactured some 5000 products and had annual sales of $4.4 billion, ranking 110th of the Fortune 500 in sales and 62nd in profits.[19]

Another significant early start-up was Varian Associates. In the 1930s Dr. William Webster Hansen's laboratory was attended by Sigurd and Russell Varian, local sons of immigrants from Iceland. The latter graduated from Stanford with a master's in physics in 1927 and returned in 1935 to do research, being then joined by his brother, an aviator from Mexico; they decided to set up a lab concentrating on navigation aids, and here they developed the electromagnetic resonator which became radar. The Klystron was announced on 30 January 1939, after three years of spare-time work by the brothers and Professor Webster. It became the basic radar used in World War II through its superiority to the British magnetron. Throughout this period the brothers were employed at Sperry Gyroscope, but they set up Varian Associates at San Carlos in 1948.[20] By the early 1950s, Varian was one of the key firms in the electronic instruments business, commanding those markets that were not dominated by Hewlett-Packard; already, the area was a major player in a key new industry.[21]

Terman's Secret Weapon

At war's end Frederick Terman returned from administering a major military project at Harvard, determined to improve Stanford's then primitive electrical engineering programme. He actively sought government and business funding on the promise that it would bring new indigenous industry to the West. His contention was that universities needed to develop a new relationship with science- and technology-based industries, and he spoke of the "community of interest between the University and local industry."[22] He was phenomenally successful: by 1955 gifts from corporations had reached $500,000; by 1965, more than $2 million; by 1976, $6.9 million.

Through Terman's careful attention to faculty building, Stanford rapidly joined MIT as one of the two best electrical engineering programmes in the country. Between 1950 and 1954 Stanford awarded 67 doctoral degrees in electrical engineering; during 1960–4, 185; and during 1970–4, 242. By the early 1960s, the annual total of Stanford's Ph.Ds. exceeded MIT's; together, Berkeley and Stanford were granting twice as many as MIT. This made it easier for small firms to recruit and provided a pool of entrepreneurs. But the large laboratories and firms also recruited nationally, and the smaller firms were then able to poach from them. Stanford's honours programme was very attractive to high-technology firms whose employees could attend university in the evenings or in company time to get advanced degrees; 32 companies with about 400 employees were participating in 1961."[23]

Critical to all this was the Stanford Research Institute (SRI). Terman was instrumental in founding it in 1946 with a broad chatter which emphasized research to help stimulate West Coast business. The Korean War and Cold War stimulated the flow of funds for electronics research and development, and the development of the ballistic missile system was particularly important. Terman reportedly used his wartime contacts to steer Pentagon dollars to Stanford; as will emerge, military prime contracts to California steadily rose during the 1950s.[24] Terman consciously cultivated a "community of technical scholars" at Stanford, saying: "Such a community is composed of industries using highly sophisticated technologies, together with a strong university that is sensitive to the creative activities of the surrounding industry. This pattern appears to be the wave of the future."[25]

At this time Stanford's main problem was how to convert university land into money, since the original Stanford land gift forbade the sale of any part of the 880-acre Farm. Terman, by now vice-president, and Wallace Sterling, president, hit upon the idea of a high-technology industrial park. The 660-acre Stanford Industrial Park, created in 1951, was the first of its kind; Terman called it "Stanford's secret weapon." Leases, necessary because of the injunction against selling, were granted to high-technology firms; originally the scheme was just a means of making money, but soon the idea developed of technology transfer from the university to industry. The first tenant was Varian Associates, the Stanford spin-off for which Terman served as board member. When Hewlett-Packard took a lease in 1954, it became the nucleus for Silicon Valley; Terman sold leases to other high-tech firms on the basis of being close to the university. In 1955, 7 companies were here; by 1960, 32; by 1970, 70; by the early 1980s, 90 with about 25,000 workers. Stanford Research Park became the model for literally hundreds of others worldwide; by 1980, prepaid leases amounted to over $18 million and the income was unrestricted, enabling Stanford to begin wooing eastern professors and building itself up into a leading position. Terman's strategy here was "steeples of excellence:" small groups of experts in narrow areas of knowledge.[26]

World War II and After: The Pentagon Effect

But all this might not have been sufficient in itself, had it not been for another intervening variable: World War II and, even more critically significant, the Cold War. In the 1940s, but still more in the late 1950s, military contracts played a crucial role in the success of these Silicon Valley pioneers. And that in turn reflects critical decisions that had been made even earlier.

Some time in the 1920s, the US army and navy determined that there would be three "strategic centres" on the Pacific coast in which additional military facilities should be concentrated: Puget Sound, the San Francisco Bay, and Los Angeles–San Diego; these were to include air bases. In the autumn of 1928 aviation enthusiasts in the San Francisco Junior Chamber of Commerce initiated a campaign to persuade the navy to choose Sunnyvale, at the southern end of the Bay, as a site for one of the bases. When, three years later, the news came that the Navy Airship Base Investigating Committee had chosen Camp Kearny near San Diego, the senior and junior Chambers joined in a campaign to persuade the committee to change its mind. The committee looked at ninety-seven sites in all, twenty-three in the Bay Area, and finally voted 4–1 in favour of Sunnyvale over Camp Kearny. To ensure that there would be no reversal of the decision, the senior Chamber pledged half a million dollars to purchase a thousand-acre site and give it to the navy. In 1931 that was not easy, but it was achieved in three months, through a Bay Area-wide campaign.[27]

> No small part of the satisfaction of Bay Area leaders in this achievement was, some acknowledged, the defeat handed southern California. But the chief interest of businessmen in the new military establishment, aside from its importance for national defense, was in the sizable annual payroll that would be added to the Bay Area economy, and in the initial expenditure for construction of hangars, air strips, hous-

ing and equipment. In the lean years of the early 'thirties nothing looked so substantial and desirable as a federal installation supported by all the taxpayers of the United States. Moreover, no one doubted that the whole Bay Area would benefit by the new base.[28]

Similar campaigns, with donations, led to the construction of Hamilton Air Force Base and the Naval Air Base in Alameda. "The addition of three new bases in an area which already had military establishments on both sides of the Golden Gate and at Mare Island and Benicia dramatized the fact that the federal government considered the whole Bay Area, in effect, one big base."[29] And this became evident by the eve of America's entry into World War II: "The Bay Area had become by the summer of 1941 a major 'arsenal of democracy.' From Moffett Field at the lower end of San Francisco Bay to the Benicia Arsenal overlooking the waters of Suisun Bay, it was an enormous complex of military establishments, some dating from the early days of California statehood, some brand new."[30] Even by spring 1941, the army alone had some 20,000 troops and a large civilian complement at work here. In 1940, Moffett Naval Air Station, between Palo Alto and San Jose, leased property to the young National Advisory Committee for Aeronautics (NACA); the Ames Research Centre later became NASA. The war stimulated the Californian economy and generated a massive population influx to cope with demand from war industries. Local industries geared up for war production. There was an initial flow of federal funding to Stanford for the development of military electronic components and equipment. Military installations and industrial centres burgeoned all around the San Francisco Bay Area: in the city of San Francisco, in Richmond and Oakland in the East Bay, and at Moffett Field.[31]

There were also new firms, appearing in small factories amid the orchards. Ampex was founded in 1944 by Alexander M. Poniatoff, a 52-year-old Russian immigrant, as a spin-off from Dalmo Victor Co. of San Carlos (where Poniatoff then worked) to make motors for Victor's radio antenna for fighter aircraft. At war's end it faltered, until its founder met Harold Lindsay of Dalmo Victor who had in turn encountered Jack Mullin at a presentation at the Institute of Radio Engineers in San Francisco in 1946; Mullin had smuggled a German "magnetophone," a prototype tape recorder, out of Germany. Painstakingly, they developed it for production and had their first commercial success with the Bing Crosby radio show in 1947–8, then moving into the first industrial videotape recorder in 1956.[32]

By the spring of 1949 the San Jose Chamber of Commerce could list no fewer than eighty new industries located in the city since 1944, many in the traditional industry of food-processing, but also including General Electric, IBM and Westinghouse. The farmers of Santa Clara County were far from happy: they could foresee orchards being rooted up by the hundreds, and they were right. Down to World War II, the San Francisco Bay area had grown around the twin cities of San Francisco and Oakland. But, because of the mountainous terrain, there was now little available land for further expansion in or near these cities; the only available land was at the south end of the Bay. In the late 1940s, suburban homes began to spread into the plum trees. From 1940 to 1950, Santa Clara added 115,598 new residents, a two-thirds increase. Most of them were using cars to get to work; and in March 1950, the county health officer reported smog to be not only a Santa Clara County but also a general Bay Area health problem.[33]

But this was just the start: for, in the early 1950s, the coming of the Cold War and the Soviet–American missile race brought a new spurt of growth. Throughout this decade, the complex of universities at the south end of the Bay, in which Stanford was joined by Santa Clara University and San Jose State University, plus the military establishments and labour pool and the climate and the lifestyle, began to attract major technology firms from outside. They included the giants of those days: Sylvania, Fairchild Camera & Instrument, General Electric, Philco-Ford, Westinghouse, Itel, and Kaiser. GE nuclear power established itself in San Jose, Westinghouse naval equipment at Sunnyvale, Sylvania in Mountain View, Philco-Ford also in Mountain View. Most important of all was IBM's arrival in San Jose in 1952 to design the first computer disk memory, later moving to Gilroy. Allan and Malcolm Lockheed from Los Gatos brought the new Lockheed Missile & Space Company to Sunnyvale in 1956, quickly becoming the Valley's largest employer, and relocating its research arm in the Stanford Industrial Park. Their move was crucial; Department of Defense purchases of semiconductors then represented about 40 per cent of total production, as against 8 per cent in the early 1980s.[34] In effect, Silicon Valley became "an information-exchange system for technical know-how."[35] Santa Clara's history as prune capital was ended. The Bay Area, with 2.7 million people in 1950, added nearly a million more by 1960—and much of this growth was in Santa Clara County.[36]

The most important reason for this phenomenal growth was military contracting.

> The industry would never have emerged when it did, nor grown as rapidly as it did without the vast impetus to innovation and production generated by military and aerospace demand for semiconductors and the vast government support for semiconductor research and production facilities. Furthermore, the nature and location of government activities were critical determinants of the spatial patterning of the industry, and especially of its development in Santa Clara County.[37]

Military demand was particularly crucial in the early years, 1950 to 1960. The percentage of military prime contracts which went to the Pacific region rose from 12.3 per cent in World War II, to 17.9 per cent in the Korean War years, to 27.5 per cent in 1961. In the semiconductor industry, production for the defence market rose from $15 million to $294 million between 1955 and 1968; the government market peaked in 1960 when it accounted for fully one-half of sales. Between 1955 and 1963, defence work ranged from 35 to 50 per cent of total production. There was now a new pattern of production, without any real peacetime parallel—at least in the United States: the Pentagon offered a huge guaranteed market at high prices and thus the promise of certain profit; the stress was on top quality, with price a strictly secondary consideration, so there was a massive incentive to innovate; the resulting solid-state semiconductor devices were far too expensive for industrial or consumer use, but then applications could be broadened at lower prices. By underwriting prohibitive investment and production costs, and by being willing to buy from new untested firms, the Department of Defense also encouraged the development of countless small new firms.[38]

Government funding also spurred innovation: between 1958 and 1974, all branches of the federal government—predominantly defence- and aerospace-related—put $930 million into the industry for R and D, nearly equal to the $1.2 billion firms themselves spent. Basically, the armed forces covered all the engineering design and development costs, thus underwriting the costs of new production lines which firms would never have developed by themselves.[39]

During this time, the concentration of aircraft and aerospace firms here gave California a significant edge, for these were the main customers of the electronics firms. As the electronic element in aerospace and military products grew, the numbers of engineers expanded rapidly: even in 1962 Lockheed employed 2200 research scientists. All this created external economies through a uniquely rich concentration of skilled labour. And the Pacific region received an overwhelming share of federal R and D contracts: 36.5 per cent for Department of Defense and 47.5 per cent for NASA in 1964. As the technology became ever more complex, there was a premium on proximity, especially for small firms which could not afford to interact over long distances.[40]

Some firms tried to keep clear of the military embrace: at Fairchild, Noyce said the maximum military support they were willing to take was 4 per cent. But they clearly depended on subcontracting from other firms which were prime defence contractors; and Texas Instruments, one of the leading firms, depended heavily on defence contracts. After the mid-1960s, Stanford and the military decreased in relative importance, and information-exchange factors rose in significance; but by that time, the basic structure of the Silicon Valley complex had been laid down.[41]

Technological Breakthrough: The Transistor

There was, however, another critical factor. The Cold War, and the resulting missile race—especially after the 1957 crisis, when the Soviet Union launched their Sputnik satellite—had transformed the nature of war. The urgent need now was to develop incredibly complex guided missiles, requiring sophisticated electronic componentry. By the 1960s some 20 per cent of aircraft costs, and at least 30 per cent of missile systems, went on electronics. For this purpose—packing electronics into a missile to be blasted into space—the old-fangled glass valves that can now be seen in science museums were useless. Hence the importance of the semiconductor. As two historians of Silicon Valley have put it: "Could Silicon Valley happen again in another place at another time? Perhaps so, but we doubt it. A 'Silicon Valley' requires a technological innovation (like semiconductors) whose time has come. So just plain luck was also involved in the rise of Silicon Valley."[42]

Semiconductors, put crudely, are pieces of material that can either conduct an electric signal, or stop it. They are the basic raw material on which the whole vast edifice of modern computer technology, with its endless binary combinations of 0 and 1, depends. They can be broken down into two main categories: discrete components such as diodes and transistors, and monolithic integrated circuits. The first and basic technology, discrete semiconductors, was developed in the late 1940s, following the epoch-making discovery of December 1947 at Bell Labs; and commercial production of these relatively simple devices began in the 1950s. The second stage of development, the integrated circuits, was developed in the late 1950s and these were successfully manufactured after discovery of the planar process at Fairchild Semiconductor in 1958; they soon came to dominate the industry.[43]

The invention of the transistor was without doubt the technological key that launched Silicon Valley. But it occurred on the opposite side of the country: at Bell Laboratories, Murray Hill, New Jersey, on 23 December 1947. The transistor is a device which uses semiconductor materials to perform functions such as amplifying or switching an electrical current. It has huge advantages over the old thermionic valve, on which the electronics industries were based during their first half-century: small size, durability, lower energy consumption, more reliability and wider range of applications. Its invention came from the research of three physicists at Bell, John Bardeen, Walter Brattain and William Shockley, but it stemmed also from the contributions of many hundreds of researchers working in many different places on related electronic technologies during and before World War II. Its discovery in the Bell Laboratories was far from accidental; it was a direct result of huge state-supported scientific and technical resources dedicated to the programme, in what was already the world's largest industrial research organization. But fundamental research in Britain may have lagged behind Bell by only a matter of weeks.[44]

By 1951 the first Bell transistor, a germanium point contact transistor, was adopted for commercial production by Western Electric, the manufacturing arm of AT&T; but it proved very difficult to manufacture in bulk and suffered from many problems of reliability. Some of these difficulties were overcome in 1951 by Shockley's invention of the junction transistor. Soon after, under the pressure of a lengthy anti-trust case, Western Electric held a series of symposia revealing their properties and applications as well as the principles underlying their manufacture, and simultaneously established a very liberal licensing policy. But commercial applications and interest in the transistor were rather slow to develop in the early 1950s, in part because of continuing difficulties in standardized mass production techniques. So there was a premium on developing further improvements to overcome these problems; and, because of the liberal licensing arrangements, there was plenty of incentive for firms to compete.[45]

One of the most crucial came in May 1954, when Texas Instruments (TI) succeeded in making a silicon transistor; it had the capacity to work at very high temperatures and proved of great interest to the military, whose support provided a major impetus to the development of transistor production in the USA over the following decade. A second was the planar process of 1959, which offered many advantages over previous methods for the standardized production of transistors, and later more integrated and compact components; it was the key that made possible the development of the integrated circuit. By making integrated circuits relatively robust and reliable, the planer process did much to set the industry on the growth path it followed for the next quarter-century; from 1959 to 1962 prices fell by 80–90 per cent; between 1957 and 1965 production increased twenty-fold by volume.[46]

With this technological evolution, a virtuous circle developed: lower cost, increased performance and reliability, increased production, hence still lower costs. With the entry of many new firms, the industry grew at unprecedented rates: by 1963 there were 108 establishments; by 1967, 177; by 1972, 325; by 1977, 547. Shipments skyrocketed from $5.1 million in 1954 to more than $500 million in 1960, to $1.5 billion in 1970, and to more than $5 billion by 1977. Between 1956 and 1962, 6000 different types of transistors were introduced. Three entire generations developed in twenty-five years, from the single circuit of 1956, to 30,000 circuits in the early 1970s, and to 75,000 by the early 1980s. As each generation developed, prices fell dramatically: the cost of a Fairchild planar transistor fell from $150 to $45 between February 1958 and January 1959, and to $22.70 by February 1960. This meant intense pressure to reduce production costs through outsourcing.[47]

One question, crucial for the future, was where all this was happening. The simple discrete devices of the 1950s were made by firms already located in the North-East, like RCA, Sylvania and of course Western Electric; they had started long before, with valves, and made the transition to transistors without too much difficulty. And so, despite disadvantages like high wages and a union presence, the North-East was the first major centre. But, from the start, some producers went outside the North-East: Motorola located in Phoenix in 1949, Texas Instruments in Dallas in 1952, and Shockley Laboratories in Palo Alto in 1955. So, for a brief period in the 1950s, semiconductor production was carried out profitably at a wide variety of locations, especially since at that point firms tended to integrate their production stages in one plant.[48]

It was after that, in the age of the integrated circuit, that Silicon Valley began to pull ahead of the rest of the pack. During the late 1950s and 1960s a number of firms located there: by 1965 the area had 4164 workers in eight establishments, only slightly more than Phoenix or Dallas; thence, employment grew rapidly to twenty-six establishments with 12,000 workers by the end of the 1960s. Neither Motorola nor TI generated such spin-offs, nor did specialist producers or subcontractors appear in Phoenix or Dallas. And, back in the North-East, firms failed to make the transition to integrated circuits, and fell out of the leading ranks.[49]

Shockley, Fairchild, Intel:
Three Semiconductor Generations

The critical event that brought about this change was the move of William Shockley to Palo Alto. When Shockley resigned from Bell Labs to start on his own in 1954, he first joined Raytheon in Boston, planning to establish a semiconductor firm with their assistance. But Raytheon was not interested, so he moved to Palo Alto because his mother lived there and because Arnold O. Beckman, Professor of Chemistry at Cal Tech, provided the financial backing for Shockley Semiconductor Laboratory; it started business in 1955 on El Camino Real in Mountain View. People jumped to join him, and he hired eight of the best: "It was the greatest collection of electronics genius ever assembled—and all of them were under thirty, at the height of their powers."[50] They included Jean Hoerni from Cal Tech, Victor Grinich from SRI, Eugene Kleiner from GE, Gordon Moore from Johns Hopkins, and Robert Noyce from Philco-Ford. It was to become the direct or indirect source of virtually all the eighty-five or so semiconductor start-ups in Silicon Valley. Shockley told friends that he was going to California to make a million dollars. He failed to do so, but passed the fever onto his protégés who were indeed successful, serving as role models to thousands of others.[51]

Shockley received the Nobel Prize in 1956, for his work on the transistor, soon after arrival in Palo Alto. A famous photograph shows a dozen men toasting Shockley on his award of the prize; many were soon to leave.[52] For Shockley had diffuse and wildly overambitious plans, and proved an impossible colleague: Terman described him thus: "He was very attractive to bright young people, but hard as hell to work with;"[53] more bluntly, one executive who knew him for years summed him up as "A genius, but a real prick."[54] He determinedly pursued R and D on four-layer diodes when his staff urged him to transfer to silicon transistors; after two years the firm had introduced only one simple diode and no transistors, while Shockley took alienation to new heights.

Finally seven decided to bail out together, in 1957. There was then no real venture capital outside a few places like Boston and New York. An investment bank in New York, Hayden Stone, found a corporate sponsorship through Fairchild Camera & Instrumentation Corporation of New Jersey; Fairchild were doubtful about the group's management capacity until they persuaded the eighth, Bob Noyce, to join. Shockley refused to speak to any of the "Traitorous Eight" for years; his firm collapsed, being sold in 1960 and closed in 1968; ironically, the building is now a stereo store. Arthur Rock of Hayden Stone later became the world's preeminent venture capitalist, backer of Intel and Apple. So—not in itself, but for the chain reaction it produced—Shockley's move was the last critical building block in the construction of Silicon Valley.[55]

The new company, Fairchild Semiconductors, was the first to work exclusively in silicon, though there were then some twenty firms working on transistors. Its leader, Robert Noyce, was the son of a Congregationalist minister in Iowa; educated at the local Grinnell College, he enrolled in the MIT doctoral programme in 1949, already obsessed by transistors, and was able to meet the pioneers at conferences; after graduation he chose to work for Philco-Ford, the smallest and most obscure company that also made him the lowest offer, because it offered varied work; here he developed the hearing aid transistor. He met Shockley at a technical conference in 1956 just as Shockley was preparing to leave.[56]

As director of R and D at Fairchild, Noyce shares with Jack Kilby of Texas Instruments, another midwesterner, the credit for invention of the integrated circuit; both arrived at it simultaneously through the obvious need to overcome what

Noyce called the "horribly inefficient" method of wiring circuits. The result was a long lawsuit between the companies. Ironically, the device had been theoretically conceived in 1952 in England and manufactured there in 1957; the first patent was filed in 1959 by Texas Instruments. But it was Noyce, together with Jean Hoerni, who in 1960 invented the planar process whereby impurities are diffused into the base, allowing volume production of silicon transistors. That now is history; the importance of the invention was that, by allowing the manufacture of many individual electronic components and functions to be embodied on a single microchip, it marks the real establishment of micro-electronics as a major new technology system. The first commercial application of integrated circuits was in hearing aids in 1963, but the military provided the most important early market; by 1970, however, with early production problems resolved and prices lowered, commercial applications multiplied and the military share fell sharply. As with the transistor, the 1960s saw progressive process innovation, which allowed increasing numbers of electronic functions to be put on a single microchip, with rapid falls in price per function plus increased reliability and range. The discrete components incorporated in each integrated circuit increased from less than 10 in 1960 to 100,000 in 1980, whilst the average price of the integrated circuit fell from $50 in 1962 to about $1 in 1971.[57]

Fairchild Semiconductor was a strange firm, which later became a legend:

> It was a company of young men who acted very old. It was the wildest-living company the Valley has ever seen, yet it was, like any good 1950s company, highly conservative and conformist. Its employees had incredible loyalty, yet it bled to death faster than most mutinous firms. The Fairchild history also seems to undermine the reputations of some of its most famous graduates. If Noyce is such a great executive, why did the plant progress so fitfully, and why was it so unprofitable? If Sporck is such a manufacturing genius, why did Fairchild always have trouble getting products out the door? And if Sanders is the marketing guru of Silicon Valley, why did he have such a reputation for irritating customers?
>
> The answer is that Fairchild was a corporate vocational school for these individuals. Here they could screw up without serious repercussions—after all, nobody else knew how the job was done either—and learn from their mistakes. That was good, because the next time round, when they were on their own, the same mistake would be fatal.[58]

In three years, 1961–3, Fairchild attracted some three dozen future presidents or vice-presidents of electronics companies, and an untold number of future millionaires. In 1965, Noyce at thirty-seven was one of the oldest people at Fairchild Semiconductor; most of the key people were around thirty.[59] The firm started the process of "Silicon Valley fever" or breakaway. "Fairchild became the mother hen of the Northern California semiconductor industry;" about half of the eighty-five or so US semiconductor companies of the 1980s were direct or indirect spin-offs from the firm. Employment with Fairchild was the gateway into the semiconductor industry elsewhere in Silicon Valley; at a 1969 conference of semiconductor engineers at Sunnyvale, less than two dozen out of 400 had never worked there.

Fairchild, a huge company, could take this; but it never rehired anyone who left.[60] "Throughout the sixties, bright young engineers spun out of Fairchild Semiconductor like so many enterprising Minervas from the head of Zeus. New start-ups abounded: three new chip makers in 1966, another three in 1967, thirteen in 1968, eight more in 1969; their names a seemingly endless set of permutations on a few basic syllables—tech, tronic, inter, micro, ics, tron, etc."[61] Job-hopping became endemic, and speeded up after the arrival of venture capitalists in the late 1960s.[62] This particularly gutted Fairchild: "It got to the point," one observer said, "where people were practically driving trucks over to Fairchild Semiconductor and loading up with employees."[63]

The people who did all this were odd people, who did not behave like people in America's older industries that then provided the staple fare of the management school textbooks. They were nearly all white men in their early twenties; many had studied engineering at Stanford and MIT, and had no industrial experience; none came from the region, and a surprising number of key figures had roots in small towns in the Midwest, sharing a distrust for "established" or "old-line" industry and the "Eastern establishment." As they moved from firm to firm, their paths crossed repeatedly, and their relationships transcended sectoral and occupational boundaries—from established firms to start-ups, from semiconductors to PCs to software, and back again. In consequence, unusually, they developed stronger commitments to one another and to the cause of advancing technology than to the individual companies or industries to which they might belong for a few weeks or months.[64] They also destroyed traditional hierarchies of employers and employees and divisions between corporate functions, creating in their place what Saxenian calls "interdependent confederations of project reams that were linked by intense, informal communications and that mirrored the region's decentralized industrial structure."[65] They saw themselves as the pioneers of a new industry in a new region.[66]

In particular, Fairchild bred Intel, its most gifted child. In 1968, after relations with the East Coast management deteriorated, Noyce left Fairchild to launch Intel with his colleagues Gordon Moore and Andrew Grove, obtaining venture capital from Arthur Rock; Noyce and Moore invested $250,000 each, Rock found them $2.5 million.[67] From the outset Intel—the name stood for Integrated Electronics—concentrated on memory chips, and it was almost accidental that it got a major boost from microprocessors, invented at Intel in 1971. However, at a conference in the late 1960s, Noyce predicted the computer-on-a-chip; when one critic said, "Gee, I certainly wouldn't want to lose my whole computer through a crack in the floor," Noyce replied, "You have it all wrong, because you'll have 100 more sitting on your desk, so it won't matter if you lose one."[68] Most computer designers were not then interested in anything but mainframes, but Noyce persuaded Stan Mazor, recently hired from Fairchild, to work on microprocessors. Just as the planar process and the integrated circuit had made Fairchild a commercial success for Noyce, so the microprocessor boosted Intel into the big time.[69] After the invention of the transistor by Bell Labs, and of the integrated circuit by Bob Noyce and Jack Kilby, it was the third truly significant event in the history of the microelectronics industry.[70]

The man who achieved it was Marcian "Ted" Hoff. He had majored in electrical engineering at Rensselaer Polytechnic Institute near his home town of Rochester, NY, and had then gone to Stanford for his Ph.D. with Terman; he had stayed on as research associate but then had been bitten by the entrepreneurial bug. In 1968 Intel had just been founded, and Hoff was highly recommended by the Stanford faculty; he was third choice but got the job, becoming the company's twelfth employee. Intel's original main emphasis was on semiconductor memory chips; but early in 1969, a few months after opening but already employing 2000 people, they received an order from Busicom, a Japanese calculator company, to produce integrated circuits for a line of desktop calculators. After a holiday Hoff realized that the new DEC PDP-8 was little more expensive than the calculator and could do more; the reason people would buy the calculator, he discovered from the marketing colleagues, was that they were put off by computers: "A computer was an instrument from the Twilight Zone."[71]

Hoff proposed a set of integrated circuits which would be programmable: a microprocessor. The Japanese were not interested. But, in October 1969, they came back and Hoff persuaded them to take exclusive rights on the chip. In 1971, aided by Fredetico Faggin who also came to Intel from Fairchild, they had the 4004 ready. Gordon Moore, Intel president, understood the momentous commercial implications: "Now we can make a single microprocessor and sell it for several thousand different applications."[72] They then designed the 8008 for Victor Poor of Computer Terminal Corporation, who second-sourced it from TI, but Intel kept ahead by adding "bells and whistles;" this was an eight-bit processor, the first that could operate on eight binary digits at one time.[73]

Intel could sell the 8008 to other buyers. They renegotiated the 4004 price downward but got rights to sell that too elsewhere. But Intel's marketing staff would not announce it until Edward L. Gelback came in as their chief; this was a classic case where the marketing people "knew what their public want" and refused to believe the engineers. Finally the 4004 was announced in *Electronics News*, a trade publication, in November 1971, followed by the 8008 in April 1972. So radical an invention was the microprocessor, that the mass media did not pick up on it for nearly a year after Intel's announcement in late 1971. All this had been achieved by less than a dozen individuals, working for a year and a half on a small budget.[74]

Intel's marketing experts were hesitant about selling chips to the general public, and in some senses they were right; for instance, to be of any use the chips needed software. Gary Kildall from the Naval Postgraduate School at Pacific Grove developed one of the first pieces of software for the new chip, PL/I; later, working at Intel, he wrote a system that evolved into CP/M, the first generally used operating system for personal computers, and the market leader until the arrival of MS-DOS.

But the Intel management were doubtful about microprocessor-controlled computers: ironically, they still thought that the chief application of the new chips would be in watches. In any event, they decided to stay with chip production, leaving computer production to the established companies. This was understandable:

Intel was still a new company with sales of $18 million, one-tenth those of Fairchild; its problem was that no one, even the youngest, could really foresee the future. Hoff recalled that everyone thought of computers as big expensive pieces of equipment; one job interviewee asked what size 360—the huge IBM mainframe of the time—they had, and, told they had none, said he wasn't interested.[75]

Then, in August 1973, Intel announced their third microprocessor, the 8080. One historian has written that it "may well be the landmark invention of the last quarter of the twentieth century. This was the chip that turned the corner. It and its second source copies and imitators sold in the millions and reshaped the modern world."[76] It went into the first personal computer, the Altair. Indeed, the microprocessor made the microcomputers possible; and the microcomputer, in turn, hugely boosted the market for microprocessors.[77] From then on, costs of chip production fell dramatically while capacity rose, with increasing sales leading to lower prices and thus to increasing sales, in a dizzy circle which eventually was to make basic computing power virtually free: firms found themselves effectively giving away the razor to sell the blades, i.e. the software and everything else needed to make the machine work.[78]

The Birth of the PC: From Albuquerque to the Bay Area

The beginnings of the personal computer really lay in a competition between two magazines, *Popular Electronics* and *Radio Electronics*, whose readers wanted a home computer but could not get one. In September 1973, *Radio Electronics* published an article by Don Lancaster on a "TV Typewriter," but that was only a terminal. At *Popular Electronics*, technical editor Leslie (Les) Solomon was looking for a story about a home computer; he had extensive contacts with imaginative people, and on a holiday visit to Albuquerque had met Ed Roberts, a business partner of his friend Forest Mims, at MITS, an electronics firm that had moved into calculators but had nearly been wiped out in 1974 as prices tumbled. In early 1974, Roberts decided to take a huge gamble on making a kit computer. He decided on the new Intel 8080 chip and got them for $75 each instead of $360. Thus he could sell the Altair for $395, only $35 more than the retail price of the chip. Finally Solomon chose it as the computer his magazine would promote. He was impressed by the need to beat the Mark-8, an 8008-based computer, which had appeared in the rival magazine in July 1974. It was a typical gambler's gesture: no one at MITS had ever built a computer, so he was staking the entire reputation of his magazine on a promise and a hunch.[79]

Solomon trusted Roberts, but Roberts was distrustful of Solomon, a man with a reputation for tall stories. The name Altair came from Solomon's daughter who was watching *Star Trek*; it was the star to which the *Enterprise* was heading. Through Solomon, Roberts was approached by Roger Melen, a Stanford graduate student who had invented a digital camera. Solomon used this to illustrate how the Altair could be linked to a security camera.[80] The article appeared in January 1975, with the cover "PROJECT BREAKTHROUGH! World's First Minicomputer Kit to Rival Commercial Models . . . ALTAIR 8800."[81] Within two weeks, Roberts and his tiny staff were overwhelmed; hundreds of orders poured in, for as many computers as they had ever hoped to sell; MITS went from one of the local bank's biggest debtors to its best customer. It was very difficult to fulfill orders for the $395 machine, and Roberts delivered it stripped down, so that it could do very little. Steve Dompier, a young Berkeley building contractor, described the machine at an early session of the Homebrew Computer Club, a motley band of Bay Area computer enthusiasts who began to meet in a Silicon Valley garage, in April 1975; they heard about the four thousand orders that had poured in, and that, more than anything, caused a spark to go round the room; they knew that "What they had been waiting for had happened. The door had been kicked open."[82] They would be the people who would make the revolution. One of the greatest among them, Chuck Peddle, described their quality: "They made the business happen. They bought computers even when they didn't work, when there was no software for them. They created a market, and then they turned around and wrote the programs that brought other people in."[83]

They had to, because the Altair had hardly anything to make it work. It had a central processing unit, a memory, and an input-output unit; no more. It even lacked any permanent storage. Its input system consisted of switches that had to be flipped, one per bit; output came through flashing lights. Until paper tape readers and a version of BASIC software became available, communication was in machine language; the BASIC needed 30,000 switch flips without error, and even then everything was lost at the end of a session.[84]

This lack of software was simultaneously the Altair's Achilles heel and the main challenge to all its users. Paul Allen and Bill Gates were school friends in Seattle's private Lakeside High School, and became early computer geniuses and hackers; Gates was able to crash the DEC operating system and CDC's Cybernet. Later on, when Gates quoted his qualifications, "He just said, 'I crashed the Burroughs; I crashed the CDC.' Then they knew he was good."[85] Later, when the 8008 was launched, Allen lured Gates into writing an interpreter, but they did not manage to finish it.[86]

Various people were trying versions of BASIC, a simple programming language that had been invented by John Kemeny and Thomas Kurtz at Dartmouth as long before as 1964; Allen, then at Honeywell in Boston, and Gates, a freshman at Harvard, called Roberts and offered him their version. They then proceeded to write it; they finished the last bit as the plane touched down at Albuquerque; Allen was hired as MITS software director, in other words the entire department. Their own company, then called Traf-O-Data, was renamed Micro-Soft, later Microsoft; this was its first sale as a microcomputer software house.[87]

The first operating system for the microprocessor was the CP/M, developed in 1973 by Gary Kildall, computer science professor in the US Naval Post-graduate School in Monterey; he started Intergalactic Digital Research, later Digital Research, with his wife, and sold CP/M to IMSAI in 1977. The first word processing program, Electric Pencil, was developed by Michael Shrayer in southern California at the end of 1976. Seymour Rubinstein left IMSAI to establish a software house, MicroPro, with another ex-IMSAI employee, Rob Barnaby; they developed WordStar, which became an industry standard, in mid-1979. The first West Coast Computer Faire, modelled on the popular Renaissance Faire, was held in San Francisco in April 1977.[88]

The remarkable fact was that Roberts, Peddle, Gates, Allen and the other computer makers were [not] interested, despite the fact that it was obviously the way to go.[89] David Ahl of Digital later said, "We could have come out with a personal computer in January 1975. If, we had taken that prototype, most of which was proven stuff, the PDP-8a could have been developed and put into production in that seven- or eight-month period."[90] Engineers put up proposals at the existing companies, but their managements rebuffed them. Hewlett-Packard rejected Stephen Wozniak's ideas; Control Data rejected Robert Albrecht's; and, most significantly, Kenneth Olsen or DEC rejected David Ahl's proposal, saying he could see no reason for anyone to want a computer in the home; Ahl soon after left DEC.[91]

After its first flush of success, MITS ran progressively into trouble, mainly due to communication problems between Roberts and his high-level staff. Paul Allen rejoined Bill Gates, working exclusively for Microsoft, at end-1976. Although MITS grossed $13 million in 1976, its products were not regarded as anywhere near the best; deliveries were slow, and service was poor. By mid-1976 there were several competing computers, all of which in principle could use the same circuit boards; and Tandy Corporation were looking for a computer that they could sell ready-packaged. Over fifty companies had entered the market; at the first West Coast Computer Faire in spring 1977, Chuck Peddle demonstrated the Commodore PET and Apple introduced Apple II. In May 1977 Roberts sold MITS to Pertec, a company specializing in disk and tape drives for minicomputers and mainframes; it was not a success, particularly when it was discovered that Gates and Allen owned the rights to the BASIC. Within two years MITS was gone.[92] Nevertheless, as the historians of the personal computer have written: "It would be hard to overestimate the importance of MITS and the Altair. The company did more than create an industry. It introduced the first affordable computer, of course, but it also pioneered computer shows, computer retailing, computer company magazines, users' groups, software exchanges, and many hardware and software products."[93] Altair's success had prompted competition: by end-1977, rivals had emerged like mushrooms all over the country. Though the search for profit was part of it, this was a revolution driven by obsessive technologists, and normal economic laws no longer applied. The phenomenon was nationwide, in such places as Denver and Bountiful, Utah, Chicago and New Jersey; but the San Francisco Bay Area was the hub. Most of the start-ups came from the counter-culture, which had a technological element. Lee Felsenstein had written for the *Berkeley Barb* before joining other computer junkies in an urban commune in a San Francisco factory building. There was a widespread belief that computer power should be given to the people. Bob Albrecht had dropped out of Control Data to found the Portola Institute which developed *The Whole Earth Catalog* and the People's Computer Company. Individuals like these two were still not thinking personal computers, only of access to computers. But they had soon found that the Altair's 4k memory boards did not work, and thought they could do better. Bob Marsh, an out-of-work ex-Berkeley engineering student, teamed up with Lee Felsenstein to start Processor Technology early in 1975; working in a garage in Fourth Street down near the railroad tracks in Berkeley, they sold boards that proved to work. A war developed: when Roberts denounced his Bay Area competitors as parasites, two Oakland hobbyists called their board company Parasitic Engineering. The only Roberts-approved company was Garland and Melen's Cromenco, named for Crothers Memorial Hall in Stanford, their dorm.[94]

The members of the Homebrew Computer Club, which held its first meeting in March 1975 in the garage of microcomputer enthusiast Gordon French in Menlo Park, eventually launched no less than twenty-two companies, of which twenty were still in operation in the mid-1980s, some of them leading companies like Apple, Cromenco, and North Star. When founded it had a regular membership of 500, mostly young and male; the name came from the fact that then all home computers were assembled from kits. A "mapping" (market) session was followed by a "random access" session in small groups, where information was freely exchanged; here Steve Wozniak handed out copies of the circuit designs for the Apple, no one yet thinking that anything would have commercial value. They soon had to move out of French's garage and into an auditorium at Stanford. One member, Fred Moore, an activist and draft protester, wanted to develop noncommercial uses of computers, but that was not to be how it worked. When several club members joined companies, the free exchange of information ceased.[95]

> In front, performing, was Lee Felsenstein. Bob Marsh and the Proc Tec group were usually assembled along one wall. Steve Wozniak and the boys from Apple and the other 6502 processor fans sat in the back. Jim Warren of *Dr. Dobb*'s sat on the aisle three seats from the back, stage left, ready to stand during the Mapping session and do his Core Dump, an extemporaneous outpouring of all the news and rumors he had heard. The front row always had Gordon French, who maintained the software library, and Bob Reiling, who wrote the newsletter.[96]

Soon there was a San Francisco branch which in effect consisted of Berkeley people. Four, George Morrow, Chuck Grant, Mark Greenberg and Bill Godbout, teamed up to build a computer. By end-1975, though new companies were springing up everywhere, the most furious activity was still in the San Francisco Bay Area, with IMSAI in San Leandro, Cromenco designing boards for the Altair, MOS Technology with its KIM-1 hobby computer, and Microcomputer Associates in Los Altos. Meanwhile Marsh and Felsenstein were developing an "intelligent terminal" at Solomon's prompting, which became the Sol computer. Proc Tec moved from its garage to an Emeryville factory, to be replaced there by Grant and Greenberg's North Star, Polymorphic, and Kentucky Fried Computers; these were just alternative identities, and soon afterwards North Star became the only plate on the door. Oakland's Howard Fulmer and George Morrow began to produce the Equinox in 1977.[97]

Meanwhile, many of the new start-up companies were following Altair into trouble: this business was a classic case of easy come, easy go. So the names disappeared from the lists almost as fast as they had appeared. Now that computers were entering a mass market, another kind of creative effort would be needed to make the hardware produce something the public would want to buy—especially in writing the appropriate software for different applications.[98]

Some competition came from a very different source: from people actually interested in money. IMSAI in San Leandro became a major competitor because it had been founded by a former sales representative, latterly data manager for the City of San Francisco, Bill Millard, who saw the firm as business people selling to business; it became a power in the industry, rivalling Altair. Seymour Rubinstein, software product marketing manager, bought the CP/M from Gary Kildall, who had developed it down in Pacific Grove, for a flat $25,000, then telling him he should have got more. But IMSAI too collapsed in 1979.[99]

Tandy/Radio Shack, "the McDonald's of the electronic world," was equally profit-oriented; in fact it was not interested in computer manufacturing and simply wanted to market the machines, but failed to reach an agreement with IMSAI and so developed its own computer at its Fort Worth headquarters; sales of the TRS-80, introduced in summer 1977, far exceeded expectations, and resistance inside the company fell away; soon the machine was upgraded. The TRS-80 was a price breakthrough, and people who knew nothing about computers began buying. Commodore, Atari and TI were competing, as was Clive Sinclair in Britain. Adam Osborne, an emigré Briton working on computer journalism, developed the first portable computer out of Berkeley and then nearby Hayward in 1981.[100]

The biggest competitor was of course Apple. Steven Jobs, who had been born the year Shockley came to Palo Alto, and Stephen Wozniak met in eighth grade where they attended the same high school in Santa Clara. Wozniak, whose father worked for Lockheed Space & Missiles, had started playing with computers in fourth grade. With Bill Fernandez he had developed a Cream Soda Computer three years before Altair, but it refused to work. It was through Fernandez he met Jobs, the only one of the three who had not come from an engineering family. Both had an irregular education: Wozniak at Colorado and then Berkeley, Jobs at Reed College in Oregon. Both worked in Silicon Valley: Wozniak with HP, Jobs with Atari. Wozniak began to attend the Homebrew Club, and soon saw that he could develop a computer around MOS Technology's new 6502 chip. He designed a skeletal machine without a case, keyboard or power supply; Jobs saw an opportunity, and they sold possessions—Jobs' VW microbus, Wozniak's HP calculators—to pay someone to create a printed circuit board. They got credit from the local Byte Shop and assembled their first Apple in summer 1976. Then they developed the superior Apple II.[101]

Jobs, "the hustler, entrepreneur type," as Wozniak described him, decided he wanted to run a large company; through Nolan Bushnell of Atari he was introduced to Mike Markkula, a former Intel executive, who agreed to come into the company on a one-third basis, contributing $91,000. It was an unlikely, therefore highly Californian, combination, a 34-year-old retired executive and two long-haired kids in jeans; but Markkula had convinced himself that Apple could achieve a record by entering the Fortune 500 list in less than five years. He set the tone for the company, helping Jobs with his business plan, obtaining a credit line at the Bank of America, and bringing in Mike Scott, a seasoned executive who had worked for Markkula in product marketing at Fairchild, to run the company.[102]

The two had very different personalities. Wozniak combined eccentricity, genius and innocence; he was the classic nerd,[103] whilst Jobs was different: "Jobs also has a genius, not in electronics—by all accounts, he doesn't particularly enjoy computers—but for hucksterism . . . He mixes young-executive patois and the shaman jive of utopianism, poster-caption philosophy and the youthful colloquialism of a self-proclaimed prophet."[104] The Apple I was Wozniak's machine, but the II was Jobs':

> With the penetrating vision which characterized much of Jobs's work during this period, the young man realized before just about anyone else that what he had was a device that could reach beyond the hobbyists to a market a hundred thousand times that size and turn the toy of a handful of nerdy young men in ponytails and Hush Puppies into a household appliance as common as a refrigerator, a piece of office equipment as pervasive as a typewriter. It sounded like crazy utopianism— and it was. But who would know more about false and real utopias than someone who have [sic] lived in a commune and chased gurus all over India.[105]

The Apple II was the first true personal computer, and it was designed to look "about as intimidating as a Granola bar."[106] It weighed only twelve pounds. Jobs was responsible for its look, which was a major factor in its commercial success. Wozniak, who was still working for Hewlett-Packard, showed them the Apple II design; typically for such a well-established company, they were not interested. Jobs added Rod Holt from Atari to handle the screen interface and power, and then brought in Bill Fernandez, plus two high school students, Chris Espanosa and Randy Wigginton, Wozniak's Homebrew friends. Finally he persuaded Wozniak to leave HP, which took some doing. Jobs got Regis McKenna for marketing, and he put an advertisement in *Playboy* to reach a new audience.[107] "Jobs's persistence persuaded McKenna as it had Wozniak, Markkula, and Holt. Wozniak made the machine, Markkula had the business sense, and Scotty ran the shop, but the pushy kid with the Ho Chi Minh beard was the driving force. Jobs was building a company."[108] They kept moving to larger offices, all in Cupertino, ten miles south of Palo Alto. The disk drive for the machine, which Wigginton and Wozniak developed, began to be shipped in April 1978 and was vital for the company, an event second in importance only to the computer itself. Apple went from essentially zero to sales of $100 million between 1976 and 1980, and the company went public in late 1980. Jobs' shares were worth $165 million on the market, Wozniak's $88 million; Jobs was then twenty-five, Wozniak twenty-eight.[109]

Apple hit a low patch with the failure of the prematurely released Apple III followed by Wozniak's involvement in a plane crash in 1981 and his return to Berkeley. But Jobs saw a new graphically based display system, which could handle pictures as well as text, at Xerox's Palo Alto Research Centre (PARC) and became convinced it was the wave of the future; the result, with $21 million spent on R and D in 1981, was the Lisa and then the Macintosh.[110] It would also lead on, of course, to Gates's Windows, the subject of an epic legal battle between Apple and Microsoft.

The real end of the heroic era of the personal computer came on 12 August 1981 with a long-awaited announcement from IBM. It was of course the IBM Personal Computer and, as everyone expected it to do, it radically changed the entire world of personal computing. IBM bought in components and software, including a word-processing program from John Draper, Captain Crunch, the ex-phone phreak. Apple were relieved because they had expected something more advanced. But clearly, there were now only two players on the block: Apple and an IBM that everybody knew but nobody knew, for this was new territory for them. This was no longer a game for obsessed hobbyists; the funky time was over, and the innovative small companies that had pioneered the personal computer began dropping out. North Star, Vector Graphic and Cromenco all felt the pinch, as did Chuck Peddle's Victor; Osborne went bankrupt in September 1983. Others fell under IBM's shadow, especially small software companies which allowed themselves to be bought by larger ones.[111]

Critical to IBM's entry was their agreement with Bill Gates at Microsoft. Already, in summer 1980, Microsoft had decided to deal with the problem of writing software for the Apple by developing a "neutral" language with chip-specific translator programs. At almost precisely that time IBM approached them with a request to produce software for their new PC. IBM originally had wanted CP/M; but Kildall at Digital Research rejected the idea. Gates then persuaded them to develop a sixteen-bit machine. Having won the contract, he was determined to make MS-DOS the industry standard; so he argued for an open system, which would allow people to develop software more easily; as someone said, he had "discovered the Wozniak principle" of the open system. The software, developed out of an existing sixteen-bit system, SCP-DOS from Seattle Computer Products, was delivered in March 1981, after a gruelling development schedule; Gates called it MS-DOS, and a whole new era of computing was born.[112]

Silicon Valley in the 1980s: New Networks

And so, by the early 1980s, there was a general feeling in Silicon Valley that the heroic age was at an end. Noyce in 1982 argued that the business had become very capital-intensive and that the garage era was over: "I don't think this industry is any different than the automobile industry in that sense. These guys all started in their garages too, and there was intense competition, and then some consolidation of the industry." Yet this was not quite like car-making, he thought: "there are still 100 or 200 companies in the business, so it's not like the Big Three in the U.S. auto industry. It will continue to be intensively competitive for a long time to come."[113]

Not all observers agreed with him. Florida and Kenney argued in 1990 that the Silicon Valley model—frequent start-ups fed by venture capital, fragmented production, great interdependence—was inimical to long-term survival; in particular, the area had not developed any strong links with consumer electronics— Watchman televisions, CD players, miniature tape players and recorders—which were the great strength of the Japanese economy.[114]

But they were wrong, and Noyce was right: more right than he knew. For already, at that time, new chip makers had emerged, taking $10–15 million to start up on average; the fastest growth of all was in customized chips for special purposes. And this pointed to a paradox: though the semiconductor industry in Silicon Valley faced a crisis in the mid-1980s, with sales plunging 35 per cent and employment declining 7000 (and with another 20,000 in linked sectors), more than eighty new firms generated 25,000 new jobs and more than $2 billion in annual sales. While the established producers were struggling to survive, several of the start-ups were recording growth rates of 45–50 per cent a year; and only a handful had failed.[115]

AnnaLee Saxenian provides the explanation: the new start-ups were creating a flexible model of production, the precise inverse of the mass production model of the established producers. These established firms, like Advanced Micro Devices and National Semiconductor, mass-produced general-purpose semiconductors; the newcomers specialized in short runs of high value-added components, including semi-customized and customized chips and standard parts for niche markets. They used "mini-fabs"—miniature chip-making plants—and extensive electronic design automation; by serving many different markets, they spread the prohibitive costs of chipmaking. They built on Silicon Valley's dense networks of social and professional relationships, and on an environment rich in skill and know-how where engineers are often more loyal to the industry and to advancing technology than to the firm.[116]

There is a rich irony here: the established firms thought that they had outgrown the networks which had nourished them in their youth; investing heavily in dedicated, high-volume fabrication lines and facilities to reduce unit costs and so compete with the Japanese, they put everything in-house. They shifted production out of the area, even out of the country. But in doing so, they abandoned the flexibility and dynamism that had made them successful in the first place. The start-ups, in contrast, had just rediscovered the traditional model for Silicon Valley success.[117]

And this was not restricted to the chip makers; in the 1980s Silicon Valley saw hundreds of new start-ups, from disk drives to electronic design automation, from networking software to test equipment. Systems firms like Silicon Graphics, Pyramid Technology, Mips Computers, and Sun Microsystems, not semiconductor firms, came to occupy the centres of the networks. As a result, Silicon Valley was no longer simply synonymous with semiconductor manufacture; by the late 1980s, computer systems firms employed as many workers as semiconductor makers, and thousands of firms had emerged in related sectors such as software, disk drives, networking hardware, and contract manufacturing. Systems firms were at the hub of emerging production networks, which are part-cause and part-consequence of this diversification. And the cannier established firms learned how to play the new game: companies like Hewlett-Packard and Apple Computers, as well as newer ones like Silicon Graphics and Pyramid Technology, organized themselves so as to recombine components and subsystems made by specialist suppliers, both inside Silicon Valley and outside it, into computer systems. In collaborating they learned together, thus engendering a continued dynamism in the local economy.[118]

In this process, during the 1980s Silicon Valley outgrew its origins as a centre of semiconductor production to become a complex of computer-related specialists. This complex continued to grow and diversify, confounding the predictions of industrial consolidation that had prevailed a decade earlier; one expert estimated that the computer industry grew from 2500 firms to 50,000 between 1965 and 1990—the majority first-time entrants of the 1980s.[119] Most of these new firms, like Sun, concentrated their resources on the design and assembly of a final system and on the advance of technologies at the core of their firm's capabilities: Saxenian comments that "Continuing to operate like start-ups, they shared the costs and risks of the development of new systems with partners and suppliers. The computer producers Tandem, Silicon Graphics, Pyramid, and MIPS all relied heavily on networks of external suppliers."[120] Silicon Graphics CEO Ed McCracken explained to AnnaLee Saxenian that "Silicon Valley is the center of the new trend toward standardization and modularization that allows companies to specialize and get products out very fast. In Silicon Valley, you can pick up modules of software and hardware easily, and then focus on specializing. This allows you to get new products out very, very fast. It would be much harder to do this elsewhere in the world."[121]

This involved a profound reorganization of the entire process of generating new and innovative product: during the 1980s, Silicon Valley firms redefined their relationships with their most important component suppliers, treating them as partners in a joint process of designing, developing, and manufacturing innovative systems, and thus allowing both customer and supplier to become more specialized and more technologically advanced.[122] And such relationships required proximity: as one former Silicon Valley manager explained, "An engineering team simply cannot work with another engineering team that is three thousand miles away, unless the task is incredibly explicit and well defined—which they rarely are. If you're not tripping over the guy, you're not working with him, or not working at the level that you optimally could if you co-located."[123]

All this meant, simply, that smarter firms were recognizing the facts of life. During the 1970s and 1980s the cost of bringing new products to market increased, while the pace of innovation also rose. It became almost impossible for one firm to stay at the forefront of all the technologies, or even produce them at all; firms had to learn to concentrate on what they did best, buying the rest in from the dense infrastructure of suppliers inside and outside the region. A classic case is Sun Microsystems, founded in 1982: it chose to focus on designing hardware and software for workstations, and to limit manufacturing to prototypes, final assembly and testing; everything, even the CPU, was bought in. This allowed Sun to introduce four major new product generations in its first five years of operation, building on the area's unparalleled agglomeration of engineers and specialist suppliers of materials, equipment, and services.[124]

Increasingly, also, these firms replaced standard components by specialized ones to satisfy product niches. The more sophisticated these computers and their components, the more the systems firms were drawn into long-term partnerships with their suppliers based on shared recognition of the need to ensure the success of a final product. Suppliers were brought into the design and development of new systems and components at a very early stage, a major departure from the old practice of sending out precise design specifications to multiple sources for competitive bids; price is rarely considered as important as product quality and reliability in selecting a key supplier. In these relationships, both parties were concerned to preserve their own autonomy. But they recognized that local contacts were greatly superior to long-distance ones; the complex collaborative relations were based on shared trust, information exchange, and teamwork, and thus on the kind of continued interaction which could not be achieved over long distances.[125]

So, AnnaLee Saxenian concludes at the start of the 1990s,

> Silicon Valley is thus far more than an agglomeration of individual technology firms. Its networks of interdependent yet autonomous producers grow and innovate reciprocally. These networks promote new product development by encouraging specialization and allowing firms to spread the costs and risks associated with developing technology-intensive products. They spur the diffusion of new technologies by facilitating information exchange and joint problem-solving between firms and even industries. Finally, the networks foster the application of new technologies because they encourage new firm entry and product experimentation.[126]

Such special, not to say unique, organizational characteristics powerfully help to explain Silicon Valley's unique geographical form. Since the entire complex logically started its process of growth at Palo Alto, "driving south toward San Jose one essentially tracks through a year-by-year history of Silicon Valley's development."[127] As the cluster of defence-related aerospace and electronics firms began to locate here, it concentrated around Stanford where pioneers like Hewlett-Packard and Varian Associates were already established. Palo Alto's land was soon completely developed, so electronics and semiconductor production began to move south to Mountain View and Sunnyvale, eventually to Santa Clara and Cupertino. Cities, seeing the virtue of a strong industrial tax base, encouraged the process. Even today, the overwhelming bulk of production is clustered in the five cities of Palo Alto, Mountain View, Sunnyvale, Santa Clara and Cupertino at the northern end of the Santa Clara Valley.

Thus developed a highly distorted pattern of land use, with a disproportionate concentration of employment in the north. Of 70,000 workers in Palo Alto in 1976, only 11,000 actually lived in the city; the five northern cities together had 243,100 jobs but only 129,000 housing units. The main concentration of semiconductor firms was in Sunnyvale, Cupertino and Santa Clara, which even by 1980 had become the heart of Silicon Valley. Intel was in Santa Clara, with AMD (Advanced

Micro Devices); Cupertino housed Apple and other newer start-ups. San Jose in
contrast became the bedroom community, growing between 1950 and 1975 from
a compact agricultural centre of 17 square miles to a sprawling suburban city of
147 square miles, half the total incorporated area of the county. It grew from 95,280
in 1950 to 551,224 in 1975, 47.2 per cent of the county's population. In particular, it became the bedroom community for the minorities—Mexicans, Filipinos,
Vietnamese—who constituted the majority of the unskilled workers; their socioeconomic status was lower than that of the northern part of Santa Clara county;
and there were more problems—traffic, smog, crime—than in the affluent communities to the north. By the 1980s, lack of land in the core of the valley was causing
electronics firms to overspill here and into adjacent suburban towns like Milpitas
and Alviso.[128]

Growing Silicon Valley: A Look Back at the History

In 1987 two Canadian authors, Roger Miller and Marcel Côté, published an academic study of high-technology growth, appropriately called *Growing the Next Silicon Valley.* They concluded:

> What makes high-technology firms agglomerate in specific areas? A complex pro-
> cess leads to the emergence of a cluster. Usually entrepreneurs nurture their own
> ventures while working in 'incubator' firms, learning about the technology and
> marketplace and slowly developing their ideas. They are encouraged by the suc-
> cesses of other entrepreneurs. Entrepreneurs use the success next door to convince
> investors, bankers, suppliers, and key colleagues to join them in new ventures.
> Their first years are usually tough. Securing key clients is usually critical. The richer
> the commercial environment is for new firms, the easier it is for entrepreneurs to
> succeed.[129]

However relevant that might be for growing the next Silicon Valley, it evidently
comes from the experience of growing the last one. If we revisit the history, we
find two sets of forces and processes working to create Silicon Valley: internal and
external. And they worked in parallel, interactively. Internally, the critical factors
were the early interest in radio and the involvement of Stanford, which by the
1920s had set up the second-best centre of radio engineering research and teaching
in the United States. And the tradition of close university–industry relationships
at Stanford virtually guaranteed that there would be an industrial outcome: even
before the great defence-driven research drive of the 1950s, Stanford was spinning
off small firms like Litton, Hewlett-Packard and Varian, which were to become
giants in the industry. Even more important, these firms were the original incuba-
tors in the Miller–Côté scheme. Terman's far-seeing strategy of the late 1940s and
early 1950s, which created first SRI and then the industrial park, simply formalized
and accelerated this process.

Yet this might not have been enough, but for the effect of external forces. The huge defence build-up in the Bay Area during World War II—neatly abetted by crucial decisions during the depression decade of the 1930s, which had resulted partly from internal pressures—provided a crucial platform for an even more massive expansion in the Cold War era of the late 1950s. There was huge military pressure for solid-state electronics to pack into the new intercontinental and cruise missiles; the only question was where these components would be fabricated. Even then, the established East Coast producers had the clear competitive advantage. But they simply failed to exploit it.

Here Shockley's decision may have been crucial. If he had stayed with Raytheon, if he had never come to Palo Alto, if he had never hired the "Traitorous Eight" to join him there, history might not have been the same. The defection of the group to Fairchild, and the extraordinary process of spin-off thus set in train, may well have proved crucial to the subsequent growth of the valley. We cannot be sure about this, of course. But an instructive contrast is with Texas Instruments, which effectively shares with Fairchild the credit for the integrated circuit, yet produced no such chain reaction in and around Dallas.

What was important was that this spin-off process, kick-started by the Fairchild breakaway from Shockley, became endemic. Most Silicon Valley firms were spin-offs from existing firms, some of them founded here in the early years before 1950, some of them immigrants from the East Coast, some early start-ups: between 1952 and 1967, fifteen firms spun off from Bell Labs alone, including its even more prolific grandchild, Fairchild. Most growth came from new firm formation and spin-offs, not from movements of existing firms. There were very low barriers to entering the industry, because of liberal licensing of technology and lack of economies of scale; a firm like Intel, starting in 1968 with $2 million from a venture capitalist, could increase its sales more than one hundred-fold in a single decade. Easy entry was also facilitated by second-sourcing, outright imitation of innovations, and the fact that professionals could move so easily from one firm to another. Thus developed the characteristic pattern of small, intensely competitive firms: in 1953 there were already 108 establishments; by 1972, 352. It was this extraordinary process of constant breakaway, constant innovation, that culminated in Intel's discovery of the microprocessor.

Significant here was that no firm had overall control of the market: between 1958 and 1972, the four largest firms accounted for 39 per cent to 53 per cent of the total value of shipments, compared with 50 per cent for one firm in automobiles or 67–75 per cent for computers. This meant that firms depended on instant access to information through networking. Surprisingly, though, most of these start-ups survived: a study showed that 70 per cent of Silicon Valley firms continued beyond the first eight years of life; the longer-term survival rate was lower, 31 per cent from the 1960s to 1980, but even so was impressive; the study concluded that this was due to the "Silicon Valley maternity ward," the infrastructure of venture capital, consultants, peer information networks, and support industries.[130]

In this process, networking—another element in the Miller–Côté scheme—was also crucial: everyone knew many other people, partly due to the high rate of job mobility, and they in turn knew others; there was an epic rate of rumour generation, and firms got a unique advantage because each had knowledge about markets and components. One company obtained a six-month lead over a London rival because of new chips smuggled out of Intel. People might give information to friends working in rival companies. They might meet in well-known bars and restaurants like Walker's Wagon Wheel Bar and Restaurant in Mountain View, close to Fairchild, where a number of the "Fairchildren" were spun off, the Cow Girl Bar in the Sunnyvale Hilton Inn, the Peppermill off Highway 101, near Intel, and the Lion and Compass founded by Nolan Bushnell. The Peppermill was a huge breakfast meeting place, for perhaps 500 people who meet regularly. There were whole distinct networks: those who worked for Fairchild, or those who worked on games with Nolan Bushnell at Atari in the second half of the 1970s.[131]

In this process of constant spin-off an equally vital role was played by venture capitalists: early on, wealthy local individuals and families from San Francisco were the main source, while management consulting houses provided advice and evaluative services; later, by the 1980s, Silicon Valley had become the prime centre of organized venture capital activity in the entire United States, drawing in money from wealthy individuals, pension funds, universities and similar institutions, and the special investment arms of banks, insurance companies and other large corporations. No less than fifty-nine venture capitalists were located under one roof at 3000 Sand Hill Road in Menlo Park, just off the Stanford campus.[132]

Given all these preconditions, firms tended to cluster, and this continued because firms all wanted to be close to their potential labour force, to specialized inputs and services, and to the very special social, cultural and educational environment. Berkeley and Stanford expanded their doctoral and master's programmes, while community colleges and vocational schools instituted engineering and training programmes. So new spin-off firms located close to their parents. Already, by the early 1960s, Silicon Valley demonstrated what in the economic jargon is called a process of vertical and horizontal disintegration, with huge numbers of internal transactions among firms, and the development of a highly specialized local labour market; thus, important agglomeration economies developed, especially for the emerging integrated circuit producers. And, once this process had set in, it deepened with the entry of yet more semiconductor makers, subcontractors and users, all concentrated in the core of the area. It is the story of Lancashire in the 1770s, all over again.[133]

The industrial complex depended, above all, on highly educated engineers and scientists, who played a threefold role: basic research, production process improvement, and application to new products and improvement of old products. There was an extraordinary concentration of skilled scientists and engineers: 40 per cent of the total workforce in the semiconductor industry in 1972 consisted of non-production workers, compared with 16 per cent in autos and 13 per cent in apparel; 34 per cent were in professional and technical occupations.[134]

That was one innovative chain, and—despite indications to the contrary—it continued to produce new firms, and consequent expansion of the complex, during the 1980s. But, beginning in the early 1970s, there was another and equally significant chain reaction that created the personal computer industry. The beginnings of that industry, recall, can be found at various points all over the United States, but, above all, in Albuquerque, New Mexico. If the location of the original invention provided the criterion, then Albuquerque, not the San Francisco Bay Area, should have engendered the PC revolution. But it did not, and a significant reason was that MITS was too isolated. In Palo Alto and in Berkeley, in very sharp contrast, the whole freewheeling tradition of entrepreneurship combined with the post-1968 California counter-culture to produce an extraordinary degree of networking, symbolized by the Homebrew Club. And out of this, following a turbulent few years, emerged the Apple II, effectively the first commercial PC.

To be sure, that oversimplifies. Tandy, a market-driven firm from Texas, were neck-and-neck with Apple into the market; Gates and Allen developed the critical software in Cambridge, in Albuquerque, and then in Washington State. But hardly any of this would have been possible without the ferment on both sides of the San Francisco Bay. In this second revolution, as in the first, California companies invented (more accurately, reinvented) a form of industrial organization—vertically disintegrated, interdependent, networked—that academia today recognizes as flexible specialization. Just like Ford in Detroit, just like Mayer and Fox and the Warner brothers in Los Angeles, they almost simultaneously discovered new products, and new ways of making them; the critical difference was only that they took the model into reverse, away from Fordism and into a rediscovery of a far older model of artisan production.

Thus, by the end of the 1980s, AnnaLee Saxenian could conclude that

> Silicon Valley has a regional network-based industrial system that promotes collective learning and flexible adjustment among specialist producers of a complex of related technologies. The region's dense social networks and open labor markets encourage experimentation and entrepreneurship. Companies compete intensely while at the same time learning from one another about changing markets and technologies through informal communication and collaborative practices; and loosely linked team structures encourage horizontal communications among firm divisions and with outside suppliers and customers. The functional boundaries between customers are porous in a network system, as are the boundaries between firms themselves and between firms and local institutions such as trade associations and universities.[135]

External forces, in the form of the Cold War, started this process, but soon ceased to be highly significant to it. Other external forces, in the form of the shift towards the informational economy and society, again helped trigger the latent demand for the whole range of products based on the microprocessor. Silicon Valley entrepreneurs brilliantly exploited the opportunities thus offered, by developing what was essentially a new form of highly networked production. As Saxenian explains:

> The contrasting experiences of Silicon Valley and Route 128 suggest that industrial systems built on regional networks are more flexible and technologically dynamic than those in which experimentation and learning are confined to individual firms

Silicon Valley continues to reinvent itself as its specialized producers learn collectively and adjust to one another's needs through shifting patterns of competition and collaboration. The separate and self-sufficient organizational structures of Route 128, in contrast, hinder adaptation by isolating the process of technological change within corporate boundaries.[136]

The extraordinary agglomeration of the Silicon Valley firms was a contributory factor, of course, but it was not the explanation, rather an expression of a deeper explanation: "Spatial clustering alone does not create mutually beneficial interdependencies. An industrial system may be geographically agglomerated and yet have a limited capacity for adaptation. This is overwhelmingly a function of organizational structure, not of technology or firm size."[137]

Silicon Valley pioneered one such product, the personal computer, but it and the rest of America were conspicuously less successful in using the basic component as a platform for building a wide range of other consumer and producer industries. That was happening especially on the other side of the Pacific, and, above all, in the congested, teeming suburbs of Greater Tokyo.

Notes

1. Rogers and Larsen 1984, 25–6; Saxenian 1981, 48.
2. Rogers and Larsen 1984, 28.
3. Rogers and Larsen 1984, 28, 58–9.
4. Saxenian 1981, 48, 62–5.
5. Saxenian 1994, 2.
6. Braun and Macdonald 1982, 27–47; Brock 1975, 10–11; Dorfman 1982, 55–6; Fagen 1975, 26–52; Fagen 1978, 355; Heims 1980, 185–9; Lampe 1984, 554–6; Lampe 1988, 3; Loria 1984, 129–33; Noble 1977, 96–7, 114–16, 136–40; Sobel 1983, 50; Wildes and Lindgren 1985, 32, 86–90, 184–98; 228–35; Wise 1985, 68–81, 131–9.
7. Dorfman 1982, 50–8, 62, 76–9; Dorfman 1983, 300–12; Fagen 1978, 355–74, 505–9, 617–21, 647–52; Fishman 1981, 212; Lampe 1984, 556–8; Loria 1984, 137–9; Saxenian 1985a, 93–9; Smits 1985, 46–9, 106–8.
8. Hart gives the date for Palo Alto as 1774; Hart 1987, 397–8; Malone 1985, 11–12; Saxenian 1981, 48–9.
9. [This poem is] quoted in Saxenian 1981, 1.
10. Scott M. 1985, 45, 48, 83, 93, 134.
11. Quotation from Scott M. 1985, 83; cf. Malone 1985, 12; Rogers and Larsen 1984, 30–1; Scott M. 1985, 82–3.
12. Malone 1985, 13–15; Rogers and Larsen 1984, 30.
13. Malone 1985, 14, 21–2.
14. Malone 1985, 19–21.
15. Quotation from Rogers and Larsen 1984, 30–1; cf. Malone 1985, 20.
16. Rogers and Larsen 1984, 31.
17. Malone 1985, 20–1.
18. Malone 1985, 27–33; Rogers and Larsen 1984, 32–3.
19. Malone 1985, 33–6; Rogers and Larsen 1984, 34.
20. Malone 1985, 51–6.
21. Malone 1985, 56.
22. Saxenian 1981, 50.
23. Saxenian 1981, 50–7.

24. Saxenian 1981, 51, 56.
25. Saxenian 1981, 70, quoting Bernstein *et al* 1977.
26. Rogers and Larsen 1984, 35–6; Saxenian 1981, 52.
27. Scott M. 1985, 221.
28. Scott M. 1985, 221.
29. Scott M. 1985, 223.
30. Scott M. 1985, 244.
31. Malone 1985, 60; Saxenian 1981, 49; Scott M. 1985, 244–5.
32. Malone 1985, 63–5.
33. Scott M. 1985, 272–5.
34. Malone 1985, 61; Rogers and Larsen 1984, 39; Saxenian 1981, 52.
35. Rogers and Larsen 1984, 39.
36. Malone 1985, 60–1; Scott M. 1985, 311.
37. Saxenian 1981, 23.
38. Saxenian 1981, 24, 56.
39. Saxenian 1981, 25.
40. Saxenian 1981, 55–7.
41. Hanson 1982, 93–5; Rogers and Larsen 1984, 39.
42. Rogers and Larsen 1984, 39.
43. Scott and Angel 1987, 879–80.
44. Braun and Macdonald 1982, 5–7, 27–8, 33, 45.
45. Saxenian 1981, 18, 47–62.
46. Saxenian 1981, 70–1, 74–8.
47. Saxenian 1981, 19–20, 35–6.
48. Scott and Angel 1987, 883.
49. Scott and Angel 1987, 884.
50. Malone 1985, 69.
51. Malone 1985, 68–9; Rogers 1985, 25; Rogers and Larsen 1984, 35–7.
52. Rogers and Larsen 1984, 37–8.
53. Rogers and Larsen 1984, 38.
54. Malone 1985, 69.
55. Malone 1985, 69, 70–1; Rogers and Larsen 1984, 38, 101.
56. Malone 1985, 75–9; Rogers and Larsen 1984, 37–8.
57. Quotation from Hanson 1982, 94–5; cf. Braun and Macdonald 1982, 103–4, 154; Dummer 1983, 141; Freeman, Clark and Soete 1982, 111; OECD 1968, 61; Rogers and Larsen 1984, 38, 101–2.
58. Malone 1985, 86–7.
59. Hanson 1982, 107; Malone 1985, 94, 104.
60. Rogers 1985, 24; Rogers and Larsen 1984, 43–5.
61. Hanson 1982, 110.
62. Hanson 1982, 113.
63. Hanson 1982, 115.
64. Saxenian 1994, 30, 36.
65. Saxenian 1994, 50.
66. Saxenian 1994, 30.
67. Rogers and Larsen 1984, 102.
68. Rogers and Larsen 1984, 105.
69. Hanson 1982, 115–16; Rogers and Larsen 1984, 103.
70. Rogers and Larsen 1984, 103.
71. Freiberger and Swaine 1984, 12; Rogers and Larsen 1984, 104.
72. Rogers and Larsen 1984, 106.
73. Freiberger and Swaine 1984, 12–16; Rogers and Larsen 1984, 107–8.
74. Rogers and Larsen 1984, 109–10.
75. Malone 1985, 144–6.
76. Malone 1985, 146.

77. Rogers and Larsen 1984, 108–9.
78. Hanson 1982, 142–3.
79. Freiberger and Swaine 1984, 28–32; Rogers and Larsen 1984, 108–9.
80. Freiberger and Swaine 1984, 32–6.
81. Freiberger and Swaine 1984, 37.
82. Freiberger and Swaine 1984, 37–9.
83. Freiberger and Swaine 1984, 39.
84. Freiberger and Swaine 1984, 41–3.
85. Freiberger and Swaine 1984, 22.
86. Freiberger and Swaine 1984, 22–3.
87. Freiberger and Swaine 1984, 39–40, 140–3, 145.
88. Freiberger and Swaine 1984, 137–9, 147–8, 153, 181.
89. Freiberger and Swaine 1984, 17.
90. Freiberger and Swaine 1984, 17.
91. Freiberger and Swaine 1984, 18–20.
92. Freiberger and Swaine 1984, 50–3.
93. Freiberger and Swaine 1984, 53.
94. Freiberger and Swaine 1984, 57–9, 99–103.
95. Freiberger and Swaine 1984, 45–9; Rogers and Larsen 1984, 86–7.
96. Rogers and Larsen 1984, 86–7.
97. Freiberger and Swaine 1984, 121.
98. Freiberger and Swaine 1984, 104–19.
99. Freiberger and Swaine 1984, 124–5.
100. Freiberger and Swaine 1984, 59–60, 68–9, 77.
101. Freiberger and Swaine 1984, 196–9, 260–3.
102. Freiberger and Swaine 1984, 205–13; Hanson 1982, 107.
103. Freiberger and Swaine 1984, 213–15.
104. Malone 1985, 365.
105. Malone 1985, 366.
106. Malone 1985, 370.
107. Malone 1985, 370.
108. Freiberger and Swaine 1984, 216–20; Malone 1985, 374.
109. Freiberger and Swaine 1984, 219.
110. Freiberger and Swaine 1984, 223–4, 227; Hanson 1982, 208–9.
111. Freiberger and Swaine 1984, 231–40.
112. Freiberger and Swaine 1984, 276–8, 280–1.
113. Freiberger and Swaine 1984, 269, 271–4, 280.
114. Hanson 1982, 153.
115. Florida and Kenney 1990, 74–9, 81–3.
116. Hanson 1982, 154, 155; Saxenian 1989, 1.
117. Saxenian 1989, 4–6, 8.
118. Saxenian 1989, 10–12, 13.
119. Saxenian 1989, 15–16, 19; Saxenian 1990, 1.
120. Saxenian 1994, 122, 125.
121. Saxenian 1994, 142.
122. Saxenian 1994, 144.
123. Saxenian 1994, 145–6.
124. Saxenian 1994, 157.
125. Saxenian 1990, 4–6, 7.
126. Saxenian 1990, 9–14, 16–18.
127. Saxenian 1990, 19.
128. Rogers and Larsen 1984, 26.
129. Rogers and Larsen 1984, 26–8; Saxenian 1981, 70–3.
130. Miller and Côté 1987, 5.

131. Rogers and Larsen 1984, 47–8; Saxenian 1981, 31, 32–3, 53.
132. Rogers and Larsen 1984, 80–2, 84–5.
133. Rogers and Larsen 1984, 63–4; Saxenian 1981, 58.
134. Saxenian 1981, 58–9; Scott and Angel 1987, 890–3, 907.
135. Rogers and Larsen 1984, 87–8; Saxenian 1981, 20–3.
136. Saxenian 1994, 2–3.
137. Saxenian 1994, 161.
138. Saxenian 1994, 161.

References

Bernstein, A., DeGrasse, B., Grossman, R., Paine, C., Siegel, L. *Silicon Valley: Paradise or Paradox?: The Impact of High Technology Industry on Santa Clara County.* Mountain View, CA: Pacific Studies Center, 1977.

Braun, E., Macdonald, S. *Revolution in Miniature: The History and Impact of Semiconductor Electronics.* Cambridge: Cambridge University Press, 1982.

Brock, G. *The U.S. Computer Industry: A Study of Market Power.* Cambridge, MA: Ballinger, 1975.

Dorfman, N. S. *Massachusetts' High Technology Boom in Perspective: An Investigation of its Dimensions, Causes, and the Role of New Firms.* Cambridge, MA: MIT, Center for Policy Alternatives (CPA 82–2), 1982.

Dorfman, N. S. "Route 128: The Development of a Regional High Technology Economy." *Research Policy,* 12, 299–316, 1983.

Dummer, G. *Electronic Inventions and Discoveries.* Oxford: Pergamon, 1983.

Fagen, M. (ed.) *A History of Science and Engineering in the Bell System: The Early Years (1875–1925).* Murray Hill, New Jersey: Bell Telephone Laboratories, 1975.

Fagen, M. (ed.) *A History of Science and Engineering in the Bell System: National Service in War and Peace (1925–1975).* Murray Hill, New Jersey: Bell Telephone Laboratories, 1978.

Fishman, K. *The Computer Establishment.* New York: McGraw Hill, 1981.

Florida, R., Kenney, M. "Why Silicon Valley and Route 128 Won't Save Us." *California Management Review,* 33, 1: 68–88, 1990.

Freeman, C., Clarke, J., Soete, L. *Employment and Technical Innovation: A Study of Long Waves and Economic Development.* London: Pinter, 1982.

Freiberger, P., Swaine, M. *Fire in the Valley: The Making of the Personal Computer.* Berkeley: Osborne/McGraw Hill, 1984.

Hanson, D. *The New Alchemists: Silicon Valley and the Microelectronic Revolution.* Boston: Little Brown, 1982.

Hart, J. *A Companion to California.* Berkeley: University of California Press, 1987.

Heims, S. *John von Neumann and Norbert Wiener: From Mathematics to the Techniologies of Life and Death.* Cambridge, MA: MIT Press, 1980.

Lampe, D. R. "Das M.I.T. und die Entwicklung der Region Boston." In Schwarz, K. (ed.) *Die Zukunft der Metropolen: Paris-London-New York-Berlin, 1: Aufsätze,* 554–9. Berlin: Technische Universität Berlin, 1984.

Lampe, D. R. (ed.) *The Massachusetts Miracle: High Technology and Economic Revitalization.* Cambridge, MA: MIT Press, 1988.

Loria, J. "Das Massachusetts Institute of Technology und die Entwicklung der Region Boston." In Schwarz, K. (ed.) *Die Zukunft der Metropolen: Paris-London-New York-Berlin, 2: Katlog zur Ausstellung,* 128–46. Berlin: Technische Universität Berlin, 1984.

Malone, M. S. *The Big Score: The Billion-Dollar Story of Silicon Valley.* Garden City, New York: Doubleday, 1985.

Miller, R., Côté, M. *Growing the Next Silicon Valley: A Guide for Successful Regional Planning.* Lexington, MA: Lexington Books, 1987.

Noble, D. F. *America by Design: Science, Technology, and the Rise of Corporate Capitalism.* New York: Knopf, 1977.

OECD (Organization for Economic Cooperation and Development). *Gaps in Technology: Electronics Components*. Paris: OECD, 1968.

Rogers, E. "The High Technology of Silicon Valley." *Monograph Series No. 4*. College Park: University of Maryland Institute of Urban Studies, 1985.

Rogers, E. M., Larsen, J. K. *Silicon Valley Fever: Growth of High technology Culture*. New York: Basic Books, 1984.

Saxenian, A. "The Genesis of Silicon Valley." In Hall, P., Markusen, A. (eds.) *Silicon Landscapes*, 20–34. London: Allen & Unwin, 1985.

Saxenian, A. *Regional Networks and the Resurgence of Silicon Valley*. Berkeley: University of California Institute of Urban and Regional Development, Working Paper No. 508, 1989.

Saxenian, A. *Regional Advantage: Culture and Competition in Silicon Valley and Route 128*. Cambridge, MA: Harvard University Press, 1994.

Saxenian, A. *Silicon Chips and Spatial Structure: The Industrial Basis of Urbanization in Santa Clara County, California*. Berkeley: University of California Institute of Urban and Regional Development, Working Paper No. 35, 1981.

Saxenian, A. *The Origins and Dynamics of Production Networks in Silicon Valley*. Berkeley: University of California, Institute of Urban and Regional Development, Working Paper No. 516, 1990.

Scott, A. J. "Industrialization and Urbanization: A Geographical Agenda." *Annals of the Association of American Geographers*, 76: 25–37, 1985.

Scott, M. *The San Francisco Bay Area: A Metropolis in Perspective*. Berkeley: University of California Press, 1985.

Smits, F. (ed.) *A History of Science and Engineering in the Bell System: Electronics Technology (1925–1976)*. Murray Hill, New Jersey: AT&T Bell Laboratories, 1985.

Sobel, R. *IBM: Colossus in Transition*. New York: Bantam Books, 1983.

Wildes, K. L., Lindgren, N. A. *A Century of Electrical Engineering and Computer Science at M.I.T., 1882–1982*. Cambridge, MA: MIT Press, 1985.

Wise, G., Willis, R. *Whitney, General Electric, and the Origins of U.S. Industrial Research*. New York: Columbia University Press, 1985.

19

The Dependent Future

J. Logan and H. Molotch

The New U.S. Cities

Ecologists build typologies of places based on population size, on centrality, or on the products or services that places provide in a national urban system. In these schemes, each place performs a useful role for the national system as a whole; there is little acknowledgment that actors or organizations in these places manipulate place to gain special advantages or that the entire system has links to the rest of the world. Places are "dominant" only in the sense that their specialized task may happen to be the coordination of tasks that occur in a large number of other areas.

In our view, U.S. cities are tied to a transnational system whose integration is accomplished through networks of purposive individuals and organizations. We have gone to great lengths to reject the notion of natural laws of urban development, of an unfolding of spatial relationships dictated by a free market that is driven by efficiency. Domination and control, achieved by interested parties, can leave different sorts of people and social groups in permanent states of advantage and disadvantage. Given the increased mobility of capital and the lower capacity of the State to enforce development conformity among localities, the future conditions of urbanization will be diverse, and so too the fates of specific groups within each type of city. The uneven capacity of areas to deal effectively with capital will make metropolitan economies "uneven" and "distorted" in and among places in ways that contradict the neoclassical theories. An uneven capacity to attract growth is the key element in our typology of cities.

In the future urban places will likely play one of five roles: (1) headquarters, (2) innovation center, (3) module production and processing, (4) Third World entrepôt, and (5) retirement site. These types are not perfect reflections of real cities or an exhaustive typology of all possibilities, but are useful categories for suggesting how use and exchange values are beginning to cluster. For each urban setting, we demarcate the underlying economic organization at work and then describe the particular rewards from use and exchange values that lie ahead for different sorts of people within them.

1. Headquarters

The decline of the United States as the dominant world economy does not make its cities unimportant to transnational capitalism. Many of the great corporations of the world are headquartered in this country and the cities that house their key activities (alternatively referred to as "headquarter," "world," "global," or "capital" cities) will remain significant. Although we here emphasize the economic role of these places, we think of their dominance as multidimensional, one that includes a cultural leadership and, as the ecologists would also assert, a centrality in transportation and communication networks (see Abrahamson and DuBick, 1977).

Although the precise measurement that is used can yield different results, there is wide agreement on which city is at the top. New York, by virtually any indicator, is number one. In 1979, 132 of the country's largest firms (including industrials, banking, insurance, retailing, transportation, and utilities) were located within the New York SMSA (Ward, 1984). This was double the number in the runner-up metropolis (Chicago) and four times that of the next leading place (Los Angeles). Even this description understates New York's position, given the large scale and international penetration of its firms compared to those in other metropolitan areas. New York is also the location of a host of other leading institutions in the arts, education, and commerce.

The most rapidly developing national center is Los Angeles; it surpasses strong San Francisco (and is gaining on Chicago) in number of headquarters and is especially important because many of its headquarters are of firms in growing sectors. Looking only at industrial firms in the years between 1971 and 1982, the number of *Fortune* 500 headquarters within the L.A. central city increased from 14 to 21.[1] Chicago and San Francisco were modest losers of big industrial headquarters over a similar period (Cohen, 1981:305; Soja, Morales, and Wolff, 1983:224).

Notwithstanding the rise of Los Angeles and some well-publicized moves to the sunbelt (for example, American Airlines relocated to Dallas in 1978), there has been an overall pattern of sustained corporate concentration in certain major metropolitan areas. Assertions of widespread "flight" from the old regions are exaggerations. Numerous studies have shown net gains or only trivial losses of firm headquarters in the frostbelt areas in the year, from 1960 to 1979 (Birch, 1979; Burns and Pang, 1977; Palmer and Friedland, forthcoming; Schmenner, 1982; Ward, 1984). Using a different indicator of "dominance," Ross (1982) found that over the 1955–1975 period, metropolitan areas in most of the frostbelt regions experienced net gains in the national labor force controlled by firms located within them (although several other regions increased employment control at a faster rate).

There has indeed been a net outflow in number of corporate headquarters from old central cities like New York (Quante, 1976), but these have primarily been relocations to the surrounding suburbs, where firms still have access to the major business centers (albeit less immediate) as well as to the surrounding transport networks. Certain types of firms have been responsible for this modest headquarter dispersal to the suburbs: industrials, retailers, and transportation companies, rather than those in banking and insurance (Ward, 1984). When firms have moved to another national region, it has again been transportation and retailing (along with utilities) that led the way (Ward, 1984). But overall, in the years 1969 to 1979, the Northeast states still lost virtually none of their dominance in industrial, banking, and insurance headquarter activities. This seems to imply that the most cosmopolitan and ecologically dominant types of firms have dispersed the least, whereas companies that more directly service specific populations have, quite reasonably, tended to spread out along with their clientele.

Part of the reason for the continuing dominance of many old headquarter cities is the geographical pattern of acquisitions and mergers. In 1983, New York firms led the country in the number of firms they acquired; California was second in acquisition activity. Just as significant, however, was that California led the country in the number of its firms that were acquired by firms located elsewhere (heavily in New York City). The major hinterland cities apparently play a role in propagating new firms that are then scooped up by other corporations (see Schmenner, 1982); some of the acquiring firms are in the headquarter cities of the sunbelt (like Los Angeles), but more are in New York (Vartabedian, 1984:1). The hierarchy of urban dominance seems to be reflected in a hierarchy of acquisition. Thus once again, declines in absolute or relative numbers of headquarters in a given city may obscure real growth in the level of headquarters activity of a place when its existing firms grow larger through acquisitions.

Regardless of the specifics used to project *which* of the large cities will be dominant, there can be no doubt that headquarters will continue to be concentrated in certain major places, rather than dispersed to small ones. This pattern supporting the continued significance of the big cities (even of the same big cities) suggests that there is a particular quality of such places that makes them appropriate for this dominant role. The difficult question is what this quality might be.

Headquarter cities are a well-known type (although not called by that name) within ecological models of the urban hierarchy. Ecologists have argued that the large size of such places not only results from their functional superiority but also reinforces that superiority. After a city first develops because of an initial physical advantage (for example, centrality), size alone becomes a dynamic factor. Large size generates a self-sufficient market for the goods that are produced, leading to a rich internal division of labor that creates economies of its own, further sustaining growth and development (Duncan et al., 1960). Thus, for example, New York may owe its origins to an excellent natural harbor, but urban greatness was facilitated by the efficient agglomerations that took over after threshold size and density had been achieved. When technological change in production causes new places to reach threshold levels of growth, which is occurring today in the West and South, cities generate their own internal markets and hence a basis for sustaining additional growth and semiautonomous development (Berry and Kasarda, 1977:276).

In a break with ecological reasoning, other scholars have recently interpreted the great metropolis as a response to the *organizational* needs of the modern corporation (see Palmer and Friedland, forthcoming), and are therefore directing attention away from physical factors, demographic dynamics, and technology. The ongoing trend toward monopolistic and oligopolistic control of product markets, for example, ipso facto feeds the administrative growth of the cities where major corporations are already established. As firms grow larger, increasing amounts of economic activity involve transactions *within* them as goods and services are moved from one plant or office to another of the same firm (Noyelle, 1983; Pred, 1977). The market mechanism (less geographically specific) is replaced by intrafirm bureaucracies, which are located at the major headquarter cities.

Concentrations of services important to modern firms thus build up in these corporate centers. Firm headquarters typically carry out tasks with an "orientation" nature (Thorngren, 1970; see also Stephens and Holly, 1980), relying on supportive services from certain other business enterprises. Compared to marketing in the past, the marketing of a particular product now uses a much larger array of specialized activities "up front." Accounting and law firms advise management on finance, personnel practices, licensing, and international contracting; engineering consultants and graphic design studios assist in product development and packaging; advertising agencies stimulate consumer demand; specialized catalog and media merchandisers produce materials that will generate orders (see Stanback et al., 1981). The American economy's much heralded shift toward "services" is actually a shift toward *producer* services that facilitate the development, manufacture, importation, and distribution of products. Producer services grew from 29 to 36 percent of the gross national product from 1947 to 1977, while retail and consumer services either remained stable or declined during the same period (Noyelle, 1983:118).

It is the producer services that cluster in the largest places and seem to have had the least tendency toward dispersal. As Stephens and Holly (1980:164) put it, "Orientation processes are extremely contact dependent: therefore, the geographical environment best suited to meeting the firm's needs for face-to-face contacts is that of the large, economically diversified urban center." Even though New York City lost over 100,000 manufacturing jobs between 1977 and 1984, it gained 192,000 jobs in business services and finance (Greer, 1984). Banking, law, advertising, and accounting, found in the largest centers (primarily Manhattan), dominate on a national and international scale.

This locational pattern is significant because it suggests *specific* kinds of advantages of cities to *specific* kinds of firms. Palmer, Friedland, and Roussell (1985) report that the presence of large corporate headquarters activities is associated less with SMSA size than with the degree of local business service specialization. Not all cities (even large ones) offer the broad range of producer services, financial institutions, and international connections that modern multinational firms require. Conversely, not all large firms require presence in a "headquarter" city. It is the changing nature of the firm, then, that affects the city and its size, not the other way around (Palmer and Friedland, forthcoming).

The importance of the organization of a firm for the nature of the urban system means we must take a closer look at exactly what benefits are being delivered by these agglomerations of "orientation" and "support" services. If these spatial arrangements increase the efficiencies of firms, then the new organizationally oriented spatial theories are compatible, albeit modified, elaborations of the older ecological models. Places grow large because they contain organizational agglomerations that serve the efficiency-maximizing goals of component firms and hence of the whole system of cities. The organizational differentiation of cities replaces the ecologists' natural bases of differentiation, but an impersonal efficiency maximization drives the urban system in both perspectives.

But if the real specialty of headquarter places is the *control* they facilitate over a firm's own operations and those of other firms, both locally and nonlocally (see Friedmann and Wolff, 1982), then we must reexamine the given theories. The difference between control and efficiency is critical. Arrangements that facilitate control can be present merely because of the advantage they provide for one group of actors *in opposition to* the interests of others. Neo-Marxians analyzing the labor process (for example, Braverman, 1974; Gintis, 1976) have made a similar distinction regarding the work process; managers may tolerate less efficiency rather than create work arrangements that might, for example, risk worker insurgency. This is a difference between "quantitative" and "qualitative" efficiency or between what Gordon (1976:31) calls "technical efficiency" and "capitalist efficiency" (see also Marglin, 1974). If capitalist efficiency is efficiency at all, it is a "crackpot efficiency"[2] in which maximization of control at the expense of production serves only a narrow, proximate rationality and not the productive system as a whole.

There are a number of reasons to suppose that the headquarter cities' control advantages (or capitalist efficiencies) are certainly as important as technical efficiencies in maintaining the role of these cities in the urban system. One evidence is that not all large firms seem to need them; big and regularly profitable corporations can exist in small cities off the beaten track. Procter and Gamble thrives in Cincinnati, Ohio (Peters and Waterman, 1982), Johnson's Wax in Racine, Wisconsin, and John Deere in Moline, Illinois. Although we have not undertaken a systematic study of firms in the "boondocks," we observe that these companies are devoted to production of kindred product lines, and are conservative in their borrowing and financial manipulations. They do well in the corporate hinterland perhaps because they are oriented toward actual production.

We thus suspect that the energy behind the growing headquarter city is something other than coordinating efficient production, in the technical sense. Instead, the real advantage of such places may be in their ability to support corporate financial assets, only loosely tied to production results. According to Fligstein (1985), corporations' finance departments have become the most powerful component of the large modern firm, replacing first the production experts and then the marketing departments that were prominent in two previous eras (see Perrow, 1970). This is symptomatic of the rise of a "paper entrepreneurialism" (Reich, 1983), which can take a number of different forms. Finance managers can use a firm's assets to merge one firm with another or, in cases of "unfriendly takeover" threats, to discourage such mergers. Observers have long been aware that this merging and conglomeration activity has no necessary connection to technical efficiency (Herman, 1981:101; Nelson, 1959:7). In some instances, an acquisition is prompted by the need of one firm to gain the tax credits of a failing firm or to depreciate (for tax purposes) the assets of a profitable one. Sometimes the aim is to get control of a "cash cow" that can then be milked for still other financial maneuvers. Increasingly, the acquiring firm or investment group uses borrowed cash to tender its offer, and then pays back the loan out of the earnings or assets of the conquered company, which it may badly weaken in the process (this is the "junk bond" phenomenon).

"Opportunism" (Williamson, 1975) is always a force in structuring markets, and the current process of mergers and acquisitions is rife with opportunities for skulduggery by those within or outside the firms. Speculators can set up a merger to earn profits on their stock, which will rise with just the *appearance* of growth and vitality (Jung, 1984). Even if an attempted takeover is unsuccessful, the stock value of a firm that is being courted by another company often rises quickly, providing payoffs to the insiders who made it happen. In another variant, those who threaten a takeover are handsomely paid off by the courted company to "go away" ("greenmail" as it is called), thereby receiving enormous profits from activities that have nothing whatever to do with enhancing productive efficiency.

Sometimes a merger is used by managers of one firm (who may fear being ousted from their jobs) to ward off a takeover from still another company (see Herman, 1981:101). The consumer products company Chesebrough-Ponds borrowed $1.25 billion to acquire Stauffer Chemicals (an unprofitable company) just to make itself less attractive to investor Carl Icahn's takeover bid. Maneuvers in which, in the words of a Wall Street analyst of the Stauffer deal, there is "little, if any, synergism between the two companies" (Hughes and Gilman, 1985:3) have become an almost everyday experience in the corporate world. Indeed, acquisitions of firms that engage in businesses unrelated to a corporation's existing products have risen continuously since the end of World War II (Fligstein, 1986).

Regardless of their wastefulness, these forms of manipulation build the existing headquarter centers because they contain the dominant firms that acquire the less dominant ones (Dicken, 1976; Smith, 1982; Vartabedian, 1984) and because of the local activity generated by the manipulations. Such maneuvers yield large fees to the supporting firms in law, banking, and accounting. The local resources that help this process along (the no doubt useful agglomeration of lawyers, financiers, and brokers) do not make production more efficient; they make control more efficient. The reported growth in the producer-service sector may be one reflection in the labor force of this increase in control activity.

Whatever the mix of control and coordinating functions, the role of headquarters places will probably continue to grow for several reasons. First, large-scale and multinational corporations are only increasing in their levels of activity. The internationalization of production is still on the rise; the multinational corporations' share of the gross world product is expected to grow from its 1971 level of 20 percent to 40 percent by 1988 (Jazairy, Kuin, and Somavia, 1977, as cited in Blackbourn, 1982:147). Unlike smaller businesses, large multinational firms can seek a government bail-out to prevent bankruptcy, whether the firm is located in the United States or abroad, as the histories of Chrysler, Lockheed, Citroen, Lancia, Leyland, and Rolls Royce indicate (Blackbourn, 1982:155). Mergers and acquisitions among firms from different countries (increasing rapidly) are also likely to increase geographical concentration. When foreign firms start up new operations in another country, they tend to be dispersed; but when they acquire control over an existing foreign company, they inject capital into the centers where the acquired firms are already located (Smith, 1982). Similarly, the continuing decline in the number of family-owned firms, which tend to be single-location operations in secondary cities (Burt, Christman, and Kilburn, 1980; Zeitlin, 1974), and the least likely to expand through acquisition (Palmer et al., 1984), will also feed geographical concentration.

A second reason to anticipate increasing concentration is the continuing trend toward ever-larger trading zones. Either through formal institutions like the European Economic Community or more ad hoc trade agreements, free trade eases the way for large firms to invest wherever they wish. Free trade gives the multinationals an advantage by limiting regulation and other "artificial" barriers to their manipulations of resources across political borders. The deregulatory climate sweeping the United States in the 1980s will also contribute to the growth of headquarter cities. Weakening of antitrust controls enhances concentration regardless of its social or productive consequences. Deregulation in areas such as banking and securities trading similarly inhibits the imposition of criteria for technical efficiency on mergers and acquisitions. Many of the results will not be easily reversed, if only because of inertia, should reform regulation eventually follow. Locational efficiencies and habits will have been established, optimizing both productive and control capacities, further entrenching the role of the headquarter cities.

Finally, the most powerful local growth machines in the country are probably those of the corporate centers and are a force in themselves: their rentier classes have the greatest resources and their corporate tenants (who are increasingly themselves local property owners) have clout at the national level. This means that a group of highly motivated and powerful people will monitor and influence national decisions, with an eye toward maintaining locational advantage for headquarter cities.

The dynamic role of these headquarter places is at present obscured by their sloughing off the activities that once marked them as major manufacturing centers. This is a process of "restructuring" (Soja, Morales, and Wolff, 1983), in which the number of jobs declines in the heavy manufacture sector as new development occurs in finance, information processing, and other producer services. Cities like New York generate growth in office and service jobs as they lose jobs in other sectors. Boston and San Francisco, both "old cities" with crumbling manufacturing plants, have experienced robust growth in the office economy (Mollenkopf, 1983). In still another variant, Los Angeles is expanding in headquarters activities while simultaneously growing in certain goods manufacture sectors (electronics, clothing) and declining in others (automobiles, tires). Whatever the rest of the mix, the headquarter cities will have as a growing part of their economic base the activities endemic to corporate control and coordination.

2. Innovation Centers

Research and development (R & D) carried out by private firms, government, and nonprofit institutions are at the top of the product cycle. Their innovations in technology and organization are then applied in other settings to specific and more routine purposes. Innovation activities, although in one sense "producer services," are not necessarily to be found in headquarter locations—or at production sites.

Malecki (1980) has outlined a number of different patterns of R & D location. Some R & D activities directly support corporate decision making and these tend to be located adjacent to other orienting functions within the headquarters city. In still other cases, each plant operating under a corporate wing must have its own R & D facility nearby (for example, a testing lab for raw materials for a steel factory). In low-level R & D, there is wide dispersal of facilities, but they are near corporate production units. Finally, some R & D activities are free of these constraints, and tend to be located near pools of professional labor and other research-related assets, like big universities (see Jobert, 1975). This is the "pure" type of R & D, in which the special agglomeration benefits peculiar to innovation can come into existence. Examples of innovation centers are Austin, Texas, Cambridge, Massachusetts, the Silicon Valley towns of Northern California, and the Research Triangle area of North Carolina.[3]

Like their headquarter city counterparts, these agglomerations are themselves by no means "natural." They are at least helped along by the capitalists and growth elites who have a use for them. We have already discussed the development of many university campuses as intrinsic parts of local growth schemes as well as the recent intense competition to attract the Microelectronics and Computer Technology Corporation's high-tech installation. But certainly as common as the recourse to centers of higher education (and often linked with them) is the use of military contracting as a means of stimulating growth and development. What we have been calling innovation centers are, to a significant decree, war preparation centers. In the post–World War II era, according to Robert Reich, "the Defense Department . . . has been the center of high-technology industrial policy in this country" (quoted in Schrage, 1984:3). The Defense Department's $35 billion annual R & D budget is about one-third of all R & D activity in the United States.

The military has long had distinct effects on the distribution of urban growth—a fact not lost on local elites. Deep South growth leaders whose areas depended on World War I and World War II military facilities always favored high defense expenditures. More profoundly, "World War II [government] investments . . . provided the basic, private capital stock for the postwar growth of Sunbelt cities" (Mollenkopf, 1983:105; see also Fleischmann, 1977: Soja, Morales, and Wolff, 1983:207). More than is the case for nonmilitary R & D, which is located predominantly outside the sunbelt (Cohen, 1977:219), the defense installations and government-financed high-tech complexes, such as those of Southern California, depend on the war machine for their survival.[4] Unlike design and production for consumer goods, security considerations preclude going abroad, making defense one of the few secure domestic industries (Keller, 1983:350; Taplin, 1984:3).

Even minor changes in defense strategy can have an immense impact on given areas. A nuclear-testing moratorium would knock eight thousand workers off the payroll at the Nevada test site alone, a prospect that was headlined in a local Nevada news report of the 1985 Soviet moratorium proposal.[5] This "vast addiction," as George Kennan (1984:78) has recently called the dependence of so many localities on war industries, prompts many growth activists to prefer a national agenda that gives high priority to defense expenditures and to the specific military strategies that will bring development to their locale. Such addiction to U.S. defense spending is even spreading to European countries. Britain has demanded a share of the "Star Wars" development budget for its own engineering firms in return for its political backing of the Reagan administration project (*New York Times*, 1985). Within the United States and perhaps throughout the world, value-free R & D may be the growth machine system's most profoundly dangerous manifestation.

3. Module Production Places

The urban areas that are becoming the sites for routine economic tasks have in common two disturbing qualities: they are dependent on control centers located elsewhere and they are expendable in the system of places. Whether the enterprises of an urban area are engaged in assembling car parts shipped in from various parts of the world, processing magazine subscriptions arriving from remote parts of the country, or distributing secret sauce to fastfood franchises in their surrounding region, they are not sustained by any of the unique organizational constellations that make up control or innovation centers. Each place will be chosen because it meets certain minimum criteria that ecological theory would imply it must: distribution centers need reasonable proximity to markets and naval stations must have water. But many places will satisfy these requirements, leaving the chosen area in a poor position to drive a hard bargain.

Some module cities achieve their utility through proximity to a natural resource (for example, mining centers) or a government function that local promoters have been able to attract (Social Security headquarters is in Baltimore). Cheap property and cheap labor are among the reasons that Omaha, Nebraska, has become the "800" telephone exchange center of the country (also helping Omaha was excess phone line capacity and operators whose Midwest diction is unproblematic for the rest of the country). Citicorp has put its credit-processing center in Sioux Falls, South Dakota, again to take advantage of inexpensive land and labor (Sassen-Koob, 1984:143). Small cities on the periphery of the large metropolitan areas as well as semirural towns are also favored . . . for their tractable, low-cost labor (Storper and Walker, 1983) and the open land favored for building sites by contemporary mass manufacture (Beale and Fuguitt, 1978:157–80; Sassen-Koob, 198–1:146).

The military can also make or break module centers by how it deploys its own routine activities, such as troop bases and maintenance sites. The Reagan administration's commitment to expansion of the country's battleship fleet is doubling defense spending in Connecticut, making that small state "the richest beneficiary of increased military spending" (Lueck, 1984:1). Simultaneously, the navy's decision to disperse its operational bases set off intense competition among potential sites. In 1984, at least seventeen Gulf Coast ports were bidding for a new base for thirty-five hundred sailors that would bring an annual payroll of $50 to $60 million, $100 million for port construction projects, and up to thirty-five hundred civilian jobs (*Schenectady Gazette,* 1984:7).

Instead of becoming the destination for new innovations, the old factory cities of the Northeast and Midwest, struggling for a viable role under the changing economic order, are likely to become module cities. But success in achieving even this future depends on the presence of obedient and cheap labor, as well as inexpensive open land for new factory construction. The efforts of elites in these old manufacturing cities to physically and socially retrofit their turf for new investment sharply illustrate the requirements for module development. Detroit is the classic case of urban decline and struggle.[6] As one of many efforts to subsidize development, $200 million in public funds was spent to clear land for a new automated General Motors factory (the Poletown project). In addition, the car companies succeeded, with local political support, in holding back auto workers' wages.

Ironically in light of the cutbacks, Detroit remains strong in some aspects of its corporate influence over the world. As measured by sales volume, assets, and the number of worldwide employees controlled by the firms headquartered within it, Detroit (in 1975) ranked second only to New York among U.S. cities in international dominance (Stephens and Holly, 1980:176). But Detroit is not now and never has been a headquarter city, even though a number of the world's largest corporations have their head offices in or adjacent to it. The auto companies are not headquartered in Detroit because of any *general* headquarters agglomeration benefits, but rather because of the circumstances that enabled the car industry to develop there—that is, access to raw materials and markets and the growth elite machinations that were effective at the time (Ewen, 1978). Suppliers dependent on one industry clustered together at the center of the "automotive realm" (see Hill, 1984:314). But these firms are in Detroit *despite* the deficiency of its headquarters support structure, not because of it.

Symptomatic of this weakness is the current dispersal of some of the auto companies' orientation activities to other places—either headquarter cities or innovation centers. Although other corporate headquarters often *absorb* such functions from the outside, Detroit seems to export them. General Motors, for example, is establishing an automobile design center in Southern California to "inject new perspective" (Boyle, 1983:1) into the building of its cars. Having a California studio, GM hopes, will help "stem the exodus of talented designers," who have gone to work in the U.S. studios of Japanese car manufacturers, all of which are in California (Boyle, 1983:2).

Similarly, in the increasingly common joint production between American and foreign firms, the most sophisticated design and development work is allocated to the foreigners—particularly the Japanese. This means that headquarters is less of a headquarters. GM's new Saturn cars, although made in the United States, are based on Japanese design and production methods, not Detroit's. Similarly GM's recent multibillion-dollar acquisition of Dallas-based Electronic Data Systems and California's Hughes Electronics will shift GM innovation activity to Texas and Los Angeles, and away from Michigan. The role of the module city thus shifts more to assemblage and coordinating local markets. For localities such as Detroit, this means that they have even less potential for developing diverse support systems for control and orientation activities.

It is not likely that a headquarter city can be created through physically rebuilding downtown. Detroit learned this lesson when it built the Renaissance Center, a downtown complex of round office towers, complete with a dramatic Portman-designed, atrium-centered, convention hotel. It is a copy of installations that have succeeded easily in San Francisco and Los Angeles. But the results have been disastrous in Detroit; the complex sits amid acres of undeveloped rubble, teetering close to insolvency (Dentzer and Manning, 1983). And too many of the tenants who were attracted to the towers merely moved in from other Detroit buildings, leaving the downtown with little discernible gain.

The future of the module cities cannot be remade by mimicking the physical structures of headquarter cities. Moreover, the glitter of rising sunbelt cities should not necessarily be taken as a sign that they are on their way to enduring dominance as major control centers. A number of these places have also had their growth tied to specific regional resources. Houston's corporate growth essentially recapitulates Detroit's development; the Texan city does not sustain corporate headquarters functions in the manner of New York City (Hill and Feagin, 1984). Instead, Houston's headquarters are wedded to the historic development of regionally based industries (oil and shipping). The implication is that as these industries decline, as they will (Texas oil will be depleted by the early 1990s), much of the local economy will be undermined. Houston will then have to join places like Detroit in searching for a routine function in the system of places.

At least Houston (and Detroit) have had their day in the sun. The lowest tier among the module places will be occupied by places serving as a social or physical dumping ground for production carried out elsewhere. Leaders of three California towns (Avenal, Adelanto, and Blythe) are courting state prison authorities, who "usually . . . don't run into this kind of reception" (Hurst, 1983), to locate a new penitentiary in their town because of the jobs and money it would bring. One rural town in South Dakota has proposed itself as a site for the disposal of low-level radioactive wastes as a strategy to develop the local economy (Daniel, 1984). Hanford, Washington, "the city that loves nukes" (Licht, 1983:5), welcomes nuclear waste as its development strategy. Although these results are extreme, the phenomenon is the same wherever places accept growth without scrutiny.

4. Third World Entrepôt

Another type of city, even more transparently tied to the emerging internationalization of American life, is the border metropolis. In the United States, these places are linked primarily to Latin American countries, specifically to those for whom the United States remains a neocolonial center. These cities typically have substantial immigrant populations and many social and organizational ties with cities on the other side of the border (Bloomberg and Martinez-Sandoval, 1982). Sensing a good growth machine strategy, but not located near a Third World country, Mayor Andrew Young of Atlanta offered to have his city play this role for the African continent (*New York Times,* January 12, 1982). Such visionary efforts aside, the important border cities are those near Central America. These cities have substantial numbers of Hispanic residents: Miami with its large Cuban population; El Paso and Brownsville, Texas (60 percent and 70 percent Hispanic in 1980, respectively); and San Antonio (now the tenth-largest American city, with half of its population Spanish-speaking). In various ways, San Diego and even Los Angeles (in addition to its other important roles) have entrepôt city attributes.

Border cities are major labor centers because of their large numbers of low-paid foreign workers, who either migrate for the day or week ("border people") or take up permanent residence (Bloomberg and Martinez-Sandoval, 1982). The aggregate potential is not trivial: the numbers of foreign-born people, primarily Latinos and Asians, who took up permanent residence in the United States during the 1970s rose sharply over previous decades (see the census report in the *New York Times,* October 21, 1984). The United States has again become the destination of more foreign migrants than all other countries of the world combined. Many of these workers, primarily the Latinos, are undocumented; their uncertain legal status makes them especially willing to accept both low wages and poor working conditions. According to some estimates, about 15 percent of the U.S. work force consists of "illegals" (Portes and Walton, 1981:178).

This labor supply is important in a number of sectors. Some of the Southern border cities are major tourist centers requiring service workers at the lowest occupational rungs (busboys, dishwashers, maids). These cities also need cheap labor for sweatshop manufacturing, particularly in those industries that do best when designers and marketing experts can have their production apparatus nearby. About 80 percent of the employees in the burgeoning L.A. area apparel industry are undocumented immigrants from Central America. Most of these are women (Soja, Morales, and Wolff, 1983:221), and about 90 percent of the firms employing them are in violation of major sections of the state labor code (Clark, 1983:282). Even in the so-called high-tech field, many small U.S. firms (of which there are a good number) require low-wage assemblers. Only the large firms can easily move abroad and thereby lower wage costs (Musgrave, 1975:13; Portes and Walton, 1991:143: see also Soja, Morales, and Wolff, 1983:226; Yago et al., 1984). Those that remain provide high-tech settings, for low-tech workers. In another variant, the border cities enable high-tech firms to solve some of their problems by putting routine manufacture on the Mexican side and headquarters and innovation activity on the U.S. side. Probably no location better provides capital with this best-of-both-worlds option than San Diego-Tijuana, where the electronics industry (for example, Infomag Corporation) increasingly distributes itself this way.

The border cities also function as trade and financial centers for importing, marketing, and distributing imported goods, including illicit materials like drugs and counterfeit brand-name products (for example, pirated music recordings or shirts with alligator logos).[7] They are also export platforms; Miami is the location for the Latin American regional offices of fifty-five U.S. multinationals (Cohen, 1977:218). Money can be laundered or otherwise dispersed in the growing Miami banking industry. Although profits fluctuate with the strength of the dollar, San Diego is a major shopping destination for Mexican nationals living on the other side of the border. The elites of Latin America use these places as centers of expertise, harbors for safe investment, and personal recreation and culture.[8] All of this is made possible, of course, by U.S. laws and administrative procedures in immigration policy, foreign trade, banking, and product copyright, which funnel a massive stream of goods and people through these specialized gates of regulation and evasion.

The border metropolises are control centers for a substantial range of hemisphere activities; though perhaps not world-class cities, they are at least Third World class cities.

5. Retirement Centers

The aging of the country's indigenous population, as well as the changing pattern of that aging, leads to a different sort of migration. People retire earlier with fewer children, and with weaker ties to grown-up sons and daughters. This has led to increasing geographical concentration of large numbers of elderly people—especially in places with good climates in the South and West. The migrations of retired people in the 60 to 70 age bracket are an important component of the growth boom of many sunbelt cities; some specialize in it. Elderly migration has also been part of the growth in states like Vermont and New Jersey, where retired people can find a pleasant semirural environment, often within easy reach of kin elsewhere in the Northeast (Biggar, 1980).

Growth strategies vary among retirement cities. Elites in some places press for more of the same; elites in others, like Tampa and St. Petersburg, Florida, seek to augment retirement with other types of industry (Mormino, 1983). The ability of the growth interests of Atlantic City to make their city a gambling resort disrupted the lives of many of the retired elderly, as well as other low-income residents (Sternlieb and Hughes, 1983). Officials and entrepreneurs in South Miami Beach, Florida, are priming their "art deco" architectural district for a conversion from old people's rooming houses to high-rent hotels and apartments (O'Connor, 1984).

Like the exclusive suburbs of the middle aged, affluent old people's towns maximize life-style benefits and services. Their residents' high private incomes substitute for some of the support that ties to kin and more youthful neighbors would otherwise provide. But we know that the typical older persons' suburb has relatively low average incomes, poor housing, and high taxes (Fitzpatrick and Logan, 1985). In these less affluent settings, whole cities are becoming dependent on pensions, social security payments, and other federal and state programs to support the local economy. Fortunes are closely linked to the future of the Social Security Administration and private pension plans. As the proportions of the very old increase, these parts of the country will face the problem of supporting medical care, home nursing, and social services at levels far exceeding local resources. If the federal government manages to make medical care and old-age social service assistance a private or local government affair, these areas (and their populations) are headed for a crisis.

With their longer life expectancy, women will make up a large part of the elderly urban population. There will also be a tendency for more of these women to have been low-wage workers with poor benefits on which to draw. Higher rates of divorce, combined with the drastically lower earning power of women in their post-divorce years (Weitzman, 1981), will also contribute to the problem. As "prisoners of space" (Rowles, 1980), the old will be penalized by local support networks that likely will be both socially and fiscally weak. There may lie ahead old people's slum cities, disproportionately female, dependent, and empty of resources.

Notes

1. Los Angeles is also emerging as a center of international banking, primarily through the purchase of California banks by foreign interests (Crocker and Union banks are British owned) and through foreign banks locating their U.S center of operations in Los Angeles (Soja, Morales, and Wolff, 1983:224).

2. The term is adapted from Mills's (1959) "crackpot realism."

3. Using three industrial sectors (aerospace, electrical and electronics, and instruments). Malecki has isolated twenty-three "innovation centers." But by using SIC codes as the basis for his typology, Malecki ends up lumping together diverse activities into a single urban type; this makes it impossible to isolate the more basic and important research functions. See Hodson and Kaufman (1982) and Baron and Bielby (1984) on the issue of sector typologies. Thus Malecki's method leads to some anomalous results; Dayton, Miami, and Baltimore become innovation centers along with Boston, San Diego, and Phoenix.

4. Hill and Negrey (1985) point out that federal expenditures generally shortchange the frostbelt region, or at least the Great Lakes states.

5. The story's lead sentence was "The Soviet Union proposed a moratorium on nuclear testing that, if adopted, would affect jobs of 8,000 Nevada Test Site workers." "Nuclear Testing Moratorium Would Affect 8000 at NTS," *Pahrump Valley (Nev.) Times Star*, April 26, 1985, p. 4.

6. Much of our discussion of Detroit is based on the work of Richard Child Hill, whose important papers are cited frequently in this book.

7. The counterfeit production of name-brand merchandise is now big business worldwide, estimated by the International Chamber of Commerce to constitute between 3 and 9 percent of total world trade (James, 1985:D=4).

8. The significance of Latin America for Miami is reflected in the prices of Miami condominiums, which dropped by 25 percent in the year after Latin American governments imposed restrictions on the movement of dollars out of Latin America by indigenous nationals.

References

Abrahamson, M., Dubick, M., "Patterns of Urban Dominance." *American Sociological Review,* 42, 5: 756–768, 1977.

Baron, J., Bielby, W. "The Organization of Work in a Segmented Economy." *American Sociological Review* 49, 4: 454–473, 1984

Beale, C., Fuguitt, G. "Population Trends in Nonmetropolitan Cities and Villages in Subregions of the United States." *Demography,* 15, 4: 605–620, 1978.

Berger, J. *The Look of Things.* New York: Viking Press, 1974.

Berry, B., Kasarda, J. *Contemporary Urban Ecology.* New York: Macmillan, 1977.

Biggar, J. "Reassessing Elderly Sunbelt Migration." *Research on Aging,* 2: 177–190, 1980.

Birch, D. *The Job Generation Process.* Cambridge, MA: MIT Program on Neighborhood and Regional Change, 1979.

Blackbourne, A. "The Impact of Multinational Corporations on the Spatial Organization of Developed Nations: A Review." In: Taylor, M., Thrift, N. (eds.) *The Geography of the Multinationals: Studies in the Spatial Development and Economic Consequences of Multinational Corporations,* 147–157. London: Croom Helm, 1982.

Bloomberg, W., Martinez-Sandoval, R. "The Hispanic-American Urban Order: A Border Perspective." In: Gappert, G., Knight, R. (eds.) *Cities in the Twenty-First Century,* 112–132. Beverly Hills, CA: Sage, 1982.

Boyle, P. "GM Will Open Southland Automotive Design Center." *Los Angeles Times,* sec. 1, pp. 1–2, March 30, 1983.

Braverman, H. *Labor and Monopoly Capital.* New York: Monthly Review Press, 1974.

Burns, L., Pang, W. "Big Business in the Big City." *Urban Affairs Quarterly* 12, 4: 533–544, 1977.

Burt, R., Christman, K., Kilburn, H. "Testing a Structural Theory of Corporate Capitalism." *American Sociological Review,* 45: 821–841, 1980.

Clark, D. "Improbable Los Angeles." In: Richard, M., Bernard, R., Bradley, R. (eds.) *Sunbelt Cities: Politics and Growth Since World War II,* 268–308. Austin: University of Texas Press, 1983.

Cohen, R. "Multinational Corporations, International Finances and the Sunbelt." In: Perry, D., Watkins, A. (eds.) *The Rise of the Sunbelt Cities,* 211–226. Beverley Hills, CA: Sage, 1977.

Cohen, R. "The International Division of Labor: Multinational Corporations and Urban Hierarchy." In: Dear, M., Scott, A. (eds.) *Urbanization and Urban Planning in Capitalist Society,* 287–315. New York: Methuen, 1981.

Daniel, L. "S.D. Town Wants Nuke Waste Dump." *Schenectady Gazette,* p. 44, January 16, 1984.

Dentzer, S., Manning, R. "Renaissance Center." *Newsweek,* p. 58, January 24, 1983.

Dicken, P. "The Multiplant Business Enterprise and Geographical Space: Some Issues in the Study of External Control and Regional Development." *Regional Studies* 10, 4: 401–412, 1976.

Duncan, O., Scott, W., Lieberson, S., Duncan B., Winsborough, H. *Metropolis and Region.* Baltimore: Johns Hopkins University Press, 1960.

Ewen, L. *Corporate Power and Urban Crisis in Detroit.* Princeton, NJ: Princeton University Press, 1978.

Fitzpatrick, K., Logan, J. "The Aging of Suburbs, 1960–1980." *American Sociological Review* 50, 2: 106–117, 1985.

Fleischmann, A. "Sunbelt Boosterism: The Politics of Postwar Growth and Annexation in San Antonio." In: Perry, D., Watkins, A. (eds.) *The Rise of the Sunbelt,* 151–168. Beverley Hills, CA: Sage, 1977.

Fligstein, N. "The Interorganizational Power Struggle: The Rise of Finance Presidents in Large Firms, 1919–1979." Paper Presented at the 80th Annual Meeting of the American Sociological Association, Washington, D.C., August 26–30, 1985.

Fligstein, N. " Anti-Trust Law and the Growth of Large Firms: 1860–1985." Colloquium Presentation. University of California at Santa Barbara, 1986.

Friedman, J., Wolff, G. "World City Formation: An Agenda for Research and Action." *International Journal of Urban and Regional Research* 63, 3: 309–344, 1982.

Gintis, H. "The Nature of the Labor Exchange and the Theory of Capitalist Production." *Review of Radical Political Economics* 8, 2: 36–56, 1976.

Gordon, D. "Capitalist Efficiency and Socialist Efficiency." *Monthly Review* 28, 3: 19–39, 1976.

Greer, W. "Business that Serve Businesses Are Pacing Job Growth in City." *New York Times,* sec. 3, p. 4, December 3, 1984.

Herman, E. *Corporate Control, Corporate Power.* New York: Cambridge University Press, 1981.

Hill, R. "Economic Crisis and Political Response in Motor City." In: Sawyers, L., Tabb, W. (eds.) *Sunbelt/Snowbelt: Urban Development and Urban Restructuring,* 313–338. New York: Oxford University Press, 1984.

Hill, R., Feagin, J. "Detroit and Houston: Two Cities in Global Perspective." Paper Presented at the 79th Annual Meeting of the American Sociological Association, San Antonio, Texas, August 27–31, 1984.

Hill, R., Negrey, C. "The Politics of Industrial Policy in Michigan." In: Zukin, S. (ed.) *Industrial Policy: Business and Politics in the United States and France*, 119–138. New York: Praeger, 1985.

Hodson, R., Kaufman, R. "Economic Dualism: A Critical Review." *American Sociological Review* 47, 6: 727–739, 1982.

Hughes, K., Gilman, H. "Cheseborough to Buy Stauffer for $1.5 Billion." *Wall Street Journal*, p.3, February 20, 1985.

Hurst, J. "Two Small Towns Believe That Crime Pays, After All." Los Angeles Times, sec. 1, p. 1, July 31, 1983.

James, B. "Fakes Are Big Business." *Santa Barbara News Press*, p. DI, 4, February 3, 1985.

Jazairy, I., Kuin, P., Somavia, J. "Transnationa; Enterprises." In: Tinbergen, J. *Reshaping the International Order: A Report to the Club of Rome*, 157–160. New York: Dutton, 1977.

Jobert, B. "Planning and Social Production of Needs." *Sociologie et Sociétés* 6, 2: 35–51, 1975.

Jung, M. "Formal and Substantive Views of the Economy: A Sociological Study of Stock Market Speculation of the 1920s." Paper Presented at the 79th Annual Meeting of the American Sociological Association, San Antonio, Texas, August 27–31, 1984.

Keller, J. "The Division of Labor in Electronics." In: Nash, J., Kelley, M. (eds.) *Women, Men and the International Division of Labor*, 346–373. Albany: State University of New York Press, 1983.

Kennan, G. "Two Letters." *New Yorker* 60, 32: 55–80, 1984.

Licht, J. "The Nuclear Waste Lottery." *Re: Sources* 6, 3:1–7, 1983.

Lueck, T. "Connecticut Growth Makes Its Economy One of Best in U.S." *New York Times* sec. A, p. 1, sec. B, p. 5, September 18, 1984.

Malecki, E. "Cororate Organization of R&D and the Location of Technological Activities." *Regional Studies* 14, 3: 219–234, 1980.

Marglin, S. "What Do Bosses Do?" *Review of Radical Political Economics* 6, 2: 60–112, 1974.

Mills, C. Wright. *The Sociological Imagination*. New York: Oxford University Press, 1959.

Mollenkopf, J. *The Contested City*. Princeton, NJ: Princeton University Press, 1983.

Mormeno, G. "Tampa: From Hell Hole to the Good Life." In: Bernard, R., Rice, B. (eds.) *Sunbelt Cities: Politics and Growth Since World War II*, 138–161. Austin: University of Texas Press, 1983.

Musgrave, P. "Direct Investment Abroad and the Multinationals: Effects on the United States Economy." *Subcommittee on Multinational Corporations, Committee on Foreign Relations, U.S. Senate, 94th Congress, 1st Session (August)*. Washington, D.C.: Government Printing Press, 1975.

Nelson, R. *Merger Movements in American Industry, 1895–1956*. Princeton, NJ: Princeton University Press, 1959.

New York Times. "Spreading Stardust in Europe." *New York Times*, A26, November 11, 1985.

Noyelle, E. "The Implications of Industry Restructuring for Spatial Organization in the United States." In: Moulaert, F., Salinas, P. (eds.) *Regional Analysis and the International Division of Labor*, 113–133. Boston: Kluwer-Nijhoff, 1983.

O'Connor, M. "A Modern Dilemma: Contrast and Conflicts in Miami Beach's Deco District." *Art and Antiques*, 43–49, May 1984.

Palmer, D., Friedland, R., Roussell, A. "Corporate Headquarters and Business Service Activity." Unpublished Manuscript, Graduate School of Business, Stanford University, 1985.

Palmer, D., Friedland, R., Singh, J. "Ties, Links, and Interdependence: The Determinants of Stability in a Corporate Interlock Network." Unpublished Manuscript, Graduate School of Management, Stanford University (forthcoming).

Palmer, D., Friedland, R., Jennings, P., Powers, M. "Testing a Political Model of Divisionalization in Large U.S. Corporations." Paper Presented at the 44th Annual Meeting of the Academy of Management, Boston, Massachusetts, August 12–15, 1984.

Perrow, C. "Departmental Power and Perspectives in Industrial Firms." In: Zald, M. (ed.) *Power in Organizations*, 59–89. Nashville, Tennessee: Vanderbilt University Press, 1970.

Peters, T., Waterman, R. *In Search of Excellence: Lessons from America's Best-Run Companies*. New York: Harper and Row, 1982.

Portes, A., Walton, J. *Labor, Class, and the International System*. New York: Academic Press, 1981.

Pred, A. *City Systems in Advanced Economies: Past Growth, Present Processes, and Future Development Options*. London: Hutchinson, 1977.

Quante, W. *The Exodus of Corporate Headquarters from New York City*. New York: Praeger, 1976.

Reich, R. *The Next American Frontier*. New York: Penguin, 1983.

Ross, C. "Regional Patterns of Organizational Dominance: 1955–1975." *Sociological Quarterly* 23, 2: 207–219, 1982.

Rowles, G. *Prisoners of Space? Exploring the Geographical Experiences of Older People*. Boulder, CO: Westview Press, 1980.

Sassen-Koob, S. "The New Labor Demand in Global Cities." In: Smith, M. (ed.) *Cities in Transformation: Class, Capital, and the State*, 139–172. Beverley Hills, CA: Sage, 1984.

Schenectady Gazette. "Japan Warns States to Go Easy on Tax." *Schenectady Gazette*, p. 36, February 11, 1984.

Schmenner, R. *Making Business Location Decisions*. Englewood Cliffs, NJ: Prentice Hall, 1982.

Schrage, M. "Pentagon High-Tech Role Debated." Los Angeles Times, IV, 3–4, October 23, 1984.

Smith, I. "The Role of Acquisition in the Spatial Distribution of the Foreign manufacturing Sector in the United Kingdom." In: Taylor, M., Thrift, N. (eds.) *The Geography of the Multinationals*, 221–252. Cambridge: Cambridge University Press, 1982.

Soja, E., Morales, R., Wolff, G. "Urban Restructuring: An Analysis of Social and Spatial Change in Los Angeles." *Economic Geography* 59, 2: 195–230, 1983.

Stanback, T., Bearse, P., Noyelle, T., Karasek, R. *Services: The New Economy*. Totowa, NJ: Allanheld Osmun, 1981.

Stephens, J., Holly, B. The Changing Pattern of Industrial Corporate Control in the Metropolitan United States." In: Braun, S., Wheeler, J. (eds.) *The American Metropolitan System: Present and Future*, 161–180. New York: Wiley, 1980.

Sternlieb, G., Hughes, J. *The Atlantic City Gamble*. Piscataway, NJ: Center for Urban Policy Research, 1983.

Storper, M., Walker, R. "The Theory of Labor and the Theory of Location." *International Journal of Urban and Regional Research*, 7:1, 43, 1983.

Taplin, R. "Women in World Market Factories: East and West." Paper Presented to the Society for the Study of Social Problems, San Antonio, Texas, August 24–26, 1984.

Thorngren, B. "How Do Contact Systems Affect Regional Development?" *Environment and Planning* 2, 4: 409–427, 1970.

Vartabedian, R. "For California, 1983 Was Year of the Merger." *Los Angeles Times*, sec.5, p. 1, May 20, 1984.

Ward, S. "Trends in the Location of Corporate Headquarters: Changing Patterns of Metropolitan Dominance in the 1970s." Paper Presented at the 79th Annual Meeting of the American Sociological Association, San Antonio, Texas, August 27–31, 1984.

Weitzman, L. "The Economics of Divorce: Social and Economic Consequences of Property, Alimony, and Child Support Awards." *UCLA Law Review* 28: 1251, August 1981.

Williamson, O. *Market and Hierarchies*. New York: Free Press, 1975.

Yago, G. *The Decline of Transit: Urban Transportation in German and U.S. Cities, 1900–1970*. New York: Cambridge University Press, 1984.

Zeitlin, M. "Corporate Ownership and Control: The large Corporation and the Capitalist Class." *American Journal of Sociology* 79, 5: 1073–1119, 1974.

20

The Post-Industrial City

H. V. Savitch

There is nothing more difficult to carry out, nor more doubtful of success, nor more dangerous to handle, than to initiate a new order of things.

—Niccolò Machiavelli, *The Prince*

Conditions of the Post-Industrial City

Just before the turn of the century, Lord Bryce wrote that the "government of cities is one of the conspicuous failures of the United States."[1] Bryce complained that political office in American cities was little more than a residue for service to the party. Once in office the politician was reduced to a string puller for the "getting and keeping of places."[2]

During the same period, a New York–based magazine, advising its readership on the best political traits, suggested that politics was fitting for "neither businessmen, professional men nor college professors."[3] Among the qualities desired, the magazine argued that the politician "must always seem to follow rather than to lead."[4]

European politicians were more actively engaged in the substance of policy, but much of their concern centered on security. In France, Paris was closely watched as "a fortress of sedition."[5] Even Great Britain's political elite was obsessed with urban security. In 1883 William Gladstone declared that the control of the police was the most important of all municipal functions and should be so for London.[6]

The political elite of the industrial city viewed its growth from a distance. In America, politicians partook of the industrial harvest with boodle and patronage.

From *Post-Industrial Cities: Politics and Planning in New York, Paris and London* by H. V. Savitch. Copyright © 1988 by Princeton University Press. Reprinted by permission of Sage Publications.

In Europe they increased their surveillance of a restless mass and built "anti-riot streets."[7]

Above all the industrial city was a "private city," built by the invisible hand of unregulated capitalism.[8] Generally speaking, industrialists and politicians carried out their businesses separately. Factories sprang up with little help from the state. Government provided some accommodation for that growth (streets, ports), but its interventions were minimal. Politics and the economy were separate and apart. Planning for a new industrial order was rare. When planning existed at all, it was sporadic and carried out without consciousness of economic design.

It was this quality of "privatism" that furnished the city with its political quality. In America, the municipality responded with machine politics—or in Norton Long's fitting words, by reducing "the politician to the role of registerer of pressure rather than responsible governor of a local political economy."[9] In Europe, royal families treated the city as a monument to kingly glory. Politics revolved around the awarding of architectural commissions and public works contracts.[10]

The rise of post-industrialism changed urban politics, both in America and abroad. Political brokerage and monumentalism could no longer suffice. Energetic and imaginative policy leadership was required. The new politics faced the task of collecting bits and pieces of the social structure in order to build a vastly more complex city. To do this, policy direction would have to replace laissez faire, and collaboration would be a better substitute for unbridled competition. Post-industrialism also required immense investment from the private sector, whose risks would be mitigated by state guarantees.

The political signs pointed toward corporatism. The drift was gradual, in some cases incomplete, and it was not always susceptible to precise measurement. But the signs were unmistakable, and today they pervade the political mood of the post-industrial city.

Adaptation is supposed to be the life-saving resource of human and animal species. The great city, too, is an organic phenomenon capable of adaptation. In order to survive, it must adapt its politics to the post-industrial condition.

One of these conditions is an increased competition between cities as well as between nations. The post-industrial city represents not only itself but the aspirations of its nation. Intranational competition results in advantages for jobs and taxes. International competition entails the higher stakes of world power, prestige, and leadership. Although the unitary governments of Europe can dampen international competition by redistributing internal income, they cannot ignore the challenge of international competition. More and more, distinctions are made between military and economic might, and though the post-industrial city can do little to bolster national defense, it epitomizes economic prowess.

The paradox is that the more competition the post-industrial city confronts from the outside, the less competitive it must be on the inside. Great cities can no longer afford a free-wheeling, "build as one might" economy. To compete effectively, the post-industrial city needs to harness its internal resources. Politics becomes both the instrument and the exemplar of this effort. In the more pluralistically laden city (New York), a politics of concertation begins to emerge.[11] Concertation is the first step in organizing formerly competitive groups by inducing them to bargain cooperatively. It gives some groups privileged access and it institutionalizes consultation between these groups and the political-technocratic elite. In New York this collaboration is still in the process of bringing a pluralist society closer to corporatism.

In those environments where the traditions of pluralism are less rooted (Paris and London), the state can more easily fashion the response. In France an already formidable state apparatus developed planning techniques to usher in the transformation. The machinery simply concerted local governments and invited organizations from the private sector to join it. In Great Britain a competent technocratic class also introduced sophisticated planning and development. Concertation of local governments and interest groups is a thornier problem whose success rests upon political consensus and the impact of Tory rule into the 1990s.

Another condition of post-industrialism is the complexity of building a brand new physical environment. Streets, highways, rail terminals, airports, office towers, shopping malls, parks, theaters, museums, houses, hospitals, universities, and research centers need to be constructed with an eye toward the demographics of the twenty-first century. Construction itself is straightforward and a matter of technical mastery. The challenge is to accomplish this smoothly while synchronizing an enormous number of transactions. Facilities need to be coordinated, finances need to be secured, and a whole new system of laws needs to be worked out. There emerges a labyrinth of negotiations between buyers and sellers, landlords and tenants, and those about to take possession and those about to be dispossessed.

Whether they want it or not, politicians are handed the consuming task of making it all work. A multitude of interests must be brought together and satisfied. No longer can the singular role of neutral intermediary be sufficient. To make it happen, politicians and technocrats assume responsibility. Whether it be Times Square, La Défense, or the Docklands, government has underwritten the investment, acquired the land, made it attractive to investors, and taken care of the dispossessed. The details of each project may vary, but the functions of the political-technocratic elite are remarkably similar.

Still a third condition of the post-industrial city has been the rise of assurer government.[12] Politics no longer ends after the ribbon-cutting ceremonies. It continues to insure all parties against the risks of change. Investors are given long-term leases with options to buy, tenants are promised priority housing with moderate rents, citizens are provided with open spaces and amenities. The single institution to which the disgruntled turn is government. Politicians become responsible for the business failures, the destruction of community, and the personal dislocations that ensue from the new environment. Despite neoconservative efforts to reduce government, post-industrialism entices its expansion. Issues that at first glance appear resolvable become pregnant with further issues. Involvement begets further involvement and obligations multiply. New York's Westway was not just a highway but a massive real estate project. Whatever is built in place of Westway will require a continuing set of commitments in public leases, park maintenance, and pollution controls. In Paris, the Secteur Seine Sud-Est will keep politicians and technocrats busy through the end of the century, and after that, the city will retain title to the new projects. London's Covent Garden still has citizen organizations that make demands and a government-supported planning team that acts upon them.

Moreover, the obligations put before politicians are often contradictory. New Yorkers may delight over higher values for their property, yet they also want their neighborhood left intact. Parisians want the benefit of an expanded economy but lament the ruination of the skyline. Londoners moan about automobiles congesting local streets while they refuse to build highways. In all three cities jobs are a major issue, and not only the national government is held responsible. Urban political leaders often stake their record on the economic issue. "The main job of government," said Ed Koch just after his inauguration, "is to create a climate in which private business can expand in the city to provide jobs and profit."[13] From his early days as Mayor of Paris, Jacques Chirac interpreted his mandate broadly and pressed for business growth. "The provinces have grown and so have the new towns," declared Chirac, "while Paris sees its own employment wasting away."[14] London's Labour Party leader, Ken Livingstone, has put the cause of full employment into a larger campaign against classism, racism, and sexism. His strongest denunciations are reserved for the privileged, whom he calls "vandals in ermine."[15]

Whatever formula urban politicians have adopted, they must engage the social and economic system. Passive politics and the politician as "caretaker" are obsolete.[16] Post-industrial politicians must exercise power on their own and must harness it to public purpose. Those purposes involve a certain amount of planning. It can be short-term, piecemeal planning or it can resemble a long-term comprehensive strategy. But once an already built environment is given the challenge of post-industrial change, planning is inevitable. The thrust for change and the planning that ensues from it help generate the policy outputs of the post-industrial city.

Policy Outputs of the Post-Industrial City

Most interpretations of urban decision making focus on conflict and clashes of interest between participants. Conflict is, of course, embedded in all change, and some scholars conclude that conflict is almost invariably resolved on behalf of the economically powerful.[17] Clarence Stone, for example, observes that "governments are drawn by the nature of underlying economic and revenue producing conditions to serve [business] interests."[18] Stone adds that "situational dependencies"[19] confer advantages to the upper strata at the expense of those at the bottom.

To be sure, disagreement, struggle, and conflict are endemic to society. These elements are the fodder of politics. But the settling of the dust also shows that a good deal of collaboration and mutual accommodation takes place. Without this, post-industrial transformation would not be possible. And when that collaboration does falter, the society becomes stuck in stagnation.

Situational dependencies certainly exist. Business classes do enjoy positions as revenue producers, and by virtue of that can be more powerful than others. But they are not always more powerful than others. Their position as revenue producers is not always a monopoly, nor is it unregulated. Government is not in business hands and it is just as certainly not helpless. Situational dependencies can just as easily be converted into situational interdependencies. Business relies on government, just as surely as government relies on business. Labor and the citizenry find their actions linked to those of politicians and businessmen.

Moreover, we cannot assume that a gain for the business class results in an automatic loss for nonbusiness classes. Alternatively, we cannot assume that beating the business interests means that labor, the community, or the urban citizenry will reap the rewards.

Our own lessons from New York, Paris, and London reject black-and-white categorization. These lessons show that policy outputs cannot be regarded as a zero-sum game. There are few sharp demarcations between winners and losers. The stakes of post-industrialism do not fall exclusively on one side of the social fence or on the other. On the contrary, costs and benefits fall in varying proportions upon varying classes, groups, and organizations. Sometimes half the residents of a community will benefit from an action while the other half loses. One class of business may reap profits while another class of business stumbles into bankruptcy. Entire communities can rise or fall with the tides of post-industrial change, affecting landlords and tenants alike.

To take another tack on this issue, some of the contemporary literature on the politics of land development interprets policy outcomes as derived from "prevailing coalitions" that join top politicians with business interests.[20] Commonly, a conflict erupts between this coalition, trying to develop land, and popular neighborhood groups, seeking to protect the environment. While this is a simple scenario, its interpretation can differ depending upon how one looks at the conflict and weighs its stakes.

Again, our own lessons show that coalitions between politicians and private interest groups can be fleeting. Politicians and technocrats form a closer bond with each other than with outside groups and are more likely to constitute a stable governmental elite. Interest groups of many and differing stripes may coalesce with that elite, but they are as apt to move out of it as into it. The elite is likely to maneuver between different groups or even to subordinate private groups to its priorities. What looks like a prevailing coalition at one moment and in one case can become a shifting or a completely changed coalition when viewed over a longer period of time and over many cases. More significantly, the scenario of top politicians and business working against popular bases in the neighborhoods dichotomizes the contest to the exclusion of other parties. Top politicians are elected from at-large constituencies; technocrats must account for the broad implications of their plan. Perforce, their choices are founded upon a complexity of different interests. For a neighborhood, development may very well be a threat to a valued way of life, but for the rest of the city it may be a chance to create a new industry, enhance city services, or "clean up" an area.

The fact of the matter is that there are few absolutes that can be stated about policy outcomes. More fittingly, there are degrees of advantage and disadvantage that can accrue. In any single outcome there are pluses (better housing for residents, more jobs for workers) and minuses (breakup of community, environmental hazards). Nor can much be said about an outcome without qualification. The absoluteness of evaluation can lead us into the thicket of making extreme value judgments (did the community truly profit by blocking development?) or into the foxhole of one or another contestant (neighborhood interests versus the city at large). Under conditions of post-industrialism and corporatism, policy outputs will emphasize the collaborative potential of the social structure. These conditions will encourage the interdependence of vital actors. Politicians, technocrats, investors, laborers, and residents will find themselves sharing the same roof. The resulting policies are best conceived as a trade-off among different options—or, in Peter Blau's conception, as a system of exchange where certain goods are bartered for others in the interests of satisfying certain ends.[21]

The Goodies Are Divisible

In earlier chapters we discussed the economic transformation brought by post-industrialism. Here we take a comparative look at the outputs of that transformation. In New York, the urban core of Manhattan bristles with jobs, office construction, and neighborhood renovation. Office rents are at an all-time high; vacancy rates are low. As the middle class rushes to the urban core, the squeeze on available apartments tightens. From all indications it appears that this new class can pay the costs of Midtown living. Manhattan not only holds the highest per capita income within the city, it also skims the high salary earners. According to the last census, Manhattan held nearly four times the number of households earning at least $50,000 than its sister counties.[22]

The urban core of Paris has also prospered. Once a city known for its proletarian vitality, its street people, and its slovenly charm, Paris is now varnished with the lacquer of propriety. Of the city's twenty arrondissements, only a handful are exclusively working class. The number of middle- and upper middle-class households has risen consistently since the 1960s, and the commercial and cultural fabric has responded to the new demand.

Notwithstanding the parallels to Manhattan, the pace and content of the Parisian embourgeoisement are different. Paris is still very much a mixed city. Class settlement is not as lopsided as in New York and urban living is still a viable choice for middle-class families. Thus the percentage of residents from the upper strata in Paris is half that of Manhattan (22 percent versus 42 percent).[23] Just as important, Paris is not subject to drastic social swings between itself and the surrounding localities. The 1982 census showed that the percentage of those belonging to the middle class was virtually identical (19 percent) in Paris and in nearby departments.[24] In contrast, Manhattan bounds ahead of its surrounding counties (twice the median income and three times the educational attainment).[25]

Despite the talk about the destruction of London's heritage, the metropolis has withstood the blitz of modern architecture. The Victorian skyline still embraces Central London, and Georgian houses continue to adorn the streets of Kensington.

Parts of Inner London have changed since the 1960s, and some boroughs have experienced both physical rejuvenation and social displacement (Camden and Islington). The upper middle class continues to occupy Central London (Westminster and Kensington-Chelsea). But of the three cities, the urban core of London is the least changed. Upper middle classes constitute a lower percentage of the urban core population (15 percent) than in New York (42 percent) or Paris (22 percent).[26] London does not exhibit the radical social shifting of New York, but neither does it show any tendency toward balancing out long-standing discrepancies.[27]

Differences among the three cities are encapsulated in several basic propositions. New York's fast-driving economy has brought an influx of upper middle classes into its urban core, and this has exacerbated differences with its surrounding counties. Paris pursues a course of growth and change that is more moderate, and its imbalances are less dramatic. Thus far, London has changed the least. Though it may be on the precipice of radical growth, it has yet to see massive social dislocation.

These generalizations are better illustrated by pointing to job growth in the three cities. Jobs translate into economic opportunities for urban residents. On the negative side, new jobs are not always given to members of the existing community and their creation can do violence to the social fabric.

Table 20.1 surveys employment patterns in manufacture since the late 1960s and early 1970s. New York, Paris, and London are examined from the perspective of their urban cores and first and second rings.

The shrinkage of manufacture is a familiar theme for the post-industrial city. Recall, however, that the exodus of factories from the inner city usually resulted in a favorable slough-off for the distant suburbs. This was true for New York and Paris, which despite their losses accommodated in their second rings over 90,000 and 61,000 manufacturing jobs. London remains the exception to this rule; its

TABLE 20.1   *Industrial Employment in New York, Paris, and London (by place of work; in thousands unless otherwise indicated)*

	New York (1971–1982)		Paris (1968–1982)		London (1971–1981)	
	number	*%*	*number*	*%*	*number*	*%*
Urban Core	−139.4	−31.4	−213.1	−42.0	−157.3	−46.4
First Ring	−201.8	−31.5	−132.2	−21.2	−231.7	−36.3
Second Ring	90.4	13.4	61.3	21.9	−7.6	−10.6
Net Regional Loss or Gain	−250.8		−284.0		−396.6	

Source: Adapted from *County Business Patterns: 1971 and 1982* (Washington, D.C.: U.S. Department of Commerce, Bureau of the Census); *Annuaire Statistique Sommaire, Avril 1978 et 1982* (Paris: Institut d'Aménagement et d'Urbanisme de la Région d'Ile-de-France, 1982); *ECONDAT: 1971 and 1981* (London: Greater London Council), Table 18 and 19; and *Employment by Sector in the OMA: 1971 and 1981* (London: Department of Employment).

manufacturing decline was uniform throughout the region. The second ring not only failed to grow but also incurred an absolute toll of more than 7,000 jobs. In addition, the net decline in manufacturing jobs was more severe for the London region than for either New York or Paris.

Although it is difficult to pinpoint the cause of London's extensive manufacturing slowdown, the blame has been attributed to conservationist measures.[28] At the same time conservationist policies have yielded desirable results. Outside the first ring, farming has survived as a way of life and green space has been safeguarded. Spreading suburbs and unsightly shopping malls have been contained. Small villages still exist in their original form. Londoners may have paid a price for ecological balance, but they do enjoy an environment that other metropolises have already brought to ruin.

Note, too, that within the Parisian region a wealthier urban core bore the brunt of manufacturing loss. This is because centralized planning plucked up Parisian factories and brought them into the new towns or the provinces. Meanwhile the pains of decline were eased for the first ring (whose older localities lost relatively fewer factories). Neither New York nor London could make this kind of transformation, which required aggressive centralized intervention and direction. In France whole swaths of industry, people, and villages were changed. The targets included labor unions, shopkeepers, and big or small businesses alike.[29]

Turning to the economic "fill-up" since the 1960s, we observe the outputs of each system. Again, the rewards are divisible, the inequities are variable, and the payoffs are dissimilar.

Table 20.2 isolates post-industrial growth and decline for each city. The format continues to emphasize intra-urban as well as interurban comparisons. Observe the changes that occur as post-industrialism takes root. The urban cores of New York and Paris have held up; London's has faltered. Manhattan's proportionate growth is the most dramatic (16.5 percent), Paris makes a steady gain (6.7 percent), and Inner London loses (–11.6 percent). In New York, the "costs" of failed growth are borne exclusively in the first ring, Paris grows in all rings, and London is the sole metropolis to incur a net loss.

The results give rise to evaluations of policy outputs and the choices that stem from them. Obviously the most desirable choice is for all parts of the metropolis to grow—or at least remain stable. Only Paris holds that enviable position, and that too is fraught with difficulties. Given the ostensibly less preferable outcome in New York, we should ask whether halting growth in Manhattan might have benefited the Bronx or any other depleted locality. We cannot say for sure, but it is unlikely that curtailing Manhattan's office towers would have caused developers to search for land in adjoining counties. The probability is that builders would have headed far beyond New York City.[30] Far from Manhattan doing damage, its boom furnished tangible benefits for people in hard-hit first-ring counties. For those who were able to find jobs, Manhattan was a source of livelihood and income. Commuters from the surrounding counties found work in the new occupations that were born of post-industrialism. Although losses in the Bronx or Jersey City might go unreplaced, Manhattan stood as a beacon. Marginal firms that might otherwise

TABLE 20.2   *Post-Industrial Employment in New York, Paris, and London (by place of work; in thousands unless otherwise indicated)*

	New York (1971–1982)		Paris (1968–1982)		London (1971–1981)	
	number	*%*	*number*	*%*	*number*	*%*
Urban Core	62.4	16.5	90.7	6.7	−95.5	−11.6
First Ring	−12.8	−10.5	309.9	45.3	66.3	6.0
Second Ring	80.9	81.5	370.4	88.4	19.0	69.7
Net Regional Loss or Gain	130.5		771.0		−10.2	

Source: Adapted from *County Business Patterns: 1971 and 1982* (Washington, D.C.: U.S. Department of Commerce, Bureau of the Census); *Annuaire Statistique Sommaire, Avril 1978 et 1982* (Paris: Institut d'Aménagement et d'Urbanisme de la Région d'lle-de-France, 1982); and *ECONDAT: 1971 and 1981* (London: Greater London Council), Table 18 and 19; and *Employment by Sector in the OMA: 1971 and 1981* (London: Department of Employment). The manner of collecting census data in each of the cities does not allow for precise comparability. But I have been able to ferret out rough indicies of post-industrial employment. For New York this consists of the FIRE section (finance, insurance, and real estate). For Paris the sector labeled "tertiary services" has been chosen. For London the relevant sector is "services, distribution, and government."

pass from the scene stayed on because of proximity to Manhattan. Clerks, secretaries, and technicians who might not be able to afford housing in Manhattan could find decent shelter within a 45-minute train ride to the urban core. As a consequence, property could be kept up and the flame of reinvestment kept alive.

These benefits are apparent in surveying the unemployment tallies in Greater London. London points up the stark dilemmas faced by the post-industrial city when economic priorities clash with social values. The failure to absorb enough post-industrial business has brought economic hardship to much of the metropolis. There can be little doubt that limitations on construction in Central London have exacerbated the plight of the jobless in Newham and Lambeth.[31] One cannot simply write off the realtors and builders as economic piranhas. They play a role in the vibrancy of the post-industrial city, and when these arch-capitalists are suffocated, so too is the local economy.

The social consequences for London are far more salutary. Mention of these inevitably brings a comparison between London's policy of containment and the Manhattan strategy. New York's approach may produce jobs but at a cost that exacerbates problems in the social ecology (severe social imbalance, neighborhood disruption) and in the physical environment. Just the other way around, London's approach has not produced jobs, but containment has managed to sort out commercial activity with reasonable equity and it has salvaged the social structure. More so than New York and Paris, London enjoys neighborhood stability. It is a metropolis of well-balanced, cohesive neighborhoods. Borough government and identity with a town hall have done much to advance this.[32] The urban core has been protected.

For London, there is still little sense of social invasion that is common in most of Manhattan and much of Paris. Piccadilly Circus attracts the tourists, but Chiswick and Hampstead are still for Londoners.

By data and outward account, Paris appears to have struck a happy medium between livable neighborhoods and jobs. On closer inspection, the axis strategy coupled to *étatisme* has wrung its costs. Citizen participation is all the more stifled and pressure groups are suffocated. A technocratic-political elite has arrogated much of the decision making to itself and with telling consequence. Parts of the built environment have been hurriedly constructed with little awareness of how it feels to live or play in the new communities. Paris contains block upon block of high-rise dormitories.[33] The French bureaucracy is well acquainted with how to achieve statistical balance, but it has paid little attention to the realities of daily urban life.

Just outside the Parisian urban core, villages have been replaced by blocks of concrete housing called *les grands ensembles.* Put up by technocrats, they were built with neither restraint nor a sensitive hand. In some places, *les grands ensembles* are nothing less than unbroken lines of mortar, steel, and squares of glass. It is as if a wall of buildings erupted in the middle of nowhere. This was done by an insulated class of officialdom who, when confronted with a housing shortage, did its job.

The Goodies Are Different: Revisiting Times Square, Les Halles, and Covent Garden

Like flagships of the fleet, Times Square, Les Halles, and Covent Garden are the products of their local command. They also underscore differences in values, priorities, and political control in the three cities.

In background and geography, the sites are remarkably similar. All three have been symbols of urban night life and center-city living. All three have been packed with an economy and society of days long past (markets, movie houses, a working class). All three lagged behind post-industrial change, until they became targets for radical reconstruction. All three sit atop land of enormous value. Even the size of their commercial targets are similar—13 acres in Times Square, 16 acres in Les Halles, 34 acres in Covent Garden.

Yet for all these similarities, the outcomes are just as dissimilar. New York and London are the antipodal points. Times Square will be radically redone along the lines of megastructure planning, for economic growth. Covent Garden has been renovated and largely conserved, with social values in mind.

The scope of each project bespeaks its underlying values. Times Square will be built upon the financial mooring of five post-industrial megastructures. Where there was once airy openness amid bright lights, the area will be shrouded by office towers and a high-rise retail mart. The exchange is governed by economics and finance. New York City will receive millions in public improvements, plus a sizable increase in taxes.[34] The developers will be given the right to build more than twice the allowable limits for height and bulk.

Covent Garden has not been so much redone as it has been refashioned. The old market building has been retained but gutted to accommodate shops and restaurants. New construction has been limited by strict controls on height and bulk. Congestion is kept down by density controls. Over three hundred sites are protected as historic landmarks.[35] Though physical conservation has not kept away the gentry, the old working class has survived. This was accomplished by GLC assurances that any resident threatened with displacement would be guaranteed housing. Other supports include a community social hall, pub, and athletic facility. The exchange is as much for the physical environment as it is for the ecology of the community. London receives a renovated habitat capable of attracting new blood and small-scale business, while the community is protected.

Even more dissimilar are the financial ramifications. Times Square is enormously expensive ($2.4 billion); the cost of Covent Garden is modest ($22.5 million).[36] Times Square is supposed to increase jobs fourfold; Covent Garden struggles to recapture earlier losses. Times Square touts an enormous boost in office space; Covent Garden worries about an invasion of too many offices.[37] Times Square trudges on with scant regard for peripheral hardships.[38] An official study admits that "the project will displace an estimated 410 businesses" and that those most hurt will be firms which are "unable to pay high rents."[39] In contrast, Covent Garden makes every effort to retain a balance between white- and blue-collar industry. The official GLC statement on the matter says that "it will be the normal policy to prevent the change . . . from industrial floorspace to other uses."[40]

Les Halles takes a third road to redevelopment. It combines New York's flair for radical reconstruction with London's temperament for a livable, civilized environment. The new Les Halles may have wiped away the old marketplace, but it does not overshadow its surroundings with megastructures. Most of it is built below the neighborhood skyline, and it contains sizable amounts of open space and parkland. If anything, the French have taken pains to respect architectural scale by digging downward to build a subterranean city. The area's eighteenth-century buildings have been renovated and the streets have been restored.

Still, for Les Halles physical decorum does not mean community protection. Unlike Covent Garden, there were no guarantees of neighborhood housing given to residents and at last count only 27 percent of the old inhabitants remained.[41] Most of these people have been scattered around, with only a few social vestiges remaining. Nor has Les Halles been bashful about ushering in the new era. Its structures are extravagant, its cost substantial ($1 billion).[42] The small factories and workshops that once sprinkled the area have all but disappeared. Today the major attractions of Les Halles consist of a cultural center (Pompidou Center), shopping for a new class of consumers, hotels, and inconspicuously placed offices. The Parisian exchange hinges on economic benefits that are more modest than New York's and social values that are vastly different than London's. Its thrust is to replace Les Halles and build it anew, for the beauty of the environment, the culture of the population, and the prestige of Paris.

Behind the redevelopment of the three sites there are significant differences in logic that express different concerns. Discussions of Times Square are filled with the need to rid the area of crime and its raunchy social life. Property value, taxes, and revenue are also major topics of concern. Covent Garden carries the most humane concerns. Much of its rationale is based on a respect for its history, its social scale, and its people. Les Halles bears the responsibility for cultural uplift and the mission of making Paris the world's premier city. Architectural prominence is another keynote for its redevelopment. Compare, for instance, these quotes on each of the sites in Table 20.3.[43]

In short, New York wanted to alter the built environment radically in order to bring about economic vibrancy. London wanted to conserve the built environment and protect the community in the interests of social salvation. Paris wanted to alter the built environment radically for cultural and aesthetic distinction.

Stating these values was not enough. Political control over capital investment was needed to accomplish differing ends. In New York private investment was channeled, but not so narrowly as to strangle private initiative. Developers needed to be given leeway; the profit motive needed to be sustained. To do this, the public sector kept control over the contours of the project. New York's Urban Development Corporation will hold title to the land for fifteen years and will supervise its redevelopment. For their part, private developers will put up the money and, in the sixteenth year, they can exercise an option to buy some of the land.

Times Square is based on the principle of private capital working under the tutelage of the public sector. Its politics is reflected in a mélange of leases, partial public ownership, concessions, and purchase options. Politicians and technocrats led the way and steered a path between competing private developers. They carefully traded on their power to award contracts in return for the resources of private investors. They also traded on a few crucial corners of Times Square in order to salvage its worn-out mid-blocks (theaters, subway entrances, walkways). Thus while private developers furnished the capital, government focused the application of that capital.

Though developers will pay a hefty price and will assume the risks, they have the opportunity of taking title to a bonanza in the heart of Manhattan. But it is a bonanza that is slated to produce over 20,000 jobs and furnish payments to the city.[44] In New York this is made possible through the powers of government (eminent domain, tax abatement, planning), which act in concert with the resources of private enterprise (initiative, risk, investment).

Neither Covent Garden nor Les Halles has the same kind of relationship with private capital. In Europe, control over capital investment is much more complete. Again, the type of control reflects desired ends. In Covent Garden, where protection and preservation are the keys, government has defrayed the costs of renovation. The public sector is the landlord for the renovated market building. Assorted small businesses rent space and pay a modest $1.12 million per year.[45]

London's tradition of publicly owned housing also goes a long way toward achieving social goals. In Covent Garden, about 30 percent of dwellings are publicly owned, thus the old community could be sheltered in buildings that did justice to its sense of camaraderie and cohesion.[46] Unlike other places, Covent Garden avoided the disastrous path of stuffing its working class in multistory cubbyholes.

TABLE 20.3   *Typical Concerns: Three Sites*

Times Square	*Covent Garden*	*Les Halles*
The Times Square redevelopment plan is the last chance of the century to eliminate the blight and social decay that threaten to transform this area from a center of commerce and transportation to a miasmal swamp awash with pimps, peddlers and purveyors of our society's greatest social ills.—*Chairman, N.Y. State Urban Development Corporation*	A major attitude which prevailed . . . was the emphasis placed on the general concept of conservation, not so much in architectural value as in terms of the general character and charm of Covent Garden . . . extensive physical change could be very detrimental to the character.—*Greater London Council, Covent Garden Team*	We must give Paris a new heart with a Latin flavor . . . The Pompidou Center will be [Les Halles'] great bridge that will allow the 20th century to make its mark on Paris.—*Mayor, City of Paris*
An estimated 4,000 people work in the project area, an extraordinarily low figure . . . a single fully occupied . . . office building alone would house between 4,000 and 5,000 employees . . . the value of the property is also depressed [which is] the direct consequence of the lack of any substantial new construction. . . . —*Environmental Impact Statement, N.Y. State Urban Development Corporation*	There has been little disruptive large or medium-scale office development in Covent Garden . . . the Council is operating a policy of firm restraint . . . special regard will be paid to the environment and the traffic aspects of proposed development. —*Greater London Council, Covent Garden Team*	A little after October of 1978 the Mayor of Paris questioned the colossal architecture for the buildings on the north side of Les Halles. He asked for a new plan which might better integrate the architecture with the surrounding environment and have a greater respect for the urban fabric, the traditional streets, and give particular care to open space.—*Director, Société d'Economie Mixte d'Aménagement des Halles*
I do strongly feel that of all the things that have taken place since I became involved in this issue 25 years ago, this is the worst that has ever emerged. I think it will mean the destruction of Times Square and we will never see it again.—*Chairman, New York City Landmarks Conservancy*	What I am not going to do is create a bonanza for the developer and if someone has bought anticipation of erecting some vast edifice somewhere it is not my fault. —*Secretary for the Environment and Inspector for Covent Garden*	The books about [old] Les Halles are very poetic, yes indeed very poetic. I lived near Les Halles when I was younger and it was a very picturesque place. Like the suks of Bangkok or Hong Kong. But Paris is not Bangkok and finally Les Halles was filthy, unhealthy and difficult to pass through. And at the time no one defended keeping the pavilions. The Prefect, Mr. Doublet, knew they had to be destroyed for the good of all of Paris.—*Chief Planner, City of Paris*

Finally, control over capital investment is augmented by the influence of community organizations and by borough government. These organizations often put the brakes on projects that threaten social well-being.

In Les Halles, where dynamic redevelopment is coupled to aesthetic value, investment control is lodged within the public sector. But it is a control insulated from direct popular influence, and it purposely incorporates large business firms into redevelopment. The City of Paris holds title to the land and retains authority over design, construction, and architecture. The mixed corporation manages Les Halles and grants construction rights to select developers. Construction rights are hedged by public plans, with which contractors must agree to comply. The formula allows for a tighter control than is the case for Times Square, yet it also permits greater private incentives than is possible in Covent Garden. Chirac can tell the developers what he wants because he is not completely dependent upon them for capital investment. Meanwhile those investors who do join the venture are able to pour their own initiative into the framework.[47]

Surely it is within the realm of politics to control development by managing the infusion of investment capital. Arrangements can vary a great deal—from the partnership with large capital in Times Square, to the fragmentation into small capital within Covent Garden, and finally to the subordination of large capital in Les Halles.[48]

Times Square, Les Halles, and Covent Garden are incarnations, *mutatis mutandis*, of the other six cases considered earlier. All sites reflect the political complexion of their habitat. The technicalities of planning cannot be divorced from the exigencies of politics: building cities is an expression of city politics.

Corporatist Politics and Change

Times are changing. Three great cities are still in the process of change, and a new politics continues to evolve. The political change is perhaps less perceptible than the physical transformation, but it is no less profound. Politics made post-industrialism possible, just as politics composed its contours and apportioned its values.

Gone are the days when buccaneers could single-handedly develop tracts of land and shape the city. Gone too are the times when hundreds of separate transactions could surface to mold the landscape gradually. The entrepreneurs can no longer build cities by secretly negotiating with political glad-handers or by paying homage to the royal family.

This is not to say that the corporatist sweep will clear the way for more popular participation or that it will do away with political corruption. Rather than disappear, these problems will take on different qualities. More people may be able to plug into corporatist modes of participation, but the impersonal nature of that participation will increase citizen alienation. Granting recognition to one group will result in the lost influence of another group. As politics becomes more complex, favoritism will be elevated to a grander scale. We can expect that corporatist politics will standardize favor-giving, that contracts will go to organizations with the most political clout, and that less organized groups will be left out. Thus, the inherent structure of corporatism will continue to pose problems.

As Samuel Beer has theorized, this is an age of collectivism.[49] It is an age of mass organization. Whether mass organizations are composed of business, labor, communities, or government, they represent the direct interests of thousands of people. Without organization these interests are just raw demands, difficult to convert into feasible action. It is organization that formulates, systematizes, and coordinates interests so they can be readied for decision making.

Corporatism is a way of rationalizing large-scale interests and making them consonant with the larger polity. Collective bargaining, concertation of interests, and planning are the tools for achieving generalized goals. The corporatist mood sets the parameters for the major actors—the politicians, technocrats, and interest groups. It conditions the things they do—their interaction, their pressures, their choices, and even their values.

Just the same, there is considerable diversity within corporatist politics. The societies, economics, and environments of New York, Paris, and London differ. The interaction, pressures, choices, and values of the major actors also differ. Much as earlier studies of elitism and pluralism showed important variations from society to society, so too does this one.[50] Each city has grown out of its particular roots and yields its particular variations. Over time, the political economies of New York, Paris, and London have created precedents that continue to shape current practice.[51] New York's pluralist-corporatist hybrid comes out of a history of fragmented government, an admiration for political entrepreneurship, and a reverence for capitalism. The politics of personality also make an imprint upon contemporary New York. In Paris, corporatism has grown out of monarchical rule and the power of bureaucracy. Private capital was less independent and the free market less sacrosanct. France is a nation in which tying capital to statist objectives is a political norm. London's liberal corporatism is drawn from an altogether different history. Its politics has been caught in an ambivalence between a respect for local democracy and a commitment to central authority. London has also inherited an ambivalence toward capitalism, drawn on the one hand from the naked industrial competition of Dickens's London and, on the other, from the moderating influence of Fabian Socialism.

Just as we rely on these traditions to understand variations between each city, so too can we make sense of continuity and change within New York, Paris, and London. The roots of urban precedent tend the branches of the contemporary city.

As New York moves into the next decade, its politics continues to revolve around two individuals—Koch and Cuomo—and around the magnetism of the marketplace. In 1986, charges of corruption rocked New York's City Hall. Though not personally connected with corruption, Koch's approval rating plummeted,[52] and along with that fall came a rise of protest against some of the city's most treasured projects, including Times Square.[53]

Scandals are not a novelty in New York; they plague the city the way locusts hit farmers. They arrive every ten years or so, do damage, and disappear until it is time to return. The significance of corruption lies not as much in its discovery as in the revelation that New York politics is exceedingly fragile. The system's reliance on political stars who link themselves, early in the decision stage, to private investors makes that relationship suspect. Even when scandal occurs elsewhere, land-use projects fall under a shadow of mistrust. Years of honest work may be tied to the fate of a single person (is any principal under indictment?), or may fall prey to the vagaries of public perception (politics is a crooked business), or may be vulnerable to a predominant mood (can we trust government to do anything?).

Fortunately for City Hall, these scandals have begun to abate. The big projects have resumed, though politicians and technocrats carry on with uncharacteristic hesitation. Some of that hesitation stems from a caution about sparking future scandals. Some derives from a spreading popular belief that areas within the urban core may have laid themselves open to excessive development. The conviction has begun to seep in that it is time to rein in the builders, preserve what little open space remains, and respect the zoning laws. Although we can expect this caution to materialize in the most densely developed parts of Manhattan, post-industrial development is likely to proceed elsewhere. Manhattan's west perimeter will continue to be suffused with residential and office towers. Planners anticipate that Manhattan's prosperity will spill into surrounding counties. Indeed, the shortage of space in Manhattan has brought about higher demands in parts of Kings County and western Queens. There are even small islands of resurgence in the Bronx.

In Paris, the centripetal forces of the system are still powerful. Chirac's role as party leader has not taken him very far from city government. He continues to reside at the Hôtel de Ville and chooses to do much of his work there. For Chirac, the mayoralty is a power base. Holding onto it means that he can dart in and out of the national government as political needs dictate. Surprisingly, Chirac continues to direct key initiatives in land-use planning. He meets regularly with top technocrats and constantly exhorts them to promote projects.

The cohesion between the political-technocratic elite that bridges state and city will bring future payoffs. The impetus toward prestige and grandeur gains momentum. On the eastern side of Paris, a new Opera House was planned by the Socialist government and criticized by the Parisian Gaullists. When the Gaullists controlled the government, they completed the project. Other public works will endow the city with more eminence. New museums dot the city, La Défense grows, and Paris heightens its appeal for international acclaim.

Of the three cities, London has traditionally been the most politically staid. Today it is the most politically dynamic. The abolition of the GLC was a first attack in a protracted Tory offensive. It deprived Labour of the chance to win over a London-wide constituency and reduced its platform for appealing against the central government. Abolition also cut off a string of benefits that tied the Labour constituency together. These included the GLC's "overspill housing" and its programs for land acquisition and conservation (the Green Belt, Covent Garden).[54]

Thatcher's 1987 victory refueled her push toward radical rightist change. The second attack against Labour is aimed directly at its borough strongholds. The Tories have led the ideological charge with their own nostrum of a "capital-owning democracy." Applied to post-industrial change, its logistics begin with tax reductions for corporations and homeowners. This is supposed to prevent high-spending Socialist councils from siphoning off private capital. The conservatives also want to create a new class of property owners. Where possible, the Tories plan to sell off public housing to tenants and other private buyers. Those renters who cannot afford to purchase their own shelter will be given the opportunity to manage public housing through tenant cooperatives or transfer housing owner-ship to special associations or independent landlords. In land development, the success of the LDDC stands as a Tory model. New development corporations will go into some areas, acquire property, supply infrastructure, and sell off the prepared product to private investors. The Tories intend to change the economic system. Not satisfied with tinkering with the welfare state, they aim to get rid of it—by cutting off Labour's roots in "municipal Socialism" and by starving its branches of politi-cal sustenance.

The Tory program may be more easily announced than accomplished. True, Thatcher has been an unwavering partisan who has moved onto ground where her predecessors dared not tread. It is also true that Thatcher's plans for housing hold a powerful appeal and, if successful, would greatly weaken Labour. Her other plans are fraught with problems. Tax reduction for the well-off, coupled to spending cuts for the poor, will increase resentment. The LDDC obtained very special property, under special conditions, and is not an easy model to follow. Other development corporations will have difficulty mimicking its success.

Post-industrial change is propelled or circumscribed by politics. Thatcher has shaken liberal corporation and heightened its conflicts, but the regime and its op-position both continue to function. The Tories came to their 1987 victory with a scant 42 percent of the vote, in a deeply divided nation, and the opposition is not likely to wither, go away, or die. London's politics is still conducted through liberal corporatist institutions and familiar routes of participation. The parties, the central government, the bureaucracy, the boroughs, the GLCS-in-exile, forums, and publicly supported interest groups (tied to these institutions) continue as the major actors in this drama. And it is impossible to separate the actors from the performance.

Abolition may have rid the Tories of an annoyance, and it gives them some immediate advantages. But the GLC's manifest and psychological functions are missed. These functions will probably be taken up by other institutions, which grow into new roles, or by a suitable replacement. For the future, the betting in the town halls, the pubs, and the university dining rooms is that some kind of GLC will come back. One study has already predicted that abolition will begin

> to falter early on in its life, partly because of effective obstruction by Labour bor-oughs and partly because of disruption caused by rate-capping. . . . Policy effec-tiveness and service levels in transport, housing, planning and other areas begin to slip. The new organization and financial arrangements are complex to operate and badly understood. A period of policy drift ensues which leaves no clear response to London's changing overall problems. In the longer term (by the mid-1990's) measures are taken to reinstitutionalize a strategic policy-making body for Greater London.[55]

The Post-Industrial City and Change

New York, Paris, and London are world cities. Examining them, we see they have more in common with other world cities than with smaller cities in their own nations. World cities are subject to similar external pressures. They command the attention of international finance, multinational corporations, and are hot spots for media and the arts.

What brings a city to world-class status? World cities are not mere ciphers for whatever new technology comes along, but actively create their own environments. The clue to their power is that they have learned to generate growth from within. Using their own resources, they convert old uses to new ones, mix these in hundreds of permutations, and pyramid one asset upon another until they have virtually re-created themselves.

Self-transformation changed sixteenth- and seventeenth-century trading cities into eighteenth- and nineteenth-century industrial ones. It now enables industrial cities to become post-industrial models for the twentieth and twenty-first centuries. New York, Paris, and London show us, in varying ways, how worn out industrial enclaves can be converted into modern CBD's, how obsolete wharfs can be turned into luxury housing, and how fruit markets or seedy downtowns can become fancy cultural centers.

Yet for all its seeming simplicity, the road to post-industrialism is complicated. There is no single path—only detours with buried treasures and hidden pitfalls. New York, with its extraordinary successes and its wrenching traumas, is almost a caricature of self-transformation. One of its offspring is an expanded, hard-driving, white-collar class. This is the middle order of New York's post-industrial society, and much of it can be found in Queens, Richmond, and the suburbs.

Two other New York social orders are more conspicuous. They live closer to one another within the municipality. One of these, affluent and hopeful, embraces a large number of well-educated, employable, small-family or single-person households. These people enjoy a new and separate world of private, highly personalized services. If they live in Manhattan, they reside in privately owned high rises, they travel by private automobile, and they work in the private sector. They are protected by private police, educated at private schools, and socialize at private clubs. Even the letters they write and packages they mail are transported by private carriers. The other social order is poor and despairing. Either post-industrialism has bypassed them or they have bypassed it. If they avail themselves of help, it comes from public services. This order occupies the city's public housing projects, rides public transit, learns in the public schools, and survives on the public dole. If they are homeless, they sleep on the city's streets; if they are attacked, they seek protection from the city's police; and if they relax, they use the city's parks.

The two orders might as well live on different planets, but they live in the same city. Both desperately need each other. The rich need clerks, secretaries, technicians—ultimately professionals. Yet the poor are ill trained, often semi-literate and unprepared for the new economy. Just as certainly the poor need the rich—if only to pay for public services. The poor also need the rich for jobs and a better way of life. These needs are increasingly unbridgeable. As the demand for post-industrial skills increases and as the poor fall further behind, the tragic mismatch grows worse. The conundrum is part of New York's post-industrial inheritance—partly a product of rapid, careless growth—and it continues to haunt the city.

Self-transformation has been much more deliberate and controlled in Paris. The city is a piece of technocratic art—carefully arranged and mixed with pre-conceptions of what things are supposed to go where. Old neighborhoods have become incredibly neat and give the appearance of contrived quaintness. Almost everyone uses public services. The working and middle classes have been slotted into public housing, the trains are packed with commuters, and cultural centers are factories of mass consumption.

Paris is becoming homogenized into a post-industrial society. Its physical transformation has seeped into the social structure. The disparate social orders, so obvious in New York, are in Paris separate classes that participate in a common order.

This is not to say that the transformation has accomplished class harmony—only that the extensive and common use of public services ease the most grotesque disparities of class. Surprisingly, to Americans, it is easier to be poor in Paris than it is in New York, because the differences are not so obvious. This observation says a great deal about a transformation whose exceptions do not so much constitute an opposite stratum as involve people who are either socially integrated (unemployed workers) or who are presumed to have a temporary status (immigrants and students).

For a long time, London's self-transformation was limited. Today it is accelerated by a freer flow of market forces and the stimulation of private investment. London is at a historic juncture, and it will be another decade before we know how it fares. The most extreme result of Tory radicalism would fragment the metropolis into bits and pieces. Greater London would more resemble subgovernments fighting to enrich their own turf than a coherent metropolis. The most vigorous development would be concentrated in parts of the CBD, the Docklands, and some outer boroughs. Many of the inner boroughs would encounter a withering corrosion. Greater London might enjoy more jobs, but the celebration of its prosperity would occur amid less balance, less conservation, and a less humane society.

This scenario would place London's post-industrialism closer to the disparate social orders of New York. Although many Londoners might profit from the rapid conversion, a whole stratum would be left behind, increasingly ill equipped and psychologically incapable of sharing in the change.

The experience of other cities tells us time radical and prodigious change can hurt. A rising tide may raise a lot of ships, but it does not raise all of them and it may leave many submerged. Some of the most exuberant Tories talk about cleaning up London's "dependency ghettos" by adopting American techniques—as if London possessed New York's problems. For the time being it does not, but it is not far-fetched to see them developing.

In a perfect world, change should maximize benefits and minimize costs. Decision makers work, however, in an imperfect world, limited by precedent, circumstance, and public habit. Even when everything falls into place, change is not easy. Some are bound to be dissatisfied and believe that other cities have done a better job. This perception is not so much wrong as it is dependent upon position. The experience of New York, Paris, and London shows us just how relative those positions can be, and why politics must always mediate planning.

Notes

1. See the classic by James Bryce, *The American Commonwealth*, vol. 1 (New York: Macmillan, 1893), p. 637.

2. Ibid., p. 642.

3. Quoted in David Hammack, *Power and Society* (New York: Russell Sage, 1982), p. 16. The original quote is from *The Banker's Magazine*, 53, 1896.

4. Ibid.

5. Pinkney, *Napoleon III and the Rebuilding of Paris*, p. 36. See also Evenson, *Paris: A Century of Change*, esp. ch. I.

6. Young and Garside, *Metropolitan London*, p. 47.

7. Pinkney, *Napoleon III and the Rebuilding of Paris*, p. 36.

8. The thesis of the "private city" can be found in Sam Bass Warner's classic, *The Private City* (Philadelphia: University of Pennsylvania Press, 1968).

9. Quoted in Lester Salamon, "Urban Politics, Urban Policy, Case Studies" *Public Administration Review* 37 (July/August 1977): 423. Salamon presents an interesting conceptual framework that uses the idea of the "private city," the "bureaucratic city," and the "policy-planning" city.

10. For how this was done in Paris, see Evenson, *Paris: A Century of Change*. For London see Donald Olsen, *The Growth of Victorian London* (New York: Holmes & Meier, 1976).

11. For an excellent discussion of pluralists and corporatism as well as "concertation," see Harrison, *Pluralism and Corporatism*, esp. ch. 5.

12. For an extended political analysis see the landmark study on America's transformation by Theodore Lowi, *The End of Liberalism* (New York: W. W. Norton, 1969). See also Yair Aharoni, *The No Risk Society* (Chatham, N.J.: Chatham House, 1981).

13. Quoted in Susan Fainstein et al., *Restructuring the City*, p. 252.

14. *Le Monde*, April 30, 1977, p. 98.

15. *New York Times*, August 2, 1982, p. A2.

16. The analysis of "caretaker politics" comes out of an earlier era of urban scholarship and can be found in Oliver Williams and Charles Adrian, *Four Cities: A Study in Comparative Policy Making* (Philadelphia: University of Pennsylvania Press, 1963).

17. The tradition is an old one, brought into vogue during the 1970s by the Bachrach and Baratz classic, *Power and Poverty*, and revitalized most recently in John Mollenkopf, *The Contested City*, and Clarence Stone, "Systemic Power in Community Decision Making: A Restatement of Stratification Theory," *American Political Science Review* 74 (December 1980): 978–90.

18. Stone, "Systemic Power in Community Decision Making," p. 985.

19. Ibid., pp. 980, 982 and passim. Another way of analyzing "situational dependencies" is to view them in terms of the things a city must do in order to function, survive, or prosper. It can be argued, for instance, that since cities must turn to private business for income, employment, and economic vitality, they must *always* favor those who are economically well off. See H. V. Savitch, *Urban Policy and the Exterior City*, pp. 61–63. Frederick Wirt makes a similar point by quoting Machiavelli's admonition about "the compulsion of necessity." See Frederick Wirt, *Power in the City* (Berkeley: University of California Press, 1973), p. 352.

20. Regarding the application to land use of the concept of prevailing coalitions, see the formidable collection of articles edited by Clarence Stone and Heywood Sanders, *The Politics of Urban Development* (Lawrence, Kansas: University Press of Kansas, 1987); for a general treatment, see

John Mollenkopf, *The Contested City*. For the application of this idea to non–land use issues, see Martin Shefter, *Political Crisis/Fiscal Crisis* (New York: Basic Books, 1985).

21. Peter Blau, *Exchange and Power in Social Life* (New York: John Wiley & Sons, 1967), p. 5.

22. *1980 Census of Population, Characteristics of People and Housing*, New York State Data Center, New York State Department of Commerce, Summary Tape File 3.

23. Statistics for Paris can be found in *Récensement de la Population de 1975 et 1982: Région d'Ile-de-France* (Paris: INSEE, 1984). Statistics for New York can be obtained from New York State Data Center, Summary Tape File 3.

24. INSEE, Observatoire Economique de Paris.

25. New York State Data Center, Summary Tape File 3.

26. For London, consult *ECONDAT Y67: 1971 and 1981* (London: Greater London Council), Tables 26 and 27 [hereafter referred to as ECONDAT]. For New York, consult *1980 Census of the Population, Characteristics of People and Housing*, Summary Tape File 3. For Paris, consult Institut National de la Statistique et des Etudes Economique (INSEE), *Récensement de la Population Région d'Ile-de-France 1982* (Paris: Observatoire Economique de Paris, n.d.).

27. ECONDAT.

28. See Hall, *World Cities*, pp. 39–44.

29. Sundquist, *Dispersing Population*, ch. 3.

30. One study that appears to substantiate this thesis is Richard Knight and Thierry Noyelle, *The Economic Transformation of American Cities* (New York: Rowman & Allenheld, 1984).

31. See, for example, Falk, "First Steps," p. 6.12.

32. Saviteh and Adler, *Decentralization at the Grass Roots*.

33. London began to construct similar kinds of facilities during the late 1960s, mostly on the dilapidated East End. After several years' experience with this kind of construction, it was abruptly halted. London's flirtation with megastructure housing was relatively brief and it reverted to the practice of building human-scale public (council) housing. In New York, megastructure-type housing was built for the poor and for the middle class shortly after World War II and in the 1960s.

34. *42nd Street Development Project: Update*, p. 12.

35. *Covent Garden Action Area Plan* (London: The Greater London Council, January 24, 1978), p. 19.

36. For estimated costs, see *Forty-Second Street Development Project Fact Sheet*, p. 6, and Tim Wacher and Alan Flint, "How Covent Garden Became a Specialty Shopping Center," in *The Chartered Surveyor*, July 1980, p. 1 (reprinted by the GLC, Covent Garden Team).

37. *Covent Garden Action Area Plan*, p. 27.

38. *New York Times*, October 22, 1984, p. 63.

39. *Environmental Impact Statement*, p. S14.

40. *Covent Garden Action Area Plan*, p. 27.

41. *Rapport à l'Assemblée Générale Ordinaire sur l'Exercice 1972*, p. 6.

42. *10 Ans d'Activé: Les Halles*, p. 49.

43. The quotes for Times Square, in order of presentation, are drawn from the *New York Times*, March 26, 1984, p. B1; *Environmental Impact Statement*, p. S8; and the *New York Times*, March 26, 1984, p. B1. For Covent Garden the quotes are drawn from *Action Area Plan*, pp. 13, 26, and from the *Birmingham Evening Mail*, January 16, 1979. For Paris, the quotes are taken from *Le Monde*, February 18/19, 1979, *10 Ans d'Activé: Les Halles*, p. 13, and a personal interview, December 14, 1984.

44. *Environment Impact Statement*, pp. S13, S14. A press release by the Mayor's office states that the project will furnish "26,000 new permanent jobs," *Press Release*, Office of the Mayor, New York, April 6, 1982, p. 4.

45. Wacher and Flint, "How Covent Garden Became," n.p. Before abolition, the GLC owned the Covent Garden's renovated market building. Since abolition, GLC property has been managed by the London Residuary Body (LRB). The LRB is supposed to function for a transitional period until all GLC affairs are terminated. GLC property is normally transferred to the boroughs, so they are likely to become Covent Garden's landlord.

46. *Covent Garden Action Area Plan*, p. 18.

47. The results can be seen in the financial accounting of Les Halles. In 1979 revenues amounted to $3.2 million, of which private developers contributed only 27 percent. The rest came from concessions granted to other public authorities, state assistance, and user fees. See *10 Ans d'Activité: Les Halles*, p. 5I.

48. Precise comparisons between the three sites are difficult to make because of different systems of accounting and different modes of payment. They can also be misleading because of different territorial definitions and because the figures are often estimates. With these caveats in mind I have constructed a brief table of comparison. The reader can note the major contrasts between Times Square and Covent Garden. Les Halles' statistics fall somewhere in between.

	Size of Commercial Target (sq. acres)	Cost of Reconstruction (millions)	Direct Revenue Paid Annually to Public Sector (millions)	Increase or Decrease in Employment (percentage)	New Office Space (thousands of sq. ft.)
Times Square	13	2,400	35.27	+500%	4,000
Covent Garden	34	22.5	1.25	−27	434
Les Halles	16	1,000	3.22	not avail.	1,666

Source: Adapted from *42nd Street Redevelopment Project: Final Environmental Impact Statement* (New York: Urban Development Corporation, August 1984); *Covent Garden Action Area Plan* (London: Covent Garden Committee, 1978); and *10 Ans d'Activité: Les Halles* (Paris: Société d'Economie Mixte d'Aménagement des Halles, 1979). Cost and revenues for Times Square are estimated figures derived from the Urban Development Corporation (author's interview, July 23, 1987).

49. Samuel Beer, "Group Representation in Britain and the United States," *Annals of the American Academy of Political and Social Science* 319 (September 1958). Also see Beer's later work, *British Politics in the Collectivist Age* (New York: Alfred Knopf, 1967).

50. For examples of these differences, compare C. Wright Mills, *The Power Elite* (New York: Oxford University Press, 1959), with Floyd Hunter, *Community Power Structure* (New York: Doubleday, 1963), and still further with the "neo-elitist" critique by Bachrach and Baratz, *Power and Poverty*. In pluralist literature there are significant differences between Sayre and Kaufman's study of New York City, *Governing New York,* and Wirt's study of San Francisco, *Power in the City.* Within this school a whole new wave of "neo pluralist literature" has surfaced. For an explanation see John Manley, "Neo-Pluralism: A Class Analysis of Pluralism I and Pluralism II," *American Political Science Review* 77 (June 1983): 368–83.

51. For an appreciation of how historical precedent shapes different kinds of corporatism, consult Philip Cerny, "The Missing Linkage: Putting the State Back into Neo-Corporatism," paper presented at the Annual Meeting of the American Political Science Association, Washington, D.C., August 1986.

52. Thus in a six-month period corresponding to before and after the revelation of the scandal, those who approved of Koch's performance as Mayor fell from 71 percent to 61 percent, while those who disapproved of his performance jumped from 23 percent to 32 percent. See *New York Daily News,* June 4, 1986, p. 5.

53. See the appeal for public support on Times Square by a former head of the Urban Development Corporation, William Stern, "Don't Punish Times Square," *New York Times,* May 22, 1986, p. A31.

54. For a critical prognosis of GLC abolition that is co-authored by a former member of the GLC, consult George Nicholson and Leith Penny, "Strategica Planning in London: The Past and the Future," *Viewpoint*, May 1986.

A "GLC comeback" could take any number of forms, as long as it consisted of a comprehensive government for a substantial part of what we know as London. These forms might include a return to three-tier government, an elected regional assembly, a council for Inner London, or the evolution of an existing institution into a broad-purpose authority.

55. Thomas Clegg, Roger Crouch, Patrick Dunleavy, and Alan Harding, *The Future of London Government* (London: London School of Economics and Political Science, 1985), p. 104.

21

The Postmodern Urban Matrix

Paul L. Knox

The Washington Metropolitan Area

At first glance, the Washington, D.C. metropolitan area may not seem a likely candidate for an exercise of this sort. Described by John Kennedy as the only city to combine northern charm with southern efficiency and by Richard Nixon as a city full of "pointy-headed bureaucrats," Washington has for a long time endured the reputation of being a rather dull federal town, lacking the dynamism of industrial centers and failing to capture the cosmopolitanism of major corporate and financial control centers. The city's material landscapes have reflected these shortcomings. The physical centerpiece of the city, L'Enfant's plan, had been allowed to leak purposelessly away in a series of compromises and missed opportunities, while the architecture of public and commercial buildings, under a height restriction of 110 feet imposed in 1910 in order to preserve the visual dominance of the Capitol and the Washington monument, made for a rather bland, stodgy and sterile urban core. In the past fifteen years, however, the Washington metropolitan area has been transformed from a federal town to a world city (Gale, 1987; Knox, 1987, 1991). Although government jobs—state, local and federal—still account for one in every four jobs in the metropolitan area, it is now a national information and communications node and a major coordinating center for all kinds of international activities, both public and private. This has resulted in a simultaneous recentralization of commercial activity and emergence of "edge cities" (Garreau, 1991); and it has created a congested, fragmented and polarized urban structure that is a good example of the postmodern metropolis.

The largest sector of the metropolitan economy is the service sector. In part, this is a product of the tourism generated by monumental Washington and the complex of galleries and museums around the Mall; but more important are the office jobs generated by the interest groups and corporations attracted to Washington by the presence of the national legislature, its bureaucratic agencies and the bureaux of major international agencies such as the World Bank. Washington contains the headquarters of nearly 200 national business, professional and trade associations and a growing number of law, accounting, real estate, computer software and high technology firms, media and communications companies, data services, mortgage banks and investment trusts and consultants ("Beltway bandits") such as economists, management analysts and scientists who do contract work for both large corporations and government agencies. Foreign-owned firms such as British Aerospace, Arianespace, Fokker Aircraft, Polaris Optics and Lafarge concrete and construction have begun to locate their US headquarters in Washington,[1] which has also become the home of a growing number of Fortune 500 companies, including MCI in the District, Martin Marietta and Mariott in suburban Maryland and Gannett (owners of *USA TODAY*), Mobil, Unisys and US Sprint in suburban Virginia. At the same time, there has been a pronounced shift away from direct federal employment toward government purchasing. Between 1979 and 1989, federal purchases of local goods and services trebled, from $3.4 billion to $10.3 billion, reaching a level that approaches the dollar value of the area's federal payrolls.[2] Thousands of local companies now live by federal contracts, with the lion's share going to companies that provide communications equipment, defense systems R&D, social services, architectural and engineering services, data processing services and professional services.

Overall, the Washington area acquired almost 600,000 new jobs—one fourth of the current total—during the 1980s (Granat and Conlin, 1990). In the process, it became an "entrepreneurial city," with one of the highest rates of growth in the nation for new business enterprises with ten or more employees and the second-highest percentage of young companies with high growth rates.[3] The result of all this growth is an exceptionally well-educated and affluent population. One in three adults are college-educated, compared to one in five in metropolitan Chicago, New York and Los Angeles and one in seven in metropolitan Detroit. In 1990, when the national average household income was $28,525, the average for the Washington metropolitan area was $43,754. One in four of Washington's black households is affluent,[4] compared to one in ten in Detroit and Chicago and one in twenty-five in Miami (Waldrop, 1990). Washington is the strongest consumer market in the country, with average retail sales per household of $22,454 in 1988. Within the metropolitan area, expenditure on men's tailored clothing, precious jewelry, imported cars, foreign vacations, imported wine, dining out and health club membership runs at more than 25 percent above the U.S. average (Weissman, 1990).

Among those at the top end of the income distribution, physicians in the Washington area had incomes that averaged $130,000 in 1989—20 percent higher than the national average; partners in large law practices had incomes in 1989 in excess of $250,000, with some[5] averaging well over $500,000; and the senior officers of 130 of the largest business and professional associations averaged almost $200,000 in 1987, with seventeen of them earning over $300,000 and four[6] earning over $500,000. It is estimated[7] that there are more than 277,000 households in the Washington area with net (after-tax) annual incomes of $75,000 or more, over 112,000 with net incomes of $100,000 or more, and more than 15,000 with net incomes of $250,000 or more—about three times the national incidence of such incomes.

The economic growth and rising affluence of the 1980s was reflected in Washington in a materialism that took its cue from the inauguration of Ronald Reagan as President in 1980:

> The staff of the Washington Post's Style section was kept busy for days counting the private jets at the airport, measuring the length of limousine queues, inspecting the quality of mink garments, interviewing Reagan's millionaire friends from California, and inventorying the first lady's wardrobe. All of this was an early indication that the Reagan years would see a renewal of the idea that the making and spending of money is a noble goal and a moral good.
>
> Van Dyne, 1989, p. 250

The ensuing development boom and consumption spree has been very visible in office, retailing and residential development. During the late 1980s, more office space was completed in the Washington area than in any other North American or European city.[8] In contrast to the plainness of Washington's federal office space, much of this office space is deliberately and self-consciously luxurious; some of it is downright outré. The executive suite of the Gannett Company's office tower in Rosslyn is decorated with snakeskin wallpaper, suede rugs, and two "neorealist" sculptures of sheep, complete with small piles of Hershey's chocolate Kisses strategically located under their rears (Van Dyne, 1989). Retailers have been quick to exploit the area's buying power. In the late 1970s, Bloomingdale's, Nieman Marcus and I. Magnin department stores appeared, followed later by Nordstrom's, Macy's, Saks Fifth Avenue and Lord and Taylor, with Hecht's commissioning the only full-sized, freestanding department store to be built in a U.S. downtown since 1945. New shopping malls and galleries have attracted upscale specialty stores such as Abercrombie and Fitch, Laura Ashley, Bally, Burberys, Cartier, Graham and Gunn, Gucci, Hermés, Ralph Lauren, Yves St Laurent, FAO Schwartz, Sharper Image, Tiffanys, Louis Vuitton and Williams-Sonoma; automobile dealerships have added Rolls Royces, Bentleys, Ferraris and Lamborghinis to the BMW, Jaguar, Mercedes Benz, Porsche and Volvo models on their lots.

The most striking outcome of Washington's development boom and consumer spree, however, is in the residential sector. The expansion of well-paid jobs brought large numbers of households in their prime home-buying years to the area, pushing up house prices and prompting a rash of construction for the top end of the market. According to real estate analysts R. S. Lusk and Son,[9] there were seventeen Washington-area neighborhoods where average home sale prices exceeded $350,000 in 1988. . . . New homes in Potomac and Great Falls stand on large lots, with circular drives and imposing gateways that create the unnerving effect of a landscape full of expensive funeral homes. . . . The houses themselves average 6,000 to 10,000 square feet, though some are the size of a three-story public school. They have elaborate master bedrooms, marble bathrooms with Jacuzzis, saunas or steam cabinets, exercise rooms, "gourmet" kitchens, libraries with computer centers, two-story foyers and 10-foot ceilings. Optional extras include cottages for guests, riding rings for horses and holding tanks for lobsters. When the boom that began in 1984 eventually slowed in 1990, such features, along with locational advantages, became critical in securing a competitive advantage in sluggish markets (Parham, 1990).

As in other world cities, economic growth and conspicuous consumption have been accompanied by an intensification of poverty and social malaise. The District of Columbia contains neighborhoods whose conditions are as shockingly bad as those in Potomac and Great Falls are ridiculously good. Their condition is less well-documented because there is less money to be made from them: for real estate analysts and marketing companies they are all but invisible. They consist of 2- and 3-story apartment buildings and some older single-family dwellings and row houses that have deteriorated to the point of no return. They are inhabited by a residual population that has been unable to participate in the expansion of the advanced service economy and so unable to escape to better neighborhoods.

Yet, while these neighborhoods are invisible to marketers and to the more affluent residents of the metropolitan area, they are the locus of two of the attributes by which Washington is best-known: homicide and drug abuse. Washington, D.C. has become firmly established as the nation's Murder Capital. With 487 homicides in 1991 (up from 456 in 1990, 438 in 1989, 369 in 1988, 228 in 1987 and 197 in 1986), the city had a homicide rate of 72 per 100,000 residents, almost exactly twice that of neighboring Baltimore. Ninety percent of homicide victims in the District were, like their assailants, black:[10] citizens of the city of the excluded, invisible until they showed up in a body bag on the six o'clock news. The link between crime and drugs is very close: two-thirds of homicide victims in recent years have had drugs in their systems,[11] and a similar proportion of defendants in the District's Superior Court have been found to be drug users.[12] Many of the homicides are the result of execution-style killings, casualties the turf wars that have proliferated in the absence of organized crime and the presence, within the city of the excluded, of an over-supply of aggressive people seeking to escape poverty or to pay for their own habit by dealing drugs.

Social Ecology

The explosive growth of metropolitan Washington has produced a good example of the "galactic metropolis." . . . Seen from the air, much of the metropolis consists of hundreds of small subdivisions, business parks, commercial corridors and suburban nodes flung over rolling, wooded countryside and loosely strung together by tendril-like access roads and a web-like highway system. Within this physical template, the overall social ecology of the metropolitan area is best captured by the "lifestyle communities" identified by consumer research. . . . Of the 40 lifestyle communities identified from national analysis, just nine account for nearly 80 percent of the Washington area's 1.4 million households.

The wealthiest communities, "Blue Blood Estates," include . . . Potomac, Great Falls, McLean and Chevy Chase. These communities account for only six percent of the area's total households but they set the standards for its materialism. They are remarkably localized, straddling the Potomac in northern Fairfax County and southeastern Montgomery County.

The largest single group consists of communities of "Young Influentials"— predominantly young, upwardly mobile singles and dual-career couples in white-collar jobs with substantial incomes. They live in places like Gaithersburg, Greenbelt and Parkfairfax, in neighborhoods strung along the major highways, with a high density of new and expensive townhouses and mid-rise apartments such as those along "Condo Canyon," parallel to I-95 in Fairfax County. Marketing studies portray them as the exemplars of Ehrenreich's (1989) yuppies: they are more than twice as likely than average Americans to go sailing, take cruises, drink bottled water and attend concerts. Their favorite automobiles are BMWs, Acuras and Alfa Romeos. They spend twice as much time as the rest of the population exercising (jogging, sailing or playing racquetball or tennis are preferred) and have little time left for television. They subscribe in large numbers to *Gourmet* magazine but are so busy that they are the area's top customers for home-delivery pizza, Chinese take-out meals and upscale frozen dinners.

The second largest group of communities—"Furs and Station Wagons"—is dominated by upwardly mobile couples in their thirties and forties with teenage children. Their neighborhoods surround the Beltway to the northwest and southwest of the city and are characterized by recently-built subdivisions with amenities such as tennis courts, swimming pools and bike paths. Two-thirds of the residents of these communities have moved into their homes in the last five years, and three-quarters of them own three or more cars, "the better to take their kids to piano lessons and soccer practice" (Weiss, 1988b, p. 254).

"Young Suburbia" communities, which account for 10 percent of the area's households, are dominated by younger households with elementary-school-aged children, on the first rung or two of the home ownership ladder, living in cheaper, high-density subdivisions in outlying suburbs like Clinton, Dale City, Herndon and La Plata. These households tend to drive inexpensive automobiles and shop in factory outlets and do-it-yourself stores but are attentive to future upward mobility, subscribing in large numbers to *Money* magazine.

Two groups of communities are dominated by suburbanizing black households. The more affluent "Black Enterprise" communities such as Brookland, Capitol Heights and Walter Reed are scattered along the northeastern and southeastern boundaries of the District and in two suburban corridors in Prince George's County. These neighborhoods are middle class, with the majority of homes worth, in 1988, between $80,000 and $150,000. Like white middle-class suburbanites, their residents are distinctive in marketing terms for their membership of book clubs, their propensity to exercise, their investments in annuities and their purchasing of lawn furniture, TV sets, VCRs, compact disc audio systems, personal computers and movie cameras. Relatively less affluent are the "Emergent Minorities," communities of predominantly black working-class households located in the middle zones of the District and is outlying enclaves within the Beltway in Prince George's County. Examples include Brentwood, Columbia Heights and Palmer Park. These are neighborhoods of rowhouses and apartment buildings where consumer tastes are characterized by above-average rates of malt liquor and menthol cigarette consumption, watching professional wrestling on TV and driving Renault Alliances, Chevy Novas, Yugos—and Cadillacs.

A third group of black communities consists of aging inner-city slum districts and housing projects—"Downtown Dixie Style." These areas are characterized by unemployment rates of around 30 percent, low educational achievement and high levels of poverty, violent crime and drug abuse. They are located to the north and northeast of the CBD and in the southeastern parts of the District: typical examples include the area around 14th and U streets, Fort Chaplin Park, and the projects of Anacostia. In marketing terms, they are of significance only for their propensity for renting television sets, buying inexpensive subcompact automobiles, reading *Soap Opera Digest* and cashing promotional coupons for check-cashing businesses and high-risk insurance firms.

Finally, the Washington metropolitan area contains two groups of communities that encompass elements of gentrification. "Bohemian Mix" neighborhoods, mostly within the District, contain pioneer, first-stage gentrification and transitional neighborhoods as well as more established but less affluent gentrified neighborhoods. Exemplified by Foggy Bottom and Dupont Circle, they are dominated by singles and divorcées, young and old, black and white, who are drawn to the urbanity of sidewalk cafes and storefront galleries set among brownstones and apartment houses. "Money and Brains" neighborhoods, on the other hand, are characterized by high-income households living near urban university campuses. Some, like Georgetown, are dominated by upscale, gentrified row houses and their infill look-alikes; others, like Spring Valley, are dominated by older, established upper-middle-class housing. They contain large numbers of accountants doctors, lawyers and scientists—Bourdieu's "new bourgeoisie". . ., who tend to buy European luxury automobiles, designer clothes and appliances, invest in stocks, bonds and securities and read *New Yorker* magazine. . . .

Packaged Landscapes

These new alliances, and the materialism upon which they are based, are inscribed most clearly on the urban fabric in the packaged landscapes of mixed-use developments (MXDs) and private master-planned communities. These are the "artful fragments" (Boyer, 1990) of postmodern urban development, serially-produced set pieces that reflect the logic of corporate consolidation, flexible strategies, product differentiation, and public-private cooperation. . . . According to the Urban Land Institute's Real Estate Project Database, there were fewer than 25 MXDs in the entire United States at the end of the 1960s. Construction began on 65 more during the 1970s and on nearly 300 more during the 1980s (ULI, 1989). This proliferation is largely the result of the restructuring and repositioning of the development industry. The increased involvement of large corporations and financial institutions in real estate made large amounts of capital available for prestige projects, while developers were impelled to put together projects that could support the rising costs of urban land while spreading design and management costs over bigger units and the same time incorporating flexibility to differentiate space for different categories of users.

In the Washington metropolitan area there are more than 40 MXDs,[13] two-thirds of which were initiated in the 1980s. They have been fostered by public agencies who view them as attractive additions to the tax base, as anchors for urban planning and design projects and for revitalization programs, as useful transition elements between different land uses and as potential stimuli, when located near Metro stations, for ridership on the public transit system. Indeed, some MXDs, such as National Place, have been publicly initiated. The District of Columbia was one of the first central cities in the United States to relax single-purpose zoning when, in 1974, it introduced a mixed-use zoning ordinance for twelve blocks of the West End (to the north of Pennsylvania Avenue and to the east of Georgetown), providing incentives and bonuses for moderate-income housing, pedestrian or cycling areas and retail or service space that might contribute to the vitality of the area. More recently, the District has encouraged mixed-use development in the traditional retail-commercial sector of downtown[14] with a zoning overlay that requires 18 to 20 percent of a new building's gross first floor area to be preferred retail, service or arts uses. Meanwhile, the Pennsylvania Avenue Development Corporation has assembled over 110 acres of land along the city's most important symbolic axis (between the U.S. Capitol and the White House) and established a planning framework that includes a number of MXDs, including National Place, the Willard Hotel complex, the Old Post Office . . . and Market Square. Altogether, eleven of the 40 MXDs in the Washington area have been assisted by significant changes in public codes or ordinances; nine have been assisted by direct public investment in supporting elements such as access improvements, garages, arenas, libraries and cultural facilities; and five have been assisted by direct public ownership or shared risk.[15]

The net result is a landscape studded with clusters of glitzy nodes. About one third are located in the CBD, with the rest in commercial nodes and corridors and in peripheral edge-city concentrations convenient to "Blue Blood Estates," "Young Influentials" and "Furs and Station Wagon" neighborhoods. The micro-landscapes of the MXDs themselves are carefully packaged, with striking architecture, luxurious-looking materials and fittings, and interior spaces planted like rain forests. Upmarket commercial and residential tenants and fashionable retail outlets are accompanied by health centers, small convenience stores, concierge services and security patrols. Some have exclusive restaurants and business clubs, fitted out in mahogany, crystal and lush carpeting. A typical example is the Twinbrook Office Center/Holiday Inn Crowne Plaza in Rockville, Maryland. Located on a 6.6-acre site across from the Twinbrook Metro Station, this $55 million, 700,000-square-foot project includes 12,400 square feet of ground-level retailing, a 315-bed hotel, two restaurants, a 19,000-square-foot conference facility, an indoor/outdoor pool and a racquetball and health club. The architecture combines a Late Modern exterior with a lush, postmodern interior space that features an atrium with a large wooden Victorian-style pavilion set amid waterfalls, ferns and meandering brick walkways. Settings such as this are an important component of the postmodern urban matrix because of their visibility and exclusivity. Like larger and even more spectacular settings based on waterfront redevelopments or festival marketplaces, they are part of the "carnival mask" of contemporary urbanization (Harvey, 1989, p. 92), settings that serve as a focus of stylish materialism while diverting attention from the refugee landscapes of the poor and the homeless.

A second important form of packaged landscape is represented by the private master-planned communities that have proliferated within the "Blue Blood Estates" and "Furs and Station Wagon" ecology of Washington's northern and western suburbs.[16] They are a response to the mass production and mass consumption of split-level suburban space, a result of product differentiation and carefully-targeted niche marketing. By exploiting PUD zoning, . . . developers can put together projects that are attractive to a very profitable sector of the residential market while retaining scope for flexibility in the composition and timing of the development. Residents of such communities are offered sequestered settings with an extensive package of amenities that typically includes tennis courts, a golf course, swimming pools, play areas, jogging courses, an auditorium, exercise rooms, a shopping center, a day-care center and a security system symbolized by imposing gateways and operated by electronic card-key systems. Housing is typically a mixture of expensive single-family homes, upscale townhouses and condominiums and a few smaller studios or apartments for young singles or the elderly, all in High Suburban style: mock-Tudor, mock-Georgian, neo-Colonial, Giant Cape Cod and so on. The entire ensemble is framed in a carefully landscaped setting that might contain a lake stocked with swans or a neoconservationist assemblage of remnant woodland, an artificial wetlands environment and plantings of wild flowers. The landscape is completed by a parade of joggers in expensive warm-up suits and by busy UPS vans delivering affordable luxuries from the mail-order branches of Spiegel, Williams-Sonoma, Sharper Image and Bullock and Jones.

These artful fragments provide the ultimate framework for the culture of stylish materialism. They are communities of affect rather than communities of interest, sharing only a dedication to the iconolatry of visible wealth and distinction, a sect that has adopted the architecture of the English gentry, the artifacts of French aristocracy and imperial China and contemporary European kitchen and automobile technology as signs of membership. The very names of the communities are carefully selected in order to set the required tone of distinction, heritage and authenticity: Hampton Chase, Lansdowne, Manor Gate, River Oaks, Stilloaks, Tavistock, Woodlea Manor and so on. Advertising imagery draws on the totemism of golf, equestrianism and pastoral landscapes, while advertising copy leaves no doubts about the status and stylishness of the product. Woodlea Manor, for example, is described as "Exclusive. But not entirely out of reach," and as a place "Where style of living matters." The slogan for Sully Station is "Sometimes It's Better to Live in the Past;" for King's Forest ("The Community That Says 'You've Arrived' Has Arrived") it is "Your Crowning Achievement. . . ." Within the Washington metropolitan area there were in 1989 some 30 private master-planned communities (including Reston, a suburban new town in Fairfax County built by R. E. Simon in the 1960s and subsequently taken over by Gulf Oil and then Mobil Oil; and Columbia, a suburban new town in Howard County built at the same time by J. Rouse, developer of Baltimore's Harbor Place, both now enjoying an expansion with the popularity of packaged residential settings) (Knox, 1991). Most of them were begun during the development boom of the late 1980s, and many are still incomplete, waiting out the recession of the early 1990s.

Reclaimed Landscapes

In many ways, the reclamation of older fragments of central-city areas through preservation and conservation can be attributed to the failure of urban redevelopment schemes. Citizen protests against wholesale demolition and renewal were an important part of the broad countercultural movement of the 1960s. Their success helped to redefine the conventional wisdom among city planners and urban policymakers. By the 1980s, historic preservation had become part of an officially-sponsored "heritage industry," bolstered by tax credits and accelerated depreciation benefits for investments in historic property (Gleye, 1988). Between 1970 and 1985 the number of properties and districts listed in the National Register of Historic Places increased from 1,500 to 37,000 (Listokin, 1989).

Yet it is no coincidence that historic preservation has been a striking aspect of urban change during the blossoming of postmodernity. Historic buildings and districts lend distinctiveness and identity to both residential and commercial users while resonating very clearly with those aspects of postmodern culture that emphasize the past, the vernacular and the decorative. Furthermore, the heritage industry is bound up in the struggle for cultural legitimacy and at the same time is an important component of the "society of the spectacle." Historic preservation not only reclaims buildings and neighborhoods from the ravages of physical decay but, much more significantly, reclaims them from the ignominy of social decline. Occupants of refurbished buildings are able to draw on the cultural capital and social prestige of earlier occupants; meanwhile, the buildings themselves become part of the scenography of the contemporary city.

In Washington, urban renewal programs had been particularly vigorous during the 1960s and early 1970s. President Kennedy had expressed his dismay at the urban decay visible along the route to his inauguration, and the Pennsylvania Avenue Development Corporation was subsequently established in order to tidy up and revitalize the axis. Then, after the riots and civil disorder of the late 1960s, office and retail activity were repelled from the old downtown area to the east of the White House, prompting the redevelopment of a "new downtown" area to the north and west (Gale, 1987). In the process, the demise of several familiar landmarks prompted the formation of an activist preservation group, Don't Tear It Down, which soon became an important element in local politics. The first victory of the group (now known as the DC Preservation League) was the prevention of the demolition of the Old Post Office, which was subsequently restored and adapted to a mixed-use "festival" space that is a key element in the Pennsylvania Avenue Development Plan. Other notable victories for the group have includes the preservation of the Willard Hotel and the nineteenth century terrace known as Red Lion Row, both on Pennsylvania Avenue.

By the time the old downtown area began to be ripe for reinvestment in the mid-1970s, Washington's preservationist movement had become a considerable force, and developers had come to recognize the demand for historic settings. As a result, the downtown townscape is now a virtual set piece of preservation projects, including Gallery Row, the National Bank of Washington, the Hotel Washington, the Evening Star Building, Woodward and Lothrop's, the Colorado Building, . . . the Sun Building, the McLachen Bank, the Southern Building, the National Theater and the Warner Theater (Knox, 1991). Overall, almost 4000 structures have now been designated under local preservation laws, twelve areas have been designated as residential historic districts, and an entire volume of the District's Comprehensive Plan is devoted to historic preservation (Gale, 1987).

The success of historic preservation fostered the spread of gentrification—a kind of do-it-yourself postmodern design that has enabled undervalued central city neighborhoods to be "reclaimed" by capital through the invasion of young professionals seeking to establish a distinctive lifestyle and habitus (Jager, 1989; Mills, 1988; Smith, 1987; Zukin, 1988). While historic preservation has had little direct effect on the value of adjacent land or buildings (Gale, 1989), designated buildings and districts have been important components of the avant garde *mise-en-scène*, part of a diorama assembled from "real" places with "real" buildings and "real" people. This "reality" is, of course, one of the first victims of the socio-spatial dialectic that accompanies gentrification. "Real" people are displaced, "real" buildings are remodelled, and "real" places are transmogrified into isolated, sanitized enclaves of urbane materialism.

In Washington, these enclaves include parts of Georgetown and Old Town Alexandria (both the object of gentrification for more than 50 years), together with a broad crescent of neighborhoods that encircle the CBD to the north. They encompass a broad spectrum of landscapes that vary according to the stage of gentrification. In the mature gentrified "Money and Brains" neighborhoods of Georgetown, Old Town Alexandria, the Kalorama Triangle area and Capitol Hill, Georgian and Federal residences valued at $300,000 to $600,000 are interspersed with boutiques, flower shops and antique stores. The neighborhoods are introverted: there is little street life, and the character of the area has to be read from the telltale glimpses of interior décor, the correctness of exterior paint and trim and the dominance of expensive European automobiles parked on the street.

At the other extreme, in the vanguard of gentrification in "Bohemian Mix" neighborhoods such as Shaw, Mount Vernon Square and Dupont Circle, it is the reclaimed homes (early twentieth-century rowhouses and 3- or 4-story walk-up apartments) that are interspersed—among dilapidated homes, crack houses, X-rated businesses and second-hand stores. These neighborhoods are extroverted, their vibrancy an important attraction for pioneer gentrifiers. The landscapes of these first-stage gentrifying areas are captured vividly by Michael Dolan (1990, pp. 21–22) in his description of Dupont Circle:

Dupont Circle is where, when the geeky bespectacled kid on the skateboard isn't about to flatten your arches, the mumbly bum is begging you for half your burrito. It's where the quiet comes and goes amid drunks blustering themselves into another dust-up and the Park Service groundsman revving the motor on his rototiller. It's where the skinheads stride by with their boomboxes and their big black boots as primly grim success-dressers ignore the lean tattoo-faced fellow haranguing them for spare change when he isn't participating in mysterious triangular transactions involving tightly folded currency and small, possibly contraband packages. . . .

It's the place where neighborhood denizens and passers-through . . . shop the daily specials at Larimer's grocery, following the European tradition of buying provender a meal at a time. It's the place where you can pick up a balalaika for $69.99—a "glasnost special"—at Ardis Music Center, or climb four flights upstairs and study tai ch'i at Great River Taoist Center, then stroll a few doors north to Food for Thought, the continually endangered eatery, on whose 20-foot bulletin board "Returned Peace Corps Volunteer (Nepal) & George Washington Graduate Student (Non-Smoker, Liberal) Seeks Housing" coexists with "Two People Wanted for Rooms in a Negative Force Steeljaw Trap House With Six Hunks and One Hussy 19–24 (We Like Bourbon, Johnny Cash, and Fungus)". . . .

Refugee Landscapes

Amid the residual enclaves of "Downtown Dixie Style" neighborhoods and the more extensive tracts of "Emergent Minority" neighborhoods in the District are landscapes where drug alleys, crack houses and shooting galleries are embedded among dreary housing projects and apartment blocks, the only refuge for the worst casualties of metropolitan economic and social transformation. While ghettos and slums are by no means new components of urban structure, these landscapes of the excluded are unprecedented in the intensity of combined poverty, violence, despair and isolation. Places that are avoided by everyone (even their own inhabitants), they are characterized by red brick duplexes and triplexes that bear the stigmata of boarded-up windows, bullet-holed doors, yellow police tape and spray-painted graffiti. Lawns and open spaces are strewn with debris; the only people who seem to spend any time out of doors are drug dealers, terminal-stage addicts and thick-legged prostitutes.

Potomac Gardens, 12 blocks from the U.S. Capitol, is a typical example of such refugee landscapes. As described in a *Washington Post* investigation,[17] nearly one third of the 306 households in the complex in 1989 had to rely on public assistance. Only ten families contained both a father and a mother; two were headed by fathers, the rest by single mothers. There were 46 vacant apartments and about twelve apartments within the complex where crack was regularly bought and used. While drug use/non-use creates a critical social cleavage in such settings, the *type* of drug preferred by users provides the basis for finer social differentiations. "[Heroin] junkies despise the "pipeheads" whose entire daily existence is often spent getting high or looking for rocks. Crack smokers, meanwhile, consider themselves superior to heroin junkies, who litter the complex with needles"[18]—and will shoot up anywhere, cooking their dope with rainwater from the ground and using the mirrors of parked cars to locate veins in necks or groins.

The going rate in 1989 for fifth graders paid by dealers to keep watch was $3; and a 12-year-old was widely known as one of the most aggressive drug dealers. "A police source said officers have seen the boy with wads of cash and residents said the boy carries a 9-mm pistol in a shoulder holster."[19] The link between drugs and violence is intimate. Potomac Gardens is part of an eruption of murder and drug dealing that covers much of the eastern half of the District. Law-abiding residents of these areas, if not literally caught in the cross fire, are caught up in a desperately bleak socio-spatial dialectic in which both the built environment and its inhabitants are increasingly isolated and stigmatized. The everyday lifeworld of many residents has already come to accommodate having to watch cars carefully in order to avoid being caught in a drive-by shooting, to lock themselves into their apartments early in the afternoon, to draw shades and blinds, to watch television from positions well away from windows and to stuff towels around doors to keep out crack fumes from the stairwells.

Equally desperate are the landscapes and lifeworlds of the city's literal refugees—the homeless. Estimates of the number of homeless persons in the Washington metropolitan area range from 12,000 to 27,000. Most of the homeless are located in the District, although Fairfax County contains several thousand homeless persons[20] and other suburban counties each contain at least several hundred. Surveys suggest that single men account for only about 35 percent of the homeless; children account for more than half. The "landscapes of despair" (Dear and Wolch, 1987) generated and inhabited by the homeless are particularly visible in the District, where the bundles and carts of homeless persons huddled over Metro grates and under freeways in winter and sprawled over the lawns and benches of public open spaces in summer make for a stark contrast with the architecture of the federal area. Despite the efforts of groups such as the Community for Creative Non-Violence (led by the late Mitch Snyder), the city's record in caring for the homeless is poor. It did have a policy, between 1984 and 1990, of providing unlimited overnight shelter to the homeless, but the shelters themselves have been shown to be characterized by filthy blankets, rats, lice and scabies, broken toilets and streams of running sewage (Gellman, 1989). Vulnerability, hunger and illness are the hallmarks of the lifeworld of the homeless; ephemerality, crowding and squalor are the hallmarks of the micro-landscapes they inhabit. Together, their lifeworlds and landscapes have become emblematic of the dualism of contemporary cities. Their continued existence, meanwhile, attests to the vicious exclusion that is the corollary of the hedonistic materialism of the postmodern city.

The Rhetoric of Postmodern Landscapes

This last point brings as to the important question of the meaning of new landscape elements and their role in legitimizing and reproducing the social order. Duncan (1990) refers to the "rhetoric" of landscapes in discussing the mechanisms by which signification takes place within the built environment. He suggests that "By becoming part of the everyday, the taken-for-granted, the objective and the natural, the landscape masks the artifice and ideological nature of its form and content. Its history as a social construction is unexamined. It is, therefore, as unwittingly read as it is unwittingly written" (p. 19). Change in urban morphology occurs relatively slowly, particularly within the contemporary context of rapid technological change and time-space compression. The emergence of packaged, restored and refugee landscapes has therefore been almost completely unnoticed, while their significance in forming the basis of a new socio-spatial dialectic has been virtually unexplored.

Notes

1. Altogether, more than 130 foreign-owned companies have selected Washington as the headquarters of their U.S. operations, about five times the 1980 number. Together these companies employ about 16,000 people (*Washington Post,* March 7, 1990, p. C1)
2. Based on data from the Greater Washington Research Center.
3. As reported by *Inc.* magazine. See J. Case, The most entrepreneurial cities in America, *Inc.,* March 1990, 41–48.
4. With an income at least five times the poverty threshold in 1988.
5. In the offices of Skadden, Arps, Slate, Meagher and Flam and Fried Frank, Harris Shriver and Jacobson. See Van Dyne (1989).
6. The executive directors of the American Medical Association, the Motion Picture Association of America, the National Cable Television Association and the Edison Electric Institute.
7. Claritas Corporation, Alexandria, Virginia; cited in Van Dyne (1989).
8. *Washington Post,* February 11, p. E1.
9. Cited in Van Dyne, 1989, p. 248
10. The Puzzle of DC's Deadly Distinction, *Washington Post,* October 30, 1989; pp. A8–9.
11. Amid Endless Killings . . . , *Washington Post,* January 22, 1990, pp. E1, E7.
12. Drug War Results 'Spotty,' *Washington Post,* April 14, 1990, p. A1.
13. Including multi-use developments.
14. Bounded on the west by 15th Street, on the north by New York Avenue and H Street, on the east by 9th Street and on the south by E Street and Pennsylvania Avenue.
15. Data from the Urban Land Institute Project Data Base, 1990
16. The essential features of these communities are: 'a definable boundary; a consistent, but not necessarily uniform, character, overall control during the development process by a single development entity; private ownership of recreational amenities; and enforcement of covenants, conditions and restrictions by a master community association' (Suchman, 1990, p. 35).
17. L. Duke and D. M. Price, A Microcosm of Despair in DC, *Washington Post,* April 2, 1989, pp. Al, A27–8.
18. *Ibid.,* p. A27.
19. *Ibid.,* p. A27.
20. These include many working poor who cannot afford the rents in the area and are forced to camp in local parks such as Burke Lake Park and Lake Fairfax Park.

References

Boyer, C. 1990 The return of the aesthetic to city planning, pp. 93–112 in D. Crow (ed.), *Philosophical Streets.* Washington, DC: Maisonnueve Press.
Crow, D. 1990 *Philosophical Streets.* Washington, DC: Maisonnueve Press.
Dear, M. and Wolch, J. 1987 *Landscapes of Despair.* Princeton: Princeton University Press.

Dolan, M. 1990 A short history of a very round place, *Washington Post* Magazine, September 2, 1990, 18–39.

Duncan J. A. 1990 *The City as Text*. Cambridge: Cambridge University Press.

Ehrenreich, B. 1989 *Fear of Falling*. New York: Pantheon.

Gale, D. 1987 *Washington, DC: Inner City Revitalization and Minority Suburbanization*. Philadelphia: Temple University Press.

Gale, D. 1989 The Impact of Historic District Designation in Washington, DC. Occasional Paper #6, Department of Urban & Regional Planning, George Washington University, Washington, DC.

Garreau, J. 1991 *Edge Cities*. New York: Doubleday.

Gellman, B. 1989 D.C. Ordered to Speed Changes on Shelters. *Washington Post,* January 8, 1989, Al–A19.

Gleye, P. H. 1988 With heritage so fragile: A critique of the tax credit program for historic building rehabilitation, *Journal of the American Planning Association*, 54, 428–88.

Goldberger, P. 1990 After Opulence, a new 'Lite' Architecture, *New York Times*, May 20, 1990, Section 2, pp. 1, 38.

Granat, D. and Conlin, J. 1990 The Sky is Falling? *Washingtonian*, 25, 7, 88–96.

Harvey, D. W. 1989 *The Condition of Postmodernity*, Oxford: Blackwell.

Jager, M. 1989 Class definition and the aesthetics of gentrification: Victoriana in Melbourne, pp. 78–91 in N. Smith and P. Williams (eds.), *Gentrification of the City*. Boston: Allen and Unwin.

Jencks, C. 1977 *The Language of Post-modern Architecture*. New York: Rizzoli.

Jencks, C. 1986 *What is Postmodernism?* New York: St Martin's Press.

Knox, P. L. 1987 The social production of the built environment: Architects, architecture and the post-Modern city, *Progress in Human Geography*, 11, 354–78.

Knox, P. L. 1991 The Restless Urban Landscape: Economic and Socio-Cultural Change and the Transformation of Washington, D.C., Annals, *Association of American Geographers*, 81, 181–209.

Listokin, D. 1989 Landmark designation: An emerging form of land use control, Paper presented to annual meeting of the Association of Collegiate Schools of Planning, Portland, Oregon.

Mills, C. A. 1988 Life on the upslope: The postmodern landscape of gentrification, *Society and Space*, 6, 169–89.

Parham, L. 1990 Washington, DC, *National Real Estate Investor*, 32, 6, W1–W16.

Punter, J. 1988 Post-Modernism: A definition, *Planning Practice and Research*, 4, 22–8.

Smith, N. 1987 Of yuppies and housing: gentrification, social restructuring, and the urban dream, *Society and Space*, 5, 151–72.

Suchman, D. R. 1990 Housing and community development. In D. Schwanke (ed.), *Development Trends 1989*. Washington, D.C.: Urban Land Institute, 28–37.

Urban Land Institute 1989 *Mixed-Use Development Handbook*. Washington, D.C.: Urban Land Institute.

Van Dyne, L. 1989 Money fever, *The Washingtonian*, October 141–5, 239–56.

Waldrop, J. 1990 Shades of black, *American Demographics*, 129, 30–33.

Weiss, M. 1988a *The Clustering of America*. New York: Harper and Row.

Weiss, M. 1988b What your address says about you, *Washingtonian*, December, 158–61, 254-60.

Weissman, E. 1990 The facts of life, *Regardie's*, February, 164–74.

Zukin, S. 1988 *Loft Living, Culture and Capital in Urban Change*. New York: Radius Books.

22

The New Urban Economy

The Intersection of Global Processes and Place

Saskai Sassen

The Formation of a New Production Complex

According to standard conceptions about information industries, the rapid growth and disproportionate concentration of many of the producer services in central cities should not have happened. This is especially so for advanced corporate services, because they are thoroughly embedded in the most advanced information technologies; they would seem to have locational options that bypass the high costs and congestion typical of major cities. But cities offer agglomeration economies and highly innovative environments. Some of these services are produced in-house by firms, but a large share are bought from specialized service firms. The growing complexity, diversity, and specialization of the services required makes it more efficient to buy there from specialized firms rather than hiring in-house professionals. The growing demand for these services has made possible the economic viability of a freestanding specialized service sector.

A production process takes place in these services that benefits from proximity to other specialized services. This is especially the case in the leading and most innovative sectors of these industries. Complexity and innovation often require multiple highly specialized inputs from several industries. The production of a financial instrument, for example, requires inputs from accounting, advertising, legal services, economic consulting, public relations, design, and printing. In this regard, these are highly networked firms. These particular characteristics of production explain the centralization of management and servicing functions that has fueled the economic boom in major cities beginning in the mid-1980s. The commonly heard explanation that high-level professionals require face-to-face interactions needs to be refined in several ways. Producer services, unlike other types of services, are not necessarily dependent on spatial proximity to buyers—that is, firms served. Rather, economies occur in such specialized firms when they locate close to others that produce key inputs or whose proximity makes possible joint production of certain service offerings. The accounting firm can service its clients at a distance, but the nature of its service depends on proximity to specialists, lawyers, and programmers. Moreover, concentration arises out of the needs and expectations of the people likely to be employed in these new high-skill jobs who tend to be attracted to the amenities and lifestyles that large urban centers can offer. Frequently, what is thought of as face-to-face communication is actually a production process that requires multiple simultaneous inputs and feedbacks. At the current stage of technical development, having immediate and simultaneous access to the pertinent experts is still the most effective way to operate, especially when dealing with a highly complex product.

Furthermore, time replaces weight in these sectors as a force for agglomeration. In the past, the pressure of the weight of inputs from iron ore to unprocessed agricultural products was a major constraint pushing toward agglomeration in sites where the heaviest inputs were located. Today, the acceleration of economic transactions and the premium put on time have created new forces for agglomeration; that is, if there were no need to hurry, the client could conceivably make use of a widely dispersed array of cooperating specialized firms. And this is often the case in routine operations. Where time is of the essence, however, as it is today in many of the leading sectors of these industries, the benefits of agglomeration are still extremely high—to the point where it is not simply a cost advantage but an indispensable arrangement. Central here has been the general acceleration of all transactions, especially in finance, where minutes and seconds count, in the stock markets, the foreign currency markets, the futures markets, and so on.

It is just this combination of constraints that has promoted the formation of a producer services complex in all major cities. This producer services complex is intimately connected to the world of corporate headquarters; they are often thought of as forming a joint headquarters-corporate services complex. But in the analysis developed in this [reading], we need to distinguish the two. Although it is true that headquarters still tend to be disproportionately concentrated in cities, many have moved out over the last two decades. Headquarters can indeed locate outside cities, but they need a producer services *complex* somewhere to buy or contract for the needed specialized services and financing. Headquarters of firms with very high overseas activity or in highly innovative and complex lines of business still tend to locate in major cities. In brief, firms in more routinized lines of activity, with predominantly regional or national markets, appear to be increasingly free to move or install their headquarters outside cities. Firms in highly competitive and innovative lines of activity and/or with a strong world market orientation appear to benefit from being located at the center of major international business centers, no matter how high the costs.

Both types of firms, however, need a corporate services sector complex to be located somewhere. Where this complex is located is probably becoming increasingly unimportant from the perspective of many, though not all, headquarters. However, from the perspective of producer services firms, such a specialized complex is most likely to be in a city, rather than, for example, in a suburban office park. The latter will be the site for producer services firms but not for a services complex. And only such a complex is capable of handling the most advanced and complicated corporate needs.

These issues are examined in the next two sections. The first discusses how the spatial dispersal of economic activities engenders an increased demand for specialized services; the transnational corporation is one of the major agents in this process. The second section examines whether and, if so, under what conditions corporate headquarters need cities.

The Servicing of Transnational Corporations

The sharp rise in the use of producer services has also been fed by the territorial dispersal of multi-establishment firms, whether at the regional, national, or global level. Firms operating many plants, offices, and service outlets must coordinate planning, internal administration and distribution, marketing, and other central headquarters activities. As large corporations move into the production and sale of final consumer services, a wide range of activities previously performed by freestanding consumer service firms are shifted to the central headquarters of the new corporate owners. Regional, national, or global chains of motels, food outlets, and flower shops require vast centralized administrative and servicing structures. A parallel pattern of expansion of central high-level planning and control operations takes place in governments, brought about partly by the technical developments that make this expansion possible and partly by the growing complexity of regulatory and administrative tasks.

Formally, the development of the modern corporation and its massive participation in world markets and foreign countries has made planning, internal administration, product development, and research increasingly important and complex. Diversification of product lines, mergers, and transnationalization of economic activities all require highly specialized skills. A firm with a multiplicity of geographically dispersed manufacturing plants contributes to the development of new types of planning in production and distribution surrounding the firm. The development of multisite manufacturing, service, and banking has created an expanded demand for a wide range of specialized service activities to manage and control global networks of factories, service outlets, and branch offices. Although to some extent these activities can be carried out in-house, a large share is not. High levels of specialization, the possibility of externalizing the production of some of these services, and the growing demand by large and small firms and by governments are all conditions that have both resulted from and made possible the development of a market for freestanding service firms that produce components for what might be called global control capability.

This in turn means that small firms can buy components of that capability, such as management consulting or international legal advice, and so can firms and governments from anywhere in the world. This accessibility contributes to the formation of marketplaces for such services in major cities. In brief, although the large corporation is undoubtedly a key agent inducing the development of this capability and is its prime beneficiary, it is not the sole user. . . .

Corporate Headquarters and Cities

It is very common in the general literature and in some more scholarly accounts to use the concentration of major headquarters as an indication of a city's status as an international business center. The loss of these types of headquarters is then interpreted as a decline in a city's status. In fact, using such headquarters concentration as an index is increasingly a problematic measure, given the way in which corporations are classified and the locational options telecommunications offers corporations.

A number of variables determine which headquarters concentrate in major international financial and business centers. First, how we measure or simply count headquarters makes a difference. Frequently, the key measure is the size of the firm in terms of employment and overall revenue. Using this measure, some of the largest firms in the world are still manufacturing firms, and many of these have their main headquarters in proximity to their major factory complex, which is unlikely to be in a large city because of space constraints. Such firms *are* likely, however, to have secondary headquarters for highly specialized functions in major cities. Furthermore, many manufacturing firms are oriented to the national market and do not need to be located in a city's national business center. Thus, the much-publicized departure of major headquarters from New York City in the 1960s and 1970s involved these types of firms. If we look at the Fortune 500 list of the largest U.S. firms, we will see that many have left New York City and other large cities. If, however, instead of size we measure share of total firm revenue coming from international sales, a large number of firms that are not on the Fortune 500 list come into play. In the case of New York, for example, the results change dramatically: In 1990, 40% of U.S. firms with half their revenue from international sales have their headquarters in New York City.

Second, the nature of the urban system in a country is a factor in the geographic distribution of headquarters. Sharp urban primacy will tend to entail a disproportionate concentration of headquarters no matter what measure one uses. Third, different economic histories and business traditions may combine to produce different results.

Finally, headquarters concentration may be linked to a specific economic phase. For instance, unlike New York's loss of top *Fortune* 500 headquarters, Tokyo has gained these types of headquarters. Osaka and Nagoya, the two other major economic centers in Japan, lost headquarters to Tokyo. This change seems to be linked to the increasing internationalization of the Japanese economy and the corresponding increase in central command and servicing functions in Tokyo, Japan's major international business center. In the case of Japan, extensive government regulation over the economy is an added factor contributing to headquarters location in Tokyo because all international activities have to go through various government approvals.

In brief, understanding the meaning of headquarters concentration requires differentiation along the variables just described. Although headquarters are still disproportionately concentrated in major cities, the patterns becoming evident in the mid-1980s do represent a change.

The discussion about producer services, the producer services complex, and the locational patterns of headquarters point to two significant developments over the last 10 to 15 years. One is the growing service intensity in the organization of the economy, and the other, the emergence of a producer services complex that, although strongly geared toward the corporate sector, is far more likely to remain concentrated in urban centers than are the headquarters it serves.

The subject of the rise of the producer services complex inevitably brings up the financial and real estate crisis of the late 1980s and early 1990s, since so much of the highly speculative character of the 1980s was engineered by financial, legal, accounting, and other kindred experts in the major international business centers.

Impact of the Late 1980s Financial Crisis on Global City Functions: The Case of New York City

The high level of speculation and profitability that fed growth in the 1980s was clearly unsustainable. The late 1980s financial crisis raises two possibilities. One is that it represents a true crisis of an economic system; the other, that it is instead a sharp readjustment to more sustainable levels of speculation and profitability. New York was the first of the major international financial centers to experience massive losses. Its post-1987 evolution may provide some useful insights into the interaction between crisis and readjustment in the dominant sector.

Employment in banking in the city fell from 169,000 in 1989 to 157,000 in 1991. Most of this loss (more than 10,000 jobs) was in domestic banking. It should also be noted that some of these losses were the result of the massive restructuring within the industry, including mergers among large domestic banks.

In the securities industry, an area that suffered some of the sharpest job losses after the 1987 stock market crisis, New York City remains strong. Ten years later, New York City housed 11 of the world's 25 largest security firms and accounted for 79% of the combined assets of these firms. City firms and their overseas affiliates acted as advisers for almost 80% of the value of all international mergers and acquisitions at the height of the financial boom in the mid-1980s. They remained strong in the financial boom of the mid-1990s. Because the securities industry is almost completely export oriented, it may well be less sensitive to crises in the U.S. economy and in New York City specifically.

Even after the financial crisis of 1997–98, New York City continues to function as an important international center and continues to be dominated by financial and related industries. According to many analysts, the 1987 crisis was a much-needed adjustment to the excesses of the 1980s. The 1997–98 crisis had far less of an impact on New York City (and London) than did the 1987 crisis. Within the United States, New York City remains the banking capital of the country, leading in total assets, number of banks, and volume in various markets (currency, options trading, merchant banking). Worldwide, it is the leading financial center along with London.

Furthermore, foreign banking is a growth sector in New York City and may well be a key factor in the continuing role of the city as a leading financial center for the world. So even as Japanese and European banks were surpassing U.S. banks in size, they had offices in New York City. Indeed, in 1990, New York City surpassed London in its number of international bank offices. By the end of the 1990s, London and New York City are the leading banking and financial centers in the world. Notwithstanding reductions in the domestic banking industry and major crises in several industry branches, New York remains truly a platform for international operations.

What emerges from these developments is that New York City may retain its central role as a financial center but with a far greater participation by foreign firms making loans, selling financial services, and assisting in mergers and acquisitions. The same is the case for London. The job losses and bankruptcies in the securities industry from 1987 pointed to the possibility of a major transformation in the role of Wall Street and other stock markets, most particularly in that large corporations can bypass stock markets to raise investment capital. But drastic change does not spell the end of Wall Street or the city of London. Furthermore, we now know that the actual change proved to be far less drastic and that by the early 1990s Wall Street was once again booming. The 1987 and subsequent crises may prove to be partly a restructuring process from which Wall Street emerged as a transformed market, but without losing an international base and continuing as a provider of the most specialized and complex services.

Conclusion: Cities as Postindustrial Production Sites

A central concern in this [reading] was to look at cities as production sites for the leading service industries of our time and hence to recover the infrastructure of activities, firms, and jobs that is necessary to run the advanced corporate economy. Specialized services are usually understood in terms of specialized outputs rather than the production process involved. A focus on the production process allows us (1) to capture some of the locational characteristics of these service industries and (2) to examine the proposition that there is a producer services complex that, although catering to corporations, has distinct locational and production characteristics. It is this producer services complex more than headquarters of firms generally that benefits and often needs a city location. We see this dynamic for agglomeration operating at different levels of the urban hierarchy, from the global to the regional.

At the global level, a key dynamic explaining the place of major cities in the world economy is that they concentrate the infrastructure and the servicing that produce a capability for global control. The latter is essential if geographic dispersal of economic activity—whether factories, offices, or financial markets—is to take place under continued concentration of ownership and profit appropriation. This capability for global control cannot simply be subsumed under the structural aspects of the globalization of economic activity. It needs to be produced. It is insufficient to posit, or take for granted, the awesome power of large corporations.

By focusing on the production of this capability, we add a neglected dimension to the familiar issue of the power of large corporations. The emphasis shifts to the *practice* of global control: the work of producing and reproducing the organization and management of a global production system and a global marketplace for finance, both under conditions of economic concentration. Power is essential in the organization of the world economy, but so is production: the production of those inputs that constitute the capability for global control and the infrastructure of jobs involved in this production. This allows us to focus on cities and on the urban social order associated with these activities.

23

Societal Changes and Vulnerable Neighborhoods

William Julius Wilson

The disappearance of work in many inner-city neighborhoods is partly related to the nationwide decline in the fortunes of low-skilled workers. Although the growing wage inequality has hurt both low-skilled men and women, the problem of declining employment has been concentrated among low-skilled men. In 1987–89, a low-skilled male worker was jobless eight and a half weeks longer than he would have been in 1967–69. Moreover, the proportion of men who "permanently" dropped out of the labor force was more than twice as high in the late 1980s than it had been in the late 1960s. A precipitous drop in real wages—that is, wages adjusted for inflation—has accompanied the increases in joblessness among low-income workers. If you arrange all wages into five groups according to wage percentile (from highest to lowest), you see that men in the bottom fifth of this income distribution experienced more than a 30 percent drop in real wages between 1970 and 1989.

Even the low-skilled workers who are consistently employed face problems of economic advancement. Job ladders—opportunities for promotion within firms—have eroded, and many less-skilled workers stagnate in dead-end, low-paying positions. This suggests that the chances of improving one's earnings by changing jobs have declined: if jobs inside a firm have become less available to the experienced workers in that firm, they are probably even more difficult for outsiders to obtain.

But there is a paradox here. Despite the increasing economic marginality of low-wage workers, unemployment dipped below 6 percent in 1994 and early 1995, many workers are holding more than one job, and overtime work has reached a record high. Yet while tens of millions of new jobs have been created in the past two decades, men who are well below retirement age are working less than they did two decades ago—and a growing percentage are neither working nor looking for work. The proportion of male workers in the prime of their life (between the ages of 22 and 58) who worked in a given decade full-time, year-round, in at least eight out of ten years declined from 79 percent during the 1970s to 71 percent in the 1980s. While the American economy saw a rapid expansion in high technology and services, especially advanced services, growth in blue-collar factory, transportation, and construction jobs, traditionally held by men, has not kept pace with the rise in the working-age population. These men are working less as a result.

The growth of a nonworking class of prime-age males along with a larger number of those who are often unemployed, who work part-time, or who work in temporary jobs is concentrated among the poorly educated, the school dropouts, and minorities. In the 1970s, two-thirds of prime-age male workers with less than a high school education worked full-time, year-round, in eight out of ten years. During the 1980s, only half did so. Prime-age black men experienced a similar sharp decline. Seven out of ten of all black men worked full-time, year-round, in eight out of ten years in the 1970s, but only half did so in the 1980s. The figures for those who reside in the inner city are obviously even lower.

One study estimates that since 1967 the number of prime-age men who are not in school, not working, and not looking for work for even a single week in a given year has more than doubled for both whites and nonwhites (respectively, from 3.3 to 7.7 percent and 5.8 percent to 13.2 percent). Data from this study also revealed that one-quarter of all male high school dropouts had no official employment at all in 1992. And of those with high school diplomas, one out of ten did not hold a job in 1993, up sharply from 1967 when only one out of fifty reported that he had had no job throughout the year. Among prime-age nonwhite males, the share of those who had no jobs at all in a given year increased from 3 percent to 17 percent during the last quarter century.

These changes are related to the decline of the mass production system in the United States. The traditional American economy featured rapid growth in productivity and living standards. The mass production system benefited from large quantities of cheap natural resources, economies of scale, and processes that generated higher uses of productivity through shifts in market forces from agriculture to manufacturing and that caused improvements in one industry (for example, reduced steel costs) to lead to advancements in others (for example, higher sales and greater economies of scale in the automobile industry). In this system plenty of blue-collar jobs were available to workers with little formal education. Today, most of the new jobs for workers with limited education and experience are in the service sector, which hires relatively more women. One study found that the U.S. created 27 clerical, sales, and service jobs per thousand of working-age population in the 1980s. During the same period, the country lost 16 production, transportation, and laborer jobs per thousand of working-age population. In another study the social scientists Robert Lerman and Martin Rein revealed that from 1989 to 1993, the period covering the economic downturn, social service industries (health, education, and welfare) added almost 3 million jobs, while 1.4 million jobs were lost in all other industries. The expanding job market in social services offset the recession-linked job loss in other industries.

The movement of lower-educated men into the growth sectors of the economy has been slow. For example, "the fraction of men who have moved into so-called pink-collar jobs like practical nursing or clerical work remains negligible." The large concentration of women in the expanding social service sector partly accounts for the striking gender differences in job growth. Unlike lower-educated men, lower-educated women are working more, not less, than in previous years. The employment patterns among lower-educated women, like those with higher education and training, reflect the dramatic expansion of social service industries. Between 1989 and 1993, jobs held by women increased by 1.3 million, while those held by men barely rose at all (by roughly 100,000).

Although the wages of low-skilled women (those with less than twelve years of education) rose slightly in the 1970s, they flattened out in the 1980s, and continued to remain below those of low-skilled men. The wage gap between low-skilled men and women shrank not because of gains made by female workers but mainly because of the decline in real wages for men. The unemployment rates among low-skilled women are slightly lower than those among their male counterparts. However, over the past decade their rates of participation in the labor force have stagnated and have fallen further behind the labor-force-participation rates among more highly educated women, which continue to rise. The unemployment rates among both low-skilled men and women are five times that among their college-educated counterparts.

Among the factors that have contributed to the growing gap in employment and wages between low-skilled and college-educated workers is the increased internationalization of the U.S. economy. As the economists Richard B. Freeman and Lawrence F. Katz point out:

> In the 1980s, trade imbalances implicitly acted to augment the nation's supply of less educated workers, particularly those with less than a high school education. Many production and routine clerical tasks could be more easily transferred abroad than in the past. The increased supply of less educated workers arising from trade deficits accounted for as much as is percent of the increase in college-high school wage differential from the 1970s to the mid-1980s. In contrast, a balanced expansion of international trade, in which growth in exports matches the growth of imports, appears to have fairly neutral effects on relative labor demand. Indeed, balanced growth of trade leads to an upgrading in jobs for workers without college degrees, since export-sector jobs tend to pay higher wages for "comparable" workers than do import-competing jobs.

The lowering of unionization rates, which accompanied the decline in the mass production system, has also contributed to shrinking wages and nonwage compensation for less skilled workers. As the economist Rebecca Blank has pointed out, "unionized workers typically receive not only higher wages, but also more non-wage benefits. As the availability of union jobs has declined for unskilled workers, non-wage benefits have also declined."

Finally, the wage and employment gap between skilled and unskilled workers is growing partly because education and training are considered more important than ever in the new global economy. At the same time that changes in technology are producing new jobs, they are making many others obsolete. The workplace has been revolutionized by technological changes that range from the development of robotics to information highways. While educated workers are benefiting from the pace of technological change, involving the increased use of computer-based technologies and microcomputers, more routine workers face the growing threat of job displacement in certain industries. For example, highly skilled designers, engineers, and operators are needed for the jobs associated with the creation of a new set of computer-operated machine tools; but these same exciting new opportunities eliminate jobs for those trained only for manual, assembly-line work. Also, in certain businesses, advances in word processing have increased the demand for those who not only know how to type but can operate specialized software as well; at the same time, these advances reduce the need for routine typists and secretaries. In the new global economy, highly educated and thoroughly trained men and women are in demand. This may be seen most dramatically in the sharp differences in employment experiences among men. Unlike men with lower education, college-educated men are working more, not less.

The shift in demand has been especially devastating for those low-skilled workers whose incorporation into the mainstream economy has been marginal or recent. Even before the economic restructuring of the nation's economy, low-skilled African-Americans were at the end of the employment queue. Their economic situation has been further weakened because they tend to reside in communities that not only have higher jobless rates and lower employment growth but lack access to areas of higher employment and employment growth as well. Moreover, . . . they are far more likely than other ethnic and racial groups to face negative employer attitudes.

Of the changes in the economy that have adversely affected low-skilled African-American workers, perhaps the most significant have been those in the manufacturing sector. One study revealed that in the 1970s "up to half of the huge employment declines for less-educated blacks might be explained by industrial shifts away from manufacturing toward other sectors." Another study reported that since the 1960s "deindustrialization" and the "erosion in job opportunities especially in the Midwest and Northeast . . . bear responsibility for the growth of the ranks of the 'truly disadvantaged.'" The manufacturing losses in some northern cities have been staggering. In the twenty-year period from 1967 to 1987, Philadelphia lost 64 percent of its manufacturing jobs; Chicago lost 60 percent; New York City, 58 percent; Detroit, 51 percent. In absolute numbers, these percentages represent the loss of 160,000 jobs in Philadelphia, 326,000 in Chicago, 520,000—over half a million—in New York, and 108,000 in Detroit.

Another study examined the effects of economic restructuring in the 1980s by highlighting the changes in both the variety and the quality of blue-collar employment in general. Jobs were grouped into a small number of relatively homogeneous clusters on the basis of job quality (which was measured in terms of earnings, benefits, union protection, and involuntary part-time employment). The authors found that both the relative earnings and employment rates among unskilled black workers were lower for two reasons: traditional jobs that provide a living wage (high-wage blue-collar cluster, of which roughly 50 percent were manufacturing jobs) declined, as did the quality of secondary jobs on which they increasingly had to rely, leading to lower relative earnings for the remaining workers in the labor market. As employment prospects worsened, rising proportions of low-skilled black workers dropped out of the legitimate labor market.

Data from the Chicago Urban Poverty and Family Life Survey show that efforts by out-of-school inner-city black men to obtain blue-collar jobs in the industries in which their fathers had been employed have been hampered by industrial restructuring. "The most common occupation reported by respondents at ages 19 to 28 changed from operative and assembler jobs among the oldest cohorts to service jobs (waiters and janitors) among the youngest cohort." Fifty-seven percent of Chicago's employed inner-city black fathers (aged 15 and over and without undergraduate degrees) who were born between 1950 and 1955 worked in manufacturing and construction industries in 1974. By 1987, industrial employment in this group had fallen to 31 percent. Of those born between 1956 and 1960, 52 percent worked in these industries as late as 1978. But again, by 1987 industrial employment in this group fell to 28 percent. No other male ethnic group in the inner city experienced such an overall precipitous drop in manufacturing employment. These employment changes have accompanied the loss of traditional manufacturing and other blue-collar jobs in Chicago. As a result, young black males have turned increasingly to the low-wage service sector and unskilled laboring jobs for employment, or have gone jobless. The strongly held U.S. cultural and economic belief that the son will do at least as well as the father in the labor market does not apply to many young inner-city males.

If industrial restructuring has hurt inner-city black workers in Chicago, it has had serious consequences for African-Americans across the nation. "As late as the 1968–70 period," states John Kasarda, "more than 70 percent of all blacks working in metropolitan areas held blue-collar jobs at the same time that more than 50 percent of all metropolitan workers held white-collar jobs. Moreover, of the large numbers of urban blacks classified as blue-collar workers during the late 1960s, more than half were employed in goods-producing industries."

The number of employed black males ages 20 to 29 working in manufacturing industries fell dramatically between 1973 and 1987 (from three of every eight to one in five). Meanwhile, the share of employed young black men in the retail trade and service jobs rose sharply during that period (from 17 to almost 27 percent and from 10 to nearly 21 percent, respectively). And this shift in opportunities was not without economic consequences: in 1987, the average annual earnings of 20-to-29-year-old males who held jobs in the retail trade and service sectors were 25 to 30 percent less than those of males employed in manufacturing sectors. This dramatic loss in earnings potential affects every male employed in the service sector regardless of color.

The structural shifts in the distribution of industrial job opportunities are not the only reason for the increasing joblessness and declining earnings among young black male workers. There have also been important changes in the patterns of occupational staffing within firms and industries, including those in manufacturing. These changes have primarily benefited those with more formal education. Substantial numbers of new professional, technical, and managerial positions have been created. However, such jobs require at least some years of post-secondary education. Young high school dropouts and even high school graduates "have faced a dwindling supply of career jobs offering the real earnings opportunities available to them in the 1960s and early 1970s."

In certain urban areas the prospects for employment among workers with little education have fallen sharply. John Kasarda examined employment changes in selected urban centers and found that major northern cities had consistent employment losses in industries with low mean levels of employee education and employment gains in industries in which the workers had higher levels of education. For example, during the 1980s New York City lost 135,000 jobs in industries in which the workers averaged less than twelve years of education, and gained almost 300,000 jobs in industries in which workers had thirteen or more years of education. Philadelphia lost 55,000 jobs in the low-education industries and gained 40,000 jobs for workers with high school plus at least some college. Baltimore and Boston also experienced substantial losses in industries employing low-education workers and major gains in industries employing more educated workers.

Kasarda's study also documents the growing importance of education in nine "economically transforming" northern cities and in Los Angeles. The jobs traditionally held by high school dropouts declined in all nine northern cities between 1980 and 1990, while those held by college graduates increased. "Los Angeles, which experienced a 50 percent increase in city [urban] jobs held by college graduates, also experienced a 15 percent growth in jobs held by those who have not completed high school. The latter no doubt reflects the large immigration of Hispanic workers and other minorities" who have little education.

To some degree, these changes reflect overall improvements in educational attainment within the urban labor force. However, they "were not nearly as great as the concurrent upward shifts in the education of city jobholders." Moreover, much of the increase in the "college-educated" jobs in each city reflected the educational status of suburban commuters, while much of the decrease in the "less than high school" category reflected the job losses of city residents, few of whom could aspire to a four-year postsecondary degree.

As pointed out earlier, most of the new jobs for workers with limited training and education are in the service sector and are disproportionately held by women. This is even more true for those who work in social services, which include the industries of health, education, and welfare. As we have seen, within central cities the number of jobs for less educated workers has declined precipitously. However, many workers stayed afloat thanks to jobs in the expanding social service sector, especially black women with less than a high school degree. Robert Lerman and Martin Rein report that among all women workers, the proportion employed in social services climbed between 1979 and 1993 (from 28 to 33 percent). The health and education industries absorbed nearly all of this increase. Of the 54 million female workers in 1993, almost one-third were employed in social service industries. Social services tend to feature a more highly educated workforce. Only 20 percent of all female workers with less than a high school degree were employed in social services in 1993. (The figure for comparable males is even less. Only 4 percent of employed less educated men held social service jobs in 1993.) Nonetheless, the proportion of less educated female workers in social services is up notably from 1989.

Indeed, despite the relatively higher educational level of social service workers, the research of Lerman and Rein reveals that 37 percent of employed less educated black women in central cities worked in social services in 1993, largely in jobs in hospitals, elementary schools, nursing care, and child care. In central cities in the largest metropolitan areas, the fraction of low-educated African-American female workers in social services sharply increased from 30.5 percent in 1979 to 40.5 percent in 1993. Given the overall decline of jobs for less educated central cityworkers, the opportunity for employment in the social service industries prevented many inner-city workers from joining the growing ranks of the jobless. Less educated black female workers depend heavily on social service employment. Even a small number of less educated black males were able to find jobs in social services. Although only 4 percent of less educated employed males worked in social services in 1993, 12 percent of less educated employed black men in the central cities of large metropolitan areas held social service jobs. Without the growth of social service employment, the rates of inner-city joblessness would have risen beyond their already unprecedented high levels.

The demand in the labor market has shifted toward higher-educated workers in various industries and occupations. The changing occupational and industrial mix is associated with increases in the rates of joblessness (unemployment and "dropping out" of, or nonparticipation in, the labor force) and decreases in the relative wages of disadvantaged urban workers.

The factors contributing to the relative decline in the economic status of disadvantaged workers are not solely due to those on the demand side, such as economic restructuring. The growing wage differential in the 1980s is also a function of two supply-side factors—the decline in the relative supply of college graduates and the influx of poor immigrants. "In the 1970s the relative supply of college graduates grew rapidly, the result of the baby boomers who enrolled in college in the late 1960s and early 1970s in response to the high rewards for college degrees and the fear of being drafted for the Vietnam War," state Freeman and Katz. "The growth in supply overwhelmed the increase in demand for more educated workers, and the returns to college diminished." In the 1980s, the returns for college increased because of declining growth in the relative supply of college graduates.

Also in the 1980s, a large number of immigrants with little formal education arrived in the United States from developing countries, and affected the wages of poorly educated native workers, especially those who had dropped out of high school. According to one estimate, nearly one-third of the decline in earnings for male high school dropouts compared with other workers in the 1980s may be linked to immigration. However, although the increase in immigration contributed to the growing inequality, it is only one of several factors depressing the wages of low-skilled workers. As Sheldon Danziger and Peter Gottschalk point out in this connection, "Immigrants are heavily concentrated in a few states, such as California and Florida . . . inequality did rise in these states, but it rose in most areas, even those with very few immigrants."

Joblessness and declining wages are also related to the recent growth in ghetto poverty. The most dramatic increases in ghetto poverty occurred between 1970 and 1980, and they were mostly confined to the large industrial metropolises of the Northeast and Midwest, regions that experienced massive industrial restructuring and loss of blue-collar jobs during that decade. But the rise in ghetto poverty was not the only problem. Industrial restructuring had devastating effects on the social organization of many inner-city neighborhoods in these regions. The fate of the West Side black community of North Lawndale vividly exemplifies the cumulative process of economic and social dislocation that has swept through Chicago's inner city.

After more than a quarter century of continuous deterioration, North Lawndale resembles a war zone. Since 1960, nearly half of its housing stock has disappeared; the remaining units are mostly run down or dilapidated. Two large factories anchored the economy of this West Side neighborhood in its good days—the Hawthorne plant of Western Electric, which employed over 43,000 workers; and an International Harvester plant with 14,000 workers. The world headquarters for Sears, Roebuck and Company was located there, providing another 10,000 jobs. The neighborhood also had a Copenhagen snuff plant, a Sunbeam factory, and a Zenith factory, a Dell Farm food market, an Alden's catalog store, and a U.S. Post Office bulk station. But conditions rapidly changed. Harvester closed its doors in the late 1960s. Sears moved most of its offices to the Loop in downtown Chicago in 1973; a catalog distribution center with a workforce of 3,000 initially remained in the neighborhood but was relocated outside of the state of Illinois in 1987. The Hawthorne plant gradually phased out its operations and finally shut down in 1984.

The departure of the big plants triggered the demise or exodus of the smaller stores, the banks, and other businesses that relied on the wages paid by the large employers. "To make matters worse, scores of stores were forced out of business or pushed out of the neighborhoods by insurance companies in the wake of the 1968 riots that swept through Chicago's West Side after the assassination of Dr. Martin Luther King, Jr. Others were simply burned or abandoned. It has been estimated that the community lost 75 percent of its business establishments from 1960 to 1970 alone." In 1986, North Lawndale, with a population of over 66,000, had only one bank and one supermarket; but it was also home to forty-eight state lottery agents, fifty currency exchanges, and ninety-nine licensed liquor stores and bars.

The impact of industrial restructuring on inner-city employment is clearly apparent to urban blacks. The UPFLS survey posed the following question: "Over the past five or ten years, how many friends of yours have lost their jobs because the place where they worked shut down—would you say none, a few, some, or most?" Only 26 percent of the black residents in our sample reported that none of their friends had lost jobs because their workplace shut down. Indeed, both black men and black women were more likely to report that their friends had lost jobs because of plant closings than were the Mexicans and the other ethnic groups in our study. Moreover, nearly half of the employed black fathers and mothers in the UPFLS survey stated that they considered themselves to be at high risk of losing their jobs because of plant shutdowns. Significantly fewer Hispanic and white parents felt this way.

Some of the inner-city neighborhoods have experienced more visible job losses than others. But residents of the inner city are keenly aware of the rapid depletion of job opportunities. A 33-year-old unmarried black male of North Lawndale who is employed as a clerical worker stated: "Because of the way the economy is structured, we're losing more jobs. Chicago is losing jobs by the thousands. There just aren't any starting companies here and it's harder to find a job compared to what it was years ago."

A similar view was expressed by a 41-year-old black female, also from North Lawndale, who works as a nurse's aide:

> Chicago is really full of peoples. Everybody can't get a good job. They don't have enough good jobs to provide for everybody. I don't think they have enough jobs period. . . . And all the factories and the places, they closed up and moved out of the city and stuff like that, you know. I guess it's one of the reasons they haven't got too many jobs now, 'cause a lot of the jobs now, factories and business, they're done moved out. So that way it's less jobs for lot of peoples.

Respondents from other neighborhoods also reported on the impact of industrial restructuring. According to a 33-year-old South Side janitor:

> The machines are putting a lot of people out of jobs. I worked for *Time* magazine for seven years on a videograph printer and they come along with the Abedic printer, it cost them half a million dollars: they did what we did in half the time, eliminated two shifts.

"Jobs were plentiful in the past," stated a 29-year-old unemployed black male who lives in one of the poorest neighborhoods on the South Side.

> You could walk out of the house and get a job. Maybe not what you want but you could get a job. Now, you can't find anything. A lot of people in this neighborhood, they want to work but they can't get work. A few, but a very few, they just don't want to work. The majority they want to work but they can't find work.

Finally, a 41-year-old hospital worker from another impoverished South Side neighborhood associated declining employment opportunities with decreasing skill levels:

> Well, most of the jobs have moved out of Chicago. Factory jobs have moved out. There are no jobs here. Not like it was 20, 30 years ago. And people aren't skilled

enough for the jobs that are here. You don't have enough skilled and educated people to fill them.

The increasing suburbanization of employment has accompanied industrial re-structuring and has further exacerbated the problems of inner-city joblessness and restricted access to jobs. "Metropolitan areas captured nearly 90 percent of the nation's employment growth; much of this growth occurred in booming 'edge cities' at the metropolitan periphery. By 1990, many of these 'edge cities' had more office space and retail sales than the metropolitan downtowns." Over the last two decades, 60 percent of the new jobs created in the Chicago metropolitan area have been located in the northwest suburbs of Cook and Du Page counties. African-Americans constitute less than 2 percent of the population in these areas.

In *The Truly Disadvantaged*, I maintained that one result of these changes for many urban blacks has been a growing mismatch between the suburban location of employment and minorities' residence in the inner city. Although studies based on data collected before 1970 showed no consistent or convincing effects on black employment as a consequence of this spatial mismatch, the employment of inner-city blacks relative to suburban blacks has clearly deteriorated since then. Recent research, conducted mainly by urban and labor economists, strongly shows that the decentralization of employment is continuing and that employment in manu-facturing, most of which is already suburbanized, has decreased in central cities, particularly in the Northeast and Midwest. As Farrell Bloch, an economic and sta-tistical consultant, points out, "Not only has the number of manufacturing jobs been decreasing, but new plants now tend to locate in the suburbs to take advan-tage of cheap land, access to highways, and low crime rates; in addition, businesses shun urban locations to avoid buying land from several different owners, paying high demolition costs for old buildings, and arranging parking for employees and customers."

Blacks living in central cities have less access to employment, as measured by the ratio of jobs to people and the average travel time to and from work, than do central-city whites. Moreover, unlike most other groups of workers across the urban/suburban divide, less educated central-city blacks receive lower wages than suburban blacks who have similar levels of education. And the decline in earnings of central-city blacks is related to the decentralization of employment—that is, the movement of jobs from the cities to the suburbs—in metropolitan areas.

But are the differences in employment between city and suburban blacks mainly the result of changes in the location of jobs? It is possible that in recent years the migration of blacks to the suburbs has be come much more selective than in earlier years, so much so that the changes attributed to job location are actually caused by this selective migration. The pattern of black migration to the suburbs in the 1970s was similar to that of whites during the 1950s and 1960s in the sense that it was concentrated among the better-educated and younger city residents. However, in the 1970s this was even more true for blacks, creating a situation in which the education and income gaps between city and suburban blacks seemed to expand at the same time that the differences between city and suburban whites seemed to contract. Accordingly, if one were to take into account differences in education, family background, and so on, how much of the employment gap between city and suburbs would remain?

This question was addressed in a study of the Gautreaux program in Chicago. The Gautreaux program was created under a 1976 court order resulting from a judicial finding of widespread discrimination in the public housing projects of Chicago. The program has relocated more than 4,000 residents from public housing into subsidized housing in neighborhoods throughout the Greater Chicago area. The design of the program permitted the researchers, James E. Rosenbaum and Susan J. Popkin, to contrast systematically the employment experiences of a group of low-income blacks who had been assigned private apartments in the suburbs with the experiences of a control group with similar characteristics and histories who had been assigned private apartments in the city. Their findings support the spatial mismatch hypothesis. After taking into account the personal characteristics of the respondents (including family background, family circumstances, levels of human capital, motivation, length of time since the respondent first enrolled in the Gautreaux program), Rosenbaum and Popkin found that those who moved to apartments in the suburbs were significantly more likely to have a job after the move than those placed in the city. When asked what makes it easier to obtain employment in the suburbs, nearly all the surburban respondents mentioned the high availability of jobs.

The African-Americans surveyed in the UPFLS clearly recognized a spatial mismatch of jobs. Both black men and black women saw greater job prospects outside the city. For example, only one-third of black fathers from areas with poverty rates of at least 30 percent reported that their best opportunities for employment were to be found in the city. Nearly two-thirds of whites and Puerto Ricans and over half of Mexicans living in similar neighborhoods felt this way. Getting to suburban jobs is especially problematic for the jobless individuals in the UPFLS because only 28 percent have access to an automobile. This rate falls even further to 18 percent for those living in the ghetto areas.

Among two-car middle-class and affluent families, commuting is accepted as a fact of life; but it occurs in a context of safe school environments for children, more available and accessible day care, and higher incomes to support mobile, away-from-home lifestyles. In a multitiered job market that requires substantial resources for participation, most inner-city minorities must rely on public transportation systems that rarely provide easy and quick access to suburban locations. A 32-year-old unemployed South Side welfare mother described the problem this way:

> There's not enough jobs. I thinks Chicago's the only city that does not have a lot of opportunities opening in it. There's not enough factories, there's not enough work. Most all the good jobs are in the suburbs. Sometimes it's hard for the people in the city to get to the suburbs, because everybody don't own a car. Everybody don't drive.

After commenting on the lack of jobs in his area, a 29-year-old unemployed South Side black male continued:

You gotta go out in the suburbs, but I can't get out there. The bus go out there but you don't want to catch the bus out there, going two hours each ways. If you have to be at work at eight that mean you have to leave for work at six, that mean you have to get up at five to be at work at eight. Then when wintertime come you be in trouble.

Another unemployed South Side black male had this to say: "Most of the time . . . the places be too far and you need transportation and I don't have none right now. If I had some I'd probably be able to get one [a job]. If I had a car and went way into the suburbs, 'cause there ain't none in the city." This perception was echoed by an 18-year-old unemployed West Side black male:

> They are most likely hiring in the suburbs. Recently, I think about two years ago, I had a job but they say that I need some transportation and they say that the bus out in the suburbs run at a certain time. So I had to pass that job up because I did not have no transport.

An unemployed unmarried welfare mother of two from the West Side likewise stated:

> Well, I'm goin' to tell you: most jobs, more jobs are in the suburbs. It's where the good jobs and stuff is but you gotta have transportation to get there and it's hard to be gettin' out there in the suburbs. Some people don't know where the suburbs is, some people get lost out there. It is really hard, but some make a way.

One employed factory worker from the West Side who works a night shift described the situation this way:

> From what I, I see, you know, it's hard to find a good job in the inner city 'cause so many people moving, you know, west to the suburbs and out of state. . . . Some people turn jobs down because they don't have no way of getting out there. . . . I just see some people just going to work—and they seem like they the type who just used to—they coming all the way from the city and go on all the way to the suburbs and, you know, you can see 'em all bundled and—catching one bus and the next bus. They just used to doing that.

But the problem is not simply one of transportation and the length of commuting time. There is also the problem of the travel expense and of whether the long trek to the suburbs is actually worth it in terms of the income earned—after all, owning a car creates expenses far beyond the purchase price, including insurance, which is much more costly for city dwellers than it is for suburban motorists. "If you work in the suburbs you gotta have a car," stated an unmarried welfare mother of three children who lives on Chicago's West Side, "then you gotta buy gas. You spending more getting to the suburbs to work, than you is getting paid, so you still ain't getting nowhere."

Indeed, one unemployed 36-year-old black man from the West Side of Chicago actually quit his suburban job because of the transportation problem. "It was more expensive going to work in Naperville, transportation and all, and it wasn't worth it. . . . I was spending more money getting to work than I earned working."

If transportation poses a problem for those who have to commute to work from the inner city to the suburbs, it can also hinder poor ghetto residents' ability to travel to the suburbs just to seek employment. For example, one unemployed man who lives on the South Side had just gone to O'Hare Airport looking for work with no luck. His complaint: "The money I spent yesterday, I coulda kept that in my pocket—I coulda kept that. 'Cause you know I musta spent about $7 or somethin'. I coulda kept that."

Finally, in addition to enduring the search-and-travel costs, inner-city black workers often confront racial harassment when they enter suburban communities. A 38-year-old South Side divorced mother of two children who works as a hotel cashier described the problems experienced by her son and his coworker in one of Chicago's suburbs:

> My son, who works in Carol Stream, an all-white community, they've been stopped by a policeman two or three times asking them why they're in the community. And they're trying to go to work. They want everyone to stay in their own place. That's what society wants. And they followed them all the way to work to make sure. 'Cause it's an all-white neighborhood. But there're no jobs in the black neighborhoods. They got to go way out there to get a job.

These informal observations on the difficulties and cost of travel to suburban employment are consistent with the results of a recent study by the labor economists Harry J. Holzer, Keith R. Ihlandfeldt, and David L. Sjoquist. In addition to finding that the lack of automobile ownership among inner-city blacks contributed significantly to their lower wages and lower rate of employment, these authors also reported that African-Americans "spend more time traveling to work than whites," that "the time cost per mile traveled is . . . significantly higher for blacks," and that the resulting gains are relatively small. Overall, their results suggest that the amount of time and money spent in commuting, when compared with the actual income that accrues to inner-city blacks in low-skill jobs in the suburbs, acts to discourage poor people from seeking employment far from their own neighborhoods. Holzer and his colleagues concluded that it was quite rational for blacks to reject these search-and-travel choices when assessing their position in the job market.

Changes in the industrial and occupational mix, including the removal of jobs from urban centers to suburban corridors, represent external factors that have helped to elevate joblessness among inner-city blacks. But important social and demographic changes within the inner city are also associated with the escalating rates of neighborhood joblessness. . . .

24

The State and the Global City

Notes toward a Conception of Place-Centered Governance

Saskia Sassen

Regulatory Capacities and Space Economies: Preliminary Notes

Current forms of economic transnationalism have a number of characteristics that matter for an examination of questions of governance. Two are particularly important (see Sassen, 1996 for a more extensive discussion). One of these is that many key components of economic globalization today do not strengthen the interstate system, in contrast to the situation during the three decades after World War II. A second one is that the state remains as the ultimate guarantor of the "rights" of global capital, that is, the protection of contracts and property rights.

There follows a brief discussion of each of these in order to set a context for the ensuing examination of global cities and the emergent transnational urban system as potentially significant sites for the implementation of mechanisms for governance and accountability in the global community.

Globalization and the Interstate System

During the Pax Americana, economic internationalization had the effect of strengthening the interstate system. Leading economic sectors, especially manufacturing and raw materials extraction, were subject to international trade regimes that contributed to build the interstate system. Individual states adjusted national economic policies to further this type of international economic system, doubtless often pressured by the hegemonic power of the United States. (Even though already then certain sectors did not fit comfortably under this largely trade-dominated interstate regime: out of their escape emerged the euro-markets and offshore tax havens of the 1960s.)

The breakdown of the Bretton Woods system produced an international governance void rapidly filled by multinationals and global financial markets. This has fed the notion of the shrinking role of the state and the debate about nonstate-centered systems of governance (Jessop 1990; Rosenau 1992; Young 1989; Kooiman and van Vliet 1993; Leftwich 1994). According to some (see Panitch 1996; Mittelman 1996; Drache and Gertler 1991), the neoliberalism of the 1980s has redefined the role of states in national economies and in the interstate system. Further, the structure of the state itself in developed countries has undergone a shift away from those agencies most clearly tied to domestic social forces, as was the case in the United States during the Pax Americana, and toward those closest to the transnational process of consensus formation.

A focus on international finance and corporate services brings to the fore the extent to which the forms of economic globalization evident in the last two decades have not necessarily had the effect of strengthening the interstate system. Further, the ascendance of international finance has produced regulatory voids that lie beyond not only states but also the interstate system. In this regard, an analysis of these industries can help bring to the fore the differences between the role of the state in earlier forms of internationalization and the current globalization of economic activity evident in some (but by no means all) economic sectors.

One way of illustrating this weakened articulation of the growth dynamic of finance and corporate services to the state and interstate system is by examining what we could think of as the new valorization dynamic embedded in the ascendance of these industries—that is, a new set of criteria for valuing or pricing various economic activities and outcomes. . . . We are seeing the formation of an economic complex with properties clearly distinguishing it from other economic complexes in that the articulation of its valorization dynamic with the public economic functions of the state is quite weak compared with Fordist manufacturing, for example.

Guaranteeing the Global Rights of Capital

Even though transnationalism and deregulation have reduced the role of the state in the governance of economic processes, the state remains as the ultimate guarantor of the rights of capital whether national or foreign. Firms operating transnationally want to ensure the functions traditionally exercised by the state in the national realm of the economy, notably guaranteeing property rights and contracts. The state here can be conceived of as representing a technical administrative capacity which cannot be replicated at this time by any other institutional arrangement (Sassen 1996); further, this is a capacity backed by military power.

But this guarantee of the rights of capital is embedded in a certain type of state, a certain conception of the rights of capital, and a certain type of international legal regime: It is largely the state of the most developed and most powerful countries in the world, Western notions of contract and property rights, and a new legal regime aimed at furthering economic globalization.[1]

Deregulation has been widely recognized as a crucial mechanism to facilitate the globalization of various markets and industries because it reduces the role of the state. But deregulation can also be seen as negotiating on the one hand the fact of globalization, and, on the other, the ongoing need for guarantees of contracts and property rights for which the state remains as the guarantor of last instance (Panitch 1996; Sassen 1996; see also Negri 1995). The deregulation of key operations and markets in the financial industry can be seen as negotiation between nation-based legal regimes and the formation of a consensus among a growing number of states about furthering the world economy (Mittelman 1996; Trubek et al. 1993). In other words, it is not simply a matter of a space economy extending beyond a national realm. It also has to do with the formation and legitimation of transnational legal regimes that are operative in national territories. National legal fields are becoming more internationalized in some of the major developed economies and transnational legal regimes become more important and begin to penetrate national fields hitherto closed (e.g., Trubek et al., 1993; Aman, 1995).[2] The state continues to play a crucial role in the production of legality around new forms of economic activity.[3]

Transnational economic processes inevitably interact with systems for the governance of national economies. There are few industries where deregulation and transnationalization have been as important to growth as in international finance and advanced corporate services. What deregulation in finance makes clear is that it has had the effect of partly denationalizing national territory: for example, the International Banking Facilities in the United States can be seen as such an instance. Yet another, more familiar instance, can be found in various forms through which manufacturing production has been internationalized: for example, export-processing zones which fall under special regimes that reduce the obligations of firms to the state, notably regarding taxes and labor legislation (see, e.g., Bonacich et al., 1994; Gereffi 1996; Morales 1994; Mittelman 1996). Insofar as global processes materialize in concrete places, they continue to operate under sovereign regulatory umbrellas, but they do so under new emergent transnational regimes and, often, under circumstances of a denationalizing of national territory.

It is through the formation of such transnational regimes and the denationalizing of national territory that the state guarantees a far broader range of rights of national and foreign capital. These rights are often in addition to those guaranteed through strictly national regimes. In this regard, deregulation and other policies furthering economic globalization cannot simply be considered as an instance of a declining significance of the state. Deregulation is a vehicle through which a growing number of states are furthering economic globalization and guaranteeing the rights of global capital, an essential ingredient of the former. Deregulation and kindred policies constitute the elements of a new legal regime dependent on consensus among states to further globalization.

Elements for New Policy Frameworks

A focus on the space economy of information industries elaborates and specifies the meaning of deregulation insofar as important components of these industries are embedded in particular sites within national territories and others are located in electronic spaces that escape all conventional jurisdictions or borders.

To help situate my particular question here in the broader governance debate let me refer to one of the working argumentations that organize the larger project on which this brief essay is based: A focus on leading information industries in a strategic subnational unit such as the global city illuminates two conditions that are at opposite ends of the governance challenge posed by globalization and are not captured in the more conventional duality of national–global. These two contrasting conditions are placeboundedness and the virtualization of economic space. . . .

Regarding the first, a focus on leading information industries in global cities introduces into the discussion of governance the possibility of capacities for regulation derived from the concentration of significant resources, including fixed capital, in strategic places, resources that are essential for participation in the global economy. The considerable placeboundedness of many of these resources contrasts with the hypermobility of information outputs. The regulatory capacity of the state stands in a different relation to hypermobile outputs than to the infrastructure of facilities, from fiber optic cable served office buildings to specialized workforces, present in global cities.

At the other extreme, the fact that many of these industries operate partly in electronic spaces raises questions of control that derive from key properties of the new information technologies, notably the orders of magnitude in trading volumes made possible by speed and the fact that electronic space is not bound by conventional jurisdictions. Here it is no longer just a question of the capacity of the state to govern these processes, but also of the capacity to do so on the part of the private sector, that is, of the major actors involved in setting up and operating in these electronic markets. Elementary and well-known illustrations of this issue of control are stock market crashes attributed to electronic program trading, and globally implemented decisions to invest or disinvest in a currency, or an emerging market which resemble a sort of worldwide stampede, all facilitated by the fact of global integration and instantaneous execution worldwide. Mexico's recent crisis and its aftermath are an illustration of this; so is the fall of the U.K. bank Barings.

The specific issues raised by these two variables, that is, place-boundedness and speed/virtualization, are quite distinct from those typically raised in the context of the national–global duality. . . . A focus on this duality leads to rather straightforward propositions about the declining significance of the state vis-à-vis global economic actors. This is partly a result of the overarching tendency in economic analyses of globalization and information industries to emphasize certain aspects: industry outputs rather than the production process involved, the capacity for instantaneous transmission around the world rather than the infrastructure necessary for this capacity, the inability of the state to regulate those outputs and that capacity insofar as they extend beyond the nation–state. And all of this is by itself quite correct; but it is a partial account of the implications of globalization for governance.

A focus on key properties of the new information technologies, such as speed, and their implications for questions of governance illuminates the extent to which we may be confronting a whole new configuration, one that cannot be addressed along the lines dominating much of the thinking about governance in a global economy. It is not just a question of coordination and order in a space economy that transcends a single state, but a qualitatively new variable: technologies that produce outcomes which the existing apparatus both private and governmental cannot handle because they are processes embedded in a speed that has made current mechanisms for management and control obsolete. It is impossible to address this subject here in depth. . . .

A focus on place, and particularly the type of place I call global cities, on the other hand, brings to the fore the fact that many of the resources necessary for global economic activities are not hypermobile and could, in principle be brought under effective regulation. But this would be a type of regulation focused not on the outputs of information industries—which are indeed hypermobile and circulate in electronic spaces—but on the material and socioeconomic infrastructure. Essential to this proposition in an understanding of the extent to which key components of the leading information industries are placebound and conversely, the extent to which key components of what we call the global economy actually materialize in places.

A refocusing of regulation onto infrastructures and production complexes in the context of globalization contributes to an analysis of the regulatory capacities of states that diverges in significant ways from understandings centered on hypermobile outputs and global telecommunications. One crucial piece of such an analysis is a detailed examination of the importance of place and placeboundedness in global economic processes. This is the subject in the remainder of this [reading].

Place and Production-Complex in the Global Economy

The analysis of the space economy developed here is centered in the notion that we cannot take the existence of a global economic system as given, but rather need to examine the particular ways in which the conditions for economic globalization are produced. This entails examining not only communication capacities and the power of multinationals, but also the underside of the global economy.

The capabilities for global operation, coordination and control contained in the new information technologies and in the power of the multinationals need to be produced. By focusing on the production of these capabilities we add a neglected dimension to the familiar issue of the power of large corporations and the new technologies. The emphasis shifts to the *practice* of global control: the work of producing and reproducing the organization and management of a global production system and a global marketplace for finance, both under conditions of economic concentration.

I see the producer services, and most especially finance and advanced corporate services, as industries producing the organizational commodities necessary for the implementation and management of global economic systems. . . . [4] Over the last few years we have seen the growth of a rich literature on the producer services, including major information industries such as international finance and advanced corporate services (e.g., Daniels 1985; Delaunay and Gadrey 1987; Noyelle and Dutka 1988; Daniels and Moulaert 1991). With a few exceptions (e.g., Castells 1989; Sassen 1991; Knox and Taylor 1995; Drennan 1992; Mitchelson and Wheeler 1994; Fainstein 1994; Stimson 1993; Corbridge et al., forthcoming) the literature on producer services and cities has not necessarily been concerned with the operation of the global economy as such, nor has it been seems part of the literature on globalization.[5]

Introducing the research on producer services into our analysis of the global economy helps us explore how the categories of place and production process are involved in economic globalization. These are two categories that are easily overlooked in analyses of the hypermobility of capital and the power of multinationals. Developing categories such as place and production process does not negate the centrality of hypermobility and power. It adds other dimensions and in so doing intersects with the regulatory role of the state in a distinct way and one that diverges from much international political economy.

Specialized services are usually understood in terms of specialized outputs rather than the production process involved. A focus on the production process in these service industries allows us 1) to capture some of their locational characteristics and 2) to examine the proposition that there is a new dynamic for agglomeration in the advanced corporate services because they function as a production complex, a complex which serves corporate headquarters yet has distinct locational and production characteristics. It is this producer services complex, more so than headquarters of firms generally, that benefits and often needs a city location. We see this dynamic for agglomeration operating at different levels of the urban hierarchy, from the global the regional. Some cities concentrate the infrastructure and the servicing that produce a capability for global control and servicing.

In brief, with the potential for global control capability, certain cities are becoming nodal points in a vast communications and market system. Advances in electronics and telecommunication have transformed geographically distant cities into centers for global communication and long-distance management. But centralized control and management over a geographically dispersed array of plants, office, and service outlets does not come about inevitably as part of a "world system." It requires the development of a vast range of highly specialized services and of top-level management and control functions.

The next three sections develop these subjects in greater detail.

Globalization and Service Intensity

The globalization of economic activity has raised the scale and the complexity of transactions, thereby feeding the demand for top-level multinational headquarter functions and for advanced corporate services. This demand for specialized services is further fed by a second major process, the growing service intensity in the organization of all industries. . . . This has contributed to a massive growth in the demand for services by firms in all industries, from mining and manufacturing to finance and consumer services. To this we should add the growing demand by firms for nonspecialized services, notably industrial services.

Two of the key variables that maize these processes relevant to cities and to the argument in this [reading] are: 1) the rapid growth in the last fifteen years in the share of services that firms buy rather than produce in-house; and 2) the existence of agglomeration economies in the production of specialized services. If firms continued to produce most of their services in-house as used to be the case, particularly with the large vertically integrated firms, cities might have been less significant production sites for services. Service activities would have moved out of cities as part of the moves by the larger firms of which they were but one component; there could conceivably have been far more geographic dispersal of specialized service jobs than there is now, though these jobs would of course have been included in the industrial classification of the larger firms, which were not necessarily service firms.

I discuss these two variables next.

The Growing Demand for Corporate Services

The increase in the share of bought services can be seen in the figures on growth in producer services jobs, in the numbers of producer services firms, and, perhaps most sharply, in the figures from the national input-output tables for the United States. Figures on employment and numbers of firms in producer services have by now become familiar and have been published widely. That cannot be said for the figures from the national input-output tables; I analyzed these figures for several years and several industries within major sectors and found a clear trend of growth in the value of bought service inputs for the industries examined.[6]

The sharp rise in the use of producer services has been fed by a variety of processes.[7] Among these are the territorial dispersal, whether at the regional, national, or global level, of multi-establishment firms. Firms operating many plants, offices, and service outlets must coordinate planning, internal administration and distribution, marketing, and other central headquarters activities. Formally, the development of the modern corporation and its massive participation in world markets and foreign countries has made planning, internal administration, product development, and research increasingly important and complex. Diversification of product lines, mergers, and transnationalization of economic activities all require highly specialized services.

For all firms, whether they operate globally or regionally, the rise of litigation, the growing importance of insurance, advertising, and outside financing, have all contributed to a growing need for specialized services. Further, as large corporations move into the production and sale of final consumer services, a wide range of activities, previously performed by free-standing, independent consumer service firms, are shifted to the central headquarters of the new corporate owners. Regional, national, or global chains of motels, food outlets, flower shops, require vast centralized administrative and servicing structures. The complexity of these will in turn generate a demand for specialized corporate services bought from specialized firms, something far less likely in the small independently owned consumer service firm. A parallel pattern of expansion of central high-level planning and control operations takes place in governments, brought about partly by the technical developments that make this possible and partly by the growing complexity of regulatory and administrative tasks. All of these trends have fed the growth of producer services in cities large and small.

A brief examination of the territorial dispersal entailed by transnational operations of large enterprises can serve to illustrate some of the points raised here. For instance, the numbers of workers employed abroad by the largest one hundred nonfinancial transnational corporations worldwide are rather large. (For detailed figures on this and the following items, see UNCTC 1993; Sassen 1994, chap. 4.) Thus about half of Exxon's and IBM's and about a third of Ford Motors' and GM's total workforce is employed outside the United States. We know furthermore that large transnationals have very high numbers of affiliates. Thus in 1990 German firms had over 19,000 affiliates in foreign countries, up from 14,000 in 1984; and the United States had almost 19,000. Finally, we know that the top transnationals have very high shares of foreign operations: the top ten largest transnational corporations in the world had sixty-one percent of their sales abroad. The average for the 100 largest corporations was almost fifty percent.

What these figures show is a vast operation dispersed over a multiplicity of locations. This generates a large demand for producer services, from international accounting to advertising. Operations as vast as these feed the expansion of central management, coordination, control, and servicing functions. Some of these functions are performed in headquarters, some are bought or contracted for therewith feeding the growth of the producer services complex.

The Formation of a New Production Complex

As for the second variable, agglomeration economies, the issue here is why has there not been more dispersal of specialized service firms, particularly since these are among the most advanced and intensive users of telematics and hence could supposedly locate anywhere. In order to understand why such a large share of these firms is concentrated in cities, and often in dense spatial concentrations reminiscent of industrial districts, we need to focus on the actual production process in these services.

The evidence on the locational patterns of the leading information industries shows sharp economic concentration in major cities. For instance, New York City accounts for thirty-five percent of earnings in producer services, compared to little over three percent of the national population, and between a fourth and a fifth of all producer services exports in the United States, which total about US$40 billion annually (Drennan 1992). London accounts for about forty percent of producer services exports in the United Kingdom, and Paris accounts for forty percent of all producer services employment in France and over eighty percent of the advanced corporate services (Cordier 1992; *Le Debat* 1994). There are many other such examples.

According to standard conceptions about information industries, the rapid growth and disproportionate concentration of producer services in major cities should not have happened. Because many of these services are thoroughly embedded in the most advanced information technologies, producer services could be expected to have locational options that by-pass the high costs and congestion typical of major cities. It is my argument that in order to understand their sharp concentration in large cities, we need to focus on the actual production process in these industries.

The production process in these services benefits from proximity to other specialized services. This is the case especially in the leading and most innovative sectors of these industries. Complexity and innovation often require multiple highly specialized inputs from several industries. The production of a financial instrument, for example, requires inputs from accounting, advertising, law, economic consulting, public relations, design, and printing. The particular characteristics of production of these services, especially those involved in complex and innovative operations, explain their pronounced concentration in major cities. The commonly heard explanation that high-level professionals require face-to-face interactions, needs to be refined in several ways. Producer services, unlike other types of services, are not necessarily dependent on spatial proximity to the consumers—firms—served. Rather, economies occur in such specialized firms when they locate close to others that produce key inputs or whose proximity makes possible joint production of certain service offerings. The top-of-the-line accounting firm can service its clients at a distance, but the nature of its service depends on proximity to other specialists, from lawyers to programmers. Moreover, it is well known that many of the new high-income professionals tend to be attracted to the amenities and lifestyles that large urban centers can offer. Frequently, what is thought of as face-to-face communication is actually a production process that requires multiple simultaneous inputs and feedbacks. At the current stage of technical development, immediate and simultaneous access to the pertinent experts is still the most effective way, especially when dealing with a highly complex product. The concentration of the most advanced telecommunications and computer network facilities in major cities is a key factor in what I refer to as the production process of these industries.[8]

Further, time replaces weight in these sectors as a force for agglomeration. In the past, the pressure of the weight of inputs from iron ore to unprocessed agricultural products, was a major constraint pushing toward agglomeration in sites where the heaviest inputs were located. Today, the acceleration of economic transactions and the premium put on time, have created new forces for agglomeration. This is increasingly not the case in routine operations. But where time is of the essence, as it is today in many of the leading sectors of these industries, the benefits of agglomeration are still extremely high—to the point where it is not simply a cost advantage, but an indispensable arrangement. This is further underlined by the centrality of the market in many of the most speculative and innovative branches of finance. Speculation and innovation in the context of deregulation and globalization have profoundly altered market operation in the industry, promoting far greater instability. Under these conditions, agglomeration carries additional advantages insofar as the market becomes a key site for new opportunities for profit and speed is of the essence. (Sassen 1991, chapters 2–4; Mitchelson and Wheeler 1994; but see also Lyons and Salmon 1995).

This combination of constraints suggests that the agglomeration of producer services in major cities actually constitutes a production complex. This producer services complex is intimately connected to the world of corporate headquarters; they are often thought of as forming a joint headquarters-corporate services complex. But in my reading, we need to distinguish the two.[9] Although it is true that headquarters still tend to be disproportionately concentrated in cities, over the last two decades many have moved out. Headquarters can indeed locate outside cities, but they need a producer services complex somewhere in order to buy or contract for the needed specialized services and financing. Further, headquarters of firms with very high overseas activity or in highly innovative and complex lines of business tend to locate in major cities. In brief, firms in more routinized lines of activity, with predominantly regional or national markets, appear to be increasingly free to move or install their headquarters outside cities. Firms in highly competitive and innovative lines of activity and/or with a strong world market orientation appear to benefit from being located at the center of major international business centers, no matter how high the costs.

Both types of firms, however, need a corporate services complex to be located somewhere.[10] Where this complex is located is probably increasingly unimportant from the perspective of many, though not all, headquarters. From the perspective of producer services firms, such a specialized complex is most likely to be in a city rather than, for example, a suburban office park. The latter will be the site for producer services firms but not for a services complex. And only such a complex is capable of handling the most advanced and complicated corporate demands.

Elsewhere (Sassen 1994, chapter 5), a somewhat detailed empirical examination of several cities served to explore different aspects of this trend toward spatial concentration.[11] Here there is space only for a few observations (see also Abu-Lughod 1995). The case of Miami, for instance, allows us to see, almost in laboratory-like fashion, how a new international corporate sector can become implanted in a site. It allows us to understand something about the dynamic of globalization in the current period and how it is embedded in place. Miami has emerged as a significant regional site for global city functions though it lacks a long history as an international banking and business center as is the case for such global cities as New York or London.

The case of Toronto, a city whose financial district was built up only in recent years, allows us to see to what extent the pressure toward spatial concentration of financial firms is embedded in an economic dynamic rather than simply being the consequence of having inherited a built infrastructure from the past, as one could think was the case in older centers such as London or New York.[12] But the case also shows that it is particularly certain industries which are subject to the pressure toward spatial concentration, notably finance and its sister industries (Gad 1991; Todd 1995).

The case of Sydney illuminates the interaction of a vast, continental economic scale and pressures toward spatial concentration. Rather than strengthening the multi-polarity of the Australian urban system, the developments of the 1980s—increased internationalization of the Australian economy, sharp increases in foreign investment, a strong shift toward finance, real estate and producer services—contributed to a greater concentration of major economic activities and actors in Sydney. This included a loss of share of such activities and actors by Melbourne, long the center of commercial activity and wealth in Australia (Daly and Stimson 1992).

Finally, the case of the leading financial centers in the world today is of continued interest because one might have expected that the growing number of financial centers now integrated into the global markets would have reduced the extent of concentration of financial activity in the top centers.[13] One would further expect this given the immense increases in the global volume of transactions. Yet the levels of concentration remain unchanged in the face of massive transformations in the financial industry and in the technological infrastructure this industry depends on.[14]

For example, international bank lending grew from US$1.89 trillion in 1980 to US$6.24 trillion in 1991—a fivefold increase in a mere ten years. New York, London, and Tokyo accounted for forty-two percent of all such international lending in 1980 and for forty-one percent in 1991 according to data from the Bank of International Settlements, the leading institution worldwide in charge of overseeing banking activity. There were compositional changes: Japan's share rose from 6.2 percent to 15.1 percent and Britain's fell from 26.2 percent to 16.3 percent; the U.S. share remained constant. All increased in absolute terms. Beyond these three, Switzerland, France, Germany, and Luxemburg bring the total share of the top centers to 64 in 1991, which is just about the same share these countries had in 1980. One city, Chicago dominates the world's trading in futures, accounting for sixty percent of worldwide contracts in options and futures in 1991.

This concentration in the top centers is partly a function of the concentration of the most advanced technical financial capabilities in these centers. And it is partly a function of various macroeconomic conjunctures, notably the perceived high risk of new markets in combination with the ease with which money can be shifted back and forth, as is illustrated by the current flight from the so-called emergent markets after the December 1994 Mexican devaluation of the peso and the ensuing financial crisis for foreign investors.

The Global Grid of Strategic Sites

The global integration of financial markets depends on and contributes to the implementation of a variety of linkages among the financial centers involved.[15] Prime examples of such linkages are the multinational networks of affiliates and subsidiaries typical of major firms in manufacturing and specialized services. Corporate service firms have developed vast multinational networks containing special geographic and institutional linkages that make it possible for client firms—transnational firms and banks—to use a growing array of service offerings from the same supplier (Marshall et al., 1986; Noyelle and Dutka 1988; Daniels and Moulaert 1991; Fainstein 1993).[16] There is also a growing number of less directly economic linkages, notable among which are a variety of initiatives launched by urban governments which amount to a type of foreign policy by and for cities. For example, New York State has opened business offices in several major cities overseas.

Whether these linkages have engendered transnational urban systems is less clear. It is partly a question of theory and conceptualization. So much of social science is profoundly rooted in the nation-state as the ultimate unit for analysis, that conceptualizing processes and systems as transnational is bound to engender much controversy. Even much of the literature on world or global cities does not necessarily posit the existence of a transnational urban system: in its narrowest form it posits that global cities perform central place functions at a transnational level. But that leaves open the question as to the nature of the articulation among global cities. If one posits that they merely compete with each other for global business, then they do not constitute a transnational system; in this case, studying several global cities becomes an instance of traditional comparative analyses.

If one posits that besides competing they are also the sites for transnational processes with multiple locations, then one can begin to posit the possibility of a systemic dynamic binding these cities. . . . I have argued that in addition to the central place functions performed by these cities at the global level, as posited by Hall (1966), Friedmann and Wolff (1982) and Sassen (1982), these cities relate to one another in distinct systemic ways. For example, the interaction among New York, London, and Tokyo, particularly in terms of finance and investment, consists partly of a series of processes that can be thought of as the chain of production in finance. Thus, in the mid-1980s Tokyo was the main exporter of the raw material we call money while New York was the leading processing center in the world. It was in New York that many of the new financial instruments were invented, and where money either in its raw form or in the form of debt was transformed into instruments that aimed at maximizing the returns on that money. London, on the other hand, was a major entrepôt which had the network to centralize and concentrate small amounts of capital available in a large number of smaller financial markets around the world, partly a function of its older network for the administration of the British empire. This is just one example suggesting that these cities do not simply compete with each other for the same business. There is, it seems to me, an economic system that rests on the three distinct types of locations these cities represent.[17] In my view, there is no such thing as a single global city, unlike what was the case with earlier imperial capitals—a single world city at the top of a system. The global city is a function of the global grid of transactions, one site for processes which are global because they have multiple locations in multiple countries (see also Abu-Lughod 1995; Smith and Timberlake 1995).

If finance and the advanced corporate services are in fact embedded in such transnational systems then this might be a rather significant factor in examinations of the possibilities on deregulation and globalization but also on a complex and dense grid of linkages and sites. The hypermobility of these industries and the associated difficulties for regulation are only part of the picture, albeit the most intensely studied and debated one; the global grid of linkages and sites within which this hypermobility is embedded and through which it flows is potentially another part of the picture, and one that will require more research to elucidate.

Conclusion: Regulating the Global Grid of Places

Including cities in the analysis of economic globalization and the ascendance of information industries adds three important dimensions to the study of economic globalization. First, it decomposes the nation–state into a variety of components that may be significant in understanding international economic activity and regulatory capacities. Second, it displaces the focus from the power of large corporations over governments and economies to the range of activities and organizational arrangements necessary for the implementation and maintenance of a global network of factories, service operations, and markets; these are all processes only partly encompassed by the activities of transnational corporations and banks. Third, it contributes to a focus on place and on the strategic concentrations of infrastructure and production complexes necessary for global economic activity. Processes of economic globalization are thereby reconstituted as concrete production complexes situated in specific places containing a multiplicity of activities. Focusing on cities allows us to specify a global geography of strategic places as well as the microgeographies and politics unfolding within these places.

The transformation in the composition of the world economy, especially the rise of finance and advanced services as leading industries, is contributing to a new international economic order, one dominated by financial centers, global markets, and transnational firms. Correspondingly, we may see a growing significance of other political categories both sub- and supranational. Cities that function as international business and financial centers are sites for direct transactions with world markets.

These cities and the globally oriented markets and firms they contain mediate in the relation of the world economy to nation–states and in the relations among nation–states. Transnational economic processes inevitably interact with systems for the governance of national economies. Further, the material conditions necessary for many global economic processes—from the infrastructure for telematics to the producer services production complex—need to be incorporated in examinations of questions of governance and accountability in the global economy. They signal the possibility of novel forms of regulation and conditions for accountability.

In sum, an analysis focused on place and production has the effect of decoding globalization; the latter is conceptually reconstituted in terms of a transnational geography of centrality consisting of multiple linkages and strategic concentrations of material infrastructure. Globalization can then be seen as embedded and dependent on these linkages and material infrastructure. To a considerable extent, global processes are this grid of sites and linkages.

The existence of such a transnational grid of places and linkages that constitute the infrastructure for the globalization of finance and other specialized services points to regulatory possibilities. Precisely because of its strategic character and because of the density of resources and linkages it concentrates, this new geography of centrality could in turn be a space for concentrated regulatory activity. But the type of regulatory frameworks and operations it would entail need to be discovered and invented, as does the meaning of accountability and democratization of the new global information economy.

Notes

1. For instance, France, which ranks among the top providers of information services and industrial engineering services in Europe and has a strong, though not outstanding, position in financial and insurance services, has found itself at an increasing disadvantage in legal and accounting services. French law firms are at a particular disadvantage because Anglo-Saxon law dominates the international transactions. Foreign firms with offices in Paris dominate the servicing of the legal needs of firms operating internationally, for both French and foreign firms operating out of France.

2. The hegemony of neoliberal concepts of economic relations with its strong emphasis on markets, deregulation, free international trade has influenced policy in the 1980s in United States and United Kingdom and now increasingly also in continental Europe. This has contributed to the formation of transnational legal regimes that are centered in Western economic concepts. Through the IMF and IBRD as well as GATT this vision has spread to the developing world. An issue that is emerging as significant in view of the spread of Western legal concepts is the critical examination of the philosophical premises about authorship and property that define the legal arena in the West (e.g., Coombe 1993). Similarly, Anglo American law is increasingly dominant in international commercial arbitration, an institution grounded in continental traditions of jurisprudence, particularly French and Swiss (Dezalay and Garth 1995).

3. Many of these changes, of course, required explicit government action. Pastor's study [*Congress and the Politics of U.S. Foreign Economic Policy, 1929–1976*] on the United States about the arduous legislative road to open up the country to foreign investment is a good case in point.

4. Producer services are intermediate outputs, that is, services bought by firms. They cover financial, legal, and general management matters, innovation, development, design, administration, personnel, production technology, maintenance, transport, communications, wholesale distribution, advertising, cleaning services for firms, security, and storage. Central components of the producer services category are a range of industries with mixed business and consumer markets. They are insurance, banking, financial services, real estate, legal services, accounting, and professional associations.

5. There is, however, a rapidly growing literature on the impact of globalization on cities, which in various ways incorporates examinations of producer services, including, besides the ones already listed above, Friedmann 1986; Fainstein et al. 1993; Hitz et al. 1995; von Petz and

Schmals 1992, Machimura 1992; Frost and Spence 1992; Rodriguez and Feagin 1986; Knox and Taylor 1995; Levine 1993; *Le Debat* 1994.

6. Using input-output tables from 1972 to 1987 we examined the use of service-based commodities in eleven four-digit SIC industries (ranging from wholesale trade to mining). The service-based industries examined as the intermediate commodity input, down to the four-digit SIC code, included among others, finance and insurance, and business services. For the sake of simplicity, the following figures cover the 1992 to 1982 period only because after this date the comparison becomes too complicated to describe in [an endnote]. Of all the industry combinations studied, the level of service inputs from the finance industry was most prominent, tripling from 1972 to 1982, in banking, wholesale trade, and insurance. The use of business services increased sharpest in the following industry groups: motor vehicles and equipment, insurance carriers, wholesale trade, and banking. The use of business services in banking more than tripled from 1972 to 1982. (See Sassen and Orlow 1995 for a full description.)

7. For a discussion of the literature and the broader trends lying behind the possibility of the formation of a free-standing producer services sector (Sassen 1991, chap. 5).

8. The telecommunications infrastructure also contributes to concentration of leading sectors in major cities. Long-distance communications systems increasingly use fiber optic wires. These have several advantages over traditional copper wire: large carrying capacity, high speed, more security, and higher signal strength. Fiber systems tend to connect major communications hubs because they are not easily spliced and hence not desirable for connecting multiple lateral sites. Fiber systems tend to be installed along existing rights of way, whether rail, water or highways (Moss 1991). The growing use of fiber optic systems thus tends to strengthen the major existing telecommunication concentrations and therefore the existing hierarchies. . . .

9. It is common in the general literature and in some more scholarly accounts to use headquarters concentration as an indication of whether a city is an international business center. The loss of headquarters is then interpreted as a decline in a city's status. The use of headquarters concentration as an index is actually a problematic measure given the way in which corporations are classified. Which headquarters concentrate in major international financial and business centers depends on a number of variables. First, how we measure or simply count headquarters makes a difference. Frequently, the key measure is size of firm in terms of employment and overall revenue. In this case, some of the largest firms in the world are still manufacturing firms and many of these have their main headquarters in proximity to their major factory complex, which is unlikely to be in a large city due to space constraints. Such firms are likely, however to have secondary headquarters for highly specialized functions in major cities. Further, many manufacturing firms are oriented to the national market and do not need to be located in an international business center. Thus, the much publicized departure of major headquarters from New York City in the 1960s and 1970s involved these types of firms. If we look at the Fortune 500 largest firms in the United States (cf. "*Fortune* Magazine 500 list") many have left New York City and other large cities. If instead of size we use share of total firm revenue coming from international sales, a large number of firms that are not part of the Fortune 500 list come into play. For instance, in the case of New York City, the results change dramatically: forty percent of U.S. firms with half their revenue from international sales have their headquarters in New York City and its environs.

Second, the nature of the urban system in a country is a factor. Sharp urban primacy will tend to entail a disproportionate concentration of headquarters no matter what measure one uses. Third, different economic histories and business traditions may combine to produce different results. Further, headquarters concentration may be linked with a specific economic phase. For instance, unlike New York's loss of top Fortune 500 headquarters, Tokyo has been gaining such headquarters. Osaka and Nagoya, the two other major economic centers in Japan are losing headquarters to Tokyo. This is in good part linked to the increasing internationalization of the Japanese economy and the corresponding increase in central command and servicing functions in major international business centers. In the case of Japan, extensive government regulation over the economy is an added factor contributing to headquarter location in Tokyo insofar as all international activities have to go through various government approvals.

10. For example, Wheeler (1986) examined the spatial linkages between major U.S. corporations and financial institutions and found that corporations do not necessarily use the firms available in their location but rather tend to work with firms located higher up in the metropolitan hierarchy, a trend that is particularly strong for large corporations. Schwartz (1992) found that large firms located in the New York metropolitan area continued to use Manhattan firms for most of their service needs.

11. A very different category through which some of these issues can be examined is that of "centrality." The spatial correlates of centrality today can assume a multiplicity of forms, ranging from the traditional central business district (CBC) as well as a metropolitan grid of economic nodes intensely connected via telematics. . . . Examining the evidence for a number of major cities I found a clear trend toward centrality, but with a far broader range of spatial correlates than the traditional CBD. Telematics and the growth of a global economy, both inextricably linked, have contributed to it new geography of centrality (and marginality). To simplify an analysis made elsewhere (Sassen 1994), there are four forms of centrality today. First, the CBD remains a hey form of centrality although there is no longer a simple straightforward relation between centrality and such geographic entities as the downtown, or the central business district, as was the case in the past. But the CBD in major international business centers is one profoundly reconfigured by technological and economic change.

Second, the center can extend into a metropolitan area in the form of a grid of nodes of intense business activity. This regional grid of nodes represents, in my analysis, a reconstitution of the concept of region. Far from neutralizing geography, the regional grid is likely to be embedded in conventional forms of communications infrastructure, notably rapid rail and highways connecting to airports. Ironically perhaps, conventional infrastructure is likely to maximize the economic benefits derived from telematics. I think this is an important issue that has been lost somewhat in discussions about the neutralization of geography through telematics. Third, we are seeing the formation of a transterritorial "center" constituted via telematics and intense economic transactions. The most powerful of these new geographies of centrality at the interurban level binds the major international financial and business centers: New York, London, Tokyo, Paris, Frankfurt, Zurich, Amsterdam, Los Angeles, Sydney, Hong Kong, among others. But this geography now also includes cities such as São Paulo and Bombay. The intensity of transactions among these cities, particularly through the financial markets, trade in services, and investment, has increased sharply, and so have the orders of magnitude involved. Fourth, new forms of centrality are being constituted in electronically generated spaces. . . . The city is a strategic site in the first three of these forms of centrality.

12. In his study of the financial district in Manhattan, Longcore found that the use of advanced information and telecommunication technologies has a strong impact on the spatial organization of the district because of the added spatial requirements of "intelligent" buildings (see also Moss 1991). A ring of new office buildings meeting these requirements was built over the last decade immediately around the old Wall Street core, where the narrow streets and lots made difficult; further, renovating old buildings in the Wall Street core is extremely expensive often not possible. The occupants of the new buildings in the district were mostly corporate headquarters and the financial services industry. These firms tend to be extremely intensive users of telematics and availability of the most advanced forms typically is a major factor in their real estate and locational decisions. They need complete redundancy of telecommunications systems, high carrying capacity, often their own private branch exchange, etc. With this often goes a need for large spaces. For instance, the technical installation backing a firm's trading floor is likely to require additional space the size of the trading floor itself.

13. Further, this unchanged level of concentration has happened at a time when financial services are more mobile than ever before: globalization, deregulation (an essential ingredient for globalization), and securitization have been the key to this mobility—in the contort of massive advances in telecommunications and electronic networks. One result is growing competition among centers for hypermobile financial activity. In my view there has been an overemphasis on competition in general and in specialized accounts on this subject. As I have argued elsewhere (Sassen 1991, chap. 7), there is also a functional division of labor among various major financial centers.

In that sense we can think of a transnational system with multiple locations (see also Abu-Lughod 1995).

14. Much of the discussion around the formation of a single European market and financial system has raised the possibility, and even the need if it is to be competitive, of centralizing financial functions and capital in a limited number of cities rather than maintaining the current structure in which each country has a financial center.

15. There is a rapidly growing and highly specialized literature focused on different types of economic linkages that bind cities across national borders (Castells 1989; Noyelle and Dutka 1988; Daniels and Moulaert 1991; Leyshon, Daniels and Thrift 1987; Sassen 1991).

16. There is good evidence that the development of multinational corporate service firms was associated with the needs of transnational firms. The multinational advertising farm can offer global advertising to a specific segment of potential customers worldwide. Further, global integration of affiliates and markets requires making use of advanced information and telecommunications technology which can come to account for a significant share of costs—not only operational costs but also, and perhaps most important, research and development costs for products or advances on existing products. The need for scale economies on all these fronts contributes to explain the recent increase in mergers and acquisitions, which has consolidated the position of a few very large firms in many of these industries, and further strengthened cross-border linkages among the key locations which concentrate the needed telecommunications facilities. They have emerged as firms that can control a significant share of national and international markets. The rapid increase in direct foreign investments in services is strongly linked with the growing tendency among leading service firms to operate transnationally. Subcontracting by larger firms and the multiplicity of specialized markets has meant that small independent firms can also thrive in major centers (Sassen 1991; Noyelle and Dutka 1988; Leyhson, Daniels and Thrift 1987).

17. The possibility of such a transnational urban system raises a question as to the articulation of such cities with their national urban systems. It is quite possible that the strengthening of cross-national ties among the leading financial and business centers is likely to be accomplished by a weakening of the linkages between each of these cities and their hinterlands and national urban systems (Sassen 1991). Cities such as Detroit, Liverpool, Manchester, Marseille, the cities of the Ruhr, and now increasingly Nagoya and Osaka, have been affected by the territorial decentralization of many of their key manufacturing industries at the domestic and international level. This process of decentralization has contributed to the growth of service industries that produce the specialized inputs to run spatially dispersed processes and global markets for inputs and outputs. These specialized inputs—international legal and accounting services, management consulting, financial services—are heavily concentrated in business and financial centers rather than in these manufacturing cities themselves.

References

Abu-Lughod, J., Lippman, J. "Comparing Chicago, New York, and Los Angeles: Testing Some World Cities Hypotheses." In: Knox, P., Taylor, P. (eds.) *World Cities in a World System,* 171–191. Cambridge: Cambridge University Press, 1995.

Aman, A. "A Global Perspective on Current Regulatory Reform: Rejection, Relocation, or Reinvention?" *Indiana Journal of Global Legal Studies* 2: 429–464, 1995.

Bonacich, E., et al. (eds.) *Global Production: The Apparel Industry in the Pacific Rim.* Philadelphia: Temple University Press, 1994.

Castells, M. *The Information City.* London: Blackwell, 1989.

Coombe, R. "The Properties of Culture and the Politics of Possessing Identity: Native Claims in the Appropriation Controversy." *The Canadian Journal of Law and Jurisprudence* 6,2: 249–285, July 1993.

Corbridge, S., Martin, R. Thrift, N. (eds.) *Money, Power, and Space.* Oxford: Blackwell, 1994.

Cordier, J. "Paris, place financière et bancaire." In: Berger, M., Rhein, C. (eds.) *L'Ille de France et la recherché urbaine.* STRAITES-CNRS Univ. Paris 1, et Plan Urbain-DATAR, 1992.

Daly, M., Stimson, R. "Sydney: Australia's Gateway and Financial Capital." In: Blakely, E., Stimson, T. (eds.) *New Cities of the Pacific Rim.* Institute for Urban and Regional Development, University of California, Berkeley, 1992.

Daniels, P. *Service Industries: A Geographical Appraisal.* London: Methuen, 1985.

Daniels, P., Moulaert, F. (eds.) *The Changing Geography of Advanced Producer Services.* London: Belhaven Press, 1991.

Delauney, J., Gadrey, J. *Les Enjeux de la societé de service.* Paris: Presses de la Fondation des Sciences Politiques, 1987.

Dezalay, Y., Bryant, G. "Merchants of Law as Moral Entrepreneurs: Constructing International Justice from the Competition for Transnational Business Disputes." *Law and Society Review* 29, 1: 27–64, 1995.

Drache, D., Gertler, M. (eds.) *The New Era of Global Competition: State Policy and Market Power.* Montreal: McGill-Queen's University Press, 1991.

Drennan, M. "Gateway Cities: The Metropolitan Sources of U.S. Producer Service Exports." *Urban Studies* 28, 2: 217–235, 1992.

Fainstein, S. *The City Builders: Property, Politics, and Planning in London and New York.* Cambridge MA: Blackwell, 1994.

Faintein, S., Gordon, I., Harloe, M. *Divided Cities: Economic Restructuring and Social Change in London and New York.* Cambridge, MA: Blackwell, 1993.

Friedman, J., Wolff, G. "World City Formation: An Agenda for Research and Action." *International Journal of Urban and Regional Research* 63, 3: 309–344, 1982.

Frost, M., Spence, N. "Global City Characteristics and Central London's Employment." *Urban Studies* 30, 3: 547–558, 1992.

Gad, G. "Toronto's Financial District." *Canadian Urban Landscapes* 1: 203–207, 1991.

Gereffi, G. "The Elusive Last Lap in the Quest for Developed Country Status." In: Mittelman, J. (ed.) *Globalization: Critical Reflections. International Political Economy Yearbook* 9, 1996.

Hitz, H., et. al. (eds.) *Financial Metropoles in Restructuring: Zurich and Frankfurt En Route to Postfordism.* Zurich: Rootpunkt, 1995.

Jessop, R. *State Theory: Putting Capitalist States in their Place.* University Park: Pennsylvania State University Press, 1990.

Knox, P., Taylor, P. (eds.) *World Cities in a World System.* Cambridge: Cambridge University Press, 1995.

Kooiman, J., Van Vliet, M. "Governance and Public Management." In: Eliassen, K. and Kooiman, J. (eds.) *Managing Public Organizations: Lessons from Contemporary European Experience,* 56–72. London: Sage, 1993.

Le Débat. Le Nouveau Paris. Special issue of *Le Débat.* Summer, 1994.

Leftwich, A. "Governance, the State, and the Politics of Development." *Development and Change* 23, 4: 363–340, 1994.

Levine, M. *Montreal.* Philadelphia: Temple University Press. 1993.

Lyons, D., Salmon, S. "World Cities, Multinational Corporations and Urban Hierarchy: The Case Study of the United States." In Knox, P. and Taylor, P. J. (eds.) *World Cities,* 98–114, 1995.

Machimura, T. "The Urban Restructuring Process in the 1980s: Transforming Tokyo into a World City." *International Journal of Urban and Regional Research* 16, 11: 114–128, 1992.

Marshall, J., et al. *Uneven Development in the Service Economy: Understanding the Location of Producer Services.* Report of the Producer Services Working Party, Institute of British Geographers and the ESRC. August, 1986.

Mitchelson, R., Wheeler, J. "The Flow of Information in a Global Economy: The Role of the American Urban System in 1990." *Annals of the Association of American Geographers* 84, 1: 87–107, 1996.

Mittelman, J. ed. "Globalization: Critical Reflections." *International Political Economy Yearbook* Vol. 9. Boulder, CO: Lynne Reinner, 1996.

Morales, R. *Flexible Production: Restructuring of the International Automobile Industry.* Cambridge: Polity Press, 1994.

Moss, M. "New Fibers of Urban Economic Development." *Portfolio: A Quarterly Review of Trade and Transportation* 4, 1: 11–18, 1991.

Negri, T. " A quoi sert encore l'Etat." *Pouvoirs Pouvoir* 25–26 of *Futur Anterieur:* 135–152. Paris: L'Harmattan, 1995.

Noyelle, T., Dutka, A. *International Trade in Business Services: Accounting, Adverstising, Law and Management Consulting.* Cambridge, MA: Ballinger Publishing, 1988.

Panitch, L. "Rethinking the Role of the State in an Era of Globalization." In: Mittelman, J. (ed.) *Globalization: Critical Reflections. International Political Economy Yearbook* 9, 1996.

Rodriguez, N., Feagin, J. "Urban Specialization in the World System." *Urban Affairs Quarterly* 22, 2: 187–220, 1986.

Rosenau, J. "Governance, Order, and Change in World Politics." In: Rosenau, J., Czempiel, E. (eds.) *Governance Without Government: Order and Change in World Politics,* 1–29. Cambridge: Cambridge University Press, 1992.

Sassen, S. *Losing Control? Sovereignty in an Age of Globalization.* New York: Columbia University Press, 1996.

Sassen, S. *Cities in a World Economy.* Thousand Oaks, CA: Pine Forge/Sage Press, 1994.

Sassen, S. *The Global City: New York, London, Tokyo.* Princeton, NJ: Princeton University Press, 1991.

Sassen, S. "Recomposition and Peripheralization at the Core." *In Immigration and Changes in the New International Division of Labor,* 88–100, San Francisco, CA: Synthesis Publications, 1982.

Sassen, S., Orloff, B. "The Growing Service Intensity in Economic Organization: Evidence from the Input-Output Tables." Department of Urban Planning, Columbia University, New York City, 1995.

Smith, D., Timberlake, M. "Cities in Global Matrices: Toward Mapping the World System's City System." In: Knox, P., Taylor, P. (eds.) *World Cities in a World System,* 79–97. Cambridge: Cambridge University Press, 1995.

Stimson, R. "Process of Globalization and Economic Restructuring and the Emergence of a New Space Economy of Cities and Regions in Australia." Paper Presented at the 4th International Workshop on Technological Change and Urban Forum: Productive and Sustainable Cities. Berkeley, California, April, 14–16, 1993.

Todd, G. "Going Global in the Semi-Periphery: World Cities as Political Projects, The Case of Toronto." In: Knox, P., Taylor, P. (eds.) *World Cities in a World System,* 192–214. Cambridge: Cambridge University Press, 1995.

Trubek, D., et al. "Global Restructuring and the Law: The Internationalization of Legal Fields and Creation of Transnational Arenas." Working Paper Series on the Political Economy of Legal Change No. 1. Madison, WI: Global Studies Research Program, University of Wisconsin, 1993.

United Nations Conference on Trade and Development, University of Transnational Corporations. *World Investment Report 1993: Transnational Corporations and Integrated International Production.* New York: United nations, 1993.

Von Petz, U., Schmals, K. (eds.) *Metropole, Weltstadt, Global City: Neue Formen der Urbanisierung,* Vol. 60, Dortmund: Dortmunder Beitrage zur Raumplanung, Universitat Dortmund, 1992.

Wheeler, J. "Corporate Spatial Links with Financial Institutions: The Role of the Metropolitan Hierarchy." *Annals of the Association of American Geographers* 76, 2: 262–274, 1986.

Young, O. *International Cooperation: Building Regimes for Natural Resources and the Environment.* Ithaca, NY: Cornell University Press, 1989.

25

Planning the American Dream

Todd W. Bressi

What is the "New Urbanism" . . . ? In one sense, it represents a rediscovery of planning and architectural traditions that have shaped some of the most livable, memorable communities in America—urban precincts like Boston's Back Bay and downtown Charleston, South Carolina; neighborhoods like Seattle's Capitol Hill and Philadelphia's Germantown; and traditional small towns where life centers around a courthouse square, common, plaza, train station or main street. For planners and architects who embrace the New Urbanism, places like these provide both inspiration and countless practical lessons for the design of new communities.

But the New Urbanism is not a romantic movement; it reflects a deeper agenda. The planning and design approaches explored in this book revive principles about building communities that have been virtually ignored for half a century: Publics spaces like streets, squares and parks should be a setting for the conduct of daily life, a neighborhood should accommodate diverse types of people and activities; it should be possible to get to work, accomplish everyday tasks (like buying fresh food or taking a child to day care) and travel to surrounding communities without using a car. The projects in the following pages show how these traditional approaches to building communities are being applied anew in suburbs and urban infill projects, places that until recently have been regarded as being altogether different from traditional communities.

The New Urbanism also represents a new chapter in the history of American city planning. For a century, this reformist profession has been guiding urban redevelopment and suburban expansion with the goals of eradicating the crowding, poverty, disease and congestion that threatened to overwhelm industrial cities, and of creating a rational, efficient framework for growth that all but rejected traditional patterns of city and town development. The result of these efforts is a metropolitan landscape that is beset by an altogether different set of problems—traffic congestion, poor air quality, expensive housing, social segregation and neighborhoods whose physical character amounts to little more than the confluence of standard development practices and real estate marketing strategies. The New Urbanists are confronting these problems with an energy and creativity that had eluded planners until now.

The planners and architects whose work is shown in this book are at the forefront of a growing group of designers who are taking up this agenda. Their work is not clouded in theory and rhetoric. It is attracting the attention of not only critics and scholars but also people who can make change happen: citizen advocacy groups, local and regional planning agencies and even private developers. There is little question that the approaches these designers advocate will be shaping the form of American cities and suburbs for decades to come.

From City to Suburb: A Century of American Planning and Urban Design

The suburban dispersal American cities have experienced in the last century has been remarkable in several ways. First, the magnitude of growth and the range of social and economic groups that have emigrated to the suburbs are unprecedented. Second, suburbs have evolved beyond their original role as "bedroom" communities; they now offer shopping, work and cultural activities, rendering suburbanites less reliant on central cities. Finally, this dispersal has been accompanied by the invention of new typologies for houses, commercial buildings and public spaces that contrast sharply with traditional forms—typologies that have been injected into center city projects as well.

This unprecedented suburban expansion has paralleled the unprecedented expansion of America's middle class and its desire to rise above urban, working-class conditions. The most powerful icon of the middle class, the single-family detached house surrounded by ample yards, has roots in Victorian–era mythology: The house was seen as a cradle, nurturing (and cultivating) the emerging independent nuclear family, and as a bulwark, insulating women and children from the industrial city's evils. The house nurtured the family by providing specialized places for socializing, private life and household work, and by offering an opportunity, through landscaping and interior decoration, for the expression of individual taste. And the house, protected in its residential enclave and surrounded by spacious yards, offered privacy and protection from outside contamination. Suburban neighborhoods and houses also offered the middle class a new connection with nature: Romantic, picturesque site planning with curved streets and lavish plantings demonstrated the proper balance between nature and human artifice; irregular house forms like porches and bay windows were considered a sign of organic complexity; and the yard was a garden that demonstrated the family's connection with the earth.[1]

The middle class's ability to move to suburban single-family homes was facilitated by transportation innovations. Before the 1920s, most suburbs grew in tandem with the extension of streetcar and railroad lines. Generally, they were compact clusters extending as far as a person might comfortably walk between home and a streetcar stop, and platted on tight grids that made land subdivision and sale efficient. Houses usually were put up by small builders who followed local practices or chose from the myriad of easily available plans. Houses came in a range of styles and typologies, depending on the region and the resident's taste and wealth—from Philadelphia's rowhouses and double homes to stately midwestern Victorians to California Craftsman bungalows.

After World War I, suburban growth was shaped by automobiles, which became the second icon of suburban life: Cars provided an unprecedented level of mobility, freeing people to determine their own travel patterns, and strengthened the suburbs' middle-class nature by excluding those who could not afford purchase and maintenance costs. Automobiles opened vast amounts of land for development, and the business of making and sustaining them boosted the economy more than efficient streetcars ever could.

As auto ownership skyrocketed, government eagerly built networks of boulevards, parkways and expressways that served as armatures for dispersing development ever more widely and thinly. Car owners found the single-family detached house especially convenient because it offered easy possibilities for storing autos. When cars were novelties, garages appeared as backyard outbuildings; as cars became household fixtures, they attached themselves to the sides of houses; and as families acquired whole fleets of vehicles, garages moved to the front. Along the way, garages doubled or tripled in size; now they can be the most dominant visual element of a house's facade or an entire streetscape.

By the 1920s the profession of city planning was becoming institutionalized. Planners sought to remake cities from within through administrative reforms, such as building codes, and aggressive actions like clearing and rebuilding blighted areas. They also sought to foster orderly suburban growth by devising plans for efficient metropolitan regions in which residential districts were safely segregated from commercial and manufacturing activities but easily accessible to them via highway networks.

The boldest attempts at restructuring cities dated from Chicago's 1893 World's Columbian Exposition, which demonstrated how a combination of Baroque planning and Neoclassical architecture could impose a sense of order, civility and purpose on chaotic industrial cities. These efforts, which borrowed heavily from France's Beaux Arts school of architecture, were christened "City Beautiful" here. City Beautiful plans typically sought to establish formal civic centers, in which architecture and public space were conceived as a unified whole, and efficient networks of arterial streets to speed traffic through traditional street grids.

The most ambitious planners, inspired by British Garden City projects and their experience designing new communities for war industry workers, sought commissions for the design of entirely new towns. They, too, found inspiration in the architecture and planning of historic European towns, meticulously documented in books such as Camillo Sitte's *Town Planning According to Artistic Principles* and Werner Hegemann and Elbert Peets' *The American Vitruvius*. But few of their proposals, outside of industrial or resort towns, attracted backers of sufficient wherewithal; the most notable surviving examples are Venice, Florida; Mariemont, Ohio; and Kingsport, Tennessee.

A concept that had more impact on suburban planning was architect Clarence A. Perry's "neighborhood unit." This idea reinforced the Victorian notion that a neighborhood was a protective domestic enclave requiring insulation from commerce, work and traffic, and held that the functional and literal center of a neighborhood should be an elementary school. Each neighborhood would be surrounded by arterial streets wide enough to handle through traffic; internal streets would be designed to facilitate circulation within the neighborhood. Local shops would be located along the arterials, preferably at traffic junctions and adjacent to similar districts.[2]

Planners found it easiest to establish regulatory frameworks in which private developers could make their own decisions about neighborhood design. Subdivision regulations governed the process by which buildable lots could be created out of undeveloped tracts of land—typically dictating lot sizes and shapes, street widths and block lengths, and open-space set-asides. Zoning prescribed the activities that could take place on a lot; the size of a building that could be developed; dimensions for front, back and side yards; and requirements for functional matters like parking.

Agencies such as the U.S. Commerce Department and New York's Regional Plan Association promulgated model subdivision and zoning laws that were replicated in countless communities, often with little modification for local conditions. These mechanisms did not presume any one type of design, but they imposed a new level of uniformity on suburban development by creating classification systems that treated hundreds or thousands of properties alike. Usually, their underlying purpose was to protect land values, foster family environments and maintain a degree of economic and social exclusion. Its practice, zoning often separated commercial and residential uses, sanctified single-family homes by isolating them from apartments and imposed liberal setback rules that required large lots, thereby driving up housing costs.

As traffic volume increased, these standards were modified to make auto travel more safe and efficient while protecting the character of residential areas. Eventually, they called for streets wide enough to accommodate both parking and traffic, turning radii so generous that service and emergency vehicles could negotiate any cul-de-sac, and T-configured intersections that minimized traffic conflicts. Planners distributed traffic through hierarchical networks of arterial, collector and local streets. Grid systems fell out of favor because they allowed through traffic on residential streets, and culs-de-sac were enshrined in the standards because they prevented through traffic.[3]

New Deal reforms that promoted home ownership and stimulated the housing industry encoded these design principles more than local planners could ever have. These reforms required unprecedented standardization—of the terms under which money would be lent, methods by which property was appraised and criteria used to determine whether a loan could be insured. In essence, a set of national criteria determined the worth and bankability of a house; these evolved into standards for house design, lot and yard configurations and street layouts that became patterns for the home building industry. Again, single-family detached homes had a special advantage—the mechanics of lending for them were much simpler than creating ownership opportunities within multi-family buildings.[4]

This standardization was complemented by changes in the home-building industry, which learned mass production techniques while building housing for war workers and had a large pool of demobilized GIs eager to step up to suburban living (thanks to New Deal and veterans housing programs). Before 1945, the typical contractor put up 5 or fewer houses a year; by 1959 the average was 22.[5] Today, developers typically bring more than 100 acres through the approval process at a time and spin off sections to different builders, who rarely undertake projects with fewer than 150 houses or 100 apartments because of the economics of planning, building and marketing. To simplify production, most builders offer only a handful of models, and regional or national builders might repeat the same models in several places.[6]

Since World War II suburbs have taken on a more diverse character; functions once unique to center cities began to follow their customers and labor pools outward. Industrial activities were lured by the ability to spread out in low-slung buildings on large pieces of land and the easy access to the rapidly expanding network of interstate highways. Regional shopping centers began to flourish in the suburbs in the early 1950s. In the 1970s, white-collar "back-office" functions found new homes in the suburbs as companies tapped into a new labor market: Suburbs were full of underemployed women, many of whom were well-educated, not union members and eager for a paying job.

Nevertheless, this development occurred piecemeal at best. Bankers, builders and planners evolved standards that extended the framework of separated uses and hierarchical, auto-friendly. traffic networks to these new types of development. Efficient land-use approval processes encouraged each commercial and residential project to be considered on its own, with little regard to the development that surrounded it. As a result, malls, offices and housing tracts simply leapfrogged to less congested areas near arterials or freeway interchanges and demonstrated little visual or spatial connection with their surroundings.

Urban renewal programs provided federal funds and legal tools for injecting these suburban approaches into cities, where architects and planners advocated tearing out "blighted" housing and industrial buildings and replacing them with modern apartment and office towers. While the ostensible rationale of these efforts was to improve urban social and economic conditions, they also cleared the way for massive infusions of capital investment by wiping out complex street, ownership and leasing patterns.

Following the ideas of architect-planners like Le Corbusier, urban renewal buildings disdained traditional urban forms and stood as isolated objects surrounded by plazas, park-like open spaces or parking lots. Cities also were reconfigured to accommodate auto traffic: Side streets and alleys were closed to create large "superblock" compounds free of cars; other streets were widened and straightened to serve as high-speed arterials. Loop and spur freeways were wrestled through central cities to pump even larger volumes of cars in and out.

What has the last century of suburb building and city planning wrought? By and large, these efforts have accomplished what they set out to do. They have liberated many people from crowded, unhealthy living conditions. They have established a social, economic and regulatory framework that unleashed enormous amounts of metropolitan development. But the land-use and transportation patterns that emerged have created problems of their own—many of which seem even more intractable than those posed by industrial cities.

Home ownership, a cornerstone of suburban life, is out of reach for an increasing number of households. Most do not fit the archetype of working husband, housewife and two children, rendering the traditional single-family, large-lot house increasingly irrelevant. The infrastructure costs for low-density, single-family development are staggering; in northern California, where such costs can add almost $30,000 to the cost of a new house,[7] even two-income households cannot afford the ideal three-bedroom, two-bathroom, three-car-garage house on a quarter-acre lot. Compounding this is the steep cost of automobility: keeping two cars can cost upwards of $10,000 a year.[8]

Sprawled, low-density suburban development is compromising the quality of life suburbs often promise. First, more and more leisure time is being spent on commuting. A one-hour commute consumes ten hours a week; congestion and mismatched housing and job locations force some people to commute two or more hours each way. Second, reliance on cars has a devastating impact on people who cannot drive or afford them: Children cannot travel to school or organized activities unless driven by somebody; teenagers, who need cars to have independent social lives, take after-school jobs to pay for their cars, cutting into studying and social time; elderly people who lose their drivers' licenses can no longer shop, visit or see doctors. Third, while suburbs might have once offered a healthy antidote to grimy industrial cities, cars are now generating tremendous air pollution, particularly in suburban metropolises like Denver, Los Angeles and Houston. Finally, attractive rural landscapes are being lost in region after region; even John Steinbeck's storied Salinas Valley is threatened.

Most problematic is the effect suburban dispersal and urban renewal have had on civic life. Social scientists debate the extent to which physical design creates or reflects social conditions. But current metropolitan settlement patterns have clearly exacerbated social, class and racial segregation and diminished the importance of common ground on which people of different backgrounds and outlooks might encounter each other. They have heightened, not ameliorated, urban social and economic decline and created vivid new symbols of urban distress. By isolating people in houses and cars and by segregating households into homogeneous enclaves, the late 20th century suburban metropolis has done little to replace the urban vitality it so aggressively replaced, and little to foster desperately needed civic responsibility in our increasingly diverse society.

The New Urbanism at Work

The deceptively simple responses the New Urbanists propose to these problems are based on one, equally simple principle: Community planning and design must assert the importance of public over private values. This principle serves as a reference for making the layers of decisions involved in creating a new community— from how the design of buildings relates to the streets they face to how land-use and density patterns are coordinated with regional transit routes. These planning and design approaches are being applied with equal vigor to new communities on the suburban edge, exurban towns and inner-city infill sites:

The center of each neighborhood should be defined by a public space and activated by locally oriented civic and commercial facilities. These places should not be relegated to leftover sites at the edge of neighborhoods, and their form and image should be strengthened by surrounding building form, architecture and street patterns.

Each neighborhood should accommodate a range of household types and land uses. A neighborhood is a place for living, shopping and working. It should include building types varied enough to accommodate this range of activities and flexible enough to be easily adapted as different uses for them emerge.

Cars should be kept in perspective. Land-use patterns, street layouts and densities should make walking, bicycling and public transit viable alternatives to driving, especially for routine, everyday trips. Streets should be safe, interesting and comfortable for pedestrians. Improving traffic flow should be only one of many considerations in platting streets and designing neighborhoods.

Architecture should respond to the surrounding fabric of buildings and spaces and to local traditions. Buildings should not be conceived as objects isolated from their surroundings; they should contribute to the spatial definition of streets, parks, greens, yards and other open spaces.

The New Urbanists draw upon a range of design traditions for inspiration. Their ideas about the relationships between planning and architecture reach back to the City Beautiful and Town Planning movements, which in turn reach back to Renaissance and Classical cities. Their ideas about connections between land use and transit draw on practices that shaped the development of streetcar suburbs and ideas that were advocated by regional planners in the early decades of the century.

One can even find a trace of 1920s "city efficient" and "city functional" influence in the New Urbanists' thinking. Peter Calthorpe and Andres Duany/Elizabeth Plater-Zyberk, whose projects and ideas have received the most attention, implicitly acknowledge that there should be some standard increment of suburban growth and that the proper focal point of any new community should be a public space that provides a locus for civic activities, local commercial uses and a transit stop connecting the neighborhood to the region. This underlying structure, they believe, gives a perceptible sense of order and identity at a range of scales.

The basic template of Peter Calthorpe's regional plans is the "transit-oriented development" or TOD, which channels growth into discrete nodes along light-rail and bus networks. A TOD, which is like a streetcar suburb-meets-edge city, exploits a basic relationship between transportation and land use: Put more origin and destination points within an easy walk of a transit stop and more people will use transit. Each TOD would be a dense, tightly woven community that mixes stores, housing and offices in a compact, walkable area surrounding a transit station. Calthorpe has written that in theory 2,000 homes, a million square feet of commercial space, parks, schools and day care could fit within a quarter-mile walk of the station, or about 120 acres.[9] In the same space a typical suburban developer might build just 720 single-family homes.

Closest to the station would be space for retail and service businesses, professional offices, restaurants, health clubs, cultural facilities and public uses—making jobs, goods, entertainment and services easily accessible to TOD residents and transit riders without requiring auto usage. Buildings near the center could have large floorplates to accommodate back-office and bulk retail uses. They could rise several stories, enabling a mix of commercial, office and even residential uses. And they could require less parking because of their location near transit and housing and because businesses with different peak periods (such as movie theaters and offices) can share parking.

Near the commercial area would be a mix of small-lot single-family houses, duplexes, townhouses and apartments—suitable and affordable for families, singles, empty-nesters, students and the elderly. Housing would be clustered around courtyards or parks that would link with larger public spaces, day care and recreation facilities. A final ring of development, in the quarter mile surrounding the core, would consist of single-family detached homes or larger-scale commercial enterprises. Although this sounds like typical suburban development, Calthorpe would encourage minimum average densities of 10 to 15 units per net acre (enough to support a bus line) and focus neighborhoods around shops, day-care facilities and parks.

Calthorpe's plans for Portland, Sacramento and San Diego propose a range of TODs: An "urban TOD" is located directly on a main transit route and is suitable for job-generating and high-intensity uses like offices, retail centers and high-density housing. A "neighborhood TOD," located on a feeder bus line, would have a residential and local-serving shopping focus. TODs could be located not only in new growth areas but also in infill or redevelopment sites, which could evolve from auto-oriented to pedestrian-oriented places. Rio Vista West, a TOD proposed for San Diego, incorporates a 120,000-square-foot discount retail operation.[10]

The "traditional neighborhood development" (TND) approach conceived by Andres Duany and Elizabeth Plater-Zyberk (their firm is known as DPZ) and others operates at a smaller scale, includes more fine-grained regulation and varies more in response to local conditions than Calthorpe's TOD approach, but it is rooted less strongly in convictions about regional planning and the importance of transit. TND-like master plans have been proposed in a range of scenarios, from resort communities (Seaside and Windsor, Florida) to redeveloping shopping centers (Mashpee, Massachusetts) to mobile home parks (Rosa Vista, in Mesa, Arizona) to traditional suburban settings (Kentlands, in Gaithersburg, Maryland).

The basic building block of DPZ's community plans is the neighborhood, which is sized (from 40 to 200 acres) and configured (a radius of no more than one-quarter mile) so that most of its homes are within a three-minute walk of neighborhood parks and a five-minute walk of a central square or common. There, a meeting hall, child-care center, bus stop and convenience store are located. Each neighborhood would include a variety of housing types suitable for different household types and income groups.

In Most DPZ projects, neighborhoods are nested and layered into larger units called villages or towns; what makes each community unique is that the patterns of overlapping and connection never repeat from one place to the next. Groups of neighborhoods form villages, which generally are separated from each other by greenbelts but connected by major streets. A village school might be located in a place where several neighborhoods come together. Civic and commercial uses that serve the village (such as recreational facilities or a cinema) or a broader area (such as a fire station, conference center or retirement home) often are located along main streets and next to public spaces.

A town, which might comprise several villages and neighborhoods, can include an even larger variety of commercial or institutional uses. Avalon Park, in Orlando, includes several towns that are specialized according to the regional services they provide. One contains a university campus and cultural facilities; another features a large component of office space and related services; others incorporate the retail activity associated with a regional mall and with a typical commercial strip.

An equally important characteristic of the New Urbanists' proposals is the way neighborhoods and communities are knit together. DPZ is a forceful advocate of platting neighborhoods with grid-like street patterns, as was common practice through the 1920s. Street networks with frequent connections, they argue, ease traffic congestion by providing a choice of paths for any trip, yet tame cars by requiring frequent stops. Such networks make pedestrian and bicycle movement easier by slowing auto traffic and making trips shorter than in places with hierarchical street systems; combined with requirements for mixing land uses, they could produce communities in which walking is a realistic choice for most everyday trips. Moreover, networks with intersections at regular intervals create a sense of scale and order not evident in typical subdivisions, improving one's sense of orientation.

The imagery of the grid does not imply that all streets will be designed similarly, DPZ's codes sometimes call for a dozen different types of streets—boulevards, streets, courts, roads, lanes, alleys and others—each with its own dimensions and specifications for street and sidewalk width, tree planting, on-street parking, traffic speed and pedestrian crossing time. Consequently, each street's character reflects more precisely its location and use, as opposed to the uniform, overscaled local and collector streets found in typical suburbs. Calthorpe's TOD plans often include a layer of radial streets emanating from the core. Radial streets, he argues, are efficient for pedestrians because they make the trip to the center of the community shorter. They serve as a powerful contrast to local streets, adding a civic presence and grandeur rarely found in suburbs, and they reinforce the clarity and identity of the center.

Just as important in Calthorpe's plans is the way TODs are connected to the region—each neighborhood is accessible to others and to existing communities through a network of light-rail and bus routes. No matter how walkable each neighborhood is, no matter how many shopping and job opportunities it provides, people in this highly mobile society will not live their entire lives within the confines of one community. Nowadays, suburban travel patterns resemble a tangled web, not a hub-and-spoke pattern with all trips leading to central cities and back. But when these diffuse travel patterns are spread over low-density areas, transit is impossible. By directing development into denser nodes, the New Urbanists channel more trips into discrete corridors that could be served by transit.

What most distinguishes the neighborhoods proposed by the New Urbanists is the importance accorded to public spaces like greens, plazas and parks. Like traditional town commons or courthouse squares, these spaces are regarded as the civic focus for neighborhoods. They are located in central, prominent places, feature local commercial uses and are often connected to major streets. Community facilities (such as day care, churches, schools or meeting rooms) are assigned special positions adjacent to these spaces, underscoring the importance both the institution and public space play in community life.

Many design strategies are used to reinforce the identity and stature of these spaces. They might be treated as figural elements; their location, shape and volume made distinct and identifiable. Buildings surrounding the space might be subject to special urban design guidelines, particularly streetwall and setback requirements that ensure they help define the volume of the space. The green in Kentlands' Old Farm neighborhood has several distinctive characteristics: adjacent to it are renovated farm buildings that convey a sense of history; lines of rowhouses and tightly arranged detached houses create enclosure on two sides; it sits at a high point in the neighborhood; and it incorporates a dramatic pre-existing stand of mature trees.

The same principles apply to street design. The New Urbanists reposition the detached house to better define the space of both the public street and private yard: A row of houses with regular setbacks can turn the street into a positive space. DPZ's codes dictate the proportion of building heights to street width, ensuring that each type of street has a distinct spatial character. In commercial and multi-family areas, buildings face public spaces such as streets and parks; parking lots are tucked behind or, if that is not possible, to the side—but not between the street and the building.

Streets also are designed to be comfortable, safe and interesting for pedestrians. At Laguna West, the main street runs perpendicular to a pre-existing six-lane regional artery so traffic, noise and pollution do not invade the central shopping and office area. Residential streets, narrower than those in most typical suburbs, slow traffic and allow for wider walkways. Trees planted in parking lanes also slow traffic and convey the sense that the street is a succession of smaller, human-scaled spaces.

The New Urbanists also pay close attention to architecture—particularly to a building's siting on its lot, massing and exterior detail—arguing that only certain types of buildings and spaces can create the range of public and private spaces that successful communities require. Most suburban zoning, for example, generates houses that are suited only for nuclear families and configures open space to surround houses and isolate them from other houses and the street. These

Victorian-era legacies leave few of the well-defined neighborhood gathering places that can be found throughout traditional towns and cities, and they provide housing for a decreasing proportion of American households.

The neighborhoods proposed by the New Urbanists generally include a richer mix of building types than can be found in conventional suburban neighborhoods—from sideyard houses, rowhouses, semi-detached houses, cottages, secondary units, courtyard apartments, mid-rise apartments to shopfronts and offices with apartments above. Development is controlled by designating for each lot the building type that might be put there, and setback regulations are used to create functional open spaces and a strong relationship between buildings and streets.

The most detailed level of planning found in the New Urbanists' work is architectural design guidelines. DPZ's codes are the most elaborate and tightly drawn—sometimes dictating the thickness of mortar bands between bricks. The codes, which vary from town to town and often are based on historic styles and local vernacular, can cover the design and placement of elements such as windows, garage doors, balconies and decorative columns; the selection and combination of materials; the massing and pitch of roofs; and more. These rules seem to exert an extraordinary level of control (particularly for mass-market housing) and generally reveal a tilt toward romantic and picturesque townscapes. But their purpose is to force greater attention to detail, thereby invigorating suburban architecture and imparting a greater level of civility to the streetscape.

Building the New American Dream

Given the enormous power that financial institutions, state highway agencies (one of them, Caltrans, has been nicknamed "the California Pentagon"), landowners and developers wield over local planning decisions, how influential will the New Urbanists be?

Remarkably, significant public sentiment is gathering behind them. In 1989, when a Gallup poll asked people what kind of place they would like to live in, 34 percent chose a small town, 24 percent a suburb, 22 percent a farm and 19 percent a city.[11] Dissatisfaction with suburban life surely contributes to this sentiment: Polls of San Francisco area residents routinely find traffic congestion and the lack of affordable housing are the most significant quality of life concerns.[12]

As unhappiness with congestion, development of sensitive lands, housing costs and air quality mounts, public agencies are being strong-armed into action. One outcome has been the unraveling of the political consensus that growth is good. Citizens routinely vote against development proposals because they expect growth will only worsen their quality of life; many communities are implementing growth controls or outright moratoria. Ironically, new development consequently occurs in ever more haphazard patterns, exacerbating these problems.

At the same time, a number of statewide and regional planning initiatives are lending credence to the New Urbanists' ideas. Air quality boards in Los Angeles and Sacramento are forcing local governments to reconsider land-use patterns that generate excessive automobile use. Washington State's tough growth management law has Seattle studying how to accommodate growth in TOD-like "urban villages" along its proposed light-rail system. Virginia's Loudoun County, responding to residents' fears that its rolling farmland would be converted into the next ring of Washington, D.C. suburbs, approved TND-style zoning that encourages traditional hamlets and villages. Recent California legislation requires localities to accommodate secondary units in some form. That state's voters have approved several local tax increases to pay for building new mass transit systems, and there is talk of lining some of them with TOD-like development.

Advocacy groups are pressuring for development policies that echo New Urbanist ideas. California's Local Government Commission published a primer, *Land Use Planning for More Livable Places*, that incorporates many of these suggestions. The Regional Plan Association, a business-sponsored research and advocacy group, is urging municipalities in the New York/New Jersey/Connecticut metropolitan region to plan TOD-like "compact clusters" along regional commuter lines; one rail agency, New Jersey Transit, is studying how to promote transit-friendly development near its stations. The citizens' group 1,000 Friends of Oregon commissioned Calthorpe to develop a regional TOD plan along Portland's MAX light-rail system; similarly, The Treasure Coast Regional Planning Council asked Dover, Correa, Kohl, Cockshutt, Valle (DCKCV), a Miami-based design and planning firm, to create a regional plan based on TND principles.

The New Urbanists believe the best way to change suburban development patterns is to change the rules of the game. They have concentrated on crafting subdivision regulations, zoning codes and regional plans—and on building the consensus necessary to win grassroots and political approval for their proposals. Their success has resulted from several factors: an inclusive approach to preparing plans, unusually powerful and carefully targeted presentations, a well-honed ability to advance their proposals as straightforward solutions to difficult problems, a persistence derived from their conviction and commitment toward their ideas and a pragmatism that enables compromise.

DPZ's on-site charettes, which concentrate most of the work for a project into several days of intense activity, have proven invaluable in building community support. During a charette, the firm confers with local officials, community leaders and interest groups; stages public meetings and presentations; and calls in local architects, planners and citizens to collaborate. The focused program becomes an event, capturing attention in ways that typical planning activities never do.

The New Urbanists place an enormous importance on communicating their proposals in terms that decision makers and everyday citizens can easily grasp, and their presentations are as strong on style as on substance. Calthorpe and Duany can be charismatic and compelling public speakers. DPZ's proposals are often accompanied by captivating if overly romantic perspectives (drawn by Charles Barrett and colored by Manuel Fernandez-Noval) that, emphasize the picturesque quality of the firm's town plans and architectural visions. DCKCV prepares realistic simulations that meld computer technology and photography in depicting existing and proposed build-out conditions.

Unlike purely visionary proposals, the New Urbanists' work demonstrates a practical concern with how they will be implemented. One DCKCV study explains how a project platted as a series of traditional neighborhoods on a grid could be developed in small components by numerous builders over many years—just like any other large-scale project. Some DPZ proposals incorporate a "regulating plan" that enables local government to reassert street platting and subdivision prerogatives that were ceded to private developers decades ago for efficiency's sake. The typical regulating plan is made up of three layers of rules; the more a proposal follows, the fewer discretionary reviews it will face. The DPZ-inspired TND-ordinance is a prototype planning document that local governments can adopt and developers can implement without staging an intensive charette. The ordinance follows the legal precedent of the planned unit development but is designed to produce traditional neighborhood layouts and architectural forms.

Nevertheless, businesses and public officials have erected their share of hurdles. Early versions of the TOD developed by designer-educators like Calthorpe, Douglas Kelbaugh and Daniel Solomon did not include a "secondary ring" of detached homes; Calthorpe introduced this feature to accommodate developers' demands for a greater proportion of single-family detached housing. When Laguna West's developers asked that the grid be replaced by a standard cul-de-sac arrangement, Calthorpe compromised again but designed pedestrian connections where through streets would have been. At Kentlands, DPZ planned a two-story day-care center to frame a nearby civic space, but no national day-care chain would agree to operate it—one-story buildings require less staff and have lower insurance costs. (A local operator ultimately agreed to move in.) The city balked at streets less than 20 feet wide, fearing that fire trucks would not be able to get through, until builders agreed to install fire sprinklers in houses along those streets.[13]

At a larger scale, it has been difficult to integrate TODs with transit. In Santa Clara County, California, where the existing light-rail line is expanding, developers have been unable to accumulate large tracts of land near stations and local officials have been reluctant to use their redevelopment powers to assemble sites. In Sacramento, although there are long-range plans for light rail to serve Calthorpe's Laguna West project, there is no guarantee. This means that transit may not be implemented until after development occurs, or that transit-oriented development may lag decades behind the extension of a transit line.

Nevertheless, one could argue that with either transit or TODs in place, it is more likely that a link between transit and denser development eventually will emerge. This is happening now around stations on the San Francisco region's BART system, where dense station-area development had been resisted for decades. Now cities like Concord, Pleasant Hill and Hayward are planning for a new generation of growth around their stations.

Notes

1. Gwendolyn Wright, *Building the Dream: A Social History of Housing in America* (Cambridge, MA: MIT Press, 1981), and Robert Fishman, *Bourgeois Utopias* (New York: Basic Books, 1987).

2. Clarence A. Perry, "The Neighborhood Unit," in Committee on the Regional Plan of New York and Its Environs, *The Neighborhood Unit* (New York, 1929), pp. 34–35, as excerpted in Christopher Tunnard, *The Modern American City* (New York: D. Van Nostrand, 1968), pp. 163–164.

3. Spiro Kostof, *The City Shaped: Urban Patterns and Meanings Through History* (London: Thames and Hudson, 1991), p. 80.

4. Kenneth T. Jackson, *The Crabgrass Frontier* (New York: Oxford University Press, 1985), pp. 205–206; Kostof, *The City Shaped*, p. 82.

5. Peter G. Kowe, *Making a Middle Landscape* (Cambridge, MA: MIT Press, 1991).

6. Jackson, *The Crabgrass Frontier*, p. 239; Peter Calthorpe, *The Next American Metropolis* (New York: Princeton Architectural Press, 1993).

7. "Fees Cast Shadow on Affordable Housing," *Housing and Development Report* (San Francisco: Bay Area Council), October 1991.

8. Calthorpe, *The Next American Metropolis*.

9. Peter Calthorpe "Pedestrian Pockets: New Strategics for Suburban Growth," in *The Pedestrian Pocket Book* (New York: Princeton Architectural Press, 1989), p. 11.

10. Much of this description comes from Calthorpe, *The Next American Metropolis*.

11. Andres Duany and Elizabeth Plater-Zyberk, "The Second Coming of the Small Town," *The Utne Reader,* May/June 1992.

12. See various issues of *Housing and Development Report* (San Francisco: Bay Area Council) that report on the annual Bay Area Poll.

13. Todd W. Bressi, "Cities to Walk In." *Metropolis*, March 1990; and Edward Gunts, "Plan Meets Reality," *Architecture*, December 1991.